The Emphatic Christian Center

Reforming Christian Political Practice

Kyle A. Pasewark & Garrett E. Paul

ABINGDON PRESS / NASHVILLE

THE EMPHATIC CHRISTIAN CENTER
REFORMING CHRISTIAN POLITICAL PRACTICE

Copyright © 1999 by Abingdon Press

All rights reserved.
No part of this work may be reproduced or transmitted in any form or by any means, electronic or mechanical, including photocopying and recording, or by any information storage or retrieval system, except as may be expressly permitted by the 1976 Copyright Act or in writing from the publisher. Requests for permission should be addressed in writing to Abingdon Press, 201 Eighth Avenue South, Nashville, TN 37203.

This book is printed on elemental-chlorine-free paper.

Library of Congress Cataloging-in-Publication Data

Pasewark, Kyle A., 1959–
 The emphatic Christian center : reforming Christian political practice / Kyle A. Pasewark and Garrett E. Paul.
  p. cm.
 Includes bibliographical references and index.
 ISBN 0-687-00225-7 (alk. paper)
  1. Christianity and politics—United States. I. Paul, Garrett E., 1949– . II. Title.
BR115.P7P295 1999
261.7′0973—dc21   99-15043
                                                                                                       CIP

Scripture quotations, unless otherwise indicated, are from the New Revised Standard Version Bible, copyright © 1989, by the Division of Christian Education of the National Council of the Churches of Christ in the United States of America. Used by permission.

The quotation noted RSV is from the Revised Standard Version of the Bible, copyright 1946, 1952, 1971 by the Division of Christian Education of the National Council of Churches of Christ in the U.S.A. Used by permission.

To

*Mark, my brother,
who keeps me centered*

—Kyle A. Pasewark

For

*my mother and my late father,
my teachers, colleagues, and students,
and
Betsy, Chris, Hans, and Emily*

—Garrett E. Paul

Contents

ACKNOWLEDGMENTS 7

INTRODUCTION 13

PART ONE
THE PREDICAMENTS OF POLITICS AND CHRISTIANITY

Chapter One: *A Common Failure: The Secularist
           State and Its Religious Critics* 25

Chapter Two: *Let Freedom Reign: Contemporary
           American Political Practice* 83

PART TWO
AN EMPHATIC CHRISTIAN CENTER

Chapter Three: *Where Shall We Go? Who Shall We Be?
            A Theology for the Christian Center* 109

Chapter Four: *Difference and Commitment: Pluralism
           and the Christian Center* 151

Chapter Five: *Taking Center Stage: The Emphatic
           Christian Center and Political Practice*.... 198

NOTES 267

INDEX 317

Acknowledgments

The Emphatic Christian Center began over coffee. That fact gives me confidence; most good things seem to begin over coffee. After that meeting, Garrett Paul and I began a short article, "The Emphatic Christian Center," published in *The Christian Century*. This article was supposed to be the end of it. To our surprise, as academics perpetually insecure about whether anyone hears what we say or cares what we think, that article generated considerable interest, and became, these years later, this book.

A book has its own spirit. After the words are on the page, it is overbearing for an author to claim it as "his" or "her" own. Acknowledgments, however, are personal and allow an otherwise questionable liberty of ownership. For me, this book arose from an odd combination of irritation and hope. Irritation at the assumed opposition between religion and politics on one side of American political discussion, and even greater annoyance at the Christian right's attempt to make *its* religion and politics the measure of truth; hope because I think that there are opportunities for a powerful exchange between religion, culture, and politics in contemporary American life.

We tried to think about the opportunities for such fruitful exchanges as well as the impediments that our culture places in their way. We also tried to do something unusual in combining several tasks: to provide a theological analysis of American culture, a theologically based political perspective (the emphatic Christian center), *and* an elucidation of some of the Christian center's practical commitments.

The analytic and theoretical work were fairly familiar ground for me. The practical turn was new. In chapter 5, I was responsible for the work on poverty, education, and sexual violence. Poverty and education were long-standing but dormant interests. Thinking about sexual violence was a newer concern, and arose from very personal circumstances. In the spring of 1993, perhaps because my own life was troubled, six women (some of whom I had recently met, some of whom were old friends) told me of events in their lives ranging from severe sexual harassment to sustained sexual abuse. Coincidentally, I was asked to write a review of Catherine MacKinnon's *Only Words*. That review turned out to be quite critical of MacKinnon's approach; at the end of the essay, I strongly urged men to begin to speak about sexual violence, and made a silent promise to myself that I would do so. This book, and my volunteer work in Fargo, North Dakota, and New Haven, Connecticut, are ways of keeping my promise.

To keep a promise and complete a long-term project are happy occasions. This book, though, is bittersweet. It is almost certainly the last theological book I will write. That is heartbreaking. I am, I think, a better human being now than I was when I began my trek through the theological and religious world a decade and a half ago. Perhaps that is enough. During the last several years, however, and largely under the influence of this book, I gradually changed directions. This shift, paradoxically, was a gift of religion and theology, whose true powers do not come to the fore in a self-contained "religious" world but in driving believers to discern the action of the divine in all the world.

I am now fortunate enough to be able to study the law at Yale Law School. I think that my studies here will put me in a better position to practice the kind of power described in this book. Still, being suspended between two worlds is uncomfortable even in its rewards. Not the least discomfort is to be forced to total the debts incurred over the years, and in an acknowledgments section to try desperately to include those who have been of particular importance over the years. In print, this is likely my last chance.

My coauthor, Garrett Paul, is also my friend. As a Lutheran of a different stripe than I, he underestimates (below) his contributions to this volume. I feel badly about that because I think he has meant more to the book (and certainly to me) than he realizes. My teachers over the years, particularly Langdon Gilkey, deserve my thanks less for what they taught me than for how they did it: more worlds and ways of thinking were opened than closed, and that, I think, is the highest compliment one can pay to teachers. Some of my students—for whom I hope I provided the same widening lens—found their way into this volume; I want especially to thank Chris Wheatley, who helped with research for the

Acknowledgments

book. Aside from being a fine student, he is also a superb human being. Sarah Pedersen and Kelly Morse, students of recent and more distant vintage, I am pleased to count as my friends.

Many colleagues gave me helpful advice and criticism about this volume and my work in general. These, too, I am delighted to count as my friends. The most difficult part of leaving the field of theology is knowing, deep down, that we will never share quite the same intimacy we once did. However, their gifts to me went far beyond the walls of the academy. Larry Alderink, Per Anderson, Sr. Shawn Carruth, Thomas Davis, Frank Guliuzza, Dean Hammer, Roy Hammerling, Stewart Herman, the late Melanie Lane, Margaret Mitchell, Jeff Pool, Richard Rosengarten, Mary Tollefson, Lee Upton, James Yerkes, and Eric Ziolkowski are friends whom I cherish.

Others did not spend as much time talking with me about this project but are wonderful friends whose gifts of joy and power I will not forget. I have known Isaac Catt, Kathy Guliuzza, Carol Hammer, and Dale Herbeck for about twenty years now, and Deborah Eicher-Catt for a few less. These, I pray, will always be with me—I cannot trace, really, what you have done for me, but know that much of what I am is due to you. Lynda Alderink, Sandra Anderson, Richard Dickson, Peggy Hammerling, the Hammerling children, Lanier Harper-Dickson, Shirley Hoden, Jean Jacobi, Linda Johnson, Betsy Paul, and Leigh Ann Wheeler, I have known for less time but their kindness and care also add fibers to my heart.

In the midst of the turmoil of the last several years, I was also held in the embrace of my family. There is first, my furry family of Cleopatra, Thug, Mug, sweet departed Dark Star, and Spooky, cats who have given me pleasure every moment of their lives. My father, Richard, my stepmother Karen; my mother, Alice; my brothers Mark and Michael; my sister-in-law Virginia; and my nephew, Eric, have been wondrous to me, well beyond anything I could ever have asked. I pray that you all have some small idea of what you mean to me, for I am not gifted enough to tell you.

Through you all, I have learned what it means to feel the embrace of divine love. I hope that I have added warmth to your lives as well.

Kyle A. Pasewark
New Haven, Connecticut
May 1999

This book would never have come to be had it not been for the authors' fortunate—providential—first encounter in 1991. We soon came to realize that we shared several common political, theological, and ethical concerns, which led to what you are now reading.

Here I have frequently played something of an Ursula Niebuhr to Kyle's Reinhold: sharpening style, clarifying substance, and strengthening prose (I know that Kyle says I underestimate my contribution; but perhaps he underestimates Ursula Niebuhr's!). Most of the ideas started out as his. This is not meant to evade any responsibility on my part. We freely challenged and adapted each other's work so that it finally became our own, and now we would be hard pressed to identify with any certainty just who wrote what on almost any given page. Nothing got by either of us that we did not, eventually, both come to accept. Only once were we compelled to leave a disagreement unresolved and to explain it in a footnote, and the reader will have to look for that.

For me the departure in this volume is to focus upon the present, for most of my published research focuses on the past, particularly Germany from 1895 to 1923 and the work of Ernst Troeltsch during that period. But in some sense this is only the practical application today of what Troeltsch tried to do then: to marshal the insights of theology, philosophy, historiography, and ethics in the service of reconstructing political culture in the midst of a crisis. Fortunately for us, the crises that confront us today are not likely to rival the one that occupied him from 1914 to 1923, something I try to remember when I become discouraged.

I tend to be a little less disclosive of my personal life than is the current norm, perhaps in reaction to the fruitless and improbable exhibition of ersatz intimacy that relentlessly stalks our daily public intercourse. But I will say that every one of the four issues discussed in chapter 5—poverty, the family, sexual abuse, and the environment—has had a direct impact on my life. Which is probably true as well for most of you reading this now.

This may be the only book on American religion and politics to be interrupted by two natural disasters—the Red River and Minnesota River floods of 1997, and the great southern Minnesota tornado of

1998. I am particularly grateful to the many municipal, state, and federal employees; the Salvation Army, Red Cross, and Lutheran Disaster Response; and the tremendous number of volunteers, who all helped St. Peter begin to recover. (But don't ask if our lives are back to "normal" yet. They never will be.) Any libertarian who complains about the evils of government ought to have to go through such a disaster without any government support.

I owe gratitude to many others. Gustavus Adolphus College supported my research and writing in many ways, including an academic leave during 1996–97. Mary Palmquist typed and retyped materials which became part of this book; and without her administrative and secretarial support for my administrative tasks, I would have contributed nothing. I am also deeply indebted to my students past and present, whose questions and comments have helped me to clarify ideas which seemed perfectly clear until I tried to explain them.

Finally, and most important, I owe a debt I can never repay to my mother and late father, to my dear wife, Betsy, and to our children, Chris, Hans, and Emily, all of whom tolerated and supported this project, and me, in ways I could never enumerate. S.D.G.

Garrett E. Paul
St. Peter, Minnesota
February 1999

Introduction

THE FAILURE OF THE VACUOUS CENTER

There is a deep discontent abroad in the land. Public opinion polls have consistently indicated considerable dissatisfaction with the polarization of contemporary politics, and a desire for what Colin Powell has called "the vast American center." This desire has led to the formation of political groups such as that led by the late Paul Tsongas, Richard Lamm, Tim Penny, and others, which presents itself as a "passionate center," to say nothing of the recent internationalization of the so-called "Third Way." A widespread dissatisfaction with political discourse also pervades religious circles (except for those which are politically energized and successful). Hence it is no surprise that similar calls for the development of a new center have appeared in religious and theological circles, as well as in scholarly literature.[1] These proposals understand the center as the mere midpoint of the spectrum of political opinion. Centrism is seen as the weight that balances political life, preventing politics from tipping too far in one direction or another.

That sort of "middle ground" is *not* what this book is about. There are compelling reasons to reject this sort of centrism; the most basic is that it cannot have principled content. A center that sees its task as nothing more than brokering compromise between political extremes is a vacuous center that, ironically, worsens the very polarization it hopes to ameliorate. A true center, an emphatic center, is defined not by the compromises it makes, but by the positions it takes; not by the principles it sacrifices in the interest of compromise, but by those that inform its very being. It is this kind of center, an emphatic Christian center, that we advocate.

The emphatic Christian center is a center because it is centered; it advocates and acts from defined commitments. What it advocates is not determined by its place on a political spectrum, but in fidelity to its core. It is also a center in a second sense: it actively centers the politics of the spectrum—left, right, and center. The politics of the spectrum in its current form are incoherent. The positions of the right and the left, no less than those of the vacuous center, lack coherent grounding and are frequently self-contradictory. To justify their political programs, both the left and the right routinely appeal to "freedom," but what they affirm in principle they often contradict in practice. The left demands freedom in "social issues" (such as reproduction and sexual "lifestyles") but decries it in the economic realm, while the right simply reverses these positions, lionizing economic freedom ("free enterprise") and yet advocating coercion on social and cultural issues ("family values"). The result is a confused and muddled politics on both wings.[2] Moreover, because neither wing reflects on its own principles,[3] politics becomes increasingly divisive and vicious, reduced to the self-validation of "opinion" and "feeling" without intellectual or public accountability for political arguments.

It is worth asking whether it is precisely the American understanding of the fact and the value of freedom that lies behind this destructive and incoherent rhetoric. But such questions are not frequently asked in public culture. The center, where one might expect to find such questions posed, is constitutionally incapable of asking them. Vacuous centrism has surrendered the political agenda to the extremes, seeking nothing more than compromise between them. Restricting itself to this cowardly task, the vacuous center fails us. It abandons any claim to coherent political principles; its primary commitment is to compromise, nothing more. This is related to its further failure to provide specific proposals for public life.[4]

Nor is the failure of the vacuous center simply benign. The 1990s witnessed an oscillation between the two most likely outcomes of centrism's failure: first comes polarization, and then disgust with polarization breeds exhaustion and apathy (after which the cycle repeats itself). At the beginning of the decade, the center actively (if unconsciously) encouraged the polarization it so desperately wanted to contain. Always seeking the midpoint, it thereby invited the right and left to become ever more extreme in an effort to tilt the compromise in their direction. The right, shrewdly understanding this dynamic, has masterfully pushed the entire political spectrum to the right by characterizing Clinton and the "new Democrats" (self-proclaimed centrists!) as the new left. As a result, what just a few years earlier was seen as moderate or even slightly conservative politics came to be viewed as the rabid dog of "liberalism."

The effects on American thinking about culture and society have been enormous. During the Reagan years, for example, no one seriously entertained the idea of eliminating minimum payments to the poor and their children. It was, after all, Reagan himself who minted the term "safety net." But the movement of the political spectrum to the right led to more and more strident calls to shred all federal and state efforts to ameliorate poverty, with shockingly little investigation or discussion of the actual successes and failure of those efforts. The "center," pulled by its mediating nose, has now moved far to Reagan's right. On the other hand, Daniel Patrick Moynihan, whose work from the 1960s through the 1980s led him to be characterized as "a racist, a victim-blamer, a neoconservative, a neoliberal, and even (by Irving Kristol) a 'revisionist progressive,' " is now "Washington's last loud liberal"—all without changing his mind.[5] In its eagerness to compromise, the center served the right very nicely during those years. The supposed virtue of such centrism (despite its incoherence) was supposed to be that it would provide for "balance" and thus political stability. In this it has been a breathtaking failure.

The politics of the spectrum is barren and empty. To conceive politics in spectral terms privileges location and not ideas, bargaining and not thinking. Incapable of principled commitment, the vacuous center is most vulnerable to flagrant manipulation. All that seems needed to enlist this vacuous center is simply to prove that one has been the most "reasonable," the most compromising. This is easy enough: just begin with the most outrageous proposal, and then *any* flexibility will seem generous. Although in the 1990s the right was the chief beneficiary of this desire for a mere centrism, things can always change. If the left turns up its own volume and makes its own proposals sufficiently preposterous, perhaps it can make the vacuous center its servant. Thus the first result of a nonprincipled, vacuous center is actually to encourage the politics of polarization.

After a sustained period of rant, however, Americans tired of it. The

1996 budget battle was the turning point. The Republican Congressional leaders began the 1996 budget stalemate with a typical maneuver, presenting a chart to show that they had moved farther in offering compromises than had the president. President Clinton, understanding what was at stake, promptly denied that that was the case,[6] as if good budget policy were defined by the extent of compromise, not the budget's content. Whatever the dubious merits of that position, the president succeeded in turning the rhetoric of compromise and moderation against the Republicans.

To dismiss this skirmish as campaigning for poll numbers misses the point; both sides were convinced that what the "vast American center" wanted was compromise, in any form and at any price. Compromise itself, regardless of content, was the perceived demand. We were drained. The budget battle provided the momentum for Clinton's tepid (43 percent) but nonetheless decisive victory. Subsequently, we seemed to enter upon a new era of political peace, at least until the impeachment proceedings. But even in the impeachment and the trial, both parties sought to appear "reasonable" and "nonpartisan," though that became increasingly difficult as the proceedings wore on. This uneasy truce is the result of a different kind of politics of denunciation—the denunciation of denunciation. Beginning with the budget dispute, it became the fashion to criticize a proposal, not for its substance, but for not being "mainstream." The president largely succeeded in his 1996 budget negotiations because the White House and Congressional Democrats successfully and incessantly portrayed their Republican counterparts as "extremists." The subsequent electoral campaign was filled with charges and countercharges of extremism, usually without explanation of what was extreme about any particular position or candidate.[7] Political alternatives were reduced to a jockeying for position. But this sort of quest not to appear "extreme" implies "that an unpopular, or even an unfamiliar, idea is per se a bad idea." This is little better than polarization. After all, as Hendrik Hertzberg notes, "The list of ideas that were good many years before they were mainstream is a long and distinguished one; it includes abolitionism, women's suffrage, social security, child-labor laws, and the income tax."[8] In such a vapid situation it becomes increasingly difficult to tell what our politics is about. George Stephanopoulos, a senior advisor to

President Clinton in the first term, left the White House after the 1996 election because the election "didn't seem to be about anything."[9]

This abandonment of actual ideas in favor of staking out the center of a spectrum has been popular, a respite from backbiting and frontal assaults (except in those moments when one accuses one's opponents of backbiting and frontal assaults). After the 1996 elections it became a case of the politics of exhaustion, until the guns of impeachment were fired. But such truces—mere interludes in between the chronic vitriol—have little to do with principle, and much to do with public weariness of the battles fought early in the 1990s. We were then properly concerned with the increasing nastiness, and even outright hatred, manifested in our political life. But the mere suspension of public manifestations of that hatred while the troops on both sides recovered their strength was no solution. As J. Glenn Gray reminds us, "Peace will never occur as a consequence of weakness, exhaustion, or fear."[10] Even if we are not—for the moment—in the midst of what James Davison Hunter calls a "culture war,"[11] Gray's warning is directly relevant to the vacuous center and its appeasing gentleness. We require not weakness but *strength;* we can realize our aims only if we become aware that "power and gentleness can coexist and become the greatest benison for an unhappy world."[12]

A political culture (like ours) that lacks a strong and emphatic center will almost certainly oscillate between polarization and exhaustion (as we have). We perpetually swing from one response to the other, alternating a tick at one end with a tock at the other. Nothing, however, fundamentally changes. The growth of polarization, and its subsequent period of exhaustion, are both promoted in no small part by the incoherence of political discourse. And this, in turn, is promoted by the absence of an emphatic center. Tick: the political wings, lacking a principled center, shout all the louder. Tock: we grow tired, charges of "extremism" gain favor and we suspend the battle, only to resume it when our energy returns. If we want to begin to overcome this oscillation between polarization and exhaustion, it is not enough to call for a softening of tone (important though that may be). We need a strong, emphatic voice that *centers* political discourse with consistent, coherent, principled commitments, calling the political wings back to their own truest insights. An emphatic center, in contrast to its vacuous counterpart, strives to combine firm convictions and gentle hearts. The politics of the spectrum are mere form and location; a productive politics must introduce content. That is why we call for an *emphatic* center.

In this book, however, we develop not merely an emphatic center, but an emphatic *Christian* center. This may be the most formidable of our tasks, for while there may be a widespread desire for a political center, there is hardly a broad cultural desire for any more religious politics.[13] Indeed, for a broad swath of American culture, any Christian (or any explicitly religious) political perspective is identified with ignorance, effrontery, fanaticism, or all three. There is no way to rule out this distrust and fear at the outset. Nor is there any legitimate way to rule out from the start the claims of those who oppose any religious involvement in politics and public life.[14] The fruitfulness of an emphatic Christian center must emerge in the course of the argument. We support an emphatic Christian center not because both authors are confessing Christians. *Fruitfulness* is the criterion. We are convinced that the Christian conception of human existence as estranged from an omnipotent, just, and loving God is descriptive of the world in which we live, and—more important—productive for a more livable world. To think and to act through the implications of these insights can help make this world a better one.

It is not that Christian conceptions are the only fruitful ones; nor that they cannot be supplemented and corrected by other religious, nonreligious, and antireligious insights; but neither can these insights be replaced by some sort of universal reason or vague personal spirituality. If the evidence showed that politics could survive or thrive without religion; or that Christian intimations of the sacred could not assist the quest for productive public and political life; or that Christianity could adequately praise God without a vibrant political chord, we would not have labored to write this book. But the evidence more plausibly shows the opposite.

THE STRUCTURE OF THE BOOK

In the first chapter, we argue that politics without religious animation (indeed, multiple religious animations) is self-contradictory and self-defeating. The effort to exclude religion in its many forms from political participation is destined to fail. The emergence of the religious right should not have come as a surprise. It was surprising only because we were under the illusion that a purely secular politics existed, and that it could provide vibrancy, life, and meaning to public culture. We insist that secularism as an ideology (as distinct from the formally secular structure of the state)[15] cannot sustain vital public life; furthermore, it usually rests on an assumption of universally accessible rationality that has long since been discredited.

Moreover, attempts to exclude religion from politics tend—altogether ironically—to encourage the dominance of those intemperate religious and quasireligious forces that destroy public life rather than enrich it. This is the subject of chapter 2, where we show how the typically American religious dedication to a warped conception of freedom has created an incoherent and destructive politics. Indeed, this concept of freedom—actually a *religion* of freedom—as the mere absence of restraint ultimately minimizes the importance of politics and public life themselves. We live in a public culture that despises public life; we practice a politics that is increasingly dedicated to the destruction of the polis. Our politics is fundamentally antipolitical.

Chapter 3 addresses the contribution the emphatic Christian center can make to the reinvigoration of politics. The contemporary political problem is not simply one of ethics (or in the term often favored by conservatives, "values"). Rather, an emphatic Christian centrism must arise from a source deeper than mere politics and morality. It is, in the first instance, theological. Its specific positions spring from a vision of existence that rests on a deep intuition of our status before God and God's revelation in Christ Jesus through the Holy Spirit. We provide three interrelated specifications of that vision: (1) a recovery of the emphasis on our *separation* from God expressed in a variety of symbols of sin, particularly including the symbol of original sin, making justice a central criterion of political and social life and providing a real ground for hope; (2) an emphasis on *love,* particularly as respect and appreciation for the depth of one's opponent's commitments; and (3) divine *power* and omnipotence, which, far from detracting from human power, is rather what makes it possible in the first place.[16] While these principles may initially appear remote from more particular political commitments, we maintain that they can open the way to a revitalized appreciation of public life and politics, not only for Christians but for others as well. We go on to elaborate some of the implications of these principles in chapters 4 and 5.

In chapter 4, we return to the question of religion in public life, addressing the concern of many thoughtful people who fear any religious involvement in the political realm because they suspect that religion is by nature exclusive and seeks to dominate the public realm. Religion, such a view holds, is intrinsically tyrannical—and "religious politics" as often does its best to confirm this perspective. Besides, it is held, "pluralism" means that since no one religion dominates the American scene, then no religion can speak. We show that the solution is not to exclude religion (which would be impossible anyway), for then it will return with ever more tyrannical aspirations. Rather, the answer lies in the transformation of such religious tendencies, both from without, and more important, from *within* the particular religions themselves. Indeed, this self-critical task is required by the principles outlined in chapter 3—sin, love, and power. This is all the more pressing because our contemporary understanding of pluralism utterly excludes the possibility that commitments can and should be changed in the course of political discussion. On the contrary, the theological principles of the Christian center (particularly the symbols of sin and divine power) have temporal transformation at their core. But this requires time—something not even mentioned in most of the current discussion.[17] Healthy social cohesion does not rest on universal agreement (as some religious and nonreligious thinkers maintain). Even less does it rest on the receding fantasy of universal reason. Rather, it rests on unity through plurality, as Christian trinitarian traditions (among others) argue. Thus the emphatic Christian center calls for the emergence of emphatic centers of equally particular traditions (both religious and nonreligious). The emphatic Christian center seeks the reinvigoration of political life in American culture, but is aware that it can be only a contributor—and, on Christian grounds, that is all it can seek. This is why, for Christian reasons, the secular structure of the state is not optional but, in fact, necessary.

Chapter 5 uses the principles of Christian centrism and its emphatic pluralism to accomplish three objectives. First, we develop a framework for political practice for intelligent and committed citizens who, like ourselves, cannot have expertise in every question that our body politic confronts. We conceptualize a coherent place for government and self-interest (each of which is despised by one political wing or the other) in accomplishing the goal of generating power for the social body.

Second, in this same chapter we deploy the theology of the Christian center on the crucial policy questions of *poverty and education,* the *family, sexual violence,* and the *environment.*[18]

All these issues agitate our body politic considerably. And all are polarizing issues, bitterly dividing the left and right. The left rages against sexual violence and the damage done in patriarchal families, and demands more governmental support for victims; while the right rages against the left's attack on the family and seeks to strengthen families and limit governmental interference. Both sides, curiously, seem to have allowed poverty to recede somewhat into the background, despite its clear links to the other issues. Vacuous centrism's attempt to find a "middle ground" somewhere between the two sides is doomed to fail, to produce half-way measures that will address the legitimate concerns of neither. Similarly, current debate about the environment is fatally limited by a politics of opposition between "jobs" and "trees," "nature" and "humanity." Although these oppositions sometimes exist, environmental politics takes them for granted even when it is both unhelpful and false to do so. An emphatic Christian center, however, will pursue all these issues in light of its principles and of the serious perils these problems pose for us all.

Third, this chapter—and the book—close with a consideration of how the Christian center might become an institutional force with infrastructure, organization, and continuing importance to American political life. The center must happen *somewhere.* Ideas do not exist in thin air, but must be embodied in discourse that takes place somewhere, between embodied selves. Much of the center's weakness stems from the obvious but neglected fact that there are few places where centrist discourse can take *place.* The Christian right's successes have been, in part, due to its dominance of a variety of media, while the left and the center have lost many of the forums they once used. The full vitality of the center requires that this question be addressed successfully.[19]

In an important sense, then, the last chapter is both the aim and limit of the book. In it, we produce an emphatic centrist agenda for the future. Not a complete agenda, it nevertheless provides a starting point for future discourse. It does so, we believe, with consistent principles that spring from the best of the Christian traditions. Although our emphatic centrism is *distinctively* Christian, however, it is not *uniquely* so. Instead, just as Christian centrism should nourish the whole body politic, other centers, both religious and secular, must nourish it. That, too, is part of redefining politics, rejecting the reigning image of politics as winning or losing contests for domination over others. We replace that image with a vision of politics as constructive public activity, exertion on behalf of the polis, for adherents of many traditions. To the extent that effort succeeds, public power rather than domination will infuse our political and social life.

This is where we hope to conclude: that Christian theology and ethics can clarify and improve our public life, and even help us to reclaim its dignity. But the full promise of specifically Christian efforts—for both Christianity and political culture—cannot be realized without other, equally particular endeavors from other quarters. Because America today is not "a Christian America,"[20] much less a Protestant one, and because many Americans—both religious and nonreligious—are convinced that, at the political dinner table, the only good religions are those which are silent, obedient, and well-mannered, we must begin our task by asking whether religion should speak in politics.

PART *1* ONE

THE PREDICAMENTS OF POLITICS AND CHRISTIANITY

Chapter 1

A Common Failure

THE SECULARIST STATE AND ITS RELIGIOUS CRITICS

Hannah Arendt, in her brilliant study *On Revolution*, observes that

> in theory as in practice, we can hardly avoid the paradoxical fact that it was precisely the revolutions, their crisis and their emergence, which drove the very "enlightened" men of the eighteenth century to plead for some religious sanction at the very moment when they were about to emancipate the secular realm fully from the influences of the churches and to separate politics and religion once and for all.[1]

This surprises us because Americans think about the relation between religion and public life largely through Roger Williams'—and then Thomas Jefferson's—famous metaphor of the "wall of separation" between church and state. Though that metaphor is under fire from various quarters,[2] and not only from those who dream of a Christian America, it retains a powerful hold on American consciousness. It is often taken to mean that religion has no place in political life, but should be restricted to "private" matters (or may be helpful in voluntary social welfare programs). This preference is not limited to those without formal religious commitments; many adherents of institutional religions also affirm the irrelevance of religion to political life. Both the pious Williams and the political Jefferson worshiped at this "wall," and although Jefferson is better known for the phrase, it was actually Williams who first insisted that religion and political life be kept separate. However valid the arguments for separation may (or may not) be, Arendt's paradox remains: Why did the French and American revolutionaries actually reintroduce religion at the very moment when it was supposed to be banished? We may also go on to ask why the liberal secular state is today on the defensive worldwide, from the United States to India to Egypt, and why, in some cases (notably Iran) it was destroyed.

Our position is this: at least in America,[3] secular cultural and governmental institutions remain healthy only so long as they permit and invite religious vivifications in cultural, social, and political meanings. Put somewhat differently, this means that *secularity* and *liberality* are viable so long as they do not become *secularism* and *liberalism*.[4] These are distinct phenomena. Secular*ity* means, for example, that governmental institutions cannot advocate particular religious views in government policies, or support them from the public coffers. Secular*ism* and liberal*ism* are *ideologies* which maintain that religion is an unnecessary (at best) or pernicious (at worst) influence in public life which should absent itself not only from government, but from the public arena altogether.

Emphatic Christian centrism maintains that secularity in our political institutions is necessary and desirable, not only for politics, but also for society, including religious people themselves (who are part of society). On the other hand, we maintain that secularism as an ideology is impossible, self-contradictory, and finally destructive. To establish this view, we must first define "religion." The entire debate over religion and politics is skewed by the simplistic and inaccurate definitions of religion used by its enemies and friends alike. Many cultural and scholarly discussions of religion and politics assume a very narrow definition of religion which rules out any careful consideration of what it means to separate religion from public life, let alone whether and how it should be done. A broader and yet more precise understanding of religion will enable us to see the contours of the issue more clearly. Only then will we be able to examine the relationship between religion and politics, and see why the exile of religion from public life is impossible to execute and dangerous to attempt. This, in turn, will require a careful review of the positions of both those who advocate and those who reject a role for religion in public life.

We emphasize that the argument of this chapter is not limited to Christianity's relation to political and public life.[5] Our concern here is with religion in the broad sense. Indeed, that must be our focus. If our argument here favors only Christianity, it will have failed, as later chapters will argue. The *public* square is just as naked with only one participant as with none.[6]

A note to readers: in the coming section, "What Is Religion?" we take a detour from immediate concern with American political and religious culture. The detour is necessary: it develops a conception of religion that provides criteria for the judgments we make in the balance of the book. However, readers more interested in the judgments themselves can easily defer the next section until later and proceed to "The Mutual Necessity of Religion and Public Life," page 41.

WHAT IS RELIGION?

A Broader Definition

The contemporary debate often reflexively reduces the relationship between religion and the public arena to a topic that is considerably narrower, the relation of *church and state* (even if "church" is often taken to include the institutional expressions of all major religions, not merely Christian churches). This confusion was once employed as a political shibboleth against Roman Catholic politicians such as Al Smith and John F. Kennedy, but has now been turned against Protestants as well. For example, in the 1996 Republican gubernatorial primary in Washington, Ellen Crasswell (a self-described "Christian radical") was accused by one opponent of stepping "over the line separating church and state."[7] But restricting the meaning of "religion" to these institutional bodies ("churches") seriously limits our understanding of religion and the religious dimensions of culture.

For now, we seek to define the boundaries of religion in a purely formal way. This question temporarily removes us from the issues of religion and politics, the state of American political culture, and the content of the emphatic Christian center. But the question is not an idle one. This identification of "religion" with "church" obscures the issues, concealing the religiosity of those secularists who oppose the mingling of "religion" and public life and yet expect their own quasi-religious comprehensive worldviews to remain in the public square. Ironically, it also serves to conceal the majoritarian tendencies of those who argue for the "right" of Christians to be heard.

"Religion" is much more than "church." What makes religious institutions (like churches) religious, as distinct from social, political, or cultural institutions, is that religious institutions primarily (although not exclusively) ask and answer a specifically religious question—the question of ultimate, determinative meaning. The anthropologist Clifford Geertz, for example, describes religion as "(1) a system of symbols which acts to (2) establish powerful, pervasive, and long-lasting moods and motivations in men by (3) formulating conceptions of a general order of existence and (4) clothing these conceptions with such an aura of facticity that (5) the moods and motivations seem uniquely realistic."[8] Franklin Gamwell defines religion as "the primary form of culture in terms of which the comprehensive question is explicitly asked and answered."[9] David Tracy maintains that religion uniquely deals with questions of "Ultimate Reality" and that theology is reflection on the "limit questions of our existence."[10] Paul Tillich's famous definition of religion as "ultimate concern" signifies (1) that religious faith is the "state of being ultimately concerned,"[11] and (2) that "God is the name for the content of the concern."[12] This conception is the most helpful, particularly if supplemented by Geertz's attention to symbolic structures (which include religious doctrines and language) and Tracy's conception of theology. Tillich's definition has several advantages, but also poses some problems. To those we now turn.

Kent Greenawalt, echoing a common concern, argues that defining religion as an ultimate concern is overbroad for purposes of constitutional interpretation (despite its actual employment in several Court decisions).[13] Because we are not concerned here with constitutional interpretation, this presents no difficulty. Even if a narrower conception of religion may be necessary for constitutional purposes, the definition of religion as "ultimate concern" is still fruitful for cultural analysis.[14] Indeed, Greenawalt's objections to "ultimate concern" focus on precisely those features which make it helpful for interpreting culture. He is right to suggest, first, that "ultimate concern" is not necessarily tied to any institutionally recognizable religion. But it is just this breadth that makes it possible to analyze religion's cultural presence both *within* and *without* various institutions, including religious ones.[15] (Indeed, in the next chapter we contend that the *real* American religion is an overwhelmingly libertarian devotion to freedom, which is at least as powerful inside religious institutions as outside them.)

Second, Greenawalt is correct to maintain that "ultimate concern" is not simply descriptive, but normative. Precisely this normative aspect, however, makes it possible to assess both the intensity and the fruitfulness of specific religious commitments. The more religious one is (or, for that matter, the more religious a religion is), the more encompassing will be one's ultimate concerns,[16] and the more every other concern will be referred to, understood, and lived in the light of the ultimate concern. Tillich's definition is largely a reformulation of Augustine of Hippo's distinction between use and enjoyment. For Augustine, "To enjoy something is to cling to it with love for its own sake. To use something, however, is to employ it in obtaining that which you love, provided that it is worthy of love."[17] In other words, the value of all existing things is determined by their relation to ultimate concern (for Augustine, God), which alone is worthy of full devotion. Correspondingly, the intensity and degree of this devotion is exactly the degree to which all other concerns are taken up into that worshipfulness.[18]

Greenawalt's third objection is that one's *professed* ultimate concern may well not be one's *real* ultimate concern: "Most people with traditional religious beliefs accept intellectually that religious concerns are ultimate, but their feelings and behavior are not always in accord with that premise."[19] Once again, Greenawalt mistakes a strength for a weakness. Of course it is neither possible nor desirable for courts to assess the truth of religious convictions (nor the truth of political convictions, for that matter), but that is precisely what theological and cultural criticism must do. The notion of ultimate concern is principally existential. Indeed, one of its chief advantages is that it points out our near-universal hypocrisy. We may be, and usually are, incorrect or self-deceived about our own religious commitment. It is possible and common to *claim* adherence with the "whole heart" to a religion that is, in fact, only a secondary concern in one's actual life.

The question is the *purpose* of one's religion (a concept central to Gamwell's account). For example, if one is a Christian merely in order to achieve heavenly bliss by means of believing and acting according to the dictates of Christianity, then one's religion is not finally the triune God but the self. In this case, the truly *ultimate* concern, that for which everything else is to be done, that which is enjoyed for its own sake—is the self. And this discrepancy between what one *claims* to worship and what one *really* worships applies not only to individuals, but to entire religious communities. This divide is the site of one of religion's most productive critical abilities. Religions and their adherents at this point can be driven to self-criticism, measuring the distance between what is professed as the ultimate concern and what is actually lived—or they may refuse. Whether or not constitutional law can productively incorporate such an existential understanding—the whole purpose of which is to evaluate religion and culture—is irrelevant to its fruitfulness as a tool for theological and cultural criticism.

A different objection comes from Hannah Arendt, who maintains that we must be careful not to confuse a thing with its function. Her 1968 criticism of the "functionalization" of thought seems to imply a rejection of Tillich's definition:

> A convenient instance [of functionalization] may be provided by the widespread conviction in the free world that communism is a new "religion" notwithstanding its avowed atheism, because it fulfills socially, psychologically, and "emotionally" the same function traditional religion fulfilled and still fulfills in the free world. The concern of the social sciences does not lie in what bolshevism as ideology or as form of government is, nor what its spokesmen have to say for themselves. Their concern is only with functions, and whatever fulfills the same function can, according to this view, be called the same. It is as though I had the right to call the heel of my shoe a hammer because I use it to drive nails into the wall.[20]

There are several responses to Arendt's complaint. First, there is no reason why a functional analysis must stop there. It is hard to see what would be lost if Communism were investigated both as a form of government and as a religion. Still, Arendt's position raises an important point. Religion and forms of culture—which we shall call "cultural forms"[21]—are distinguished by the questions they explicitly and primarily address.[22] A cultural form remains nonreligious only so long as it does not promulgate an interpretation of ultimate meaning. But a cultural form can be religious as well as economic and political. A political institution can remain political even when it is more than political, that is, when it claims that a certain political action or stance is ultimately meaningful and fulfilling. And religious institutions are never only religious, but also political and social. Religious groups never *only* ask and answer the question of ultimacy. They do other things besides (at a minimum, they have an internal political organization). Political analysis of religious institutions and theological analysis of political institutions are equally legitimate. Problems arise when only one type of analysis is performed.

Moreover, if we ignore the religious functions of supposedly nonreligious cultural forms, we limit our understanding. Our common discourse recognizes this by speaking of a variety of activities as requiring "faith" or being "religious."[23] Consider the example of Communist-restoration organizations such as the "Spiritual Heritage Society" in today's Russia;[24] or Robert Bork's claim that a constitutional amendment to ban flag-burning should be supported because the flag is a "sacred symbol"; or Presidential candidate Bob Dole's bald assertion that "if the American flag is not held sacred then nothing is sacred."[25] To describe such pronouncements as simply political misses a key dimension. If the flag is a sacred symbol, then what it symbolizes, the nation, is a sacred object; if it is the very litmus test of the sacred, then the nation is supremely sacred. It has become God. A theological analysis of culture then must ask: is the nation *truly* sacred? No strictly political analysis can address this question, nor can it simply disregard claims to "sacredness." Nor can it grasp the potent union of religion and nationalism worldwide. In such cases, theological examination (whether performed by theologians, political theorists, or other cultural critics) is not merely optional.

Arendt's objection also underestimates change. One thing often comes to take the place of another because it performs a function better. If the heel of a shoe were a better hammer than a hammer, doubtless it would come to be sold and marketed as a hammer; and what we now call "hammer" would become a curio in a museum in which future generations could pity us for our backwardness. Likewise, religions grow, die, and are replaced by other religions.

Finally, we (like Tillich) do not understand religion *solely* in terms of its function. The ultimate functions religiously only because it is understood to *be* ultimate; its function depends on its perceived referent, its content.

The Criteria of Ultimacy: Comprehensiveness and Self-transcendence

Religion, then, has two sides: an *objective* side (the divine, the sacred, or God) and a *subjective* side (in classical Protestantism, faith).

The objective side entails the claim that *what* is worshiped is truly ultimate, while the subjective side consists in the believer's *experience* of it *as* ultimate, a defining preoccupation that affects and remakes all the self's other concerns. A religion's personal and cultural influence (as well as its function) depends on what is *claimed* and *lived* as God.

This two-sided character of "ultimate concern" is just what makes Tillich's understanding of religion both fruitful and difficult. We have already identified one of these fruitful complications—what a religion claims to be ultimate need not correspond strictly with what its believers do and say. There can be a looser or tighter fit between the dominant forms of a tradition and its adherents. In fact, we can distinguish five possible religious relations to ultimacy, with infinite gradations between them.[26] First possibility: a religion's symbolic form expresses ultimacy in a relatively adequate way; that is, it proclaims as ultimate that which really is ultimate, and relates reality to it with some facility. At the same time, the believer actually experiences this ultimate *as* ultimate. This is the ideal case, in which both the religion and the adherent have an ultimate concern that is really ultimate.[27] Second possibility: the religion expresses ultimacy in a relatively adequate way, but the believer misappropriates that expression and places ultimate concern in something else which is *not* truly ultimate, but which the believer nevertheless experiences as ultimate.[28] Third possibility: the religion expresses ultimacy well, but the believer fails to be moved by it, that is, does not *feel* it as ultimate; there may be a "God," but it makes no decisive difference to the believer.[29] Fourth possibility: the religion proclaims something which is *not* ultimate, and the adherent appropriates that false ultimate. Both stake their existence on this false ultimate. Fifth possibility: the religion expresses ultimacy poorly, but the believer knows that to be the case, and has a more adequate grasp of what ought to be of ultimate concern. In this instance, the believer has a fuller ultimate concern than the religion. In the second and fifth instances, where there is a perceived discrepancy between the religion's and the adherent's ultimate concerns, each may attempt to transform the other, depart from each other, or eliminate each other. The same is largely true of relations between religions.

This is not merely a descriptive, but also a *normative* account of religion. In order to distinguish more and less adequate versions of ultimate concern, there must be criteria by which such judgments can be made. We have already introduced the question of hypocrisy, but it will not do to stop there. Sincerity is not a sufficient criterion (though one much beloved of Americans)—there is no reason to believe that Hitler or Stalin was not sincere. The dedicated fanatic is more dangerous than the middling hypocrite. True ultimacy requires at least two additional criteria: *comprehensiveness* and *self-transcendence*.

Ultimacy as Comprehensiveness

First, comprehensiveness: God (or the gods) must be related to *all* realms of being. Conversely, all forms of being must participate in God, and all meanings must be encompassed in, and participate in, the defining meaning that is God. This involves comprehensiveness[30] in two senses: (1) breadth, that is, no *type* of being, species, or entity is excluded from participation in the divine; and (2) depth, that is, no *aspect* of those realms can be excluded either. An adequate system of religious symbols must relate every dimension of being, in its breadth and depth, to the object of worship,[31] and must preserve the believer's human "openness for absolutely everything, for being as such."[32]

There are many ways in which the object of religious faith can fail this test of comprehensiveness. Indeed, it is doubtful that any historical religion has fully satisfied it.[33] First, a religion may simply exclude a given realm from relation to the divine, either consciously or because of certain cultural or theological proclivities. Until recently, Christianity did this with the natural world. In such cases, the fullness of the deity is not being worshiped. The god that is worshiped is a god, not God. If God or a panoply of gods lacks comprehensiveness, then something more truly ultimate could be worshiped, namely the divine which does *not* exclude any sphere of existence from relation to it. This is not only a matter of thought. It carries existential implications, for both believers and the realm thus excluded. The believer's life is limited by its incapacity for any conceptual or practical relation with that realm.[34] But the excluded realm is impoverished as well. This was, according to Augustine, the problem with the Roman Empire. It was not that the pagans were impious. Rather, drawing on his distinction between use and enjoyment, Augustine argued that Rome's ultimate demise was due to its having made a disastrous choice for its final object of enjoyment: the empire's glory (which was the true Roman religion). This allowed Rome to inflict all manner of injustice upon other peoples, who eventually revolted. Rome's problem was not too little religion, but too much (albeit distorted).[35]

Augustine mistakenly thought that Christianity precluded idolatry because Christians do not worship a God limited to a particular place and time, and therefore could not accept or inflict injustice against any people. It remained for Ludwig Feuerbach (followed by a host of others) to turn Augustine's analysis against Christianity itself.[36] One of Feuerbach's most telling points was his claim that the Christian focus on attaining of heavenly bliss effectively devalued the world. The elevation of God implied the debasement of humanity. Feuerbach was correct: a religion that does not relate to all things will ignore and probably denigrate what it excludes. Similar roads are well traveled in politics. Those who advocate the separation of religion and politics say something, not only about themselves, but also about politics or religion. Some Christian sects ignore political life because politics is unimportant or positively harmful to the soul; political visions that eschew religious participation in public debate usually view religion as similarly irrelevant or harmful.

Vital religions do not long manage to exclude entire realms of being. A religion that participates in the truly ultimate divine cannot exclude any such realms for long. Religions routinely reestablish comprehensive relations with the whole of being; if one religion fails, another will fill the void—if there are no hammers, a heel will do. This usually requires an internal reformulation of the religious tradition.[37] One method of reestablishing comprehensiveness is to reintroduce the excluded realm by positing a purely negative relation to it, identifying it as antithetical to ultimate meaning and purpose. In Christian thought, this is usually the category of sin. That which is sinful is not removed from relation to God, but excluded from a directly positive relation.[38] For example, many nonpolitical sects quickly became antipolitical, asserting the sinfulness of political activity—just as pacifism does not lack a relation to physical violence, but has an exclusively negative relation to it. Another way to restore comprehensiveness involves incorporating the formerly excluded dimension of being into worship, ritual, and symbolic frameworks.[39] This requires the new claim that the divine is really and positively related to this previously unregarded realm, and that this is either new or was simply heretofore misunderstood. (This is beginning to happen in Christianity's relation to nature.)

What we have grown accustomed to calling "conservative" and "liberal" religious movements in America largely correspond to these two respective strategies: conservatives posit a negative relationship to the new, liberals a positive one. Of course, these are frequently mixed, and there is often much inconsistency between what is said and what is actually done. Thus conservative Christians have almost completely embraced divorce (without ever having actually admitted it), while liberals have remained more traditional in their desired family arrangements than their rhetoric about nontraditional arrangements might lead one to expect. Even the opponents of change are transformed by the very act of opposition. A denomination or congregation which opposes the ordination of women, for example, is not the same as it was before the issue was raised—and some of their daughters go elsewhere to be ordained. For our purposes here, however, the essential point is that the whole symbolic system can be judged minimally on how well it incorporates all aspects of all beings into participation with God.

The Inevitable Loss of Ultimacy: Finitude and History

Religion is defined by the question of ultimate, determinative meaning. Comprehensiveness—or the lack of it—is one criterion by which this can be judged. So far, we have noted only the palpable fact that religions lose and gain in comprehensive adequacy. "Loss" and "gain" are the proper terms, for there has never been, nor will there ever be, a religion that is fully comprehensive. Religions and religious people worship the divine; they are not themselves divine.

How do these losses and gains occur? The aim of religions, and the cultures they vivify, is what Tillich called "theonomy": the cultural situation in which all finite cultural forms point toward and participate in "their transcendent meaning,"[40] God. No culture or religion has been utterly theonomous, but there have been approximations (Tillich thought that the high Middle Ages were a period of relative theonomy). But such periods do not last. There are at least two reasons for this. Both are, as far as we know, permanent structures of human life and its conditions.

The first such problem is human finitude (which is *not*, in itself, evil or sinful).[41] One of the tasks of a religion is to relate our obviously limited and incomplete lives to ultimate religious meaning. Indeed, religious doctrines and symbol systems can be understood as responses to the problem of the relation of the infinite to the finite, the ultimate to the particular. However, any specific religious solution to this problem is unavoidably particular and finite. This creates an insuperable difficulty: to be truly comprehensive, a religious system of meaning would have to hold all particularities (including nature) in its grasp, simultaneously and in their proper proportion and relation. It would also have to relate this comprehensive system of meaning to the divine. The challenge to religion—to include all realms in relation to the divine, each in its proper place and weight—is formidable.[42]

However difficult it is to maintain theonomy in the face of finitude, a second feature of human being—the ambiguity and relativity of history—strains theonomy even more. If history were the story of progress, or even just benevolently neutral, we could think that women and men of goodwill and acute intelligence in each succeeding generation would purify the limitations of their forebears, standing like Sir Isaac Newton "on the shoulders of giants." This was, it seems, part of the nineteenth-century confidence in the progress of history that was largely blind to the possibility that we might be more petty, more limited, and less intelligent than our forebears. Such confidence is not merely foolish; it is, ironically, ahistorical. As finite beings, we are embedded in history. If every realm of being must be related to the divine for a religion to be adequately comprehensive, then any adequate religion or faith must also understand history in relation to the ultimate. Conversely, if God is truly divine, God must be history's God, and the real changes history brings at each moment must be placed within frameworks of ultimate and determinative meaning.

American liberals and conservatives alike have dealt badly with history. Although both attempt to incorporate historical change into a comprehensive meaning, they frequently operate with a truncated notion of history. Conservatism strives to preserve the past because it is the past, and cannot recognize the possibility that the God of history might usher in something new that transforms life's possibilities for the better. For the conservative, history is but a fall from paradise. Primitivist American Protestants who enshrine a past moment (the New Testament church, for example) as normative for all time clearly exemplify such an interpretation of history.[43] For other religious groups, the nation's founding is the normative moment,[44] and all departures from which are descents into various hells. Subsequent history is the devil's playground, not God's province.

Progressivism correctly recognizes that history transforms, and that such transformation may well signify a greater meaning than previously available. But progressive interpretations of history—which view conservative fears as simply backward, because history steadily progresses and improves—are finally as antihistorical as the conservative. Just as in Rauschenbusch's theology and (arguably) Dewey's philosophy, history is usually seen as the mere unfolding of latent potentialities; the "new" is safely encased in the old.[45] For Dewey, change emerged from the development of scientific method; for Rauschenbusch, the very content of the future emerged from present potentialities.[46] The new was simply the old come out of hiding. Progressives are sanguine about change.[47] After all, nothing has really changed in essence; only appearances differ. Moreover, the "new" is inevitable. Conservatism confronts the possibility of radical change more adequately than progressivism because it recognizes that the new can just as easily be disastrous as beneficial. Curiously, however, neither can countenance the possibility that the new is a manifestation of power, an irruption of meaning not fully traceable to the past and sometimes superior to it. H. Richard Niebuhr rightly observed that, for both conservative and progressive interpretations of history, "time does not affect either the ideas or their actualizers in any very significant fashion."[48]

This account of progressives and conservatives is oversimplified. Progressive theorists of history such as the Social Darwinists advocated social policies similar to those of conservatives;[49] the progressive Rauschenbusch laced his thought with a heavy dose of Protestant primitivism; much contemporary conservatism persists in Reaganism's primitivist confidence, and Reaganism often expressed the primitivist restoration of an idyllic past in the future by means of the very modernity this conservatism professes to despise, and particularly by means of a quite antiprimitive technology.[50] "Liberals" and "conservatives" often maintain both attitudes, largely depending on the change that appears or is contemplated. Liberals seek to conserve social welfare programs, while conservatives argue for "traditional values." Meanwhile, both sides attack each other for being insufficiently progressive on these issues. But *these* are views of history between which they oscillate, not others. Nor are these views as different as they first seem. If the new is not really new, then perhaps the clock *can* be turned back to the archetypes from which all else emerged. For both, history "cannot be sundered from the concept of homogeneous, empty time"[51] a paradisiacal age of innocence that is, in reality, no time at all.[52]

Whatever else history may bring, it does usher in the really new, manifested in self-positing power, unpredictable on the basis of known potentialities.[53] Two implications are worth mentioning. First, the new realms of being which history brings must be integrated into frameworks of ultimate meaning. Second, and more subtly, the powers of being undergo transformation over time and space; their relation to ultimacy changes, growing greater or lesser.[54] Real historical change, like the structure of human finitude (which it compounds), precludes any fantasies about steady progress toward ever more adequate ultimate concern. This also brings all utopian fantasies, whether futurist or restorationist, to an end.

All conceptions and symbols of ultimate fulfillment contain a reflective content, and such content lives from the past. Søren Kierkegaard correctly noted that life can only be lived forward, but can only be understood backward. Following Kierkegaard, Arendt notes that an action's "meaning never discloses itself to the actor but only to the backward glance of the historian who himself does not act."[55] We understand and act upon what has already pressed itself on us. Religion, even as it seeks to discern and evoke the future, is always catching up to the time in which it lives. The processes of history and its actors bring new realms of being into existence. The development of the nation-state, the waxing and waning of species, and the advent of cyberspace are all events which any religion that claims true ultimacy must discern in relation to the divine. Environmental questions have grown more pressing on a crowded, technological planet where every action increasingly outstrips our ability to understand its consequences for the earth. Conversely, changes in religious symbol systems and practices will alter what we see as the core problems of civilization in any particular time.

Thus, the question of meaning in any particular religious tradition involves a religious intuition of the central problems of meaning for its time. There is no escape from particular history. This should be no cause for despair, for history is also the ground and support of all productivity. Still, for religion, it creates the particular risk, even the inevitability, that ultimacy will be lost.[56] Time and finitude themselves (even without the help of any perversity or sin) rob religion and culture of theonomous relation if religion remains static. This means, as we explain more fully in chapter 4, that *no religion could be fully adequate in a single form in history.*

Self-transcendence and the Recovery of Ultimacy

This is why the second criterion, self-transcendence, is necessary. Comprehensiveness and ultimacy can be lost in many ways. Symbols and doctrines can become truncated and sterile. Religious teachings, like all reflective conceptual systems, need time to anticipate as well as to respond to every new situation to and in which they must speak. The difficulty is particularly severe for religions because they seek to embody comprehensive structures of meaning. Particular symbols may be intensified to such an extent that they overwhelm the whole, creating narrow molds into which all comprehensive meanings are forced. Anything which does not fit is either made to fit or ignored. This was Augustine's complaint about Roman religion. Similarly, certain historic Christian symbols, productively intensified at flashpoints in the history of the church, have sometimes outlived their usefulness. The Lutheran Reformation's emphasis on faith obscured the importance of political life long after the sixteenth century (and perhaps played a role in delaying Germany's political maturity). Similarly, pronounced stress on either inner experience or external action, while often necessary to correct distortions in practice, has often become the exclusive emphasis in some sectarian traditions. Every new movement is in danger of overshadowing the whole with its special symbol; every old one is in danger of losing comprehensiveness by clinging to the old symbols.

When a particular symbol is emphasized to the exclusion of all others, this does not make the symbol wrong; it rather *skews* the meaning of reality as a whole. It was not wrong for Americans to sense a special calling and divine mission for the nation. Indeed, it is difficult to see how such a nation could survive without a sense of mission. But it was and is wrong when the symbols of a chosen people, manifest destiny, or the sacred mission[57] of bringing democracy to the world obscure the ambiguities of the nation, license oppression of indigenous peoples, and foster a nativism and xenophobia that extend from the anti-Catholic, anti-immigrant invectives of the nineteenth century through the Pat Buchananesque suspicion of things foreign.[58] A system that fixates on a single symbol forces everything else into submission, or simply isolates religion from the whole and makes it irrelevant. Reinhold Niebuhr was fond of noting that the destructive potential of a religion is directly proportional to its ability to create a powerful sense of fulfillment for its adherents.[59]

Finally, the symbols themselves may become distorted. This was the core of Feuerbach's argument against Christianity, later taken up in America by Dewey (who applied it to all historical religions). According to Feuerbach, as we have noted, Christianity's symbols necessarily devalued the world and the self even as Christians actually worshiped the self in the guise of God. The aim was eternal life, and that aim was essentially self-interested. What Feuerbach thought constituted the "essence" of Christianity we think are distortions, a topic addressed in chapter 3. For now, however, the point is that comprehensiveness is not a sufficient criterion of religious fruitfulness. Self-transcendence is necessary.

Religions have powerful resources with which to recover and to construct a better sense of ultimacy in relation to all being. The inner multiplicity and diversity of religious symbols, combined with venerable traditions and future anticipations, constitute rich sources for transformation. Religious traditions can keep alive a host of symbols and possibilities that cannot be actualized by all believers at all times and places but remain available for future recovery. There are intimations of future openness and transcendence in traditional eschatologies. In other words, religions have resources at their disposal which can lead them to transcend themselves. This is the criterion of self-transcendence: every religion must seek to transcend its own present configuration. Most have the resources to do so, though nothing guarantees that they will choose well.

Limitation, distortion, and the unavoidable risk of self-transcendence are inescapable because of the particularities of tradition and culture in which every religion is present. Particularity is a gift, for it is how we are real. It is also a danger. No matter how much it attempts to be comprehensive, every religion (like every language) is particular, and conceals as well as reveals. There is no escaping this. The pretension to fully adequate universality was, like the autonomous ego, "mortally wounded when it was found that language was not its instrument."[60] Absolute universality is not an option; even self-transcendence cannot accomplish it.[61] This can tempt a religion or a culture to sloth and indifference: disavowing the call to self-transcendence because it can never become universal. Or it can tempt a religion to pride: the pretense that it is fully universal when it knows that it is not. But properly understood, this discovery is an opportunity: the multiplicity of cultural and religious traditions, their interactions, their reinterpretations and criticism are the *means* to combat idolatrous distortions of the particular (though they can also simply be an occasion for more idolatry). A theonomous situation is not a universal, ahistorical position, but one in which all particularities participate in and point to the God that transcends, incorporates, and heals each.

We have, then, two formal criteria for judging religious symbol systems and assessing their fruitfulness: (1) comprehensive grasp, both in breadth and depth; and (2) a capacity (and willingness) for self-transcendence combined with a denial of idolatry, especially self-idolatry. Now we are able to return to the question with which we began: What kind of religion, if any, should be valued in the public sphere? The initial answer is that a religion's value for public life will be directly proportional to its drive toward comprehensiveness and its capacity for self-transcendence.

THE MUTUAL NECESSITY OF RELIGION AND PUBLIC LIFE

With these criteria in mind, we are in a better position to analyze and to evaluate current proposals concerning the proper place (if any) of religion in American public life. Broadly speaking, these proposals fall into three broad categories: the *inclusionists*, who argue that religion (sometimes meaning only conservative Christianity) should be included; the *universalist exclusionists*, who want to exclude religion because it is not universal; and the *particularist exclusionists*, who want to exclude religion because it causes conflict. We repeat: our evaluation of these proposals is *not* distinctively Christian—specifically Christian criteria do not enter the debate until chapter 3. Here our judgments are based only on the formal criteria of comprehensiveness and self-transcendence. In other words, our argument for the legitimacy of *Christian* participation in public life emerges from more general standards by which the claims of *all* religious groups—including a *variety* of Christian groups—are evaluated. The public square must remain public.

One reason we took such a substantial detour into the question of *defining* religion and ultimacy is that the question of religion's role in public life hinges on the question of what religion *is*. As we shall see, neither inclusionists nor exclusionists have thought carefully about this problem. Some exclusionists, as we have already noted, simply equate "religion" and "church." Others simply presume that all religious claims are irrational or incommensurable, and hence authoritarian, repressive, supernaturalistic, arbitrary, and tyrannical; therefore the forces of public "reason" must oppose religious claims. But most inclusionists have an equally uncritical view of religion; they refuse to ask *what kind* of religion ought to be valued in public life (usually presupposing that conservative Christianity, and maybe Judaism, are the only serious contenders). Their assumption seems to be that religion is reducible to morality, and that if we want morality in public life, religion is an unproblematic way to achieve it. Like Dwight Eisenhower, they believe that "our government makes no sense unless it is founded on a deeply felt religious belief—and I don't care what it is"[62] (although they dissent from Eisenhower's final qualifier).

One more point before we take up the arguments of the inclusionists and exclusionists: our current political practice is *antipolitical*. In contrast to the great respect public life enjoyed among the ancient Athenians and the early Americans, ours is an era in which politics is constantly devalued. Candidates from Ross Perot to Morry Taylor garner support by proclaiming that they are not politicians, but despisers of politics who will bring the resources of private business to bear on political problems (generally in autocratic ways). Perot's politics was purely mechanical—"just get under the hood and fix it." Lest Perot and Taylor be dismissed as cranks, we should remember that Perot was supported by just under 20 percent of the electorate in 1992. Even candidates of the major parties routinely employ the same tactic, running for governmental office by running against government's legitimacy. The term "politics" is almost always used even by officeholders to denote shady intention and partisan advantage rather than public benefit. The surest insult is to call someone "political." Politics becomes at best a necessary evil, not an honorable calling. In other words, political and public life have lost their religious quality, the sense that they participate positively in God's meaning and purpose.

Public life now enjoys the same enviable reputation as public toilets. It is not a vocation through which one can honor God.

Politics' loss of a religious dimension cripples public life for believers and nonbelievers alike. The political challenge facing us today is, in part, religious: how to imbue the public sphere with meaning. Because of their commitments to religiously grounded politics, one might expect the inclusionists to help reinvigorate public life, value, and meaning; to some of them we now turn.

Arguments for Inclusion: The Triumph of Formalism

THE ARGUMENT FROM RIGHTS

The most forceful arguments for including religion in public debates, unfortunately, do not get us very far. Their exclusive focus on merely formal questions of freedom and rights prevents them from engaging religious content and asking whether this content might be *productive* in public debate—and if so, just what kinds of religious content will prove most helpful.[63] Just like their liberal opponents, inclusionists generally limit the term "religion" to institutional religions, not the broader definition of "ultimate concern" we have defended. (Our use of the term "religion" for the remainder of this chapter should be clear from the context. When we say "religions," we generally mean the narrower understanding of institutional religion that both the inclusionists and their liberal exclusionist opponents presuppose.)

Inclusionists confine themselves to asking whether religions have a *right* to participate. But this right almost no one is in fact inclined to disallow. It is the right to be *heard* that is in question.

The focus on rights is a deeply rooted American tendency. The recent case in which the Supreme Court enjoined a school district in Mississippi from conducting morning prayers was less interesting for the decision itself than for the debate that surrounded it. In several national media, including *The Oprah Winfrey Show*, friends and enemies of the practice alike argued almost exclusively in terms of their "right to speak" or their "right not to have personal religious opinion infringed." The defenders of school prayer imitated their opponents' language of pluralism, claiming that religious voices are entitled to equal hearing. Moreover, both sides also assumed that the only legitimate means to resolve the dispute were legal, namely, the Court. Since both parties understood the dispute to be about inviolable freedoms, how could it be otherwise?

Though the influential works of Stephen Carter and Richard Neuhaus are more subtle than this, both still focus almost exclusively on questions of rights. Neuhaus, for example, has considerable sympathy with fundamentalist complaints that God has been "taken out of our public schools or out of our public life." Although "God, being God, cannot be 'taken out' of anything . . . it is the case that truth claims and normative ethics that have specific reference to God or religion have been . . . excluded."[64] Carter makes the same mistake, though more understandably so because he is a legal scholar; but both Neuhaus and Carter carry their legal reflections over into the arena of public debate without alteration. Both refuse to engage the *content* implied by the plural option they support, namely *what* it is about religion that makes it important for political debate and decision making. Indeed, Carter makes (but does not defend) the assertion that there are no standards by which one could judge the relative adequacy or productivity of religious positions: "*The truth* is that outsiders have no standpoint from which to judge what counts as a 'superior' or 'inferior' position."[65] Really? And if there are no criteria, why are those who seek to exclude religion for the public square unjustified in doing so? How is Carter able to judge *their* truth from the outside? Carter and Neuhaus open the door for a halfway relativism—outsiders cannot judge the adequacy of faith commitments, but those with faith commitments can judge the truth claims of others.

What would ever lead sophisticated scholars to embrace such a problematic view without bothering to question it? The unexamined assumption is that a legal conception of rights is the sole consideration, and is sufficient to establish not just the possibility of participation in public argument but also its *desirability*. There is a comic sadness in defenses of the Mississippi school district. Complaining bitterly about "secular humanism" and "individualism," the inclusionists nevertheless build on a cornerstone of liberal individualism—the primacy of rights.

The argument from rights may be partly correct. But it is certainly inadequate. Because we are concerned here with political decision making and public debate, and not just the institutional relationship of "church and state," the argument has little mileage. The rhetoric of rights[66] violates its own boundaries when it becomes an all-purpose defense of desirability. Simply put, *the right* to engage in a given conduct does not *make* that conduct *right*. In our law-obsessed culture, however, that difference is blurred. Consequently, inclusionist arguments are regularly reduced to questions of rights, fairness, and purely formal pluralism.[67]

Worse still, our moral language seems unable to escape the shackles of legal language. Kent Greenawalt, who attempts to meld liberalism with limited religious inclusion, promises that he is "not talking mainly about legal propriety" but about "how people make (and can be expected to make) moral evaluations."[68] Though he generally thinks it unwise for those who participate in religious institutions to give religious grounds for their political choices, he concedes that if there are no "commonly accessible reasons" by which such choices are made, religious grounds may be offered. Why? Because it would be unfair for religious grounds to be excluded. "I do *not* rely on any claim that depriving public decisions of religiously based understandings will result in *bad laws or policies, impoverish political dialogue*, or *undermine the stability of law and government*. Rather my argument is based on *simple notions of fairness and tolerance* for diverse beliefs."[69] Morality is here reduced to legal morality.

Similarly, Michael Perry, who properly emphasizes the distinction between legal right and moral ought, nevertheless restricts what counts as a moral argument so severely that the distinction is all but erased. Perry asserts that his question "is not about what citizens should be legally permitted to do. Rather, the inquiry is about what . . . citizens should do *as a matter of political morality.*"[70] Yet he later retracts this effort on grounds that sacrifice this more robust morality for the legal morality of a liberal, pluralist democracy: "It is deeply misguided to construct an (exclusivist) ideal [in which Perry includes his own earlier conception] of political choice purportedly for all of us Americans, or even most of us, partly on the basis of theological views, or epistemological views, that many Americans not only do not embrace, but reject." Such would not constitute a valid "principle of restraint."[71] (This despite the fact that his *Love and Power*[72] did attempt to generate criteria for desirable public involvement by those committed to institutional religions.) Whereas his original focus was on full moral desirability, Perry now talks only about restraint: pluralism without regard for content, and the right to speak, all of which are certainly moral considerations, but limited ones.

The Argument from Facticity

When the freedom-right-fairness defense of inclusion does get beyond mere legal considerations, it often extends no farther than hurt feelings. Carter, for instance, is outraged on behalf of religious persons that the demand to exclude religion from public life "represents a sweeping rejection of the deepest beliefs of millions of Americans, who are being told, in effect, that their views do not matter."[73] Maybe so—but perhaps they are being asked to change their views for the better. The sometimes petulant assertion that one is not being "taken seriously" implies that one should be. Worse, it quickly lapses into an argument based on mere facticity: since religious views *do* influence politics, they should not be excluded. It also assumes that no religious position can be criticized or improved by another. This argument boils down to a particularly bankrupt version of rights, namely, the "right to my own opinion." Neuhaus dismisses any questions about mixing religion and politics with the simple assertion that "they inescapably do mix, like it or not."[74] Carter echoes,

> When the guardians of the public square inveigh against religious dialogue, or when pundits worry about the influence of religion on politics, they are worrying . . . against history. The battle for the public square is already over. The rhetoric of religion is simply *there;* it is far too late in America's political day to argue over "shoulds."[75]

We ought to be troubled by these seemingly innocent assertions. First, we repeat, the argument from facticity refuses to engage content; givenness is not sufficient justification. Ought and is may converge for basic structures of being (for example, it does not make much sense to ask whether one should have been a comet instead of a human), but not for historically contingent religious institutions. Defense is needed, not mere declaration. There may be good reason for religious action in the public arena; but that reason should be articulated.[76]

Second, these analyses either overlook history and change, or, like Carter, simply declare that the historical tide has irreversibly turned. But historical trends are notably reversible: like the wind (and the Spirit), they often blow where they will, and what turns one way this year may reverse itself the next. There was no "war to end all wars." The Republican Party was supposed to have died in 1964; the Democrats, in 1988. The Soviet bloc was supposed to be a perpetual threat; and now Jiang Zemin declares the "liberation" of Tibet to be incontrovertible "progress." Inclusionists such as Carter and Neuhaus reduplicate these errors in declaring themselves to be on the side of history. Besides, the argument from facticity self-destructs when applied to political life. If institutional religion is irreversibly in the public sphere, why complain about its exclusion in a few areas? And if it is excluded, is this not also a given "fact" to be appropriately applauded because it is the way things are?

A halfway Hegelianism that affirms that "whatever is, is right," is impossible if one wants to criticize *any* aspects of what is. Any analysis which relies exclusively on rights and the "way things are" is strikingly ill-suited to analyze the adequacy of various positions, both religious (in the narrow sense) and nonreligious. This is the question that Carter dismisses and that Greenawalt and the later Perry refuse to ask. If this be pluralism, it is a pluralism of neglect, alternately vacuous and dangerous, and easily transformed into a virulent antipluralism.[77] To assert that religion should play a role in political life simply because it exists or because its adherents have rights endangers that selfsame religion's continued vitality. Any religion—any position, for that matter—that stakes its claim merely on its current social dominance or its "right to its own opinion" grows flabby and complacent, ripe for defeat by opponents who at least take the trouble to argue about what *should* be the case. In the 1970s, the welfare state relied on its assumed inevitability; now it is a nearly empty shell. Until the 1970s, Protestant Christianity relied too much on its factual dominance of American political speech; now that it has been rightly challenged, it must do what it should have been doing all along—rethink its appropriate place, if any, in contemporary public life.

Majoritarian Antipolitics

Neuhaus, unlike Carter and Perry, does argue for the importance of religious involvement in the public sphere in several ways. His first claim derives from his argument from facticity, but shades that position into a disturbing majoritarianism.[78] He protests that the exclusion of the institutional religion, "this sanitizing of the public square" as he calls it, "has not been subjected to democratic debate or vote."[79] Would sanitization have been acceptable had it been submitted to the rule of the majority? Apparently Neuhaus's answer to the stock parental query, "If most of your friends decided to jump off a cliff, would you follow?" would be "Yes!" He presents his majoritarian impulse as pluralism. But it is a strange pluralism indeed that insists that any opposing arguments about religion's role in the public square deny "who we are."

Who are the "we" who matter? The majority, the Christian.[80] Neuhaus argues that "*only* the biblical tradition is democratically supportable in this society."[81] Why? Because Christians are the majority. "Democratically supportable" means that the majority assents:

> Surrounding the [public] square, pressing to get in—are those who sing the songs not of Athens nor of Havana but of Jerusalem. They say they represent the future, and at the same time they say they represent the past. Most insistently, they say they represent the majority of us. And, to an extent, for better and for worse, their claims are true.[82]

It is not that Neuhaus is not sometimes critical of the majority; he is.[83] But he seems unable to conceive of democracy as anything other than the exclusive rule of the majority—a tyranny that *the American constitutional republic was specifically designed to prevent.*[84] We do not put everything to a vote precisely because then the majority would dictate. Liberalism rightly fears the move from facticity to majoritarianism, particularly when facticity is wedded to authority. Whether liberalism should fear every religion is another question, but it is justified in hesitating before the claims of some.

Neuhaus slips into majoritarianism so easily because he does not attend to the question of religious content. He needs to keep the argument purely formal—because he is (evidently) unwilling to subject the *content* of religion to public scrutiny—and the principle of simple majority rule fits the bill. Moreover, his inattention to the content of religious convictions leads Neuhaus to treat it as static—it is all simply "religion," usually equated with Christianity, because that is "who we are." Who we might become, whether we are now as we were, or whether we ought to be as we are, are questions Neuhaus's purely formal argument cannot ask. The religious beliefs, attitudes, styles that have the "right" to be in the public square are timeless, simply given. And because these beliefs (whatever they are) are held by a majority, they apparently have greater rights. This is dangerously tilted toward majoritarianism.

Neuhaus's second argument for institutional Christianity's participation in public life is more interesting, but again possible only because he limits himself to purely formal considerations. Institutional religion, he says, prevents totalitarianism. How? The secular state, if it succeeds in eliminating all ideological opponents, becomes a total ideological system, and then proceeds to totalitarian domination. Religion is the principal institutional check against totalitarianism, because it opposes the state's claim to totality. Neuhaus explains,

> The notion of the secular state can become the prelude to totalitarianism. That is, once religion is reduced to nothing more than privatized conscience, the public square has only two actors in it—the state and the individual. Religion as a mediating structure—a community that generates and transmits moral values—is no longer available as a countervailing force to the ambitions of the state. Whether in Hitler's Third Reich or in today's sundry states professing Marxism-Leninism, the chief attack . . . is upon the *institutions* that bear and promulgate belief in a transcendent reality by which the state can be called to judgment. Such institutions threaten the totalitarian proposition that everything is to be within the state, nothing is to be outside the state.[85]

Neuhaus is correct that the state *can* become an "ersatz religion" (i.e., an ultimate concern), because "transcendence abhors a vacuum."[86] And he is right that some totalitarian societies have furthered that objective by forcing religion out of public life. He is also right to argue that mediating institutions, including religious ones, can serve as a check on the totalitarian tendencies of the state. (They do not seem, however, very effective as a check on the totalitarian tendencies of the marketplace!) But he is wrong to imply that only Christian institutions can do so or that they have always done so.

It is surely too much to say that "the disestablishment of religion leads to the establishment of state as church" and that there is "no conceptual alternative to a *de facto* state religion once *traditional* religion is driven from the public square."[87] Is the threat of tyranny less because it is carried out by a majority or because the proffered civil ideology is Christian rather than Marxist? Whatever the answer, it requires a normative, theological content of Christianity that Neuhaus is unwilling to subject to criticism. Moreover, nonreligious institutions have certainly opposed totalitarianism vigorously. Finally, Neuhaus's dichotomy—either traditional (Christian) religion or the totalitarian state—ignores the fact that statism can be linked with religion and is arguably more dangerous when it is. It is not obvious that Soviet-style totalitarianism was worse for its citizens than Marcos's rule of the Philippines, Latin American dictatorships, Duvalier terrorism in Haiti, apartheid South Africa, or American slavery, all of which invoked Christian Scriptures and Christian churches for their oppression. Majoritarianism not only fails to prevent such state terrorism, it can foster it. This Neuhaus ignores.

Neuhaus abstracts from the content of any actual state and any actual religious commitment. The significance of Christianity is only that it is not the state—a very thin justification indeed. The question is not simply whether "the state" is dangerous, nor whether "religion" is critical of the state. Instead, the issue is whether the American state is dangerous (and in what ways), and whether religions in America ought to be engrossed in public life. Neuhaus virtually equates the state with totalitarianism. Furthermore, like many neoconservatives, Neuhaus conflates "the state" and "government," which should remain distinct. But what is the *evidence,* in the current American context, that government and politics are *solely* concerned with domination, that all government does is assault freedom?[88] Of America's many dangers in the late twentieth century, totalitarianism seems far down the list. Neuhaus himself points out that politicians make careers by running against politics.[89] In any event, if politics is essentially totalitarian in character, then the object of political involvement must be explicitly antipolitical; we would then act politically only insofar as necessary to keep the ever-present totalitarian wolves at bay. The only reason for this kind of political involvement is to stop politics.

All inclusionist arguments that rely primarily on the right to participate and refuse to engage the question of religious content run aground on the same issues. They are majoritarian, and treat religion as static, unchanging, and unambiguously good. Indeed, the sort of static Christianity Neuhaus presupposes lacks any self-transcendence whatever. Ironically, Neuhaus's most fervent opponents—the liberals who wish to exclude religion from public discourse—agree with him completely on the static nature of religion.

Arguments for Exclusion: Universalist and Particularist Claims

As we have seen, many current defenses of religious involvement in political life are shallow, frequently building on religion's "right" to be in the public debate. This right is not in question. Almost no one denies religion's *right* to speak about public issues. What *is* in doubt—a doubt articulately expressed by some liberal political theorists—is whether religion *ought* to be part of public debate. Religious adherents, of all people, should understand the difference. Sadly, they often do not. To be *heard* is not a right but an *achievement.* In the case of politics, it requires that one show that one brings nutritious food to the public meal. And that is what a good many liberals deny that religion can do. They know that the focus on rights is one of liberalism's achievements, and are worried those who insist on religion's "right" to be heard seem intent on occupying the house and grounds carefully built and nurtured by the liberal heritage—all in order to destroy it. Many inclusionists excoriate precisely that liberal heritage as pagan and valueless, summed up in the epithet "secular humanism." Rights-inclusionists cannot have this both ways: they cannot vilify the very culture of rights upon which they stake their own claims. Liberals justly fear that the intellectual dishonesty of rights-inclusionists may be an indication that, having occupied the house of liberalism, they will expel its former tenants in the name of the "majority," "values," or "God."

Whatever the errors of the inclusionists, though, these errors do *not* justify the exclusion of religious conviction from public debate. They *do* mean that if religious conviction is either desirable or necessary to productive debate—and we believe it is both—it must run the gauntlet of liberal criticism. This will require analysis of the liberal arguments for exclusion (in the balance of this chapter), evaluation of the *content* of both current public religion (chapter 2) and evaluation of a more desirable alternative, the emphatic Christian center (chapters 3 through 5). If, however, liberal arguments are not adequately answered, questions of rights are simply irrelevant: there is no religious "right" to be heard.

Liberal political thought often grounds its arguments for the exclusion of religion in the classical division between reason and faith—itself a thoroughly Christian, indeed Protestant opposition.[90] Political discourse should supposedly be conducted solely within the confines of reason, both because of reason's self-evident value and because rational language meets the vaunted criterion of "neutrality." Religion, since its judgments are based in faith and are therefore not neutral, should remain quiet, or at most, should speak only when religious conviction is independently supportable by reason.

Such positions make certain crucial assumptions about religion, and particularly about the nature of faith. They are *assumptions;* rarely in liberal literature does one see any examination of religion or religions, or any supporting argument or evidence. The discussions of religion are spectral, describing nothing and no one in particular, with just enough resemblance to be recognizable.[91] In some cases, of course, it is an accurate picture.

The central assumption of liberal theory is that religion is extrarational. Extrarationality can be conceived variously, running a gamut from subrationality to antirationality, irrationality, and suprarationality. Most liberal arguments do not distinguish these various forms, although they make a great deal of difference. The result is that liberal theory takes it for granted that religion and the religious have no *arguments* by which their positions could be made plausible. It is as if religious convictions derived from coded communiqués between God and the believer. (It is, of course, true that *some* believers make this sort of claim; but the question is whether this is true of all, or even most, religion.) This assumption is frequently supplemented by the tacit or explicit claim that reason presents arguments, but religion is emotional,[92] reproducing the hoary opposition of reason and emotion that has been broadly and justly condemned by feminist thought.

In addition, some liberals follow Thomas Hobbes in assuming that religion has to do almost exclusively with the supernatural (a realm outside rational investigation) and that any political involvement for religion is an illegitimate extension of the supernatural (and nonrational) into the natural, which should be investigated solely by rational means. Finally, to the extent that religion is antirational, it is also authoritarian, suppressing all rational investigation that might come to a different conclusion. Insofar as religion has these characteristics of nonrationality, it should not be welcomed into the public sphere. Liberalisms that object to participation of religion in public matters do not do so, as Carter thinks, because they "trivialize" religion (though this may be the effect on the broader culture).[93] To the contrary, they believe religion to be preternaturally *dangerous* to democratic decision making.

The liberal exclusionist case is complex, partly because liberalism is not unified. It is useful to distinguish two versions: *universal* liberalism (which, though losing ground in philosophical circles, is still broadly popular in American culture), and *particular* liberalism (which commands support in both scholarly literature and the broader culture). The difference between them is that universal liberalism maintains that reason is universally accessible in both form and content, while particular liberalism has given up the hope of universal reason, instead maintaining that all forms of reason are culturally and historically conditioned. Consequently, particular liberalism discards the idea of a pure "reason" in favor of more qualified terms such as "public reason," "public criteria," and "rational argument."

Two Strands of Universal Liberalism

The American tradition of universal liberalism established itself as a force in the generation of the founders, an era which also created a distinctively American attitude toward religions and public life. The liberal tradition always contained internal variations, which meant that very different arguments were used, although with the same exclusionist result. Two distinct though related facets of the liberal tradition are especially important: the Federalist tradition, which gave us the rationale for the Constitution (represented by James Madison), and the more strongly rationalist tradition (represented by Thomas Jefferson and Thomas Paine).

The Federalist Strand—Defusing "Factionalism"

According to the American constitutional tradition, the existence of good government depended on whether it could stop the "perpetual vibration between the extremes of tyranny and anarchy."[94] The habit of conceiving proper government as falling between these two poles has continued into the twentieth century.[95] "Law and order" advocates and assistant principals everywhere have almost immediate recourse to the specter of chaos and anarchy, while their opponents appeal to the ghosts of totalitarian dictatorship. Although the opponents of constitutional government understood the principal danger as tyranny and favored a weak central government (positions echoed by today's right[96]), the constitutionalists thought a hodgepodge of independent governmental units fatal to the prospects of union. Alexander Hamilton claimed that "nothing can be more evident . . . than the alternative of an adoption of the new constitution or a dismemberment of the Union."[97]

Constitutionalists, of course, shared the fear of tyranny. Consequently, the Federalist leaders of the constitutional movement embraced two possibly incompatible demands: to provide for a united nation, but without generating that unity through domination. Largely because the Federalists bequeathed to us their style of thought, their problem resembles ours: how to bring a good society and rational justice out of divergent and opposed political and religious interests, that is, how to create unity in the midst of plurality—E pluribus unum. The anti-Federalists supposed that unity and diversity were conflicting principles;[98] the Federalist burden was to design their compatibility. The Federalists, however, were not interested in a "common ground" for its own sake, but in the *correct* common ground, which they (and many of their opponents) understood as the confluence of reason and justice.

Madison understood the multiplicity and conflict of interests as the problem of "factions." "By a faction," he says, "I understand a number of citizens, whether amounting to a majority or minority of the whole, who are united and actuated by some common impulse or passion, or interest, averse to the rights of other citizens, or to the permanent and aggregate interests of the community."[99] He defines particular interests and passions as whatever is harmful to the good of the whole or the rights of any one. Of course, these individual rights are universal in two senses. First, they were understood by the founders, the Declaration of Independence declares, as "inalienable" in Hobbes's sense that without them, humans would be less than human. Therefore, in the second place, each and every person possessed these rights. The problem, then, is how to relate the particularity of faction to the universality of rights, reason, and justice.

This opposition between the particular and the universal also determined the founders' perspective on religions and the public order. The most influential founders, including Federalists such as Madison and non-Federalists such as Jefferson, had a curious perspective on particular religions that can be summarized as "suspicious toleration." That is, they strongly believed in toleration of particular religions (or "sects," as they called them) but at the same time distrusted them deeply and preferred that they have no special impact on public life. *Religions were factions* and therefore subject to all the evils thereby entailed. This attitude has been handed down for two centuries and remains symptomatic of much liberalism today.[100] Religions are to be tolerated but distrusted.

How was the political and religious problem of factions to be solved so that adequate unity could subsist in the new nation? Two characteristic solutions were the Federalists' institutional solution and Jefferson's rationalist one; even though Madison was a universalist, his answer resonates through the newer, particular liberalism, whereas the rationalist solution was more influential upon thinkers like Dewey. According to Madison (here departing from Jefferson), the problem of factions was intractable to political discourse and rational persuasion. To be effective, persuasion would have to give "every citizen the same opinions, the same passions, and the same interests."[101] This is impossible, not only because of reason's fallibility, but also because the citizen's "reason and self-love, his opinions and his passions will have a reciprocal influence on each other. . . . The latent causes of faction are thus sown in the nature of man."[102] Nor can the problem be solved by "majority rule," for the majority is equally capable of betraying the common good and is especially dangerous to minority liberty. Indeed, Madison says, the "great object to which our inquiries are directed" is not the problem of factious minorities but "to secure the public good and private rights against the danger of" a majority faction.[103]

Because individuals alone cannot achieve this, Madison proposes structural answers. One feature of Madison's solution particularly bears on the question of religion. He saw that the bane of factions could be turned to the advantage of the new republic by allowing many factions to exist, so that none would gain sufficient might to quash the others.[104] Hence he extends the claim from religious to political plurality and presents the two as strictly parallel: "In a free government the security for civil rights must be the same as that for religious rights. It consists in the one case in the multiplicity of interests, and in the other in the multiplicity of sects."[105] A republic wants many interests and sects rather than fewer.

Madison and Hamilton were convinced that a central advantage of large republics is that they generate more interests and sects. Hamilton turned the anti-Federalist appeal to Montesquieu against them by arguing that Montesquieu himself held that a federal republic was the way to extend popular government while "reconciling the advantages of monarchy with those of republicanism."[106] In *Federalist* 51, Madison asserts that the partiality of factions is removed when a large number of them must compete for loyalty in an expansive republic:

> In the extended republic of the United States, and among the great variety of interests, parties, and sects which it embraces, a coalition of the majority of the whole society could seldom take place on any other principles than those of justice [which is the purpose of government and civil society[107]] and the general good.... The larger the society, provided it lie within a practicable sphere, the more duly capable it will be of self-government.[108]

Size matters in two ways. A large republic is beneficial in itself, and also because it spawns a greater heterogeneity of sects and interests, which prevents a factious unity of the majority.

Extending the argument to religion, Madison claims that the force of sectarian factionalism is contained, paradoxically, by increasing the number of sects and interests that vie with each other for the supremacy which their sheer number renders less likely. Particular interests or sects, then, have a strategic value. They duel with other particularities with the effect that what is particular is canceled out, leaving only the wheat of universal truth and justice to emerge. Madison was a dialectical theorist.[109] Religious toleration was the mechanism by which just results emerged from unjust motives. It was necessary in order to respect inalienable rights,[110] and it was useful and necessary in order to prevent one sect or interest from being able to constitute a faction that could actually influence public policy. The desired effect of individual denominations on public policy was, in Madison's view, nugatory.

The Rationalist Strand—Rational Religion

Madison's ingenious defense of pluralism is that it is necessary indirectly in order that universal justice may proceed. That solution is echoed today in some particular liberalism. However, throughout most of the nineteenth and early twentieth centuries, when confidence in reason ran high, universal liberalism tended to another route, illustrated in Jefferson's thought. Like Madison, Jefferson believed that particular religions should not play a role in public debates and policies. Whereas Madison believed that particularism and sectarianism were produced by the individual will (and not the individual's *reason*, which sectarianism corrupted), Jefferson was a more thoroughgoing rationalist. He begins his defense, *A Bill for Establishing Religious Freedom*, with the claim "that the opinions and belief of men depend not on their own will, but follow involuntarily the evidence proposed in their minds."[111] Moreover, God ordains to "extend [religion] by its influence on reason alone."[112] Jefferson's confident praise of reason was hardly isolated in late-eighteenth-century America. Thomas Paine, Benjamin Franklin, George Washington, John Adams, and others also believed reason's potential to be unbounded: it was the only necessary and acceptable tool for philosophy and religion.[113]

The distinguishing features of this rationalism were: (1) Reason reduced religions to their lowest common moral denominator and maintained that this was sufficient truth for religion. Indeed, (2) religious doctrine beyond this minimal morality was not only unnecessary but harmful. True religion was universal; particularity was the enemy. Particularity was the fruit of power, reason's mortal enemy. This meant that (3) reason became freedom's ally in the battle against power. Finally, there can be little question that (4) rationalist universal liberalism was therefore religious in character. These all have significant implications for rationalist conceptions of tolerance. Here too, despite their differences, Jefferson's and Madison's claims about the place of institutional religions in public life coalesce in substance.

1. Reducing reason. For the rationalists, moral precepts were universal and the only necessary components of religion because they were, in the end, all that concerned God. In a letter to the Quaker William Canby, Jefferson avers "that he who steadily observes those moral precepts in which all religions concur, will never be questioned, at the gates of heaven, as to the dogmas in which they differ."[114] Nor was there much ambiguity about what constituted moral truth. According to Paine, morality was transparent to reason, for "the God in whom we believe is a God of moral truth, and not a God of mystery or obscurity. Mystery is the antagonist of truth. . . . Truth never envelops *itself* in mystery, and the mystery in which it is at any time enveloped is the work of its antagonist."[115] Nothing more

was needed (or possible) than a deism which reformed "moral doctrine to the standard of reason, justice, and philanthropy," and inculcated "belief in a future state."[116] These were universal truths, and simple ones at that;[117] there should have been no controversy about them. But there was.

2. *Particularity, power, and the forces of evil.* Those convinced of the transparent rationality of their truth cannot quite understand how anyone could differ with them. The rationalists were lackadaisical in succumbing to this danger. For them, there could be no rational dispute about essential morality (or presumably, about what moral terms such as "freedom," "theft," "power," "murder," etc., meant). Everyone who did not share their opinions was *eo ipso* antirational. What perversity of heart would cause anyone to oppose reason? For the rationalists, as for much of the Western tradition, the answer was a lust for "power."[118]

Once upon a time, the rationalists believed, there was a pure and unsullied rational truth. For Jefferson and Paine, it lay in the moral teachings of Jesus, who taught a universal "system of morality" that was "the most benevolent and sublime probably that has ever been taught,"[119] and which Jefferson's own cut-and-paste surgery on the New Testament attempted to reconstruct. (Jefferson's reconstruction bears similarity to current attempts to retrieve the historical Jesus— Jesus begins to bear the features of the constructor.)[120] Jefferson had no doubt that what Jesus taught was "the principles of a pure deism";[121] Paine's heartier primitivism declared that "Adam, if ever there were such a man, was created a Deist."[122]

Unfortunately, most citizens were not minimalists or rationalists, and still held to fanciful doctrines. Something had to explain the fall from the primitive state of unblemished rationality. For the Deists, the Satan behind this original sin was *power.* Jefferson's account of the fall from the purity and simplicity of Jesus' religion is explicit:

> But a short time elapsed after the death of the great reformer of the Jewish religion before his principles were departed from by those who professed to be his special servants, and *perverted into an engine for enslaving mankind, and aggrandizing their oppressors in church and state:* . . . the purest system of morals ever before preached to man has been *adulterated and sophisticated, by artificial constructions, into a mere contrivance to filch wealth and power to themselves.* . . . They raise the hue and cry of infidelity, while themselves are the greatest obstacles

to the advancement of the real doctrines of Jesus, *and do in fact constitute the real Anti-Christ.*[123]

For Jefferson, the real purpose behind this "adulteration" and "sophistication" of religion was to take power and oppress others. He never bothered to explain exactly how this was the case in any particular instance (how, say, the doctrine of the Trinity oppressed); power's hostility to reason was a dogma of Deist faith. Particular religions, according to Paine, are born only through the rejection of reason and the lust for power. That "ONE that is true"[124] must purge the contagion of religion that the disease of power brought. Reason banishes the "religion" of "human invention"[125] and leaves the rational, fair soul only one church. Rejecting all creeds, whether "by the Jewish Church, by the Roman Church, by the Greek Church, by the Turkish Church, by the Protestant Church, nor by any church that I know of," Paine eloquently declares, "My own mind is my own church."[126] Particularity and power are together the forces of evil; reason and simplicity are pure, innocent, free of sin's stain.

3. Reason militant and the place of freedom. It followed inexorably that if reason failed to advance, it was because of despotic power, "the impious presumption of legislators . . . and rulers . . . who . . . have assumed dominion over the faith of others." On this point Jefferson and Madison concurred.[127] Power "destroys all religious liberty."[128] Reason may be sanguine and nonaggressive by its nature, but it must zealously if reluctantly do battle for the truth when irrationality and power seek to hinder it. Reason had to attack *all* particular features of every religion, because they were *nothing but* a contrivance of power to meet its own self-serving ends. Power had to be defeated in order that truth could triumph.

This is what made religious liberty necessary. Religious liberty is the only way in which reason can exercise its rightful self-dominion. Jefferson has no doubt that "truth is great and will prevail if left to herself . . . unless by human interposition disarmed of her natural weapons, free argument and debate; errors ceasing to be dangerous when it is permitted freely to contradict them."[129] Under the tyranny of the particular, truth could emerge only if reason could be free of power. Alpha and omega, beginning and end, were certain as long as power could be defeated. Reason required a public space free of the tyranny of particular religions, which would enable it to conquer them. Freedom was therefore valued because it was *the means to the truth* that reason was destined to attain.

4. The rationalism of Paine, Jefferson, and others can only be described as religious. Jefferson admits as much when he turns the apocalyptic image of the Antichrist against the Christian churches. We have already seen Jefferson's invocation of God's providence for reason, Paine's claim that his mind is his church, and so on. Jefferson's famous oath, "I have sworn upon the altar of god eternal hostility against every form of tyranny over the mind of man," comes in the midst of a discussion about irrational "sects."[130] The belief that if only power were conquered, history would recapture its paradisiacal past, is manifestly religious, even messianic; it is one more permutation of what Langdon Gilkey argues was Western culture's core religion in the nineteenth and early twentieth centuries—progress.[131] Reason was worthy of ultimate commitment and would finally emerge victorious. The religiosity of the rationalist claim persisted into the twentieth century, notably in John Dewey's influential *A Common Faith*.[132] Thus we arrive at one answer—itself paradoxical—to Arendt's paradox: Why did the "enlightened men" of the eighteenth century appeal to religion when they were about to eliminate it? *To remove politics from the influence of the churches.*

The implication of these rationalist positions for the place of institutional religions in public affairs is obvious: such religions are fraudulent attempts to seize power by keeping people ignorant, and are therefore inimical to any public truth. If they minded their own business, they could be tolerated; otherwise, they had to be attacked. Reason could tolerate a variety of particular beliefs only so long as those beliefs knew their place, which was outside the important business of the commonwealth. It might be necessary for the sake of public order[133] to tolerate particular religious positions, but their particularity had no public value. No one with loyalties to a particular religious tradition will be much comforted to discover that, after Paine's sustained offensive against the intelligence and even the humanity of such believers, he makes the magnanimous concession that everyone may "follow, as he has a right to do, the religion and the worship he prefers,"[134] no matter how preposterous. This is tolerance for the harmless idiot. The suspicion and outright hatred shown Catholicism and Lord Baltimore, as well as Jefferson's malicious remark about the "degraded state" of Jews before Jesus,[135] were supposedly legitimate weapons in reason's battle against the dangerous forces of unreason.[136]

Herein lay the rationalist contradiction. Reason eschewed all power, but also understood itself as the supreme power. It had to use power to attack power. And so it did, refusing to take seriously any claims it understood as "particular," dismissing them out of hand as irrational. As Michel Foucault never tired of noting, reason becomes positively oppressive at this moment. Knowledge conceals its own power by portraying any attempt to oppose it as no mere resistance to one power among others, but as resistance to truth itself.[137] All the while, the picture depends on a caricature of reason, its removal from history, and the ritual disparagement of religions as irrational.

Rationalism carried force well into the twentieth century, only recently falling out of favor with the philosophical elite. Clive James's remark that "reason was ... religion"[138] for Bertrand Russell also applies to Dewey and a broad swath of American culture, and it has continued to determine secularist conceptions of tolerance. Rationalist religion assumed that only the universal could be true. "Particular reason" was a contradiction in terms. The vaunted principle of tolerance was constricted from the start. Universal liberalism's tolerance is essentially this: *it tolerates particular traditions only so long as they do not interfere with liberal rationalism* (or in Madison's case, rational justice) *and therefore make no real difference to it.*

This vision makes sense only if the universal religion of reason is in fact universal. And this is just the claim that grew more and more implausible at the end of the twentieth century.[139] The self-contradictions of universal reason have become painfully evident. The claims made on its behalf were manifestly particularistic. First, the conception of reason was peculiarly British and Scottish;[140] the reason of the German Enlightenment, and of Hegel in particular, is still considered idle speculation in many American philosophical circles. Jefferson's parsimonious disdain of Plato and the rich Platonic tradition—"Nonsense"[141]—neatly dispensed with another major rival. Second, the rational religion that was forwarded as reason itself was distinctively Protestant (and mostly sectarian Protestant at that), particularly in its antihistorical emphasis. Its conception of history was clearly Protestant—innocence at the beginning (the New Testament church or the teachings of Jesus), a fall associated with the accretion of "human tradition" (Martin Luther's mantra, repeated by Paine), and finally the glorious recovery (or its beginnings) in the present, when pure reason (taking over the role of Protestantism's "pure Word") rules and mere traditional power is stripped naked for all to see. Third, the rationalists were religious reductionists. Only a few principles were necessary to establish proper religion. Universalism and primitivism combined forces. Rationalists felt no need to examine particular religious practices or beliefs because these were later accretions and departures from a primitive purity. They felt no need to argue on behalf of their primitivist and progressive assumptions, or their vehement dislike of Catholicism in particular and all tradition in general, or their specifically British and Scottish philosophy. Indeed, they felt no need to make arguments at all, and were thereby guilty of the very charge which they brought against "religion."

Rationalist liberalism attempts to insulate itself from all criticism by denying its particularity and thereby enshrining itself as the only legitimate ultimate. Little wonder, then, that so many religious persons as well as pluralists of all political persuasions decline to accept its condescending munificence! Religious inclusionists are right to recognize that the pretensions of universal liberalism belittle their convictions without giving them a serious hearing.[142] Liberal universalism embodies the sort of oppressive blindness of which only a religious perspective is capable.

It comes as no surprise, then, that large numbers of liberals have abandoned universal liberalism and now seek to justify both the liberal project and the exclusion of "religion" from public life on *particular* grounds. These particular liberals, however, have not made any adjustments in the liberal conception of religion, and thereby both misunderstand religion and, ironically, imperil the secular state they so desperately want to protect.

PARTICULAR LIBERALISM: RELIGION AND THE NEW REASON

Universal liberalism, although it still commands some support in the broader culture, lies virtually abandoned in philosophical and academic circles. Even its defenders, such as Gamwell, are unable to tell us even in general terms what the content of important political, moral, or religious truth might be. Enlightenment confidence in the progressive, smoothly proceeding discovery of truth in matters of morals, politics, or religion is at an end.[143]

Within the tradition of liberalism, the preferred option in academic and philosophical circles has become "particular liberalism." John Rawls, its most distinguished advocate, formulates its central question in this way: "How is it possible for there to exist over time a just and stable society of free and equal citizens, who remain profoundly divided by reasonable religious, philosophical, and moral doctrines?"[144] Rawls reflects the central insight of particular liberalism: we must conduct public life in circumstances (1) of diverse claims about the nature and content of "truth" but (2) without a "reasonable" way to decide between competing truths of religious perspectives. The latter claim is what separates particular liberalism from universal. Competing claims to ultimate truth cannot be judged by "pure reason" because there is no impartial observer who possesses that faculty. Any assessment is irretrievably bound to the particular culture and subcultures of the assessor. Particular liberalism recognizes the ideological pretensions of its universal ancestors, eschews their arrogance, and defends instead a less ambitious proposal: what we as a political culture possess is not "truth" but *consensus* about certain matters; not "pure reason" disjoined from any culture but *public reason* that is tied to American culture and possesses no obvious truth value outside that context. Not that the break is complete, however. Particular liberalism perpetuates its universalist ancestors' hostility to external authority and religious tradition, summed up in Jefferson's maxim, "We should all then, like the Quakers, live without an order of priests, moralize for ourselves, follow the oracle of conscience, and say nothing about what no man can understand, nor therefore believe."[145] But it departs from Jefferson in this crucial respect: whereas Jefferson expected all men to come to the same conclusions independently, particular liberalism knows that all men—to say nothing of all women—will *not*. Politically, particular liberalism argues that what we *should* do is all that we *can* do—preserve and extend the consensus. Truth is beyond our reach.

Meaningful universal truth is unavailable to us because all truths are entangled in particular languages and cultures. Here too particular liberalism recapitulates universalist liberalism, fearing that irresolvable fractious squabbling will undermine political life. Democratic stability is undermined in the absence of universal standards to which we can appeal. This is, once again, Madison's fear: faction. Madison was confident that there was a rationally identifiable general good that could be adequately achieved by just procedures. But for particular liberals under the influence of postmodern thought, *all morality and politics are factional.* No public good transcends the factions. And since there can be no appeal to the common good, politics degenerates into what, in many ways, it has already become—a contest for domination in which the aim is to eliminate enemies rather than convert them, be changed by them, or—heaven forbid—love them. Foucault's judgment that Clausewitz's axiom should be reversed, that politics is "war continued by other means,"[146] is echoed by former Christian Coalition leader Ralph Reed's desire to put his opponents in "body bags."[147] Thus Bruce Ackerman formulates the contemporary political problem as "how people who disagree about the moral truth might nonetheless reasonably solve their ongoing problem of living together."[148] For Rawls, the fear of divisiveness is paramount, which is why he rejects any suggestion that truth is the aim of politics, for truth is much too divisive an issue. Rodney King is another particularist liberal; his question, too, was not "What is the case?" but "Can't we get along?"

"Getting along" requires that factions—which now include every political position—be kept within tolerable bounds. One does not want to add to the confusion. That is why particular liberalism generally perpetuates the older liberalism's suspicion of religion in public life, though its rationale differs. It is now time to examine the more prominent particular liberals and their views of political life, public debate, and religion in more detail: Ackerman, Greenawalt, and Rawls. Whatever their differences, it is their common—and undefended—assumptions that are most intriguing.

The Demise of the Political: Ackerman and Greenawalt

In the face of ineradicable plurality and no agreement on truth, what are we to do? Ackerman's solution is simple, consistent, fair, and inadequate. He suggests that all political-moral commitments derive from one or both of two sources: (1) "faith," defined broadly as the answer to "whom should I trust?" or (2) an "appeal to myself" instead of "external authority."[149] Disagreement occurs when people confront others who accept differing authorities.[150]

How to resolve the problem? Conventional liberal attempts to find (1) neutral ground or (2) a common starting point for argument are fruitless, according to Ackerman. Any such method forces one party to affirm "moral principles" that that person "think[s] are false"[151] or "to speak a political language that obliges" one "to falsify primary moral beliefs in systematic fashion!"[152] The solution is to admit that there is no way beyond the impasse except "restraint."[153]

> When you and I learn that we disagree about . . . moral truth, we should not search for some common value that will trump this disagreement. . . . We should simply say *nothing at all* about this disagreement and put the moral ideals that divide us off the conversational agenda of the liberal state.[154]

We may, of course, talk about such matters of disagreement privately; but *politically, silence is golden:* "We need not lose the chance to talk to one another in . . . more private contexts."[155]

Ackerman's proposal entails a significant advantage: he does not differentiate between "religious" and "secular" ultimate commitments in terms of their reliance on "faith." He overcomes universal liberalism's tendency to use the notion of "religion" ideologically. Instead, *all* ultimate perspectives are, in the broad sense of "ultimate concern," religious. Still, one wonders just what this accomplishes, and for whom. The very simplicity of Ackerman's position proves its undoing. Two difficulties are obvious, and will also haunt other particularist proposals. First, it is difficult to imagine a more antipolitical proposition. If political life is not supposed to include disagreement, what, exactly, is it supposed to do? If we cannot discuss or argue about matters that are controversial—including what our society ought to be, or what, on the basis of any such vision, we might do for each other—what remains? A politics limited to unanimous agreement, which is to say, no politics at all. Ackerman's proposal risks reducing politics to technique without vision—the Ross Perot approach, and a frequent criticism of President Clinton as well. But no politics has ever been so severely curtailed. Even Perot and Clinton air controversial ideas in public.[156] Ackerman's proposal presumably means that no candidate could speak about controversial matters. What would be the point, anyway? Having taken office, no one could act unless there were already unanimous agreement.

The second problem is implicit in the first. Political action is paralyzed. Lacking any capacity to deliberate, politics must also forswear conscious decision and action. Just how, precisely, should the Civil Rights movement have been conducted in "more private" spheres? Should the Southern Christian Leadership Conference have abjured sit-ins and nonviolent political demonstrations and waited patiently to press for legislation until Bull Connor and George Wallace were persuaded privately? Should abolitionists have waited to bring their arguments to the political sphere until all slaveholders were convinced of the error of their ways?[157] Must health-care policy await the unanimous assent of all providers and recipients? Ackerman's proposal virtually guarantees that *whatever is, will be*—at least when it comes to moral issues on which we disagree. New decisions cannot be made; the moral decisions of the past, made in the heat of controversy, all stand. This is deeply conservative. Real debate is impossible unless, miraculously, there is already a unanimity which would render the debate—and probably action—superfluous. In millennial America, social strife is, to be sure, a substantial problem; but the cure must be at least less life-threatening than the disease. Ackerman's proposal muzzles all political speech and risks obliterating a meaningful public arena.

Other particular liberals do not go so far. In their effort to maintain some sort of political dialogue in which decisions can be made, Greenawalt and Rawls develop conceptions of "public reason." Greenawalt argues that public debate in liberal democratic America should be conducted exclusively on the grounds of "publicly accessible reasons," namely "rational in the sense of resting on reasoned arguments whose force is generally understood."[158] More specifically, this means at least that we must argue on the basis of "shared premises,"[159] which include (1) "ordinary empirical knowledge, based on observation and common sense reasoning"[160] (Greenawalt is apparently unaware that the fundamentalist religious "reasons" he seeks to exclude appeal to "common sense"),[161] (2) certain kinds of "intuitive" judgments,[162] and (3) practical judgments that obey commonly accepted criteria of "generality, coherence, and regularity."[163]

The specifics of these categories need not detain us here. Several points are relevant for our purposes. First, Greenawalt defends these restrictions not on the basis of their truth, but on the ground that they preserve "ordinary notions of liberty" and "ordinary notions of satisfying preferences," which "definitely rest on premises that are virtually universal in this society" and are commonly accessible.[164] Second, religious convictions are routinely excluded from legitimate public discourse. Why? Primarily because he believes that "religious morality and religiously grounded moral judgments" are "beyond shared premises and publicly accessible reasons."[165] This is because religious convictions are "personal"[166] and "particular."[167] Greenawalt's debt to the Enlightenment attempt to exclude particularity from public discourse is clear. But according to the new liberalism, all positions are particular. So why is religion singled out for exclusion? Because specific religious convictions are not sufficiently part of the democratic consensus to be generally accepted. Greenawalt imposes a high—nay, impossible—bar for any "nonconsensual" reasons. With respect to religion, he argues:

> Can publicly accessible reasons and shared premises actually establish the *truth* of some *particular* religious position? If we assume that a substantial number of religious perspectives, including here atheism and agnosticism, can meet minimal requisites of rational scrutiny and ethical acceptability, how is an individual to choose? If he cannot make a defense on grounds of publicly accessible reasons and shared premises, then any ethical position that critically derives from the religious perspective cannot be so defended.[168]

That is to say, because religions cannot defend themselves in their entirety as *complete* truth (how could any religion *or anything else* do so if truth is historical?), they cannot invoke *any* of that system to posit more specific positions. Shared premises—public reason—do not have to meet the same requirements, since we *already* (supposedly) *agree about them.*

Still, religious convictions are not completely disallowed. Greenawalt allows two exceptions to his exclusionary position. First, he argues (curiously) that although one should not rely on religious reasons in *public* argument, it remains true that "if all people must draw from their personal experiences and commitments, people whose experience leads them to religious convictions should not have to disregard what they consider the critical insights about value that their convictions provide."[169] Thus, although it is morally acceptable to rely on whatever grounds one wants *privately,* the *public* case for one's position should be made only in the language of publicly accessible reasons. Greenawalt's second exception reflects similar presuppositions. He believes that certain debates—about animal rights and abortion, for example—do not admit of a full solution by means of publicly accessible reasons. Our *universal* language of liberty and preference does not lead smoothly to obvious resolution. In such borderline cases, all citizens will have to appeal to standards that are not reasonable; on the grounds of fairness, "religious" nonrationality should not be excluded any more than its nonrational "secular" counterparts.[170]

Greenawalt's exceptions to his exclusionary rule are both odd and revealing. Religious convictions are disallowed because of their relative particularity in comparison with the "consensus" values of the liberty to pursue one's own preferences. On the other hand, when positions derived from religion can be translated into such "reasonable" language, it is acceptable to rely on religious convictions, so long as one does not say that that is what is being done. Such a move encourages hypocrisy externally and schizophrenia inwardly. Externally, Greenawalt tells religious persons that it is desirable to lie about the reasons for their positions. Robert Audi—who agrees that liberal reasons are the only legitimate public ones—rightly denounces this strategy. He argues that if the basis of one's positions is not acceptable to secular democrats, one should avoid public debate entirely (even if one could, deceptively, claim a secular basis for the same position.)[171] At least Audi does not advocate hypocrisy in the name of a dual alliance to religious conviction and secular argument.[172] Greenawalt's solution may be psychologically destructive. It encourages exactly the kind of split between private and public personae that is properly the subject of much feminist criticism.

Three more points. First, Greenawalt's recommendation simply cannot be accepted by those who are religiously and theologically serious. Worship attempts to integrate all aspects of life into some sensible whole, and seeks—although it never achieves—comprehensiveness. To rule out *a priori* the entire realm of public life from the legitimate objects of religious and theological investigation is to strangle religion as an ultimate concern. Second, political life is also constricted. To the extent that either Greenawalt's or Audi's recommendation is accepted, politics is stripped of any self-transcending meanings. (This problem will reappear when we discuss political liberalism's strange conservatism and its concomitant tendency to reinforce an antipolitical mentality.) Finally, Greenawalt's argument presupposes that what matters in public debate is not the grounds for one's position (which is why it is irrelevant whether one has religious reasons for them), but the position itself. This is because *rationale*—particularly if it is "religious"—is unarguable. (This problem too will return, at the conclusion of this chapter.) Does Greenawalt really mean to say that it makes no difference *why* one takes positions? Apparently: political discourse "mainly involves advocacy of positions arrived at."[173] This is probably because these reasons are not universally held. But for some of us who are busy formulating and reformulating our perspectives, it matters a great deal whether, for example, someone opposes cash maintenance systems for the poor because (1) the poor deserve their lot and are morally inferior, or (2) the cash assistance system does not do as good a job as another system at helping the poor out of poverty. The second, if true, is persuasive, whereas the first is false and disgusting. *This is true even if the policy position is the same;* and as informed citizens consider their own positions, grounds for argument matter. Why are they relatively unimportant to Greenawalt? Because he assumes that we formulate positions in our "private consciences," not in public debate. That, we believe, is a failure not only in Greenawalt's position but in liberalism more generally. It renders political argument superfluous.

The Weakness of Liberal Assumptions: Rawls

These problems are both ameliorated and accentuated in the recent work of John Rawls, the subtlest proponent of the new particular liberalism. Unlike most other particularists, Rawls does not restrict his notion of liberal democracy to formal procedural matters, but argues that specific policies of distributive justice follow from his basic principles of justice.[174] He thereby implies (but does not articulate) a more sophisticated, less individualistic notion of freedom.[175] He is also clearer about liberalism's limitations and, accordingly, the 1996 "Introduction" to *Political Liberalism* has a more nuanced view of religion's place in political debate.

On the other hand, Rawls agrees with Greenawalt that "public reason" defines the legitimate moral bounds of political argument. He begins with the presupposition that all citizens in liberal democratic regimes have "comprehensive" moral, philosophical, or religious commitments about "truth."[176] For him, "comprehensive" means what Tillich and we mean by "religious," a perspective which embraces all arenas of existence, including the political. Of course, such comprehensive-religious convictions may include a commitment to the ultimate truth and meaning of liberalism itself. Like Ackerman—and unlike Greenawalt or Audi—Rawls recognizes that liberalism itself is religious. But he views the comprehensive-religious convictions of citizens as—borrowing a phrase from postmodernism—"incommensurable." There is no "reasonable" way to resolve differences between comprehensive standpoints. This is not because all such standpoints are preposterous, but because so many are "reasonable." If they were "commensurable," politics would be left at an impasse.[177] The implications for political life are far-reaching.

This immediately limits the legitimate range of state force: "When there is a plurality of reasonable doctrines, it is unreasonable or worse to want to use the sanctions of state power against those who disagree with us."[178] The purpose of government is not to pursue the true or the good, but to foster a stable, ordered pluralistic society with multiple incommensurable views of truth and the good. Rawls does not deny the importance of "truth," but argues that *political arrangements* in pluralistic societies should not pursue it; *political* (as distinct from comprehensive-religious) liberalism does without the concept of truth."[179] Rawls believes that we can do without "truth" in politics precisely because the political realm is not comprehensive. Therefore, discussions of "truth" can occur in private settings as well as in associational venues such as churches, synagogues, universities, and so on.[180] It is *only* the *political* structure, insofar as it deals with constitutional essentials and matters of basic justice, that can (and must) do without a comprehensive-religious account of truth. And this is not only possible, but desirable:

> The advantage of staying within the reasonable is that there can be but one true comprehensive doctrine, though ... many reasonable ones. Once we accept the fact that reasonable pluralism is a permanent condition of public culture under free institutions, the idea of the reasonable is more suitable as part of the basis of public justification for a constitutional regime than the idea of moral truth. Holding a political conception as true, and for that reason alone the one suitable basis of public reason, is exclusive, even sectarian, and so likely to foster political division.[181]

Factional particularity is the problem once again.

Rawls is clearer than other particularists about the changed character of factionalism. Where Madison had denounced "factions" for their pursuit of narrow interest at the expense of the general good, Rawls dispenses with the general good as politically normative; "right" has priority over "good."[182] To enthrone one vision of the good over others (as even Madison assumed was possible) is a "civic humanism" that we can no longer afford if we are to keep the peace.[183] Now *all* perspectives are inevitably *particular,* and are dangerous just insofar as they *masquerade* as *universal truth* or *good.* Competing theories of the good cannot be resolved; therefore, the attempt to impose one or another of them is *mere domination, nothing more.* And this is just as true of *liberalism* as of *any other religious viewpoint.*

So how, given Rawls's perspective, might our political structure be organized? He argues that our liberal society already contains an "overlapping consensus" about the priority and value of freedom and equality in a fair system of cooperation.[184] From this we should be able to infer more specific contents of justice as well. He argues that all "reasonable" comprehensive doctrines can endorse these basic claims *without* invoking the entirety of the religious worldview from which they spring.[185] This political consensus is the "public reason" that defines the principles and arguments to which one might morally appeal in public debate. The moral duty of civility requires that participants "be able to explain to one another . . . how the principles and policies they advocate and vote for can be supported by the political values of public reason."[186]

For example, a comprehensive liberal might endorse a particular policy on the basis of innate human freedom and equality, while a Christian might endorse the same policy on the basis of God's gift of creation, holding that freedom and equality are not inherent to humans but the results of that gift. According to Rawls, this Christian and this humanist need not argue about the proper basis of human freedom. The truth of their wider views is suspended for the sake of political agreement (though they may well argue it in private and associational settings). Besides, Rawls suggests, there is no real gain to be had from invoking the comprehensive perspective in most cases. What, exactly, would it contribute to political life? Public debate should be parsimonious and avoid conflict wherever possible.

Rawls's solution is shrewd. It has several advantages over other particularist liberal viewpoints. First, he maintains the vitality of the political sphere and retains scope for disagreement about specific questions of policy and law. Second, his conception is not merely descriptive (like Greenawalt's notion of "publicly accessible reasons"). Rawls does not merely take an opinion poll to determine what the consensus is, but argues that, having established actual agreement about basic matters of freedom and equality, we can proceed to matters of distributive justice and fairness. His political conception of justice is not merely descriptive but also normative.[187] Third, he reverses his previous, more restrictive attitude toward institutional religious presence in political debate, an attitude that was always inconsistent with his broader project. Now any reason, religious or not, may be invoked in public debate as long as it is consistent with "public reason." Even *nonpublic* (nonconsensual) reasons may be introduced into public debate as supplemental or introductory to public reason: "Reasonable [comprehensive] doctrines may be introduced in public reason at any time, provided that in due course public reasons . . . are presented sufficient to support whatever the comprehensive doctrines are introduced to support."[188] Thus, the invocation of Christian, Jewish, Muslim, liberal, and other comprehensive views is legitimated—whether or not there is consensus about those reasons—*if* public reasons are forthcoming. Rawls neither privileges nor disfranchises the participation of religions in public life, so long as they are in sufficient accord with public reason based on conceptions of all citizens as free and equal. Precisely because Rawls rejects liberalism's ideological view of "religion," he is able to place institutional religions in proper relation to other "comprehensive" doctrines. All are equally religious and equally particular under the conditions of human knowing and fallibility.

In chapter 4, we will have more to say about Rawls's overlapping consensus and his claim that conceptions of the good in pluralist society are incommensurable. Here, the advantages of Rawls's theory notwithstanding, it is important to note that it remains tightly bound to several of liberalism's unexamined assumptions. These assumptions leave liberalism in a weaker position than it should be, and leave the secular state itself vulnerable to its critics, many of whom make their criticism on religious grounds. (This is true despite the fact that many of their religious critics, ironically, share the first two of these assumptions.)

First assumption: there are no *defensible reasons* for holding one religious (or comprehensive) view rather than another. The qualifier "defensible" is important. Liberalism does not argue that there are no reasons for holding a religious view, but that the reasons are "incommensurable"; that is, they operate in different and incomparable universes of discourse. Moreover, the particularists seem to assume (Greenawalt is explicit) that if one cannot defend the totality of one's religious worldview, it is impossible to defend any particular part of it on religious grounds. This is doubtful. Does one really have to be able to prove the truth of the Christian doctrine of the Incarnation in order to defend the importance of charity and humility? Why would that be? Nor is there any obvious reason to assume that religious worldviews can offer no credible and defensible reasons for the positions they take. In fact, liberalism merely assumes the impossibility of religious argument. Particular liberalism maintains its ancestral heritage by sharply distinguishing "reason" and "faith." Reason is associated with freedom, faith with authority, just as in the Enlightenment. Whereas Ackerman and Rawls both recognize that institutional religions are not necessarily more subject to this problem than other comprehensive perspectives, now they assume that *no one* is capable of such arguments. Ackerman attributes the impasse in public life to the fact that all citizens presumably rely on "faith," that is, which authority should be trusted, whether themselves or some external authority.[189] Rawls remains suspicious of institutional religions even as he recognizes that no other comprehensive viewpoint is privileged either: religions rely on "external authority"[190] rather than public reason, and are divisive and intolerant.[191]

Similarly, Audi maintains that "religious disagreements are [more] likely to polarize government," because religion cannot convince "except through *nonevidential* factors deriving from . . . *independent religious commitments.*"[192] Likewise, Greenawalt presupposes that religious reasons are not arguable; that is why they can only be invoked legitimately when no publicly accessible reasons are decisive. He reflexively equates "rational" and "secular,"[193] and routinely reduces "religious" to a supernaturalistic base.[194] In other words, "nonreligious" reasons are real reasons, while religious convictions rest on authority. Greenawalt's examples of religious argument are, as one might imagine, marginal. How many people take political positions on the basis that

"God has communicated to him directly" or base their positions exclusively on a confidence in miracles?[195] Liberalism persists in an outdated and bizarre image of religion, the simplistic contours of which were drawn centuries ago by the rationalist liberalism of Paine, Jefferson, and others. The image is hardly accurate, however ideologically useful it might be. Even if Pat Robertson's famed profession of power over hurricanes counts as an example, it is scarcely typical of religious argument.

Liberalism's caricature of religious argument also misses religion's normative thrust. We have already noted that religion's drive toward comprehensiveness requires it to incorporate rationality into its interpretation of existence. Religion *cannot* exclude rationality without a significant *loss* of comprehensiveness and religiosity. This is true for all religious worldviews. Also, if all realms of existence are expressions of the divine purpose—a particularly important point in monotheism—then to abandon "reason" for a "revelation" that contradicts reason diminishes the worship of God. If divine power does not extend to reason, monotheism is contradicted; if God's revelatory authority is employed *against* reason, God's revelation battles God's creation.[196] But this cannot be true monotheism—reason *must* belong to God. When Christians, Jews, or Muslims invoke revelation in contradiction of reason, they no longer worship the God they claim to honor.[197] Such an appeal to revelation by Christians is as illegitimate on religious grounds as "secular" ones.

To the contrary: *Religious argument contains no essential antirationality.* It proceeds with the same standards and criteria as any other argument. To be sure, there is suprarationality in at least one religious claim: religion as ultimate concern contends that there *is* something about which one should be ultimately concerned. In other words, the primary act of faith in religion is the confidence that there is some meaning available in existence or beyond it, and not encompassed by any finite reality—nation, culture, public reason, science, or even religion or the Bible.[198] It is not obvious that there is much more evidence for ultimate meaning than for meaninglessness. Religion takes the leap and says, beyond the evidence, that meaning triumphs over meaninglessness. This is suprarational, *not* antirational. Beyond that religious assertion, shared by many philosophers, political theorists, theists, janitors, mathematicians, and bank examiners, there is no reason to believe that the arguments of religion are antirational or proceed in some secret, publicly inaccessible way. Religious arguments can and must be coherent even to those who do not share, or who doubt, or construe differently, religion's confidence in an ultimately trustworthy meaning. Liberalism's inability to distinguish antirationality from suprarationality makes its image of religion particularly unhelpful.[199]

Second erroneous assumption: what is "publicly" rational and legitimate in public debate should be confined to the preexisting (liberal) consensus. Inclusionists such as Neuhaus and Carter rightly object to this assumption, though they frequently reverse the prejudice. We previously criticized Neuhaus and Carter for taking the fact of religious commitment as sufficient warrant for its desirability in public debate. Liberalism makes an analogous short circuit. It maintains that the fact that liberal principles are accepted automatically validates them. Just as the inclusionists refuse to discuss religious content, liberalism seeks to immunize *itself* from criticism. Indeed, liberals go one step farther. Without any evidence that liberal society (1) cannot survive discordant voices that call liberal interpretations of freedom and equality into question or (2) that these critical voices have a damaging effect on political debate, they nonetheless assert that social stability would be so damaged. In effect, liberalism enthrones itself by the same logic as that of the inclusionists: an alleged consensus justifies restricting public debate to liberal principles. Anything that calls this consensus into question is dismissed as immoral and irrational simply because it has the temerity to question liberalism's adequacy. The supposed suspension of the truth-question is for all practical purposes meaningless. If all nonliberal perspectives are eradicated from public debate, it is scant comfort to learn that this does not mean that they are false, only irrational and immoral.

Although inclusionists are justly frustrated by this heavy-handed dismissal of their position without argument, they are guilty of the same error. Liberals and inclusionists are right and wrong. They are right to claim that their perspectives are American traditions. They are wrong to say that that fact alone should restrict the scope of allowable public debate. Both have privileged the "right to one's own opinion" in religious-comprehensive matters as a freedom beyond meaningful public challenge. Both sides have lost the most vital of Madison's insights—also a part of the American tradition, and arguably its real genius—that the majority is more prone to tyranny than minorities. Liberalism and inclusionism, however, advocate themselves in largely majoritarian terms.

Similarly, liberals and inclusionists are equally conservative about their heritage. The difference lies in which aspect of the American political heritage each wants to conserve. Both perspectives are ultimately concerned about their specific heritage, and are therefore religious.[200] However, both are inadequately religious. Both seize upon a specific historical circumstance and try to freeze it in time, assuming that its truth and value are not subject to change. Both thereby sacrifice history as a realm of new meaning. Principled change becomes impossible.[201] Only the sheer force of will remains viable in the political sphere. If the pre-democratic monarchies had followed their own "public reason," democracy would not have even emerged to begin with—criticism was not part of that consensus. Early democracy did not obey the "public reason" of its day, and it certainly threatened public order. To defend liberalism by enshrining the *present* public order is—to say the least—historically unconscious.[202] It also presupposes the suspiciously universal-sounding claim that liberalism is the *final* and *best* governmental system for pluralistic society.

We are already seeing the effects of this truncated notion of reason and value, and they are likely to grow. When these forces encounter each other in public debate, no argument about the adequacy of religious-comprehensive views is possible. As with Ellen Crasswell's run for governor, Pat Robertson's candidacy for the presidency, and countless other debates over the place of religion, political speech degenerates into a formal battle between liberal charges of irrationality, and inclusionist appeals to the right to speak. The substance and adequacy of the arguments cannot be examined. The shared presuppositions of liberals and inclusionists alike render meaningful public discussion about religions and their consequences impossible. Politics becomes the war carried on by other means (even though that need not be the case). We lose meaningful discourse about what public life should accomplish and why. These are assumed to be questions resolved in "private conscience" (as in the title of Greenawalt's latest book) or at best in the "associational debate" that Rawls allows even as he rules it out of the political sphere.

Is it any wonder, then, that politics seems to be a sphere of mere tactical, unprincipled decisions? Or that it seems inevitably and unnecessarily polarized? The political peace that followed the 1996 elections was based on enervation, not principle, as the reheated impeachment imbroglio of 1999 showed. It was particularly ironic that Bill Clinton was elected in 1992 in part because George Bush was said to lack "the vision thing" and that in Congress the Republican majority was also elected on the basis of its vision in 1994. The truce which followed was due to exhaustion—of parties and the electorate alike. And yet we decry (as we should) the abandonment of principle for mere tactic. But if we do not begin to allow space for political debate of these principles, polarization returns and likely is even more extreme.

The first installment has already come. In 1998, Republican strategist Frank Luntz advised the Republican Party that "principles are more important than policy or politics,"[203] and recommended that Republicans lower the volume in the criticism of President Clinton. What happened instead was intraparty cannibalism after the 1998 election debacle, and renewed intensity of attack on Clinton. At least in part, this was because these presuppositions of liberals and inclusionists rule out debate about (as distinct from declaration of) principles, and because we are so badly out of practice, we doubt that these twin objectives of debating principles and decreasing vitriol can be accomplished simultaneously in the current environment. Rather, we will have to begin to reconceive politics as a place in which (1) all principles are available for argument, (2) none are immune from it, and (3) the purposes of the public sphere are open to critical analysis. The truncated character of the current debate reduces politics to technique, and debate to name-calling. All this contributes to the nasty reputation of "politics." But the reason that there appears to be nothing honorable or genuine about politics is that we will not allow it. We hide behind majoritarianism and our "rights" as we fire broadsides at opponents about their unfairness, irrationality, or immorality. Of course politics seems to be reduced to dirty battles of domination. That is because we reduced it.

Third assumption: The state can survive and prosper without religious animations.[204] Liberalism in its several forms effectively removes from the table, often in a majoritarian way, the *reasons* to value freedom, equality, or the secular structure of the state. And it deigns those who dare to raise these and other issues from religious points of view to be immoral or irrational because they do not conform to the public reason of liberalism. But how likely is this strategy to work? Far from strengthening the liberal state—which we believe to be desirable and necessary—contemporary liberalism weakens it. There are, first of all, empirical data. If the secular state is so strong, why is it embattled worldwide? Why does the Turkish military have to threaten to uphold it by force if necessary? Why did Iran turn from secularism to Islamic fundamentalism? Why, outside the Middle East, did the former Yugoslavia disintegrate so quickly into religious and ethnic slaughter? Why has Russia thought it necessary to privilege the Russian Orthodox Church in its process of "democratization"? And why, in America, do Catholic bishops' statements influence support for particular policy initiatives and directions? Is it accidental that two of the most successful recent social movements in the United States—the antiabortion movement in the 1970s and the Civil Rights movement in the 1960s—were firmly grounded in particular religious principles? Neither appealed to the liberal state in the *first instance;* rather, they achieved their rhetorical and conceptual power precisely because they placed these issues within frameworks of ultimate, religious meaning. Their religion did not conform to political liberalism; rather, their religion shaped political concerns and animated their involvement in politics. It is not likely, but neither is it impossible, that the Christian Coalition has "the possibility of selecting the next President of the United States," as Robertson claims.[205] It is certain, however, that the Coalition will influence the election more than it would as a "secular" organization.

Liberalism has not helped the situation by its refusal to engage religious claims (other than its own) seriously. The argument from facticity is an assertion of mere domination that properly angers those who are excluded from the "consensus," just as those who do not belong to institutional Christianity are justly upset at the effort to privilege conservative Christianity on majoritarian grounds. Thus, liberalism becomes precisely that which it claims not to be—an authoritarian religious claim which is inadequate precisely as a religion. And it is also inadequate as politics. When nonliberals enter the political debate, liberalism has no other response than impotent moralizing—flabby and ineffective. One cannot simply pass off one's opponents' positions as morally inadequate without showing why this is the case. The claim to defend "public order" and "divisiveness" rings false to those who do not see the link between the secular state and broader purposes of political and moral life. To respond to challenges with nothing but "whatever is, is right" opens the door to disaster. The fate of the welfare state is a good recent example. The decades-long complacency of the welfare state's supporters left them unable to mount a successful and persuasive defense when the attacks began. They too had assumed that American history had stopped with a consensus, and they too were wrong.

Such problems are particularly severe for most liberalism, which (with the exception of Rawls and a few others) restricts itself to procedure and form, studiously avoiding questions about the relationship between these procedures and the "good." That is, political procedures become their own end. But procedures and form are poor and unpersuasive symbols by themselves. During the German Weimar Republic, Tillich predicted correctly the victory of National Socialism over procedural democracy. A major reason, he argued, was that cultured, post-Enlightenment society lacked symbols that could powerfully connect it to experiences of ultimate meanings.[206] National Socialism touched the powerful symbols of blood, soil, and nation, and with them transformed itself into a massive public power, horrible and demonic though it was.[207] The secular state could not and did not survive without content-filled symbols, a need to which it was blind. In America, the refusal to engage the question of "God" and God's will for politics, including the concretion of that symbol in "family values," is a similar error. The drift to the "religious state" is likely to grow if it is not checked by the development of symbols that grow from within the same traditions as the religious state's advocates. But liberalism's general contempt for nonliberal religions, as well as its confidence in reason without symbols, leave it and the secular state vulnerable and endangered.

There is no evidence that politics can be healthy over the long term without being connected to realms beyond politics, that is, without being placed in a framework of ultimacy. This may enable us to reclaim the dignity of politics, upon which productive public life depends. This is not to say that the procedural emphasis of liberal defenses of the secular state is unimportant—indeed, it is vital. The antiliberal appropriation of "freedom" demonizes the political sphere rather than vitalizing it; its arguments are largely designed to serve a private, nonpublic morality. But liberalism has not shown *how* the secular state and its procedures are important for religious vitality as well. Consequently, the Christian right has made hay by portraying secularity as the enemy of Christianity, and humanism as the opposite of God's will. This, we will try to show, is fraught with peril not only for secularity but for Christianity itself. And it is on these religious grounds that the criticism of "secular humanism" (whatever that is, *exactly*) must be met. But liberalism's weak response to the charge has opened up a vacuum of symbolic power, and simultaneously turned liberality and secularity into the religions—albeit largely empty ones—of liberal*ism* and secular*ism*.

While liberalism and secularism have so far withstood many assaults, that is because they have had a virtual monopoly on the symbol of "freedom." Even now, one cannot read any liberal literature without reading again and again that freedom depends on liberalism. That is the liberal religion, but it is also the real (and inadequate) American religion, as we argue in the next chapter. So, it is not quite true that liberal defenses of secular politics entail *no* reference to religious dimensions of meaning. Nor is it accurate to say that liberalism and secularism are entirely powerless religions.

But liberalism's monopoly on the ideology of "freedom" is finished. Inclusionists, to say nothing of the advocates of the Christian state, now attack the liberal exclusion of religion precisely on the ground of freedom. Advocates of school prayer appeal to their "right" to pray, antiabortion activists proclaim the "right to free speech" as justification for protests anywhere, anytime. The antiliberal opponents of the secular state have appropriated for their own use the only powerful symbol that liberalism and secularism have! Moreover, their appeals to freedom are set in a religious framework that goes beyond politics to include the contents of morality and the divine will. Liberality and secularity cannot withstand this challenge without engaging these broader religious arguments. Summary charges of immorality and irrationality will not do. The precarious situation of the secular state in the rest of the world should serve as a warning. America is not necessarily an exception.

Inclusionists and particularist liberals alike make it impossible for us to have a public discussion of the aims of public life, the honor of politics, or the legitimacy of religions because they both assume that no discussion of the *quality* of religious commitment is possible. Their appeal to the "right to our opinion" turns religion into a matter of faith *as opposed* to reason. This, in turn, reinforces the oscillation between polarization and exhaustion. American culture believes that what is ultimate is personal, and it neither can nor should be defended. This is a serious mistake.

Where Do We Go from Here?

Unless we are able to breach this prison wall which surrounds our political discussion, the situation is likely to degenerate further. We believe that the breaches are there, and the balance of this volume seeks to identify them as part of a different political perspective, emphatic Christian centrism. But Christian centrism is not the only religious-political option available; indeed, a healthy Christian centrism requires the presence of other religious-political voices which animate the secular state with religious meanings. We aim, therefore, for "public" religions. *Public* religions should not be confused with *civil* religion. Civil religion theorists analyze the texture of a common religion that animates American culture. We maintain that "freedom" has become our civil religion, and it is inadequate. We advocate public religions, which acknowledges a plurality of religious commitments, holding that such a plurality energizes public life.[208]

At this point, both a review and preview may be helpful. In review, we maintain that secularists and their critics, despite their frequent enmity, make similar errors. These include: (1) their unwillingness to pass beyond formal considerations, largely because (2) they hold that there is no way to evaluate religious views publicly (either because they are incommensurable, or because individuals have a right to their own opinion); (3) the consequent reduction of the political sphere to a conflict of wills that can end only in domination of others, and (4) their common conservative-majoritarian impulses (both liberals and Christians would do well to remember that they, too, were once minorities). Secularists and inclusionists alike are unable to promote pluralism that includes criticism of their own treasured consensus, despite the fact that both assert their own claims on the basis of pluralism.

Such is the lamentable state of affairs when we reduce the debate over religion and public life to the formal rubric of "church and state." (1) To the extent that religion is banished from public participation, religion and religious adherents are diminished, their worldview no longer able to comprehend both the public and the private realms. (2) The significance of the public itself is damaged. Public life surrenders its claim to participate in interpreting meanings, and, lacking a relation to any ultimate meaning, loses significance. Politics becomes increasingly suspect, contempt for the political process increases, and politics finally becomes antipolitical. (3) Finally, however, because politics endures despite its self-cannibalization, religion re-enters the public sphere in forms more virulent than those against which liberalism had inoculated it. The purely secular conception of politics is wounded, perhaps mortally.

The issue is not *whether* it is permissible or desirable that religion be politically significant, but rather what the *content* of such religions should be. The issue is not one of religion or no religion, but of religions better and worse. This, then, is why the leaders of eighteenth-century revolutions sought religious sanction at the very moment they tried to separate church and state. As Gilkey says, "The organs of government and the persons associated with them always participate in ultimacy and sacrality."[209] The American secular structure was not non-religious. The very lifeblood that flowed through its secular veins was religious, in two very different ways: first, there was a mostly Protestant "civil religion" that was assumed, even by the rationalists who thought they opposed it; second, secularity was underlain by a confidence in reason, which sometimes supported and sometimes opposed the Protestant civil religion. By no means did the secular structure ever stand free of religious support. Nor does it today. Inclusionists, exclusionists, and others have religious predilections that are overtly or covertly brought to their political claims. It is the question of "which religions" or "what kind" that occupies the remainder of this volume.

Up to now, we have dealt with the problems of the *politics* in "religion and politics." Now we must turn to the inadequacies of the *religion*. This requires an examination of the current American religion: the religion of freedom, which feeds the common failures of secularism and its critics. Only then will we be able to construct a productive alternative—emphatic Christian centrism—to help overcome the difficulties that the religion of freedom has bequeathed us, and that neither end of the political spectrum seems able to resolve.

Chapter 2

Let Freedom Reign

CONTEMPORARY AMERICAN POLITICAL PRACTICE

FAITH AND FREEDOM

The year 1949 saw the publication of *The Vital Center* by Arthur M. Schlesinger, Jr. In that book, he tried to show that both the political right and left had failed in their mission. What should their mission have been? Schlesinger argued that a successful political liberalism must be based on freedom, "a fighting faith."[1] The book was subtitled "The Politics of Freedom." Like most successful books (it was reissued in 1962), *The Vital Center* both responded to its time and helped to propel it into the future. But if at midcentury both the right and the left had failed to maintain "the fighting faith," that is no longer the case.[2] Both the right and the left—and, in light of President Clinton's frequent appeal to "the vital center," even the center—have adopted it. Indeed, they fight over this faith constantly.[3] We have already observed how inclusionists and liberal exclusionists alike have constant recourse to freedom and rights. In both cases, freedom is their justifying rationale; without it, their cases crumble.

Like Jefferson's use of religious imagery to portray reason's battles, Schlesinger's language too manifests a religious dedication to the mission. In America, *freedom* is a *faith* equal in force and function to any conventional religion. Americans—believers and unbelievers, theists and nontheists, gnostics and agnostics alike—agree with Schlesinger. Freedom is our faith, our civil religion. One measure of the religiosity attached to any ideal is the frequency with which it is invoked. In millennial America, freedom is invoked to support virtually every policy. On the single weekday of November 6, 1997, the *New York Times* reported the following stories: the overwhelming passage in the House of Representatives of a bill including a 28-point "Taxpayer Bill of Rights"; Oregon voters' reaffirmation of an assisted-suicide law hailed by one of its supporters as a victory that overcame "the political machinery of those who oppose choice"; up the road, the defeat of a Washington State handgun safety bill, opposed by the National Rifle Association on the grounds that it was an "invasion of privacy and a ploy to infringe on the constitutional right of U.S. citizens to bear arms"; and testimony in the Murrah Federal Building bombing case that the defendant, Terry Nichols, carried an antigovernment article which declared that "the enemies of freedom" must know that "we will physically fight! They must know we will not shrink from spilling their blood." Finally, the *Times* reported that the defeat, two days earlier, of an initiative to abandon affirmative action policies in Houston, was due largely to the fact that "affirmative action supporters kept its opponents from seizing the high ground of equal opportunity and civil rights."[4] It was apparently another busy day for "freedom" and for "rights," preceded but a few days earlier by a Presidential advisory commission's recommendation for a "patient bill of rights" for health care. But it was hard to tell exactly whose side the god of freedom was on: on the right and against government, as in the taxpayer bill of rights, Nichols's photocopy, and the defeat of the handgun law? Or on the left, as in Houston and Oregon? About the only thing that *is* clear is that "freedom" and "rights" consume American political rhetoric. Virtually no one can win a political victory without first convincing us that their program will increase freedom and choice, and that their opponents are oppressive thieves of freedom.

Freedom's deification is evident in many other ways. The cultural dominance of a myth—and freedom is a *powerful* myth[5]—is visible not only in its plausible and profound moments, but also in the banal lengths of absurdity to which it is taken. It is not always clear what freedom actually has to do with instances in which we nonetheless invoke its sacred name and pray at its altar. Senator Trent Lott did not explain just how the 1997 budget agreement was the "beginning of a new era of freedom."[6] Perhaps he might have, had he been pressed. But he was not, and did not. Lott's obeisance to freedom was merely questionable;

others are patently ridiculous. What conceivable meaning does it have for Kellogg's Corn Flakes to be advertised with the slogan "Let freedom pour"? Or for Goodyear tires to be jingled as "serious freedom"? One can only imagine that high-priced advertising firms produce commercials with such language because they believe it will strike consumers' spiritual center (even when that language has nothing to do with the product being sold). And they are right.[7]

From the important to the implausible to the absurd, "Freedom" Almighty, its only-begotten Child "Rights," and its Spirit "Choice" are the ubiquitous Trinity of American culture. We are not the first to have noticed the compelling force of appeals to freedom in contemporary American society. Robert Bellah and his associates launched a broadside against the culture of privacy and personal choice in *Habits of the Heart* (1985). Mary Ann Glendon's *Rights Talk* (1991) argued that appeals to rights and personal choice are an ultimately counterproductive conception of the American constitutional tradition as well as a despoliation of political discourse. Ultimately, for Glendon, the absolutism of "rights" in legal talk and its filtration into American political discourse damages the very tradition of rights it attempts to protect. John McGowan's *Postmodernism and Its Critics* (1991) persuasively argues that the postmodern movement is hypermodern in one significant respect: its unquestioned devotion to freedom.[8] Indeed, McGowan shows that postmodern literary theory has raised the importance of freedom to a level beyond that of the moderns who first highlighted it.

We will not repeat the arguments of these authors and others, although in chapter 4 we will consider why postmodernism worships freedom even more than the Enlightenment did. For now, our point is that that freedom is the "civil religion" of millennial America, the deity to which appeal is made in order to trump all other values. Freedom has a sacred status; it is our "ultimate concern."[9] Nowhere is this clearer than in the Christian Coalition's 1994 *Contract with the American Family*. One might have expected (given fundamentalist views on the inerrancy of Scripture) to find the *Contract* riddled with biblical texts. Not so.[10] What one *does* find instead is the assertion of a variety of rights and freedoms that the Coalition expects to be passed in the form of coercive law. Three of the Coalition's first four initiatives were: "Restoring Religious Equality: A constitutional amendment to protect the religious liberties of Americans in public places," "Promoting School

Choice," and "Protecting Parental Rights: Enactment of a Parental Rights Act and Defeat of the U.N. Convention on the Rights of the Child."[11] On the other end of the spectrum, in a 1998 mailing, Ira Glasser, executive director of the American Civil Liberties Union, reduces the *entirety* of moral contest to "freedom vs. authoritarianism." He continues, "That's what the struggle over competing visions of morality is all about."

As we have already argued, religion has two sides: the subjective side of ultimate concern (whether an ultimate concern is *felt* as ultimate—"all about" meets this criterion easily) and a referential side (the ultimate concern itself, whether a nation or ideology or some other god or gods), concerning which we both can and *must* ask, "Should this god be God?" In this case, our answer is *No*. Freedom, as Americans understand it, is undoubtedly important. However, making it our dominant religious commitment produces catastrophic consequences for our public and private lives.

One of our chief concerns in this volume is with the damage that the religion of freedom wreaks on our public life. In this chapter, we approach the topic in two ways. First, we examine facets of the contemporary political spectrum of center, left, and right, as those three terms customarily are used. Our second task then will be to analyze the nature of this American interpretation of freedom more closely. The political impasses of American political life, we will argue, are directly related to a particularly narrow interpretation of freedom combined with an exaggerated estimate of its importance. As long as we retain that understanding, political and cultural impasses such as those we now see are inevitable. The American conception of freedom finally devours itself as well as its worshipers—it is a *demonic* religion whose creativity is inseparable from its destructiveness. The analysis of the American religion of freedom will put us in a position to propose an alternative (but not the *only* one), the emphatic Christian center, in chapter 3.

THE POLITICAL SITUATION: THE VACUOUS CENTER AND ITS RADICAL ADVERSARIES

The "Victory" of the Center

When we first published on this topic,[12] the political situation seemed very different from what it became a few years later. Then, extremism was in fashion; soon after, it seemed out of style. Then, the political center seemed hopelessly befuddled, and that confusion was among the factors that produced a striking victory for the Republican Party, which captured a Congressional majority for the first time in several decades, largely under the steam of the "Contract with America." But a short time later that contract, and the Christian Coalition's copycat "Contract with the American Family," seemed antiquated. Then, the news resembled a broadcast by Sally Jesse Raphael, in which the most extreme (and yet banal) voices received the most attention. Later, despite the persistence of the Sally-like "Crossfire" on the Cable News Network, a political truce seemed to ensue—a cease-fire only violated by occasional sniping on either side, but with nothing much happening publicly. Compromise seemed to have become, as we noted earlier, the aim of politicians on both sides of the political spectrum, a desire fueled, in part, by the demands of the electorate and even some political pundits.

We seemed to have tired of the brittle polarization of the eighties and early nineties, and polarizers on both sides seem to have recognized that (for the moment, at least) continuing to spout vitriolic attacks was not to their political advantage. A good thing? Yes, if American politics were not still rudderless; if the current truce were a sign that our conflicts had actually been resolved; if the peace were due to something other than exhaustion; if, in other words, the political culture had improved, clarified its principles and aims, and put us in a better position to make considered political judgments about what we want America to become.

Sadly, none of that has happened. The "victory" of the compromising center was empty. Its temporary nature was nowhere clearer than in the impeachment mess, a personal hatred masquerading as the "rule of law." Real issues have not been resolved, but merely suppressed, like disagreeable topics shunned at a family reunion. Clinton's rhetoric of the "vital center" as neither liberal nor conservative, both right and left, leaves us in doubt about just what it is, exactly.[13] Al Gore's talk of the "magnificent middle" is equally without content.

It is unfair to blame our elected leaders entirely for their inability or unwillingness to provide a content for the center of the spectrum. In a democratic nation, the fault is primarily the public's. That makes it worth examining what happens when our politics turns from polarization to compromise. In 1992, President Clinton was elected largely on the strength of his promise to reform the American health-care system, and because of a sense that George Bush lacked the "vision thing." We said we wanted leadership, and especially on health-care policy. Clinton raised that issue, made it national in scope, and tried to deliver on his promise. The Republican Party, in response, did nothing except block every proposal and compromise the president offered. The "vast American center" that wanted vision in politics, however, promptly shattered the eyeglasses offered it. Republican popularity skyrocketed and Clinton became nearly as unpopular as Richard Nixon at the height of Watergate. The Republicans were poised to produce a countervision, the "Contract with America," which they rode to a new congressional majority in 1994. They too tried to deliver on their promises. The President and the Democrats did little else but block Republican efforts (with the exception of welfare policy), and this time the president's popularity soared while the Republicans' plummeted.

Both parties learned the obvious lesson: when Americans say they want leadership, don't believe them. Instead, either promise much and make little effort to deliver, choose safe targets (the current attack on the IRS is a good example), or take aim at those without a political constituency (such as welfare recipients). This is the victory of the empty center: unprincipled, without a core, sacrificing the very vision it demanded in a quest for compromise at any price. That is why Clinton's health-care plan could be derided as extreme, and the president could turn the charge of extremism into a persuasive mantra against Republicans two years later. In neither case was there serious public examination of the content of actual proposals—what mattered was the purely formal consideration of where they fell on a spectrum. This much is clear: the center of a spectrum is an empty place to stand. It is vacuous, and it is where, at the moment, we are.

It is unlikely, however, that we will remain here for long. Unless we find ways to discuss principles for public policy and public objectives, we will be squeezed in a vise between two equally unattractive alternatives of our own making. On the one side, vacuous politics—the politics which allows the loudest polarizer of the spectrum to set its agenda in order to achieve "compromise"—and on the other side, renewed polarization. There is reason to suspect that a new polarization is around the corner. The time will not be too long unless an emphatic center, with emphatic, principled positions, emerges.[14]

Defeat in Victory, Victory in Defeat: The Paradox of the Vacuous Center

The unhealthy dual possibilities of empty victory and repeated repolarization are not accidental. If our argument in the preceding chapter has any merit, this is what we should expect. If politics without religious animation of some kind is both self-contradictory and self-defeating, then we should expect to find our political culture riddled with inconsistency and plagued with excess, or, alternatively, engaged in a quest for truce without principle. Although the heavier guns are only infrequently fired, so that we no longer believe that we are in the midst of what James Davison Hunter (and later Pat Buchanan) called "culture wars,"[15] the smell of smoke is still in the air. And there is no reason to suspect that new ammunition is not being loaded. In the 1980s and 90s, political discourse—both religious and secular—was monopolized by extremes which, despite whatever good points they make (and there are several), sought to push the debate in their direction by pressing toward ever farther extremes. Largely, the right succeeded, so that the centrist politics of the Clinton administration bore little resemblance to what was considered the "center" even a decade earlier. The center has not found a principled voice, despite the fact that (or perhaps because) nearly all data on public opinion suggest a desire to find a middle ground. This is largely a problem of the center's own making. Centrism harbors an internal failure that must be confessed if it is to be overcome.

The term "center" has at least two connotations. It can signify a *midpoint*, a passive (or even reactive) center between two extremes. But it can also signify a *substantive core of conviction* that actively centers us as individuals and as a society. It is this second meaning of "center" that we advocate. Yet it is the first meaning which dominates our culture: the "middle ground" or "common ground" (Clinton's term) defines itself solely in terms of what surrounds it. This sort of empty, passive centrism remains utterly dependent on the very extremes it seeks to mediate. It attempts nothing more than to keep the peace at all costs. In so doing, it turns the agenda over to the extremes. It is reactive, even reactionary, with no commitments of its own. In other words, it is a *vacuous center*, which is limited to only three possible responses to the extremes: protest, "dialogue," and silence.

The vacuous center can *protest*, as when Robert Hughes complains about the "culture of complaint."[16] This protest is legitimate and necessary, born of our weariness in hearing for the umpteenth time that we mere mortals must once more listen to the most recent righteous discoverers of absolute and final truth. True, it is precisely this complaint which led to both political parties' effective exploitation of charges of "extremism" after 1992. But these charges were made only as an attempt to block proposals, not to forward counterproposals. Complaint alone cannot produce renewal. Without a positive content of its own, protest is but petulant whining, which can prevent action but not take it.

The vacuous center can also demonstrate how empty it really is by issuing calls for *"dialogue,"* "further study," or "education." These are the siren calls of paralytics who fail to recognize their paralysis. By themselves, dialogue and study say nothing; in the current political climate, they have become pleas without substance. Religious denominations and higher education seem particularly adept at this art of evasion. As soon as the specter of disagreement raises its head, church offices call for "study," as if too little information were the root of all our differences. If not "Let's study," then "Let's dialogue." James Davison Hunter could produce a penetrating analysis of the polarized American culture of the early 1990s, but even he could recommend nothing better than "dialogue" to replace the culture wars. Nor is it only churches and universities that are so anemic. We share a widespread cultural faith that "education" is the postmodern aspirin for all that ails us. We assure ourselves that conflicts over sexuality can be overcome by better sex education; or that diseases ranging from HIV infection to smoking-related illness can be conquered merely by educating those who engage in risky practices. It seems not to occur to us that no one—save the willfully ignorant—is unaware that unprotected sex followed by a pack of cigarettes is unlikely to lengthen life expectancy.

To be sure, discussion, information, study, and education are all essential; but they are not enough. They are merely *formal* means, devoid of content and incomplete without an end outside themselves. They propose to mend the tears in the social fabric by providing a sewing kit—minus the thread. We must ask: "Education for *what?* Dialogue about *what?*" Few oppose sex education, but the right inveighs against the forms of sex education that they view as an "attack on the family," while the left directs its ire at those who "preach" abstinence, claiming that this type of education limits freedom and impedes moral development. Similarly, the president's "cure" for the miserable condition of American race relations came to nothing more than to appoint a study commission, the results of which so far have added little to what reasonably well-informed people already knew. Dialogue is meaningful only when participants bring their own specific analyses and positions to the table. This the vacuous center has not done; it has remained content with empty formalism, just as in its protests against extremism.

Finally, the vacuous center is often simply *silent,* not knowing which way to turn. This is the way of the paralytics who recognize their paralysis. It sees the relative truth of all the extremes, but does not know how to respond to their obvious deficiencies. The centrist is in much the same position in which John Updike found himself during the Vietnam War: "All sides of the issue spoke to me, and the effect possibly was numbing."[17] But if centrism takes this alternative, it provides us with a vivid demonstration of its own irresponsibility. Responsibility, as H. Richard Niebuhr taught us, means answerability.[18] If the irresponsibility of the polarizers—on both wings—lies in their refusal to be answerable instead of merely commanding submission to their gods, the irresponsibility of the center lies in its unwillingness to speak forcefully and concretely. In other words, the vacuous center has been unwilling to become an *emphatic center.* It remains captive to the ends of the political spectrum, capable only of reacting against or being manipulated by them.

Ironically, the vacuous center's hesitance also constitutes its promise. If the center mumbles when it should speak, this very failure arises from a deep sensitivity and power: its unique desire to understand the commitments of those who inhabit the political and religious extremes, and its sympathetic response to what is plausible and powerful in each position. But to realize its promise and power, it must become an emphatic center.

An emphatic center must take actual positions. The failure of the politics of polarization makes the oxymoron of a politics without positions seem attractive. As Alan Brinkley points out, the "image of a consensual, bipartisan politics is an old and attractive one," likely to garner considerable support in a campaign. But "campaigning and governing are two different things," and there "is nothing—either in our history or in the present, fractious political moment—to suggest that there is a nonpolitical route to progress." A true vital center (Brinkley continues) "will fight for what [it] believes and exhort others to follow—not seek refuge in the myth of a world without politics."[19]

As things stand, the center creates its own defeat even when it appears to be victorious. It is beholden to the conceptions of the political extremes because it has no center of its own. Thus, we must ask: If the center is captive even when it appears victorious, to whom is it captive? And by what, if anything, are the very extremes that determine the condition of the center themselves determined?

The Radical Adversaries

The political—and, we will see, religious—extremes of both wings are subject to a common ideology in differing arenas, and therefore with opposite implications: the civil religion of freedom. Despite their obvious differences, both agree on an impossible interpretation of freedom: (1) they define freedom as "negative freedom," the ability to do what one wants without restraint or responsibility to anyone; and (2) they treat this freedom as an absolute value.[20] Even more remarkable is the fact that both wings routinely contradict this definition when they arbitrarily demand the right to coerce their opponents into submission. They both thereby document their own lack of a coherent center. Nor will the center itself make much progress unless it can begin to resolve this typically American conundrum of freedom, coercion, and responsibility.

Both extremes understand "freedom" as the ability to act as one pleases without interference. Their principal difference concerns *where* they think such freedom is legitimate. Generally speaking, the left insists on the value of absolute freedom in matters of personal preference, but is perfectly willing to countenance coercion in matters of economics; while the right is happy to coerce matters of personal life, but insists on the fullest freedom in economic activities. The left regards it as self-evident that one should be able to express "personal freedom," to choose one's own "lifestyle," and so on. This canonization of conscience and personal choice is not universal, even on the left. Its less consistent adherents trumpet some personal freedoms, but are more than willing to impose codes against "hate speech," as long as they themselves can determine what is hatred and what is not. On the whole, however, the left's highest principle is personal freedom, and it is no accident that "choice" and "pluralism" are its regular mantras.[21]

This worship of personal freedom that seems so obvious to the left proceeds from some seriously flawed assumptions. It worships the human desire to do what one wants, or more basically treats wants and desire as unquestionable (and as indistinguishable from needs). The proliferation of the language of "rights" brings these claims to their highest pitch, as Glendon shows.[22] Everything from health care to art to eyeglasses (in an advertisement for a national eyeglass distributor)—from the momentous to the ridiculous—is claimed as a right. In this scheme of things, whatever one wants is likely to become one's right. And since it is my desire and my right, so the reasoning goes, it is therefore also good. Oliver Stone's claim that any criticism of the media is tantamount to censorship, and that he would "pretty much do anything," would be a fantastically unfair caricature of the left—if one of their own had not said it.[23]

What holds this chain together is the stunning assumption that there cannot be anything essentially wrong with my private desires, my will, or my reason. "That's my choice" or "I have the right to my opinion" can be the last words only if we believe that there is no perversion in most of our choices, that there is no real original sin *in* us beyond that which law may forbid or allow. This assumption of essential innocence permits the implausible leap that maintains that because something is legally permissible, it is morally defensible. From 2 Live Crew to Oliver Stone, the assumption of essential innocence is the unquestionable dogma of the American left. Kathleen Norris asks, however, "If I'm O.K. and you're O.K., and our friends are O.K., why is the world definitely not O.K.?"[24] A good question—and one the left is ill-equipped to answer. The answer of the Christian center is: "No one is O.K."

The right, of course, has a different answer. It gleefully understands the immensity of sin—other people's sin, that is—and is happy to label all forms of conduct it finds offensive, from speech to sexual behavior, as sin. This immediately translates into demands for legal restraints on "offensive" or "sinful" lifestyle choices. But the right also lacks consistency, for it exempts one lifestyle—its own—from any such restraint. Concerned Women for America, a Christian organization endorsed by Ronald Reagan, George Bush, and Jack Kemp, illustrates this bizarre mixture of freedom for "us" and coercion for "them." In a 1993 mailing, the "freedoms" it advocated were "Providing parental choice in education," "Protecting religious freedom," "Protecting the right to life of pre-born babies," and "Reducing the tax burden on families." But it advocated an equal number of coercions: "Mandating the teaching of abstinence to school children" (which presumably does not interfere with parental choice), "stopping the 'Homosexual Rights' agenda," "Mandating AIDS testing of health care workers," and "Eliminating illegal pornography." The vision of the right, no less than the left, is driven by the assumption that *its* adherents are pure while its enemies are mired in sin. (The left faults its enemies for "ignorance"; but this quickly becomes, in a quite Jeffersonian way, *willful* ignorance—they *could* know better, but don't *want* to—which is the left's version of "sin.")

Even this does not exhaust the strangeness of the situation. When the debate shifts to economic issues, the positions are simply reversed: the right demands absolute and unfettered freedom, while the left advocates coercion.[25] The right, which wants to regulate personal lifestyles because of the presence of sin, now miraculously discovers that the free pursuit of economic self-interest is good. How, exactly, do those who are so deeply flawed in their "lifestyles" become pure when they venture into the economic world—interacting with others whose lifestyles also require supervision? This is evidently a mystery too deep for explanation. This contradiction in the right's program appeared in the conservative Christian attempt to boycott the Disney Corporation when Disney offered its gay employees "family" benefits. Economic self-interest turned out not to be so unproblematic after all! And the left, for which subjective choice in personal matters is sacrosanct, just as suddenly discovers the evil of mere self-interest when it comes to economics, and demands control of the economic process. In liberalism, those who can do no wrong in their private lives suddenly become wolves when they encounter others of equal sanctity in economic life. The incoherence of both would be fantastic were it not so commonplace.[26]

The Empty Debate

In the final analysis, political debate today consists of little more than saying "I have a right to my opinion," and "My opinion will decide whether you have a right to yours." *Or,* "We will not discuss this or other disagreeable topics." No wonder, then, that the present cultural climate consists of a series of holy wars, the point of which is not to *convert* others, but to *dominate* them—alternating with periods of exhaustion, in which we try to *ignore* the other. Both wings invest two structures with absolute authority: the free self ("my opinion, my choice") and coercive law. They differ only over which spheres of life they wish to remain free, and which to coerce. (For the right, it is economics and personal morality, respectively. For the left, it is just the reverse.) They recognize no mediating structures. Under such conditions, the only real possibility is the attempt to eradicate one's enemies utterly, as we have seen in Ralph Reed's desire to exterminate those who differ with him. Or, failing that, one can simply pretend that they, and their issues, just don't exist.

The extremes are devoted to such incoherent and self-contradictory positions, and to the domination and elimination of their enemies, because of a warped and inadequate *religious conviction*, a devotion to the civil religion of freedom. The center, moreover, is unable to mount a sensible, centered criticism of even the most outrageous claims emanating from the ends of the political spectrum because it, too, subscribes to this American religion. This brings us face-to-face with the real American religion: freedom.

LET US PRAY: AMERICA'S DEVOTION TO FREEDOM AND ITS CONTRADICTIONS

Freedom the American Way

The signal importance America accords to freedom has had salutary effects both at home and abroad. Philosophies of freedom from the age of Enlightenment and Locke through Spencer and Mill in the nineteenth century were undoubtedly important in creating respect for—and perhaps even the concept of—the person. Emphasizing autonomous human reason, moral decision making, and artistic creativity, they helped to weaken and even to abolish oppressive authorities. The effects of these philosophies of freedom in the West were particularly pronounced in France and America, whose revolutions embodied freedom.

However, there can be little question that the significance of freedom has been transformed. The *concept* itself has not changed much: American freedom was always a negative freedom, a "freedom from" restraint rather than a positive "freedom for" anything in particular.[27] Still, as we have seen, the American conception of negative freedom was circumscribed by a positive goal for the devotees of the Enlightenment. Freedom was reason's tool; it provided *content* and a *goal* for the purely *formal means* of freedom. Thus freedom was held in a parenthesis, enclosed by the dark past on one side and the triumph of reason on the other.

What *has* changed is not the concept of freedom, but its place. When the god of reason was deposed from its throne, freedom took its place. Freedom has become, in other words, the aim and source of the right, the good, the true, and even the beautiful (in art, we praise nothing more than "creativity"). Freedom, which formerly was but a *means*, has now become its own *goal* as well. But it is a merely negative freedom—it lacks content—so that at the same time we made freedom the object of our devotion, we became worshipers of form alone. There was something salutary about this movement. Universal reason made a poor religion and needed dethroning. We may ask, however, whether taking away the parentheses that enclosed freedom and turning it into our civil religion was such a good idea. A tool is not a purpose; but the American religion of freedom tries to convert the former into the latter, creating irresolvable contradictions.

The problems of deified freedom become apparent when we consider the favorite synonyms for "freedom" in American culture (for the moment we omit sophisticated analysts such as John Rawls). As we have seen, "choice" and "rights" are quite popular. The greater the number of choices, the greater one's freedom (so the argument presumes). A recent advertisement for a satellite cable company proclaims its 200-plus channel availability as "Freedom Gone Berserk." It is not often that "berserk" is a good thing. But now any limitation of choices is perceived as a limitation of rights, as if there were a "right to choose" in absolutely all circumstances (as pro-choice abortion advocates argue in relation to abortion). The distressing thing about such language is that it is undifferentiated. There may indeed be rights that involve expansion of choice as well as arenas in which negative freedom should be increased, but the simple and absolute equivalence of rights, choice, and freedom is merely assumed in contemporary rhetoric. One language slides into the other. The number of choices is taken as the extent of freedom; the right to do as one pleases is the same as the right to choose without constraint; it is all freedom.

Such a notion of freedom carries with it two main assumptions. First, its conception of decision making is solipsistic. It imagines an ideal, solitary decision maker who is involved in others' choices only insofar as she chooses to be. The American vision of freedom deifies *independence*.

The Declaration of Independence was once a political document. However, its status as American Scripture, as Pauline Maier calls it, is less as a political document (especially in an antipolitical time) than as a philosophy of life. Virtually the only portion ever quoted in popular rhetoric (other than the title) is one phrase from the opening: "All men are created equal." The *political* ramifications of that claim are ignored, except sometimes by feminists and African Americans, who rightly note that neither women nor slaves were included. The Declaration's real force today is as a *personal* validation, transmitted culturally.

The second assumption is that there is nothing basically wrong with human beings. This is the assumption that Christian thought's doctrine of original sin (which we will discuss in chapter 3), and Hinduism's and Buddhism's doctrines of ignorance all deny. For contemporary American society, however, human "potential" is unlimited—this is a dogma. It is difficult to find a single instance in cultural (or sadly, even in religious) rhetoric where the intrinsic limitations of our moral and intellectual capacities are grasped adequately. It is true, of course, that we are attentive to external constraints on our potential, but only as constraints from which we believe we must be *freed* (or free ourselves).[28] This universal unlimited potential used to make exceptions for the "retarded," but people with mental retardation are no longer exempt from its demands. It is a dogma of the American religion of freedom that our moral potential is unlimited. There is nothing *essentially* wrong with humanity that education or family values or psychology could not correct.

It has not always been so with freedom. In the classical political thought of Locke, for example, the ground of freedom was not the innocence of the person, but the freedom of private property. Founders such as Madison were still quite conscious of evil and human limitations. But the late twentieth century saw any awareness of universal *inner* limitation steadily recede. If we are not smart or good, that is not because human beings are often not smart or good—let alone that all people might in some ways be ignorant or morally suspect—but because particular people have not tried hard enough (according to the right) or are subject to external limitations and oppression that prevent them from reaching their unlimited potential (the left's preferred explanation). It is not that either of these claims are necessarily wrong; they are often (but not *always*) right. What *is* misguided is the assumption that only *some* persons are, by some accident of personal choice or external circumstance, inwardly limited. We are *all* limited, and inevitably so.

Hence *independence* and *innocence* are the chief tenets of the American religion of freedom. They have brought us to a time in which, as many have documented, personal desires and beliefs are not subject to external review. "I have a right to my opinion" also means "I am right because it is my opinion." Intellectual conclusions are not subject to debate in such an environment. In religious circles, "faith" often substitutes for opinion, unassailable from outside: "That is my religion" or "This is my belief" are sure discussion-stoppers. But it is not only or even especially "religious" persons who have recourse to the fortress of faith—the sanctity of "opinion" serves the same purpose. And in tandem with opinion's unassailability, moral beliefs become sacrosanct as well. There is no significant difference between claiming that a given faith or moral opinion or choice is unreviewable—because "This is my lifestyle choice" or because "I believe it is God's will"—so long as choices and beliefs cannot be examined by others, discussed, challenged, or modified by argument. From a purely formal viewpoint, the words mean the same thing. My autonomous *decision* to believe or to act has *become its own justification,* and the decision *itself* is an *exercise in freedom.* If anyone asks for more justification, it must spring from an authoritarian desire to limit freedom.

The classic text of freedom as independence and its attendant assumptions is Henry Thoreau's *Walden.* Virtually unknown in the nineteenth century, when it was written by a minor figure in the transcendentalist movement, it is now one of the most-read classic texts in America. It is one of the few books in the American tradition that many college students read without its being assigned to them.[29] *Walden's* appeal, however, is not surprising. It is virtually *the* text of (non)political freedom, and it illustrates today's American temperament in much the same way that Rousseau illustrates the French. Moreover, *Walden's* abject failure when it was published[30] and its great success a century later indicates that the mood it illustrates and reinforces is much more twentieth-century than nineteenth-century. This point is confirmed by the definition of "freedom" given by American youth in a 1989 survey: freedom is what makes America special (a whopping 63 percent),[31] and freedom is overwhelmingly the right to do as one wants *without limits.*[32]

(One doubts that adults would have differed much in their responses.)

The innocence of unencumbered humanity is *Walden*'s cardinal presupposition. The prescribed cure for the "quiet desperation"[33] in which most of us live is escape and independence. This included independence from those with whom one seemingly must interact but would rather not, including tradespeople and others who provided services to Thoreau. Thoreau's problem was that as he grew to require such niceties of civilization, people gained "authority" over his freedom.[34] Help and cooperation were regarded as oppressive just because they inspired counterobligations. Nowhere was this clearer than in the case of government, which Thoreau's treatise on civil disobedience requires him to resist because government does not always support or agree with his own conceptions of what it ought to do, although Thoreau provides no argument about the quality of his own position. He does not need to; it is *his* position, after all. Thus, in *Walden*, government becomes the paradigm of the devil, inescapable and evil:

> I was seized and put into jail, because . . . I did not pay a tax to, or recognize the authority of the State which buys and sells men, women, and children, like cattle, at the door of its senate-house. I had gone down into the woods for other purposes. But, wherever a man goes, men will pursue and paw him with their dirty institutions, and, if they can, constrain him to belong to their desperate odd-fellow society.[35]

Thoreau does not much argue for the *political* justice of his cause because he does not need to. *He* is his *own* cause, his independence and freedom—from which society and its institutions inevitably detract. Society, because it is *society*, is *guilty*.

Thoreau, on the other hand, is *innocent* because he is an *individual*. Divinity is within, Thoreau declares.[36] And so, of course, evil is without—in society. In an intentional reversal of the Calvinist catechism, Thoreau maintains that the "chief end of man" is to recover the capacity to make "choices" that will return every individual to his or her original, innocent simplicity:

> When we consider what . . . is the chief end of man . . . it appears as if men had deliberately chosen the common mode of living. . . . Yet they honestly think they have no choice left. But alert and healthy natures remember that the sun rose clear. . . . No way of thinking or doing, however ancient

can be trusted without proof. . . . What old people say you cannot do, you try and find that you can. Old deeds for old people, new deeds for new.[37]

The aim, then, is to recover simplicity, and simplicity is independence.[38] Only the authority of others can prevent the recovery of innocence. All marks of civilization are profane; even poverty and disease are attributed to civilization.[39] *The fall is civilization.*[40] Sin in all its forms would disappear, Thoreau maintains, if *everyone* adopted his approach of simplicity: "If all men were to live as simply as I did, thieving and robbery would be unknown. These take place only in communities where some have got more than is sufficient while others have not got enough."[41] There are, in other words, no internal limits on humanity, only external limits, although one wonders precisely how the motives for inequality could have arisen in Thoreau's state of nature. How did innocents (in which Thoreau still includes "savages," animals, and children[42]) get the idea to construct the dirty institutions of civilization in the first place?

Thoreau embodies the primitivism and antihistoricism so characteristic of the American consciousness. And the same antigovernmental, antipolitical, privatistic valorization of presocial innocence is still reflected today in society's constant invocation of childlike innocence, the animal rights movement, and the rebirth of the myth of the "noble savage" in films such as *Legends of the Fall*. Paradoxically enough, the way back to simplicity leads through advance; and even though Thoreau's notion of "progress" is antitechnological (the re-creation of innocence through a romanticized nature[43]), it remains true that the "new" is sacred[44] ("new deeds for new people"). Moreover, for Thoreau, education could re-install innocence,[45] though just how that would avoid the problem of evil authority is rather obscure.

If we are sufficiently independent, so the myth of *Walden* runs, we can recover our original state of innocence. The technocratic version of this myth of innocence employs precisely the opposite means as Thoreau's but to the same purpose: the renewal of innocence, the insulation from all outside authority, and the triumph of the individual. Garry Wills's brilliant subtitle for *Reagan's America*, "Innocents at Home,"[46] captures this perfectly. Although Reagan loved the fantastic technology of the "Star Wars" satellite defense system, the motive for technological advancement was to insulate the "home," in two senses. First came the insulation of America.

But that was for the sake of protecting the *private* home of American families. Reagan's antigovernment agenda had fundamentally the same presupposition as Thoreau's: innocence was private—the "home"—and sin was anything that interfered with that realm of sinlessness and innocence. The myth of the *home* supplanted Thoreau's pond. Moreover, the Reaganesque "morning in America" of the 1984 campaign not only communicated the same ahistorical drive to recover innocence (and the same identification of innocence with the new), it even used Thoreau's imagery. If Thoreau is more admired on the left, and Reagan on the right, this should not obscure the fundamental identity of their perspectives. The differences between them involve means alone; the ends are nearly identical.

It seems odd that both Thoreau and Reagan felt the need to make their visions public. Moreover, although one might think that the devotees of freedom as complete independence would be more willing to accept others' (innocent) independence, it is difficult to imagine a less tolerant work than *Walden*. Thoreau's contempt for everyone who lives unlike him is palpable, oozing through almost every page. It is remarkably (though not surprisingly) similar to the right's disdain for "families" that are unlike the "normal" family. The right's inattention to questions of child abuse and spousal battery under the frequent guise of—again unsurprisingly—parental "rights" raises the most striking and disturbing result of the religion of freedom: the drive for independence often leads, as it apparently did for the violent reincarnation of Thoreau, Theodore Kaczynski, to an effort to *force* others to submit to one's own version of independence. Thus does freedom come to coerce independence.

Freedom as Domination

When freedom became heir to reason's divine throne, it inherited reason's old enemy: power. It is a particular conception of power, to be sure, that godlike freedom must oppose, namely power as equivalent to control or domination. But for freedom, that is what all power is—domination. For Jefferson, power and reason were implacable enemies; but reason was also (paradoxically) the greatest power, which, if left unfettered, would compel adherence to the truth. The trouble was that reason was not unfettered. The evil hosts of domination, who wanted to obscure reason for their own purposes, held it in bondage. Consequently, reason had to enlist its opponent, power, so that it could dominate the forces of unreason. Reason's opposition to domination turned into the very domination it despised.[47]

The same blind opposition to power, and the same inadequate conception of power as mere control and domination, have now been appropriated by reason's successor, freedom. On this view, freedom, to be effective, must be negative. It must negate "power." This is equally true of both the popular rhetoric of "personal choice" and the scholarly literature of liberalism. We have already seen how the latter often conceives the battle between freedom and domination as an institutionalized war between secularism and religion. Inclusionists fight the same war, simply taking different sides. For both, the relation between freedom and power is dualistic: freedom is innocence, power evil. Thoreau's never-answered question of what could lead innocent people to develop such evil tendencies is reflexively obvious for most Americans: the lust for power. This fragment of Jefferson's worldview continues unabated. The right's protest against the excessive power of the IRS is a case in point. It is not the specific performance of the IRS that is at issue, as Rep. Bill Archer freely admits, but the "power" of the government to tax at all.[48] Similarly, the hymn of the left that one should not "legislate morality" (what law does *not* do this remains a perpetual mystery) is a protest against power over individual self-determination. The stark opposition between freedom and power also appears in other ways. The antigovernment movement of the congressional Republicans in the wake of the 1994 elections attempted to use governmental power to dismantle itself.[49] On the left, disdain for those with social influence often leads to support for government, but only as a check on the unfettered dominating power of those who are influential outside government (usually in the economic sphere).

Thus in America, power is used to control power *for the sake of freedom.* Freedom is placed in the odd position of, first, abjuring power as its enemy, but second (because power constantly threatens freedom), *employing power to defeat power.* Freedom's need to expand requires that it be in control; it must *be* power and *exclude* power at the same time. Moreover, because power is the sworn enemy of freedom, it can never be trusted. Every exercise of power must be opposed on grounds of freedom, but every exercise of freedom requires an involvement with power. Freedom turns on itself and becomes its opposite. What began as an attempt to escape domination, in the end *requires the domination of others* for the sake of one's own freedom.

This movement by which freedom becomes domination is worth exploring more fully. We must pass over a substantial contributor to the process, the human need to belong to some society. The other aspects of freedom we have delineated, however, are sufficient to demonstrate its near-inevitable transformation into its apparent opposite. Negative freedom is essentially solipsistic. It desires an unfettered life of its own and subjection to nothing outside its own wants and desires. In short, freedom as the ultimate value wants to become what many religious traditions conceive as available only for God, to be *a se*, by itself. To do so requires, however, that all counterinfluences, all that could exert "power over" oneself, be either eradicated or made completely subject to the one whose freedom is paramount. Freedom as *religion*, in other words, intrinsically aims at the self's all-controlling omnipotence.

A devotee of freedom could in principle simply isolate herself from all outside influences, as Thoreau attempted. But if it was not possible for Thoreau, in a relatively sparsely settled land, how much less possible is it for us now? Anyone who visits Walden Pond and sees the throngs of meditators attempting to reproduce Thoreau's experience along with hundreds of other fellow isolationists, knows the answer. Still, negative freedom demands isolation. This gives a particular cast to America's obsession with rights. It is not accidental that the "right to privacy" was articulated as a constitutional right in the twentieth century. It is the logical outcome, the term, of all other rights thus construed. It is the right to freedom par excellence.

Therein lies the problem. The right to privacy, like many of the other rights that Americans hold so dear, is (by the current American definition) a *nonsocial* right, that is, it carves out a range of what one is able to do free from others' interference, and especially in private.[50] But the exercise, protection, and definition of these rights are accomplished socially, not privately. The right to free speech is a case in point. To say, as advocates of school prayer do, that one has a right to do as one pleases when one pleases (to pray in public schools) is to assert a private, nonsocial right in social, public circumstances.[51] Taken to this extreme, an undifferentiated "freedom to speak" would enable the private domination of any and all public spheres and spaces. The American language of rights and freedom (not *all* languages of rights and freedom) asserts an unlimited nonsocial prerogative in a society.

How can we deal with such nonsocial claims in social settings? We tend to one of two responses. First, we may try to maintain our isolation as best we can, joining with others whose thoughts, inclinations, and desires match our own, creating "lifestyle enclaves," the union of same with same.[52] Or second, we perpetuate the illusion that some natural harmony of desires is possible. After all, if all true[53] desires are innocent, perhaps our freedom, despite our apparent disagreements, will allow us to hold something in common. This accounts for the fuzzy political appeal to "common ground," from which we are supposed to be able to make harmonious beginnings.

The romantic rhetoric of the "common ground" that President Clinton so cheerfully employed against the "extremists" is more damaging than helpful when that ground is freedom. Our common religion of freedom devotes us to a god that is inevitably fragmenting and divisive. If religion, derived from the Latin *religare,* is supposed to bind together, this religion of freedom must inevitably fail; it binds us together formally, but divides us as soon as a content-filled decision must be made. *Our common ground is the devotion to freedom; but what freedom demands is that we all have separate ground.*

Yet we cannot have that separate ground in a mass society. Our absolute devotion to freedom confronts others who also want absolute freedom, but the content of what each of us wants is different. If our freedom is to be actualized, it must have a content: concrete desires and wants. But these will necessarily encounter resistance and opposition: resources are finite, all desires cannot be met, the realization of some desires excludes others, and so on. When that happens, the god of purely formal freedom has no resources with which to resolve the dispute. Because everyone's freedom is valuable, and because others' choices inevitably limit our own (except in rare circumstances), our own absolute freedom requires *control of others' freedom.* What began as a desire for complete freedom becomes a demonic domination of others who want to assert their freedom in an incompatible, or even merely different, direction.[54] It is no accident that the American religious denominations founded on the most strident proclamations of freedom became the most authoritarian of all.[55]

The only option available becomes to use force against one's opponents or to collapse into inaction. It was easy for a recent presidential commission to affirm a patient "bill of rights" in health care; it proved impossible for that commission to agree on any course of action to enforce it.[56] Any enforcement mechanism would have to trample on others' "rights." If the choice for action is made, freedom becomes a robber-god; it deprives us of all other ways to resolve our differences, particularly when combined with the self-affirming message that there is nothing wrong with what I want (since I, the *innocent* at *home,* sincerely want it). A consistent devotion to freedom has as its result either powerlessness or Ralph Reed's elimination of opposition. If Americans find such an alternative distasteful, that is our hope: that most of us will instinctively shrink from the implications of the worship of the god of freedom, whatever our antisocial and antitraditional social traditions tell us. From this perspective, the Concerned Women for America's equal mixture of freedom and coercion is not the result of an inconsistent execution of freedom, but precisely what is to be expected from the civil religion of freedom. The militia movement's violent devotion to freedom is equally unsurprising, as is the oft-bemoaned litigiousness of American culture, which is the fault, not of lawyers, but of clients—as Pogo said, "We have met the enemy and he is us." When every question becomes a matter of freedom and rights, and when freedom is our religion, every political question becomes a question of domination and coercion.

We now have an account of the dynamic by which American political rhetoric is constituted. It clearly has a pronounced religious dimension, and can even be described as a religion; but it is a destructive religion which tends to become private and absolute at the same time. It is antipolitical even when it enters the political arena, and issues in the two alternatives for public life that have characterized recent American political culture: polarization without hope of reconciliation, and exhaustion. We will oscillate, but between *these* alternatives. A purely formal godlike freedom, which, in turn, becomes domination, empties public life of content by eliminating all criteria for public debate save one: freedom itself (which, being purely formal, is empty). As a religious commitment, freedom, far from providing opportunities to bind us together, actually divides us. Like reason before it, freedom is a good idea but a poor religion—though for different reasons. Freedom not only fails to produce the self-transcendence that would yield a better religion, but in its current American form, forbids it.

We might have expected that Christians and others committed to institutional religious traditions would criticize this civil religion of freedom. But we have already seen that—for the most part—they do not. Rather, their own narrow (and therefore inadequately religious) conceptions of God largely serve to reinforce the antipolitical tendencies of the religion of freedom. If we are to overcome the oscillation between polarization and exhaustion, between professions of freedom and exercises of domination, both of which are *religious* problems, we will have to find an adequate religious language. Moreover, that language cannot be a *universal* language, but will have to arise from specific traditions. Above all, it will have to address freedom's viciously circular tendency to become domination.

To do this, a religious perspective must disclose an understanding of the character of human beings that presupposes neither our essential innocence, nor society's and civilization's total degradation (nor, for that matter, the reverse). And it will have to conceive of power more productively, not as mere opposition to freedom.

PART 2 TWO

AN
EMPHATIC
CHRISTIAN
CENTER

Chapter 3

Where Shall We Go? Who Shall We Be?

A Theology for the Christian Center

*I*n the early fifth century, during the collapse of the Roman Empire (graphically illustrated by the sack of the "eternal city"), Augustine depicted the fate reserved for those who dared object to the Roman religion of freedom:

> The worshippers and lovers of these gods, whom they delighted to imitate in their criminal wickedness, are unconcerned about the utter corruption of their country. ... Anyone who disapproves of this kind of happiness should rank as a public enemy; anyone who attempts to change it or get rid of it should be hustled out of hearing by the freedom-loving majority; he should be kicked out, and removed from the land of the living.[1]

Although we do not expect to be "removed from the land of the living" for saying so, our claim that freedom is a poor religion makes us American heretics, dissenting from the one and only article of faith on which all seem to agree—liberals, inclusionists, left, right, center, all. And yet, like Augustine's critique of the Roman religion of "glory" and "pride" (in which freedom was a minor god), our indictment of the American religion of freedom is that it does not—and cannot—deliver on its promise of total fulfillment. It is an idol.

Until now, we have expressly refrained from any reference to specifically Christian categories in our argument (except for purposes of illustration). We have examined the role of *religion* (broadly construed) in American politics, not Christianity. Our arguments that comprehensiveness and self-transcendence are necessary for religion and religious validity, that exclusionists and inclusionists alike fail in their arguments, that secular*ism* (as opposed to formal secularity) is self-defeating, and that the real American religion is freedom, have all proceeded specifically without reference to Christian understandings of God, the world, sin, redemption, Christ, and so on. That stage of our argument is over. Just as universalist liberal arguments have weakened, fractured, and crumbled under the impact of contemporary pluralism and philosophical analysis, no "universal" religious beliefs[2] or views (including the supposedly universal "scientific atheism" of Marxism) remain available to us today. Ours is a proposal for an emphatic *Christian* center—and if not Christian, it would have to be something else.[3] There is no center in the air. That this does *not* mean a "Christian state," a "Christian country," enactment of biblical law-codes, or even "universal" principles like love, tolerance, and brotherhood (that just happen to coincide with a liberal reading of the Bible), will become clear in the course of our argument. The Christian center embraces plurality[4] and secularity, but it is Christian. It cannot be nowhere.

Many of the significant difficulties of American politics, as we have argued at length, are produced by our devotion to the distorted and distorting god of freedom. This is a *religious* problem, and it requires theological reflection if we are to make headway against it. In this chapter, our task—now a theological one—has two main parts, one critical and the other constructive. First we review and criticize Christian complicity in the American idolatry of freedom. Far from criticizing this god, Christians of all stripes fold the Christian God into the tares of freedom's idolatry. American Christianity is captive to our civil religion of freedom. Our second, constructive task is to identify other theological resources available to Christians, resources not captive to the idol of freedom. We will identify three, which will be the theological principles of the emphatic Christian center: original sin, love, and power. Original sin will seem implausible to those who embrace freedom's dogma of human innocence, while love and power will strike them as irreconcilable opposites. Yet the incoherence and destructiveness of freedom's religion make them necessary. First, however, we turn to our criticism of American Christianity and its captivity to freedom's idolatry.

GOD AT THE AMERICAN MILLENNIUM: ANGRY JUDGE OR FUZZY AFFIRMER? GOD IN CONTEMPORARY AMERICAN RELIGION

Liberty or Liberation?

The American religion of freedom, with its characteristic confusion about freedom and power, extends to organized religion as well (though with some important differences from its more secular manifestations).[5] We saw numerous examples of this captivity in the foregoing chapter. Now, a more sustained analysis of the condition of American political Christianity will bring us hard against the theological work that emphatic Christian centrism must do.

Of course it is the new Christian right, with its strident emphasis on "liberty" (especially religious and economic liberty), that has garnered almost all the attention in recent years. It has made its presence felt on a variety of issues, including the Equal Rights Amendment, abortion, homosexuality, and military spending. Yet there is also an American religious left, which is devoted to a *different* gospel of freedom: the good news of personal growth, self-esteem, and "liberation" from external limitations (whether economic, political, racial, or sexual). Sometimes this takes the form of one of the liberation theologies: movements for liberation and social justice, usually African American, feminist, or gay.[6] More often, however, the religious left is much less specifically defined. Neither highly visible nor well organized (except in select, low-profile institutions), it has little public presence. In contrast, the American religious right, now centered about the powerful personality of Pat Robertson and the Christian Coalition[7]—backed up by his considerable wealth and his even more considerable ability to raise money—is extremely well organized and remarkably influential, though the actual extent of its power remains subject to question.[8]

Appeals to God in American politics have lately attained a new visibility and urgency. But such appeals are neither novel nor rare; indeed, the America of the mid-1960s through the 1970s was noteworthy for the relative absence of God-language by comparison. Nor are such appeals to God the exclusive possession of the right or of Republicans (though so it may seem to the casual observer of the present scene); we need go back no farther than Adlai Stevenson's presidential campaigns of 1952 and 1956 to find a Democratic candidate who did not hesitate to appeal explicitly to God and Christianity and to cite Scripture in his campaign speeches, nor even earlier than 1963 to find a Democratic President who referred to prayer at a press conference.[9] And the Civil Rights movement, the left's last substantial triumph, was steeped in the rich religious language of the African American Baptists who led the Southern Christian Leadership Conference, as well as the less influential but still significant rhetoric of the Nation of Islam.[10] Nor is the right's current dominance of religious rhetoric of long standing; in the 1960s, it was the right that objected to "mixing religion and politics" in the persons of John Kennedy, Martin Luther King, Jr., Malcolm X, and others.

There can be no question, however, that political appeals to God have gained in both intensity and frequency during the 1980s and 1990s, perhaps more than at any time since World War I. Moreover, the character of these appeals has also changed in important ways. The role played by the new Christian right in this resurgence and transformation of political God-talk is widely recognized, however much its actual political influence may be debated. But while the Christian right's theological rhetoric is relatively prominent in American culture, the Christian left's political rhetoric also makes its own appeal to God—in a very different way. The most striking of these differences is in the God to whom they appeal: the right exuberantly refers to a stern and righteous Father who has showered America with blessings—especially *liberty*—but is losing His patience with America for its sins and is now on the verge of withdrawing His blessings; meanwhile, the left usually refers tentatively to a vague, amorphous Love which can set us *free* to be the people we were meant to be, and which ought somehow to inspire us to be more loving; or the left may become more assertive and insist on a theology of *liberation*, whose God is still primarily Love but also begins to resemble the vengeful God of the right in some ways. In either case, the American religion of freedom is at work, whether in liberty or liberation. Before we explore these contrasting metaphors for God in more detail, however, we should identify more closely just who it is we are talking about.

The New Christian Right and the Christian Left—Who Are They?

Who do we mean when we talk about the "new Christian right"? And what is this nearly unknown, largely invisible but nevertheless significant "Christian left"?[11]

The new Christian *right* is largely defined by political issues such as family values (meaning the two-parent nuclear family and an emphasis on abstinence in sex education),[12] opposition to official sanctions of homosexual relations, support for a strong military, free markets, capital punishment, school prayer, opposition to abortion-on-demand, and support for Israel. Racial issues, urban issues, sexual violence, poverty, and the Third World are noteworthy by their absence.[13] Perhaps most striking is the utter absence of any environmental issues.

Underlying the Christian right's political stance is a vision of "Christian America."[14] This Christian America is the nation which was founded by practicing Christians who emigrated for religious reasons and sought to embody Christian values in their government and social structures. This is the America founded by the Pilgrims, the America of the Great Awakening and the nineteenth-century revivals, the America that prints "In God We Trust" on its money and administers its presidential oaths on the Bible. It is not the America of Native Peoples, of the Catholic missions of the Southwest and the archdioceses of Chicago or Boston, nor the America of New England transcendentalism or the South's slavery, nor even the Protestant America of Dutch Reformed, English Episcopalians, or German Lutherans.[15]

The new Christian right is politically very astute, and evidently well financed. (Appearances can be deceiving, however; Pat Robertson's "Family Channel" and the Christian Coalition may be well financed, but teachers at "Christian" schools and Bible Colleges consistently earn far less than their counterparts in public schools, liberal arts colleges, and state universities.) The movement has widely known and well-recognized leaders such as Robertson, Tim LaHaye, Jerry Falwell, Lou Sheldon, and James Dobson. And while the Christian right may occasionally soften its identity in order to broaden its appeal to the electorate, its members leave no doubt about who they are; they clearly identify themselves as "Christian," not merely as "religious" or "spiritual."

Institutionally, the Christian right thrives outside traditional denominational structures and bureaucracies (with the notable exception of the Southern Baptist Convention), in huge independent congregations (often with several thousand members), and in various "para-church" organizations, that is, Christian organizations that are not a church or a denomination, but sponsor "ministries" of various kinds, such as Operation Rescue or Dobson's Focus on the Family. There are conservative coalitions in some of the larger denominations (such as the Good News caucus in The United Methodist Church), but they do not appear to be closely allied with the new Christian right. The new Christian right communicates its agenda and does its business primarily through these local congregations and organizations as well as through "Christian" radio and television, direct mail, and political caucuses.

The Christian *left* in America, on the other hand, is neither as visible nor as well-defined as the right. There are certainly attempts to build and lead a Christian left, among them (on economic issues) the American Catholic Bishops, Jim Wallis's *Sojourners* and *Cry for Renewal* (although Wallis thinks of his agenda as "beyond partisanship"), and various African American churches. Still, the left is far from having a clear sense of its own identity. It is not politically astute, nor does it constitute a clear social movement. Lacking many nationally recognized leaders, it is nevertheless quite influential in its own right. But its influence is felt in very different venues from those preferred by the right—particularly in denominational leadership, seminary and college faculties, and various peace and justice organizations. On the other hand, it seems quite unable to make any impact on the mass media.[16] In some respects it longs to be the chaplain of an American culture that no longer desires its services; people would now rather shop around for their spiritual needs.

The Christian left is largely defined by its support for nonviolence, feminism, gays and lesbians, and a pro-choice position on abortion. It opposes military spending, capital punishment and racism, and advocates for AIDS victims, the poor, battered women, the homeless, Native Americans, and the Third World. It is also characterized by opposition to capitalism (though this has perhaps weakened of late), and it embraces diversity and multiculturalism. Its concern for environmental issues is passionate. Powerfully opposed to anti-Semitism, it nevertheless frequently sympathizes with Palestinians in Israeli-occupied territories.

Noteworthy by their absence are any significant concerns for marriage and family life, for lower-class and poor white males, and any positive sense of how military and police powers might be used creatively.

This Christian left is much less likely to identify itself as "Christian," and more likely to describe itself as "spiritual" or "religious," as in the various "women and spirituality" gatherings that take place throughout the country. This is done partly out of respect for Jews and nonbelievers, but also largely because the group shares little if any common identity. Clearly an ecumenical movement in intention, it nevertheless remains a largely Christian (or post-Christian) phenomenon, even if it sometimes deludes itself into thinking that it represents some purportedly universal "religiosity" or "spirituality."[17]

Although the Christian left has been around a long time—its roots reach well back into the nineteenth century, including the abolition, prohibition, and woman suffrage movements—the formative experiences for its current leadership were the Civil Rights movement and the Vietnam War, in which broad coalitions of diverse people were able to focus the nation's attention on great evils and bring them to an end, not by winning elections (at which they have never been much good), but by a variety of tactics that served well at the time, and yet failed to build any enduring organization.[18]

The Christian left is not politically savvy in comparison with the right. But institutionally, it is very well represented in the leadership and bureaucracies of the larger, older, more traditional "mainline" Protestant denominations (American Baptist, Episcopal, Lutheran-ELCA, Presbyterian [U.S.A.], United Church of Christ, and United Methodist churches), and in their seminaries, colleges, and universities. It often controls important agencies or departments. Indeed, many "mainline" denominations are rather divided between a somewhat more liberal national leadership and somewhat more conservative members (this division should not be exaggerated, however).[19]

Dissent from the program of the Christian left is relatively rare in many "mainline" seminaries and church bureaucracies, and critics of the left can find themselves marginalized. Some important icons of the left, such as feminism, gay and lesbian rights, and liberation theology are virtually exempt from criticism among nonfundamentalist religious scholars. (It is nearly impossible, for example, to find *any* intelligently written theological treatises that even hint at criticism of the gay and lesbian agenda.)[20]

A significant number of the religious left are Catholics, particularly lay Catholics and members of certain orders, such as Maryknoll, which is deeply involved with Latin American liberation theology. Many Catholics are active in peace and justice groups and in social action groups. The American Catholic Bishops have been influential in the antinuclear campaigns and vocal in their criticism of capitalism (as well as of abortion).[21]

America as seen by the Christian left is quite different from that of the right: it is the America of homeless shelters and soup kitchens, of AIDS epidemics and battered women, of grotesque wealth that breeds even more grotesque poverty, of decaying cities and suburbs so expensive that the people who work there cannot afford to live there, of inadequate schools and health care, of hungry children and gangs.

Of course, these portraits have been painted in broad strokes, and many exceptions can be found on both sides. There are Evangelicals diligently working for social change on behalf of the poor, Catholics who are both pro-life and antiwar, Catholics who are pro-choice, and denominational leaders who are politically conservative. There are well-financed liberals and underfunded conservatives. And African American churches in particular defy simple categorization.[22] Yet the preceding generalizations are not too misleading if they are not taken as universals.

There are, then, substantial differences in the visions of America predominant in the Christian right and left, as well as different foci in their diagnoses of what is wrong and right with the nation and the world. Their outlook on the world, however, bears the imprint of their view of God. And it is in their metaphors[23] for God that they are most strikingly different, and yet—because of the common appeal to "freedom"—startlingly alike as well.

God of the Left: Love and Liberation

The Christian left in the United States is now limited almost exclusively to one metaphor for God: Love. God is Love. And Love—accepting, uncritical, undemanding Love—is God. Or at least so it seems. Half a century ago H. Richard Niebuhr observed that liberal Christianity reduces Christ almost exclusively to this one virtue, love, resulting in a seriously deficient and one-dimensional portrait of Jesus;[24] his observation needs little updating. The only difference is that this view is now even more widespread and exclusive in most historical Protestant denominations. Jim Wallis, for example, develops three "tests" of politics, the first of which is "compassion."[25] Compassion grounds Wallis's other tests (community and civility), so that virtually the only God-metaphor employed in Wallis's attack on the Christian right is "love."

In many respects this is the sole content of many Christian education and Sunday school programs. Children are told that God loves them, and that is about all. Not long ago at a conference of church-related colleges, the director of a famous college choir complained that the theologians and the humanists at the conference were making things too complicated: "I thought it was all pretty simple. God loves you, love your neighbor, God is love." One cannot help wondering how he might have responded to someone saying that music is supposed to be simple, and that such matters as tempo, phrasing, and dynamics are too complex.

It is not surprising, therefore, that many members of liberal churches find the only description of God that they know useless in times of pain, suffering, and death. "If God loves me, how can he let this happen to me?" they ask, and it is a good question if God is love and nothing else. In the 1960s, an atheist or agnostic college student would probably have given intellectual reasons for not believing in God—evolution and the enormous age of the earth, Marxism's critique of religion as false consciousness, or Sartre's criticism of religion as bad faith. But the college student of today who comes to question belief in God is more apt to give personal reasons—God let my father die, God let my mother get cancer even though she took good care of herself, God lets people be homeless, God permits war. They ask, "How could a loving God let this happen?" and, on those terms, no adequate answer can be given without "complications."

Similarly, for the Christian left, questions of ethics and politics become reduced to the question of love. John McNeill, a gay Catholic and former Jesuit who has struggled for years to get the church to acknowledge the legitimacy of faithful gay relationships, argues that a loving God could not have created millions of homosexuals and then denied them the right to sexual intimacy.[26] But presumably a loving God would also not have created tornadoes and earthquakes and cancer. Nor, on these terms, would a loving God have made it so difficult for people of all sexual orientations to find true intimacy. Nor would a true God (in this sense of love) have made the law of gravity unexceptionable in cases where its application results in death or destruction, nor have made nature "red in tooth and claw," in Tennyson's memorable phrase.[27] Yet all these states of affairs indisputably exist. Don Browning, in a study of Protestant denominational studies of sexuality, has noted how the only metaphor for God they employ is God the redeemer (primarily construed as love); the metaphors of creator and governor are lacking.[28]

The following may serve as an instructive example of this perspective's laudably deep sensitivity but pathetic impotence. Several years ago a small Midwestern town was horribly devastated by a powerful windstorm that struck in the early morning hours without warning, catching the residents in their beds. About twenty people, including very young children in their parents' arms, died. At an outdoor memorial service for the victims, the pastor chose a text from 2 Kings 11, in which the prophet Elijah goes into the desert to seek the Lord. A whirlwind comes and rends the mountains, "but the Lord was not in the whirlwind." The pastor used this text as an occasion to assure the mourners that God was not in the tragically destructive whirlwind that had come upon their town. Such a statement may (or may not) be of comfort, and is surely superior to proclaiming that God had some secret purpose that required the death of small children that night (or the death of anybody else, for that matter). One must not judge the pastor harshly, for the occasion was calamitous, and the grief profound. Yet such a claim raises many difficult questions. If God is not in the tornado, then where? Is God not present in our suffering? Will God not be present in the hour of my death? Is all suffering and death simply apart from God? Does God love us, but is unable to help when fate overtakes us? Is God then simply a compassionate but powerless co-sufferer? Is God, then, merely a god whose power is always in danger of defeat by another deity or natural force? And if so, why should we worship this god rather than another, apparently victorious divinity?[29]

The metaphor of God as love is further compounded by the *kind* of love usually implied; it is, often enough, a saccharine, maudlin, sentimental kind of love that has nothing to do with the embodied, passionate, sensual, and even fierce nature of incarnate love. It is, in short, a love without power. Such sentimentalism is impotent in the face of suffering. The growing attack by the Christian left on calling God "Father"—which, in some forms, is not simply an argument for expanding our language to include "female" metaphors for God, but rather a call for *eliminating* "male" metaphors—is intimately related to this sentimentalization. Traditional "male" virtues like courage, power, fierceness, strength, directness, and unsentimentality—which are, of course, embodied in both women and men—are utterly absent from this kind of love, just as they are utterly unacceptable to the culture of the left.[30]

The pathetic, vacuous kind of love that is the sole metaphor for God employed by the Christian left—and by most of liberal mainstream Protestantism—is in perfect harmony with a bourgeois American culture that is so embarrassed and ashamed of suffering and death that it must pretend that they do not exist. A culture in which any sadness is sign of poor adjustment is unable to think that God could exist for any reason other than to help human beings reach their full potential. God becomes a giant teddy bear that you squeeze to make yourself feel good, but of no help in real suffering. The final effect is to make God distant and irrelevant, even if somewhat affectionate. The God of the left is a God without power, for the left understands power only as the opposite of freedom.

Such love is simply ineffective in the public sphere. Lacking any outward direction, it has little to offer outside of one's inner life. In America it usually takes a passive form, where God's function is restricted to being a personal security blanket that offers comfort but makes no demands. Or it may take a more active form, in which God is the inner force that enables us to become all we can be. But the only thing we (and God, in this scheme of things) can provide for others is acceptance, support, and encouragement. Anything else would not be "loving." But under the cloak of love and acceptance lurks domination in disguise: seductively coaxing people to domesticate their ultimate concern into just another ware in the spiritual marketplace, to be consumed like meat, vegetables, or entertainment. All spiritual commitments are honored if only they make no demands contrary to the American religion of freedom, which requires that all spiritualities be considered equal—even if only equally irrelevant. Commitments that *do* make demands are ruthlessly subverted and marginalized because they are not "loving" or "accepting." The only crime then becomes the failure to accept—and all cultures and religions that insist that some things remain unacceptable are themselves ruthlessly judged unacceptable, so that love reintroduces domination in a covert form. Even love cannot avoid the temptation to dominate, if only passive-aggressively.

Or, if we tire of this God's ineffectiveness, growing frustrated with mere love's inability to produce a truly loving world, we can turn it into an insistent demand. This is the path taken by much liberation theology, which, rightly rejecting the inward and therapeutic turn taken by most liberalism, insists that love must work on behalf of justice. This holds much more promise of becoming a public force. In liberation movements, a deep empathy with suffering victims transforms love into an active force. Here the God of love is seen as actively working on behalf of the oppressed, seeking to remove the causes of their oppression, but now something besides love seems to be introduced. In many respects this God bears a striking resemblance to the God of the right—angry, even vengeful, except that here God's anger is directed at an entirely different set of wrongs. Even so, the American religion of freedom returns fiercely: liberation is understood primarily in terms of removing all limitations on personal development and self-expression—especially economic, racial, and sexual limitations.[31] In some liberation theologies the path that leads from love to domination is much more straightforward: there is always the temptation to conclude that anything which interferes with a loving world must be eliminated. Thus does liberation theology speak of God in terms that recall the Christian right: a righteous God of judgment (but rarely a Father)[32] who fights for the poor and oppressed. The Achilles' heel of Marxism, which permitted and even demanded all manner of injustice in the name of ultimate justice, haunts liberation theology.[33] Alternatively, if this crusading aspect of the left does not affect its metaphors for God, it still may infuse the tone of the left's proclamations. Jim Wallis's *Who Speaks for God?* is an example of this tendency. Despite his tests of compassion, civility, and community, his assault on the Christian right is sometimes venomous. That attack may or may not be justified, but clearly it is not consonant with the "civility" or "compassion" of which Wallis speaks. Love morphs into its opposite; because Wallis determines that he speaks for compassion, he violates the limits of political discourse he sets for others.

This God of love alone, whether passive or active, whether sentimental and comforting or liberating and freeing, either remains ineffective in the public sphere, or threatens to reintroduce domination in the more subtle form of liberal "acceptance" or the more blatant forms of liberation. But the new Christian right is much more practiced, in America at least, at reintroducing domination in the name of freedom.

The God of the Right—Judgment and Liberty

The new Christian right has no trouble at all with the sort of metaphors for God that the left tries to avoid. Their God is a patient but vengeance-prone Father.[34] He patiently continues to shower blessings on America because of our faithful Christian past, but He is now on the verge of revoking them if we test His patience much more with our new unfaithfulness. Jerry Falwell, for example, began his programmatic book *Listen, America!* with precisely this claim: God has showered blessings on America because of our moral convictions, but will soon punish us because of our toleration of abortion on demand, homosexuality, military unpreparedness, and the like.[35]

The contrast to the Christian left (and to most mainstream American Protestantism) could scarcely be more vivid. God is rarely described in terms of love, at least when it comes to social and political issues; and when He is, it seems that God loves only those who keep his commandments and are faithful to Him, that is, conservative Christians. Otherwise, the metaphor of God as Judge seems to be dominant. God will judge the world for its sins, and will judge America for its sins—especially the sins of liberals. Only those who follow God's laws have access to God's mercy. Otherwise, condemnation will be the only word spoken.

Hence the Christian right does not seem overconcerned for those millions in worldly hells of poverty, oppression, prison, violence, homelessness, racism, domestic abuse, inadequate health care, and hunger. Its answer is to emphasize achievement, effort, and personal righteousness as solutions; it seems largely blind to how social structures might foster such agonies. Nor does the Christian right shrink from wholesale condemnations of homosexuals and nontraditional families (although divorce now seems to be acceptable to the Christian right— they helped elect our first divorced President, Ronald Reagan). Nor does it scruple to act as though atheists, Muslims, Hindus, and liberal Christians are aliens who do not truly belong to Christian America.

The same filter is applied to history. The role played by non-Christian deists in shaping the American Revolution and Constitution, to say nothing of loyalist Christians[36] who opposed the revolution, is ignored.[37] The right has bitterly, and sometimes correctly, complained about the exclusion or exclusively negative portrayals of Christianity in history textbooks,[38] but it seems no less blind when it portrays the Declaration of Independence and the Constitution as documents of a Christian country.

The God of the right, the angry Father and Judge, fits well with at least one important facet of contemporary American culture: the rage and anger felt by many that they are being denied their birthright to an ever-improving life, and, perhaps worse, that they are losing control of their lives and becoming marginalized in a culture they once thought they understood. This anger is frequently directed at scapegoats of various forms: feminists, homosexuals, liberals, welfare recipients. The pervasive anger that afflicts much of middle-class and lower-middle-class America[39] is nicely reflected in the righteous anger of the right's God.

But at the same time that the God of the right is vengeful toward those who do not follow His rules, He is remarkably uncritical of conservative American ideology. The Christian right's generous endorsement of free market capitalism—with absolutely no recognition of its devastating impact on the unemployed, uprooted, and marginalized people it creates—is a case in point. Indeed, it becomes quite difficult to see any difference between this God's economic agenda and that of conservative Republicanism (though they do differ considerably on questions of personal morality).[40] Also remarkable is the complete absence in the Christian right of any sense of repentance for social sins. It is true that groups such as the Promise Keepers have recently returned to a salutary emphasis on personal repentance. But when it comes to social issues, it appears that the only thing of which Christian America has to repent is not having been tough enough on liberals, homosexuals, feminists, and welfare recipients.[41]

The American religion of freedom is unmistakably present in the Christian right. *Liberty* is the version of freedom preferred on the right, while the left prefers "choice" or "liberation." For the new Christian right, liberty means chiefly two things: (1) religious freedom, including complete freedom of religious (or only Christian?) expression, and (2) freedom from government. The two are closely related: in the Christian right's version of American history, the founders sought to found a Christian country free of government interference in religion—or economics, or much of anything except personal morality. Indeed, the growing number of freedoms that Americans have surrendered to the government is one of the sins frequently enumerated as a reason that God may withdraw His blessing of liberty from us.[42]

Of course, on the right there is no need to conceal the drive to dominate. There is really no question about it: America is a Christian country, and though Jews are assured of strong support for Israel,[43] this is a distinctly Christian political vision in which non-Christians must accept a subordinate role, a point made oddly by Richard Neuhaus when he argues that Christianity is the guarantor of pluralism. Christian America has been attacked and severely weakened by a conspiracy[44] of liberals, socialists, communists, occultists, and the like, and the call is clear: Christians must take back their country. Robertson in particular is harshly critical of non-Judeo-Christian religions.[45] The chief weapon in reasserting Christian control is prayer and the ballot box, but the rhetoric is clearly one of eliminating the enemies who threaten America's very existence through their moral corruption.

In the end, it remains difficult to tell God the angry Judge apart from the anger of middle-class and lower-class white Protestant America. If the left's favorite metaphor for God is Love without Power (except perhaps to free others from power), the right's has become Power without Love (except for those who are like us). On both sides, there is little room for those who deviate from these views. Both visions, moreover, are directed toward the rhetoric of freedom as their guarantor of righteousness. As for most of America, so too for the Christian left and right—a god who is not the god of freedom above all else, is not God.

Metaphors in Question

Reinhold Niebuhr's remark that religion is often mere "self-assertion in terms of the absolute" is confirmed in much of the rhetoric of the Christian right and left.[46] The Christian right has tailored for itself a God who is a fierce Judge of those who are different, and perhaps of its own members' personal shortcomings, but never of the right itself. Yet the same is true, perhaps more true, of the left: never does its God seem to criticize the left itself *or* its members' personal behavior, except perhaps for their complicity in racism, sexism, and poverty.[47]

The skeptic or cynic will no doubt take this as further verification that Christians of all stripes do not know what they are talking about when they talk about God, and that appeals to God are worse than useless in political discourse. And there is a fair measure of truth in the skeptic's conclusion. Both the Christian right and left seem to have lost any idea of a God that transcends their own particular cultural and political concerns. Neither meets the criterion of comprehensiveness. And both fail to perceive that God may be Judge of them, and Lover of their enemies.

Both the left and the right are irreligious—as well as downright unimaginative—to limit themselves to one metaphor for God, as well as to employ their chosen metaphors so one-dimensionally. In short, their metaphors lack depth and richness. There are many more metaphors for God available from the many Christian traditions: God as Sovereign, God as Ruler, God as Husband, God as Mother, God as Midwife, God as Creator, Sustainer, and Redeemer, God as Mystery, God as Hidden, God as Infinite, God as Ultimate Concern, God as Lover, God as Warrior, God as Crucified, God as Liberator, God as Covenant-Partner, God as Ruler of the Nations, God as Redeemer of the World (not just America), the Ancient of Days, and many more besides. Christian piety might even benefit from appropriating something like the Islamic devotional practice of reciting the one hundred names of God. Thus, the difficulty of the Christian right and left, contrary to the skeptic's claim, is not that they are religious, but that they are not religious *enough*.

On the other hand, a careful reading of the historical evidence from biblical and other historical Christian sources also demonstrates that the left and right are *both correct.* There is ample precedent for both metaphors for God, Love and Judge. Nor is it true, as is sometimes supposed, that only the God of the Hebrew Scriptures is vengeful, while the God of the Christian Testament is loving. Both metaphors are present in both testaments. Jewish biblical scholars in particular have rightly denounced any attempt to portray the God of their Bible as unloving and unforgiving. Christians as far back as Marcion in the mid–second century have wrongly argued that the God of the Jewish Scriptures is vengeful and violent, while the New Testament God is loving and merciful. Marcion went so far as to reject the Old Testament and remove it from the Christian Bible. But he erred. The Old Testament God loves, and the New Testament God judges.

In this connection, it would be well for both the Christian left and the right to reflect on that most ancient of Christian symbols for God, the Trinity. For the Trinity, far from being a quasimagical reference to strange and meaningless numbers, is a profound attempt to describe how God can be both Many and One, Creator and Sufferer and Inspirer, Judge and Lover and Comforter, and many other things besides, without compromising the essential divine unity. In particular, the Christian left needs to recognize that the God who is Lover and Friend is also Judge and Avenger, and that that judgment may be directed particularly against *them,* even at the cost of innocent suffering.[48] And the Christian right needs to recognize that the God who is both Lover and Judge may turn that judgment precisely against those who invoke his name falsely—saying "Lord, Lord" (Matt 25:11, 37, 44) is no guarantee that the invocation is genuine. Indeed, God may be Love precisely to those people who hate his self-appointed advocates.

Here we begin to see the connection between the theological proclivities of the left and right and American political practice. It is a commonplace, and largely correct, to say that the right is hypocritical—quick to judge its opponents and enemies, but very slow to criticize any of its own deficiencies. But the hypocrisy of the left is also abundant. It fears and criticizes any and all power, and conceives God almost exclusively in terms of love, and never power. Yet it can be dismissive and almost violent in its coercive pursuit of equality and freedom.

The political commitments of the Christian right and left are, therefore, seriously confused and severely constrained. As we argued in the first two chapters, however, attempts to repress the role of religion in politics reflect a misunderstanding of both politics and religion. Indeed, such attempts are as little likely to be successful as attempts to repress sex in matters of human conduct. The role played by both conservative and liberal Christianity in shaping American culture—in history and in the history which is to come—can no more be disregarded than the growth of Mormonism, the presence of Islam, and the shadow of the Holocaust. Indeed, the vengeful God of the Christian right is a response to just such attempts to repress human religious instincts.

This is not to say that either the left or the right is devoid of political insight. Both have insight, even when some of those insights are couched in the hyperbolic fantasies of a Pat Robertson. But they are narrowly conceived and deeply implicated in the American religion of freedom. Both left and right are bound to the presuppositions of that destructive civil religion. They accordingly presume that their own desires are innocent (which allows them reflexively to conceptualize God as simply another name for their own political and social desires); that their opponents must be demonized or eradicated (as freedom becomes domination over freedom's enemies); and that power is the fruit of precisely that domination which threatens freedom, even if freedom must make use of it.

American political life, religious to its freedom-loving core, will not resolve its contradictions unless the religion of freedom and its assumptions about innocence and power are challenged. That confrontation is the theological burden of the emphatic Christian center, and it is to that task that we now turn.

THEOLOGICAL PRINCIPLES OF THE EMPHATIC CHRISTIAN CENTER: SIN, LOVE, AND POWER

The emphatic Christian center has three chief theological resources, or criteria: original sin, love, and power. A fourth criterion, *justice*, pervades the other three. The first will seem implausible to that broad swath of Americans who embrace the civil religion of freedom, in whatever form. The doctrine of original sin repudiates one of that religion's most crucial assumptions: human innocence. We have already argued that this assumption is implausible, nonempirical, and self-defeating, culminating not in freedom but in domination. The second, love, will seem more congenial to the expansive "tolerant and liberal" segments of American culture. The vacuous center and some of the left appeal to love and tolerance almost exclusively in their political reflections. But we now know that, important and indispensable though love is, the results of that effort are nugatory. So emphatic Christian centrism introduces a third resource, power, which for us reflects the theological affirmation of divine omnipotence. This, in turn, means that the usual identification of power as domination and control is specious; power itself needs to be reconceived. Far from being freedom's enemy (as the Enlightenment wrongly thought), power is an indispensable component of the productive, *public* freedom that can revitalize political discourse.

Original Sin

In the foregoing chapter, we showed how the American view that human beings are fundamentally innocent and unlimited in potential derives from, and reinforces, the civil religion of freedom. Without that assumption, the freedom of utter self-determination becomes less attractive. The freedom to be oneself is more appealing in an idyllic meadow than in a garbage dump. Americans, however, are convinced that if we are not actually in such a meadow, then surely the return to Eden is just around the corner. Whether we really believed it or desperately wanted to, Ronald Reagan's "Morning in America" was the message that warmed us. In American Protestantism, the return to the "pure" New Testament church and the commanding significance of the "original," "simple" ethics of Jesus reflect the American conviction that renewal is always possible, if only we will apply ourselves to it. Or, if we are not Christians or admirers of Jesus, then the Founding Fathers, Native American civilizations, or UFOs will do—somebody, somewhere must have had (or have) the perfect society to which we should return (or advance). Children seem unsullied and innocent, leading adult Americans to romanticize childhood at the same time that they try to recover their own in various therapeutic fountains of youth. These tendencies are accentuated by the American ideal of equality. The "image of an ideal perfection," Alexis de Tocqueville noted, "for ever on the wing, presents itself to the human mind" relentlessly under the influence of that ideal.[49] We overestimate the scope of human perfectibility, while underestimating the role of history in *closing* certain options even as it opens others. The American vision of equality, like its perspective on freedom, is thoroughly ahistorical.[50]

Contrary to American notions of human perfectibility there stands a long but now suspect stream of Christian thought, exemplified radically in the hoary doctrine of original sin. It is not a popular doctrine. Daniel Maguire, for example, attacks the "gloom of 'original sin' ";[51] in contemporary American theological works, it is difficult to find "original sin" in the index. Like predestination before it, original sin seems to have been carefully hidden away in the attic, like Rochester's crazy relative in *Jane Eyre*. This is understandable; it is surely less pleasing to hear about the universal limits of humanity than to believe that all limits are conquerable in history. Paul Tillich summarized the contemporary perspective well when he remarked that the modern (and now postmodern) world believes that humanity "has shortcomings, but there is no sin and certainly no universal sinfulness. The bondage of the will, of which the Reformers spoke, the demonic powers which are central for the New Testament, the structures of destruction in personal and communal life, are ignored or denied."[52] Even if we're not all "OK," it seems, we can be—and soon.

Those who cling strenuously to conceptions of original sin are more persuasive. That current of Christian thought runs from Augustine through the Catholic traditions in Thomas Aquinas and others, was radicalized in Protestantism by Luther and Calvin, and maintained in the twentieth century by Reinhold Niebuhr, Tillich, Glenn Tinder, and Langdon Gilkey, among others. These spoilsports insist that original sin is both more descriptive of our actual situation and ultimately more optimistic than the belief that human potential always tends to the good, and that all evil is ultimately a matter of correctable errors.

The most compelling argument in favor of original sin is also one of the earliest and simplest, proffered by the founder of the doctrine, Augustine. Augustine was challenged by the Pelagians, especially Julian of Eclanum, who argued that Augustine's dogma of original sin was, well, gloomy—and a denial of the human freedom to choose the good.[53] According to the fifth-century Pelagians, Erasmus a thousand years later, and most Americans today (as the bevy of analytic philosophical discussions of the "free will" demonstrate), the will is unconstrained, free in its choices. Against the Pelagians, Augustine issues a simple challenge: if they are right, it should be possible to find people whose lives are, in fact, utterly righteous. The doctrine of original sin is above all an interpretation of existence. Evidence to confirm or deny it can be adduced from the world's condition. In his defense, Augustine begins *The Spirit and the Letter* by repeating his frequent claim that "moral perfection as an end [is] never reached or likely to be reached by any man in this life save only by the one Mediator . . . remaining altogether without sin." If the Pelagians believe otherwise, their burden is clear: "to establish their assertion . . . if they can,"[54] to show that humans *can* be fully righteous by pointing to some who really *are*. Augustine was confident that they could not. There is no evidence in the intervening sixteen hundred years that Augustine's challenge has been met.

The Christian doctrine of original sin asserts that sin—not mere shortcoming, but real corruption and degradation—is present in every human being of whom we have historical knowledge. It is a condition that (even if it can be shaped, mollified, exacerbated, and otherwise changed) is ineradicable so long as we are in history.[55] There is no historical reason to call these claims into question. Indeed, those who think that they have overcome this basic human condition are the most likely to dominate others. To deny the presence of sin in oneself or one's group cuts a wide channel through which a deluge of wrongdoing will flow.

Three aspects of sin are especially important for the Christian center: (1) sin is both moral *and* cognitive (against attempts to limit sin to "moral" evil); (2) sin is *both* personal *and* social in nature (against false claims that it is one or the other); and (3) the injustice of sin cries out for a doctrine of justification that issues in new justice (not one that ends in a "forensic" forgiveness).

ORIGINAL SIN AND CORRUPTION—BOTH MORAL AND INTELLECTUAL

The paradox of sin is that it is *religious*. As both Reinhold Niebuhr and Langdon Gilkey maintain, sin is fundamentally the religious problem of "an ultimate religious devotion to a finite interest."[56] And this entails the corruption of the whole of human life—not just moral, but intellectual corruption as well. In the first chapter, we saw that the finiteness of religions renders them vulnerable to making fraudulent claims of comprehensiveness and self-transcendence. This peril is not limited to institutional religions, however; *every* social movement and personal fulfillment is subject to this tendency.[57]

Nor can we restrict the doctrine of original sin merely to *moral* corruption, as the Christian tradition often has. Even the principal advocates of the doctrine, such as Augustine and Luther, exempted some *intellectual* activities from the *effects* of original sin. The Catholic Augustine studiously avoided laying the charge of original sin against church doctrine, which he believed was under the power of the Spirit. The Protestant Luther, who thought the Roman church especially subject to original sin's effects, nevertheless excluded the clear and plain sense of the Word—and therefore the proper interpreters of the Word—from the effects of original sin. However inconsistent these exemptions were with the broader insights comprehended in the doctrine, they helped animate the ecclesiastical imperialism of Roman Catholicism and the bibliolatry of Protestantism. In Catholicism, the church's finite character is sometimes ignored in favor of what is in effect an infinite devotion to it; the same thing happens in Protestantism with respect to the Bible. Church (in Catholicism) and Bible (in Protestantism) are often held to be accurate and nearly complete representations of God, not finite and likely corrupt pictures of the infinite God in finite history.[58] To unmask the destructive consequences of these idolatries, the concept of original sin must include not only moral perversity but also the intellectual arrogance that claims to depict eternal truth adequately and for all time. It should be clear that we do not thereby suggest that the finite is of no significance; rather, we submit that all finite actions, conclusions, and conditions are historical and significant in their own right and as creatures of God—but they are not God.

The corruption of our intellectual capacities (as well as our moral judgment) has several important political implications. First, because of the universality of intellectual corruption, there can be no privileged knowledge of the divine will that is not subject to external criticism. Neither Catholic authoritative tradition nor Protestant bibliolatry or primitivism trumps critical inquiry. Indeed, appeals to revelatory authority, if they are meant to *exclude* or to *defeat* all counterargument, are not protections against sin; *they are sin*—intellectual (and inevitably moral) hubris. The same applies to *all* methods of inquiry given sacred status (such as "scientific method," "dialectical materialism," "positivism," "deconstruction," etc.) as exclusive means to "truth." No single form of critical inquiry can trump all others.

A second (and related) implication is that appeals to *universal* moral or intellectual privilege are also excluded; they are examples of sin rather than its opposite. This is a special problem in new movements of "identity" politics (whether asserted by women, men, or ethnic or racial groups), older formulations of liberation theologies, and some manifestations of "narrative" theology.[59] A biblical preference for the poor or a prioritization of children, for example, does not demonstrate that the poor or children are morally or intellectually superior. These are policy parameters, not reflections of ontologically privileged status before God or humanity. Privileges are mobile and cannot exempt anyone, even the oppressed, from intellectual or moral critique.

This leads directly to the third implication, which is especially important for ethical perspectives *as a whole*. Because moral and intellectual error are inevitable, political advocacy of policies and perspectives that fully uphold one's own *self-interest* are presumptively suspect. This is a common claim in Christian theology, and has become more common in philosophical circles since Nietzsche's focus on the claimant ("who speaks") rather than the content of the claim ("what is being spoken"), as well as Marxist critiques of "ideology." But it requires careful analysis.

Mid-twentieth-century Protestantism sometimes reduced sin to self-interest or "selfishness," a trend continued in such thinkers as Tinder.[60] Our position is not quite theirs. In Tinder's thought, for example, advocacy of one's self-interest virtually rules out the truth of the claim. Thus, the wealthy could not properly advocate a policy that would increase their wealth. It is true that such a perspective takes the reality of sin seriously; it is correct in recognizing that we often exaggerate our own needs and privileges, and that human vitality, because it is not simply a will to live but also a will to excess, cannot be voluntarily contained.[61] But this is a blunt instrument for adjudicating political claims.[62] Moreover, it particularly discriminates against the poor, who frequently have no other advocates than themselves. Our point is more subtle: not that any particular political appeal is suspect merely because it coincides with the apparent short-term interest of the advocate (though that may count as evidence), but that legitimate political perspectives cannot *in every detail* further the interest of the advocate. We return to the criticisms of religion offered by Augustine's *City of God* and Feuerbach's *The Essence of Christianity* and *Lectures on the Philosophy of Religion*. The arguments of both (Augustine against Roman paganism, Feuerbach against Christianity and finally all institutional religion) lead to a common conclusion: if one's religion uniformly supports the narrow self-interest of the devotee or his group, that is compelling evidence of sin's presence. Thus, a religious or political perspective that consistently trumpets the moral rectitude of claims that serve its constituencies' interests deserves a high degree of suspicion. In essence, such groups claim that *they* are innocent and righteous, that *the* good is coextensive with *their* good.

This suspicion is not only necessary in evaluating the political and social claims of others, but also of oneself. The person whose claims for the good invariably serve his or her own immediate interests claims also to be without sin. Conversely, one mark of political courage is to advocate some positions that do not serve the immediate interests of one's constituency or oneself in some significant respect.[63] The universality of sin, as depicted in the doctrine of original sin, disbars all claims to utter congruence between self, group, nation, race, class, gender, and so on, on one hand, and the good, on the other.

ORIGINAL SIN AND JUSTICE: BOTH PERSONAL AND SOCIAL

A second significant dispute concerns *where* sin originates: is sin due fundamentally to perversion of the will or heart, or is it forced upon us by social structures? Like the raging secular debate between "nature" and "nurture," the choice is a red herring. Sin's origins are *both* personal and social. The current religiopolitical discussion of "sin," however—largely because the religious right dominates the stage—emphasizes failures of personal righteousness. Every politician pays homage to the evils of drug use, alcohol abuse, tobacco usage, and the like (the tobacco issue is a rare instance of the left's turning a question of personal habit into a moral problem). Even questions with obvious social and economic dimensions—poverty, unemployment, lack of education—are reduced to personal initiative, ambition, and the presence or absence of wholesome desires.

The right's tendency to reduce issues of morality to individual choice, to "just say yes" or "just say no," is well known. Not that it is wrong to emphasize personal decision; but as we noted in the first chapter, the exclusive use of any one symbol to the exclusion of all others is a religious failure. The left tends to reverse the right's bias. Although the rhetoric of "social causes" for deviant behavior is currently out of favor politically, it is still widely (if quietly) believed by many that inherent human goodness is corrupted chiefly by society and is correctable by social reform. Thus, it is supposed, smokers smoke mostly because they have been unwittingly duped by "big tobacco," and others (except sometimes white-collar criminals) in trouble are victims of a bad economic system, a miserable family upbringing, gender or racial bias, and so on. The left is no more wrong than the right, but is equally incomplete.

Christian theology often duplicates this division between "personal" and "social" responsibility in conceptions of original sin. Sustained reflection on this theological dispute offers us a way out of what is finally a quite hopeless and unnecessary debate. The tendency of the Christian left to reduce original sin to "social" sin is manifest across denominations, including some theologians who are difficult to categorize along a left-right continuum, such as Karl Rahner.[64] Similarly, the moderate liberation theologian Elsa Tamez specifies the force of universal sin when she claims that "human beings in their intelligence *(nous)* are able to do justice, but the logic of sin reigning in the society enslaves them, making them incapable of complying with justice."[65] On the North American scene, the great social gospel theologian Walter Rauschenbusch argued that because sin is "selfishness," the notion of "private sin" was senseless.[66] He further insisted that "hereditary social evils are forced on the individual embedded in the womb of society and drawing his ideas, moral standards, and spiritual ideals from the general life of the social body."[67]

Rauschenbusch's position is revived in leftist political theology, feminist critiques of patriarchal society, and liberation criticisms of capitalism. This stress on the "social" origin of sin is altogether correct; it is the necessary antidote to tendencies to reduce all sin to "personal choice," a view that blinds us to the role of social structures. That view—that all who do evil simply chose to do so, and could just as easily have chosen not to do so—is rooted in a long tradition, both Protestant and Catholic (although its strongest current advocates are Protestant). Pietist traditions rooted in John Bunyan, Philip Spener, and others, ignored society in their quest for personal piety.[68] This tendency is classically illustrated in Protestantism in the political thought of Martin Luther. Luther's focus on Romans 13:1 ("Let every person be subject to the governing authorities") and 1 Peter 2:13 ("For the Lord's sake accept the authority of every human institution") drove him and large segments of the subsequent tradition to political passivity.[69] Moreover, Luther's political theology reflected the barrier he erected between external conditions and the inwardness of faith.[70] Essentially, this meant (for Luther) that no external *political* state of affairs could influence the strength of faith in any way, much less create conditions for its destruction or increase.[71]

Unfortunately, in Lutheran as well as in introversionist sectarian traditions, this rigorous separation of the inner (religious) and outer (political) spheres dismisses society's significance. Moreover, the heroic image of faith as immune from all external oppression (if only it is strong enough) tends toward an exclusive personalization of sin. Whatever the social pressures or conditions, sin is inevitably viewed as only a personal matter, which could be resisted by a sufficiently strong faith.[72] In this perspective, original sin originates inwardly, period. Political structures and social conditions have little to do with it.

For Luther, original sin was so potent that no completely good work is possible in history.[73] This ameliorated the dangers of his otherwise personalist approach. But the American tendency toward perfectionism (strongly influenced by the Puritan and Methodist movements), combined with a pietistic emphasis on the personal character of sin, easily issues in the moralistic condemnation of all wrongdoing as solely the responsibility of the individual. It de-emphasizes social reforms that might ameliorate oppressive social conditions. After all, no external condition is spiritually relevant. The gospel becomes an exclusively "spiritual" document, and the spiritual and the material are unrelated.[74]

There is a third, more perceptive position on the relation of inward and external sin, advocated in the twentieth century by such thinkers as Reinhold Niebuhr, Tillich, and Gilkey. These theologians maintain that although the origin of sin lies in the corrupt desires of individuals, sin has political dimensions. That is, although evil cannot "take you any way you don't already know how to go" (to paraphrase The Eagles),[75] the forms of corruption change over time and can be addressed, within limits, by politics. As Calvin observes, government and politics can foster virtue and promote justice, in addition to controlling sin,[76] even though government cannot finally eradicate sin because unlimited selfish desire is inherent in universally corrupted human beings.[77] Self-assertion, according to Niebuhr and Gilkey, knows no natural stopping point; enough is never enough, there is always more to be had.[78] Moreover, the social forms and temptations to fulfill limitless desire are malleable, and human beings can manipulate them to their benefit in ways even they do not understand. For some, material goods may constitute the means for selfishness; for others, it is patriotism, a social cause, religion, and so on. Still, for all these thinkers, the origin of sin in every individual life remains inward.[79]

This position is appealing because it includes the need for social and political reform as well as the need for individual conversion. Moreover, it reflects the complex ways in which the inward and external dimensions of life interact. No governmental structure is immune from human ingeniousness and selfishness; all can and will be perverted so long as sin remains a vital force.[80] Therefore, government should be designed to balance the domination of competing self-interests. It should be no surprise that this perspective coincides with Madison's conception of how factions are controlled (pitting one against the other so that they will thresh each other out). Moreover, if original sin affects us all, it is clear that we cannot expect what the utopian American belief in innocence does: an Eden reestablished on the American continent or in a small corner of it. There are no innocents at home. However, it should be equally clear that the quest for social and political justice *can* create improvement not only in political justice but also by providing the conditions for lives of inner dignity and meaning. It cannot guarantee that those opportunities are taken, but material contributors to spiritual meaning are not dismissed, as they tend to be in more personalistic understandings of sin's origin.

We amend this mutual relation between the inward and external constitution of sin in one significant way. There is no need to insist, as Gilkey, Niebuhr, and Tillich did, on the invariably inward origin of sin. There seems to be no compelling evidence for determining finally which is more significant. We turn instead to the felicitous language of Friedrich Schleiermacher, who described original sin as "in each the work of all, and in all the work of each."[81] That is, the sinfulness of all is expressed in the sinfulness of each, and the sinfulness of each is expressed in the sinfulness of all. Such, for example, is the character of child abuse; the abuser likely expresses abuse he experienced as a child, and that abuse in turn is likely (tragically) to be expressed later on by his child. More than that, the one who does not abuse her children can never be certain that she, if she had been exposed to the same conditions as the abuser, would have done any differently. This does not mean that she cannot and should not intervene; she should. But it *does* mean that the abuser she confronts is not some alien being; it could just as well have been *she* herself, exposed to different circumstances. The social and personal dimensions of wrongdoing can be distinguished, but not separated.[82]

There is no advantage to answering the question of original sin's mechanics definitively. Sin's universality and seeming inevitability stand on their own, and original sin is the symbol that describes that condition and our limited power in resisting it. Recent feminist criticism of the hegemony of self-interest as an adequate concretion of original sin is accurate and to the point.[83] The core of sin is not the same in all groups and persons at all times and places.

In fact, even though Augustine himself is largely the source of these mistaken attempts to pinpoint the origin of sin,[84] his *Confessions*, where he first introduces the term "original sin,"[85] provides a far more nuanced understanding, just because he does not seek to determine its mechanism. Augustine's discussion of the development of his own sin from early childhood (which is what leads him to the language of "original sin") equally targets both his own distorted will and his environment and upbringing. Augustine believes that his parents and teachers—including his pious Christian mother, Monica—bear responsibility for twisting his desires away from the worship of God and toward his status in school and later, his profession.[86] But their responsibility does not detract from Augustine's own fault and sin. He could have resisted the desires of others but did not. He gladly indulged others' wishes and made them his own, even adding more distortions such as his confessed callousness toward women.[87] This entire package of sin depended *both* on the wishes of others (ranging from his teachers and friends to his later career and its rewards) *and* his own warped desires. Augustine presents, then, a charged dynamic in which social pressures and private desires are *mutually originating and reinforcing*—in each the work of all, and in all the work of each.

Social and personal sin *both* are *co-original*.[88] The originary character of each dimension may not be equal at all times for all persons, of course. There may be times when the isolation of social or personal idolatry and sin is more appropriate. But neither will ever be the sole source of original sin. As Rauschenbusch tried to say, original sin is both social and individual. Jim Wallis is correct, as is President Clinton, to stress social structure *and* personal responsibility.[89]

This has important consequences. If we focus on either the social or the personal to the exclusion of the other, we distort matters. If we emphasize only the *social* origins of sin, we will likely be incautious about the effects of large-scale social reforms; we will expect too much and be slow to recognize failure, forgetting that an apparently just structure cannot remove evil from our midst. Not only "bad people" pervert just designs to unjust purposes, but all of us, "good" and "bad" alike. Conversely, while there may be "heroes of faith" for whom almost no oppression will break their basic personal decency or integrity, it is too much to expect that such persons can become commonplace, or that they can endure indefinitely. Personal integrity and corruption are fostered and promoted by public policy, popular rhetoric, and political economy. In light of the universality of sin, the challenge to public life is to make improvements in justice—both political and social justice and personal "justification." To the extent that these goals are achieved, they are achieved in concert.[90]

Original sin and the sins which result from it, therefore, impel the Christian center toward a cautious justice that is attentive to both inward desires and social structures.[91] The right wing is correct to insist that moral suasion is vital for advances in justice; a focus on personal justification, integrity, and righteousness is appropriate and necessary. Social justice is best advanced by relatively just persons. But the left is also correct. The integrity and justice of persons is either encouraged or frustrated by economic, political, and social structures. Personal integrity cannot be expected to develop within or to withstand the assault of degraded and oppressive conditions of poverty, homelessness, violence, inadequate education, or a concupiscent culture. When decency, integrity, and justice do survive these assaults, it is wonderful—but wonders are by definition rare. A heroic image of faith is appropriate for heroes; the rest of us cannot be left to wallow in mire.[92]

Finally, those on the right and the left who are politically and socially active are both correct that the message of Christianity cannot be reduced to a "heavenly" promise of salvation. When it is so reduced, Christianity stands convicted of Marx's caricature of religion as "opium" for the oppressed. Few theologians of the Christian tradition understood the gospel to be about heaven alone. The historic disputes about various versions of salvation in Christian thought were also about how these schemes enabled or hindered just and decent lives here on earth. Because God is the God of creation and the earth, not an ethereal Nero who fiddles with the angels while the world burns, it could not be otherwise. The attempt to cast God out of the world, or to remove the world from God's salvific will, is irreligious; it fails the criterion of comprehensiveness miserably. The first theological commitment of the emphatic Christian center, then, is two-sided: negatively, it recovers a vital conception of original sin; positively, it means that justice—halting, fleeting, personal, social, ever-tenuous, and never complete in history—is the proper and necessary response to that sin.

Love: Its Political Manifestations

Justice, not love? The distinctive contribution of the Christian gospel to the world is usually thought to be limited to "love." This view is wrong on several counts. First, it sometimes makes love seem unique to Christianity, despite such parallels as the mercy of Allah in Islam and Buddhist compassion, which, although not identical with Christian "love," are analogous. Second, as we argued earlier, Christianity's richness is often reduced to love and love alone. Third, the very notion of what love *is* is restricted to ineffective sentimentality or, if it becomes effective, insular and self-serving domination.

However, love *is* a significant feature of the Christian traditions, and we should delineate its present political function. We maintain that love—especially its sentimentalist version—cannot be a political objective; instead, it must be submitted to the criteria of justice (above) and power (below). Love is a political aim insofar as it is made concrete by effective power, usually in the form of justice. That does not exclude love from an important place in emphatic Christian centrism. Instead, love—manifested by power, and in service to justice—retains at least two roles. First, it sustains an appreciation for the depth and power of one's opponents' commitments. Second, it has a political role made concrete in forgiveness.

First, however, we must disabuse ourselves of sentimentalist conceptions of love. Love is not an adequate aim for politics unless it is combined with power and justice. This is especially true of "love" interpreted as vacuous acceptance. For all his political myopia, Luther was right that politics cannot operate according to the gospel principles of love and acceptance.[93] That justifies neither Luther's own political passivity nor his radical suspension of judgment with respect to the actions of the "authorities." But his central claim *is* accurate. If one *could* organize and operate a society solely on the basis of Christian love, then social coercion would be unnecessary. In other words, the presence of law already signals a distortion in the social fabric that precludes noncoercive love from becoming the highest political principle. Calvin understood this clearly. Far from believing that a "Christian commonwealth" (in which all professed to be Christians and worshiped properly) obviates the need for government, Calvin contended that the universal force of sin made government necessary *for all*. We who have witnessed religious fanaticism and its utter lack of love (under love's cover) ought to know this well. Love cannot be used as a political trump; the concretion of charity in politics is justice.[94]

Love as Appreciation

Love remains, however, a valid political principle to the extent that it serves specifically political purposes. One such purpose, in the current American environment, involves the need to create and maintain a *public* space of debate, argument, and difference. The civil religion of freedom and "the right to one's own opinion" destroys such space. Instead, we vent vitriol and trumpet personal "narratives" that place themselves outside the bounds of possible criticism.[95] What makes these attractive is the assumption of innocence that pervades American culture. Since it is "my opinion" and I am innocent, I need not answer for what I say, and thus responsibility is eliminated from politics.[96]

For the emphatic Christian center, however, love is thoroughly conditioned by an awareness of sin. Because it rejects the idea that desires and narratives are politically self-validating, it is free to recognize and to accept what is valuable in its opponents' views. This is a considerable advance beyond the charity either extreme is willing to show its opponents. Thus, a second task of the Christian center is to appreciate the depth of commitment of the extremists and the real truth that resides in their claims and symbols. Appreciation is the forgotten side of criticism, and it desperately needs rehabilitation. Appreciation does not mean mere acceptance. One who loves does not say only "yes" or "no"; she must say both, and expect others to speak as honestly and appreciatively to her. Appreciation can help to open the political space that America has padlocked. It provides the conditions for specific arguments about what politics is supposed to accomplish. Appreciation instills an attitude more than it provides content, however. Love can and must do more than this.

Love as Forgiveness: Forgiveness and Justice

In the last several years, theologians and others have increasingly argued that forgiveness has a political role to play. The tentative Japanese approaches to apologize for its troops' abuse of Korean "comfort women" during the Second World War; the pained, repentant reflections of many Germans on the culture that brought forth Nazism; the Vatican's repentance toward Protestants and its apparent determination to be reconciled with Jews;[97] French Archbishop Olivier de Berranger's apology to Jews for his church's silence during the Vichy regime;[98] and Congress' aborted attempt to apologize for slavery in America are just a few recent examples of the infusion of forgiveness into politics.

As a relatively new topic for theological reflection, the significance of political forgiveness is unclear. We will not provide much new insight into this question, except to point to the promises and dangers of the use of forgiveness for political life. The Christian center should be eager to employ forgiving love politically, but should not do so without clear purpose and clear awareness of the dangers of cheap forgiveness. Great damage has been done, especially in Protestantism (in both its liberal and conservative forms), by simplistic demands that individual Christians must forgive great evils done to them without ever raising the question of justice.

Despite the promise of political forgiveness, there is considerable danger that we will simply superimpose our already inadequate understanding of interpersonal forgiveness on our political life. Christianity has been criticized for being too quick to forgive, and not insisting upon justice. The African American entertainer Sammy Davis, Jr., when he converted from Christianity to Judaism, said "that the Christian religion preaches love thy neighbor and the Jewish religion preaches justice, and I think justice is the big thing we need."[99] There is much to this observation, particularly in political matters. Forgiveness without justice quickly becomes sentimentality even in personal relationships; when social and political relationships are involved, it becomes catastrophic. In race matters, one need only recall the clichés about "some of my best friends" and the paternalist justifications offered by many Southern whites for racial injustice. Feminist criticism likewise has properly highlighted the close relationship between the personal and the political spheres of life. Untold damage is done by well-meaning pastors who counsel rape victims to forgive their assailants.[100] To do so cheapens and trivializes both the victim's suffering and forgiveness. Dietrich Bonhoeffer protested against cheap *grace*—when the church offers grace casually, with no sense of its cost or its gravity.[101] Cheap *forgiveness* is similar: it urges people to forgive casually, almost thoughtlessly, with little sense of the cost involved—and assures them that their own wrongdoing is easily and casually forgivable. And, ironically, cheap forgiveness comes only at a great cost—the cost of belittling and demeaning the suffering and injustice inflicted on the *victims* of sin (which include us all).[102]

Part of the problem is that we tend to think of forgiveness as an event, something that happens quickly. We say, "I forgive you," and think that there is nothing more to it. But there is. Even personal forgiveness of a serious wrongdoing (let alone a great social wrongdoing such as slavery) is not that simple. It is not an event. It is a *process*, which takes *time* and cannot be *rushed*.[103] Much of the problem is also traceable to liberal and sentimentalist unitarianisms of love, which make "unconditional love" (often interpreted as acceptance of anything, no matter what) the *sine qua non* of all relationships, personal or social. But the problem also stems from a failure to see the relationship between forgiveness and justice.

Whether forgiveness is interpersonal or political-social, it must also serve justice. "Justification"—the technical term in Christian theology for God's forgiveness of human sinners—has the same root as "justice." A bitter dispute over the meaning of this word was at the heart of the Reformation. The conflict between Roman Catholic and Protestant understandings of grace at the dawn of the Reformation included precisely this issue: which conception of forensic justification could better provide for justice in the world? Although the debates focused on personal rather than political justice, the *criterion* is a good one for politics as well. Space does not permit a detailed investigation of this controversy here. Both Catholicism and Protestantism agreed that God's righteous anger at human sin had to be satisfied. Protestants insisted that only Christ's death on the cross could satisfy it, and that for human beings to think that they could do any more was unnecessary and blasphemous. "Grace alone," in Luther's phrase, was all that was required. Catholicism insisted that the Christian must cooperate with God's grace, and make satisfaction for her own sin through penance, and, if called, by celibate religious vocation. Catholics believed Protestants were abolishing the institutions of religion in order to do as they pleased; Protestants accused Catholics of adding unnecessary and dangerous "man-made" requirements to God's sole demand of faith.

Today we are faced, broadly speaking, with two incompatible and unsatisfactory versions of forgiveness: the demand that forgiveness be preceded by complete restitution (or retribution) for past wrongdoing; and the demand for "unconditional love and acceptance" regardless of the wrongdoing. The former is not forgiveness; the latter leaves no room for justice. *Especially* in politics, we need both. Protestants in particular have tended toward the latter view: forgiveness as simple acceptance, without need for restitution or reform. The Protestant right has always restricted this forgiveness to personal relationships, insisting on retribution in matters of public justice. Protestant liberalism has applied forgiveness to social relationships as well, often with a loss of concern for justice. However applied, it is inadequate. God's forgiveness is understood as universal and unrelated to any change in the forgiven's character, simply an admission ticket to eternal life no matter what. The Protestant notion of justification by forgiveness, in other words, lacks a substantive connection with "justice."[104]

This error derives from a tendency to sunder God from God's own creation. "Watchmaker deism," which thinks of God as distant from the world after its creation, present only in rewards and punishments (except that a "forgiving" God only rewards), is a pervasive American conception of the divine. Bette Midler's refrain, God is "watching you, from a distance," captures this attitude.[105] Although the right's incorporation of judgment is certainly preferable to the left's dreamy unconsciousness of it, the right is often equally deistic—their God rewards and punishes according to strict merits of faith without room for grace and divine gifts as the Christian traditions have historically understood them.[106] Even so, the right often outdoes the left in demanding that Christians forgive the wrongs *personally* done to them by others. Americans, in other words, accept Thomas Hobbes's complete division between the religious-heavenly and secular-earthly spheres. We would do well to remember that Hobbes made this separation for Royalist purposes and precisely to insulate government from religious and theological criticism.[107]

Still, one need look no farther than the former Yugoslavia, the Middle East, Rwanda, or the state of American race and gender relations to be convinced of Donald Shriver's claim that if we "are not to be derailed" from productive political association when we have harmed one another and suffered harm at others' hands, we will have to engage in "a collective form of forgiveness."[108] But if politics cannot operate productively without the nourishing waters of forgiveness, this forgiveness must yet be related to the political objectives of justice and power.[109]

"Forgiveness" cannot become an excuse to ignore or—worse—to perpetuate injustice and powerlessness. Rather, as Calvin understood, forgiveness is a condition of the unjust sinner's repentance[110]—and, we would add, of an unjust society's repentance. It opens a space for the unjust to confess their unrighteousness in an effort to *repair* it, not to continue in it, happily oblivious to its consequences. That is, forgiveness is a *means to justice and justification* rather than a self-sufficient "cheap grace." The purpose of supererogatory forgiveness is the powerful creation of a new future for both forgiver and forgiven. It is the means of laying the crimes of the past to rest in the practice of justice and power. This is as true of personal offenses as social ones. But this still leaves the problem of what to do when forgiveness is offered but not taken, or taken and yet the same evil deed is repeated again and again.

Love as appreciation and love as forgiveness, then, are both helpful ingredients for the building up of millennial American political life. But love—though essential—is not the *telos* of politics. Love must submit to the criterion of political justice; whether it is helpful in any particular instance is a function of the third and determinative political principle of emphatic Christian centrism, power.

The Aim of Politics: Power and the Christian Center

To select power as the central and irreducible principle of politics seems both natural and terribly perverse. Natural, because of the overarching importance of power in current cultural and academic discussions of politics, to say nothing of social and even domestic life. Justice and love, the previous centers of Western political life, now seem at best hopelessly naive, at worst conscious or semiconscious ideologies behind which the realities of power are concealed. Perverse, because power is widely viewed as an evil that taints (even poisons) all human and political relationships. Moreover, one of our principal objectives here is the attempt to overcome the opposition between power and reason or freedom.

The left heaps scorn on the right for ideologically cloaking its power behind noble words of justice and love. We think the left is naive. In its disdain for power and its quest for reason and freedom, it too dominates in ways that are neither rational nor free. However, the right's consistency makes it no more helpful. Its tendency to sever power and reason issues in a Realpolitik that lacks any principle, save that of quite narrowly conceived self-interest.[111] The Christian right in particular elevates power as domination—at least against its opponents—to the rank of a principle that virtually excludes love in political life. The problem of power in contemporary society and political life is an enigma that we must address.

We know that our decision to treat power as the cardinal political commitment—indeed, as the goal of politics itself—in a Christian political theology will strike some as dubious, and others as simply crude. It may seem as though we are abandoning Christianity's loftiest insights at the very moment when utter callousness in the name of religion looms on the horizon. We must ask indulgence until we can make the case (here and in the following chapters) that these suspicions are unjustified. In particular, we are entitled to ask forbearance from those who hold reason or love in high regard. Rationalists should suspend judgment until the argument is complete, and those who esteem love should gladly exercise its political manifestation—appreciation.

We should reciprocate that charity by acknowledging the gravity of these concerns. Should not politics aim at something more elevated than the tawdry quest for power? And if not politics in general, then surely religiously influenced politics? These objections derive from the general modern Western suspicion of power.[112] Even the postmodern emphasis on power's ubiquity has not diminished the moral scorn for power which has dominated the post-Enlightenment West. Lord Acton nicely summarized the modern (and postmodern) view: "Power tends to corrupt and absolute power corrupts absolutely."[113] In this view, power leaves an indelible stain of sin on its user. This perspective on power, of course, coupled with a corresponding (and self-contradictory) lionization of freedom, is a major contributor to the antipolitics that now infects the West, and especially America.

Politics involves power (however power may be understood). As the case now stands, most Americans subscribe to the bizarre theory that power is legitimate only insofar as it serves its opposite, freedom; but since freedom is power's opposite, the only service power can render is to *eliminate* itself—and the public sphere (which depends on power) along with it. That is our initial answer to the critics: to oppose power is necessarily to oppose public life, which, despise it as we might, we cannot live together without.

This answer alone suffices, for it shows that the "cultured despisers" of power are involved in a contradiction. They depend on the fruits of public life and politics even as they decry it. Such disdain for power is like unto the snobbery of those who look down at the people who perform the labor that they themselves need. But the consequences are even worse. We do not deny that involvement with power taints one with the stain of sin; that is inevitable in a morally ambiguous world in which *no* important decision or action is pure. But the refusal to use power is *no less tainted*.[114] It seems to us far better to acknowledge the ambiguities of power than to pretend that one is "above" it and thereby to engage in a domination yet more insidious. Of course power entails a similar risk that it will be transformed into domination and control. But power can be conceptually distinguished from domination and control, particularly if one begins with a theological interpretation of power.

POWER AND DIVINE OMNIPOTENCE

In the modern West, it is nearly impossible to broach the topic of power without conjuring up images of tyranny and autocracy. This was not always the case. The equation of power and domination seems to have been produced by the Enlightenment worshipers of reason, who sought to distinguish themselves from the hated tyrants they endeavored to depose. There is no question that their "reason" served an ideological function; it concealed its own manipulations, intolerance, and control even from those who used it. Postmodern philosophy has persuaded us of that much. But should we not also suspect that the other side of the equation—the postmodern pronouncement that power is nothing but mere domination—could be similarly ideological? This possibility has not seeped into postmodern consciousness, which has ideologically proclaimed freedom the new god. Even Michel Foucault, a postmodern thinker who tried to reclaim power's "productivity," remained, for all his valiant protest, chained to a political conception of power that reduced it to domination.[115]

The consensus of the modern and postmodern West about the evil of power is deeply misguided, theologically, ontologically, and culturally. It persuades us to eschew, disdain, and disguise our participation in an unavoidable feature of our common existence, to say nothing of our political life.[116]

We begin with the theological problem. G. van der Leeuw, in his pathbreaking study, *Religion in Essence and Manifestation*, makes the persuasive claim that what inspires worship is the experience of power. Power is what makes the divine divine; a god without power is oxymoronic.[117] Rudolf Otto's

The Idea of the Holy (which strongly influenced Tillich), argues that awe and fascination are the phenomenological spurs to worship and that both are born of mysteries of power.[118] Otto and van der Leeuw develop their arguments through examination of many religions. If power, as lived and experienced, is vital for religious life in general, it is particularly so for Western monotheistic religions, as in Tillich's claim that God is the "power of being."[119] Each of these religions asserts a final victory for God and a final validation of meaning for the worshipers of God. This is why the affirmation of divine *power* in Christianity comes before that of love or justice.[120] Love and justice require effective and victorious power to make them real. Despite the realities of injustice and hatred, the Christian conception of God's omnipotence affirms that they are not finally the meaning of reality or existence. Were the "powers" of evil finally victorious, the most that one could do would be to resign oneself to valiant—but futile—resistance.[121] Only if power finally validates reality's meaning can despair be conquered and life be worth living.

There is, to be sure, no obvious evidence that meaning will finally triumph over meaninglessness. This is the point at which religious argument must be nonrational. For each fragment of evidence that suggests that our struggles of existence finally do matter, there are others that suggest the opposite. And yet, religious and "nonreligious" people alike, consciously or not, act *as if* what they do adds to, subtracts from, or alters meanings. To do that requires that we believe that the quest for meaning is significant, that it will not be washed away in a torrent of evil, that what we do and say matters. And to continue to act in such ways even when it is clear that many meanings *are* washed away can only be called an act of faith—faith that somehow, in some way, meaning is more powerful than meaninglessness.

The Christian doctrine of divine omnipotence expresses this connection between worship and meaning. This means, in brief, that power is a "communication of efficacy." Power is not domination and control; these are distortions, not power fulfilled.

Power as Communication of Efficacy

What does it mean to say that power is communication of efficacy? First, it means that we accept the postmodern (and premodern) view that power is inescapable, present in every personal, social, and natural relation. Power is *ubiquitous*. The ubiquity of power, in turn, implies that power and domination are not identical, if reality ultimately fulfills beings rather than demeans and destroys them. If all being is saturated with power, we cannot avoid asking whether the power of being is ultimately destructive or supportive of beings. If the former, then existence and reality themselves are a cruel and senseless joke, immersing us in meaningless, inevitable destruction.

Furthermore, were power identical with domination and control, then *all* being would be self-contradictory in its deepest, ontological dimensions. Domination requires an Other to dominate. It must try to destroy that Other, since that Other is always a threat to domination; as a distinct center of power itself, the Other limits domination's power to dominate. Domination seeks to create puppets, but the puppet is never controlled by the puppeteer utterly. If it were, it would cease to be an Other, and there would be nothing left to dominate. Were power mere domination, power (and all being) would be self-defeating and self-contradictory.[122] Theologically speaking, if power and domination were identical, it would mean that the omnipotent God is our arch-nemesis, the undefeatable enemy of all creation. We would be created for meaningless destruction. If power merely dominated, it would eliminate the freedom of the creature; and if controlling power were the fundamental ontological structure,[123] God would be justifiably *(but impotently)* despised. Under such conditions, God

> deprives me of my subjectivity because he is all-powerful and all-knowing. I revolt and try to make *him* into an object, but the revolt fails and becomes desperate. God appears as the invincible tyrant, in contrast with whom all other beings are without freedom and subjectivity. He is equated with the recent tyrants who with the help of terror try to transform everything into a mere object, a thing among things, a cog in a machine they control.[124]

According to this view, the more power one being has, the less there remains for others. Domination is a zero-sum game with no winners.

The Christian tradition offers a quite different symbolism of power. The symbol of *creation out of nothing* puts forth the claim that the world's power participates in the divine power, indeed, that the world is produced by God's power. But God's power creates something *other* than God, powers not identical with the divine. God's *omnipotence* is defined by the production of a *power* that is *not God,* not by God's domination and control. In other words, the power which belongs to

God is precisely the power to bring an other into being. It rests not in domination but in the gift of power. (Here the connection to love should be obvious.) Divine power communicates power; it is a communication of efficacy.[125] Power as communication of efficacy, including but not restricted to sovereignty, is an ontologically adequate category. There could not be anything at all without continuing communications of efficacy. There can be no being without power.[126]

If communications of efficacy, and not domination and control, are what power and divine omnipotence are all about, several consequences for Christian centrism follow. First, power and freedom: far from being freedom's opposite, power is *necessary* for freedom. It is impossible to evade power in existence. But because freedom as we now understand it aims at solipsism and complete self-sufficiency, it has more commerce with domination than with fulfilling power, which is *communicative and plural*.[127] Freedom must participate in power, and therefore must serve power in order to maintain its own possibility. Freedom must seek to generate power. Only then will freedom cease to be our ultimate concern, and become plural rather than solipsistic. Far from being freedom's opponent, *power is its ground.* Freedom is legitimate and desirable insofar as it generates power for others as well as its exerciser. Complete independence—the current American civil religion—is not even a possibility, much less a valid goal. To the extent that we are confused about that, freedom warps itself into mere domination.

The intrinsic plurality of power leads to a second, related result. The American religion of freedom is destructive of politics; but power, properly understood, reinvests significance in the realms of plurality, notably the political sphere.[128] Politics is not optional because power is not optional. The basic ontological and theological status of power gives a place of *honor* to the public realm of politics. To paraphrase Reinhold Niebuhr, politics and power are given by God and reflect the divine majesty.[129]

Third, because communications of efficacy are ubiquitous in all existence, power is thoroughly *historical*. This, in turn, implies that everything participates in power—including truth, good, and beauty (to use Kant's triad). Hence all manifestations of power—divine and terrestrial—are subject to the risks of history. Because efficacy must be communicated and received in order for anything to persist, power cannot be guaranteed for anything that has being.[130] Although he meant it quite differently than we do, Marx was right to say that the end of power is the end of history. As long as the book of power remains open, there can be no closure regarding questions of truth, good, or beauty. Action and thought are always local, and always risk their own powerlessness as well as the temptation to become not power but domination. Politics and power cannot return to Eden nor rest in a future utopia; in history, neither could ever be or have been.

Finally, power's ontological standing as a communication of efficacy entails a judgment against weakness. Those on the left (and especially the religious left) are particularly prone to abjure power and to claim a higher moral ground for weakness. It is true that mere weakness does not dominate. But it also cannot bestow any life-sustaining and enriching power. Insofar as weakness is mere powerlessness—failing to communicate or to receive efficacy—it is merely worthless. Domination is a demonic distortion of power; weakness is the opposite of power, without strength even to be demonic. Domination is kin to the sin of pride; weakness, to the sin of sloth.[131] Consequently, the objection that perfect justice or love cannot participate in power is both true and false. True, in that neither could participate in power because neither could exist in history. False, in that a justice or love that does not participate in power occupies not a higher (much less perfect) moral ground, but no ground at all. The close connection in Islam between truth and effectiveness is to the point: Allah is not true without power, and the adequate worship of God involves making truths effective. All action ventures into dangerous waters; every action involves risk. It is impossible to determine fully in advance whether any given action will be lost in weakness, distorted in domination, or productive of power. Indeed, the risk can never be fully measured, for history is the realm of the unpredictable. But the risk must be taken, in confidence and with hope of justification and meaning, in spite of the possibility that power might fail to appear or may appear as domination and control.[132]

CONCLUSION

The initial theological framework for emphatic Christian centrism is now in place. Our principles of sin, love, and power have put the traditional theological categories of love, power, and justice at its core. However, we arrange this triad in a way quite different from that of the majority of post-Enlightenment Christian theologies, making *power* the determinative criterion of politics. We do so to avoid both the soporific evaporation of love into ineffective, abstract conceptions of justice (which tend toward powerlessness) and the illusion of innocence and worship of freedom (which tend toward dominating distortions of power). Not only does this give us a way out of the seemingly frequent contradiction between love and justice, it also is pro-political. It combats the destructive and antipolitical American civil religion of freedom.

Moreover, this view is theologically responsible. God's omnipotence is seen as the condition of the possibility of divine justice and love. Omnipotence grounds the divine creativity, issues in the world, the providential power that sustains the world, and the redemptive meaning that fulfills the world. The *imago Dei* (God's image in human beings) is defined by human participation in divine power, *in this world*. Justice and love are concretizing moments of power, of course; they move, conduct, and direct it. But it is power to which divine activity and human responses are directed. Love is surrounded by the specifically political principles of justice on the one side, and power on the other. The content of the justice that should *now* be sought depends on the possibilities of power available in this historical situation. And sin conditions every expression of love, power, and justice.[133]

Justice, love, and power are *Christian*[134] political principles, and quite traditional ones at that, even if we arrange them in a way quite different from that of most current American theology. This is largely because we oppose the civil religion of freedom, favoring instead a commitment to power in which freedom is included, but *not* as an "ultimate concern." Still, the palpably (though not exclusively) Christian character of these principles leads to a very important question: Is the specifically Christian character of these commitments ultimately self-defeating and (perhaps more to the point) dismissive of all those who are not Christian? In other words, have we attacked the present chauvinism of the Christian right only to substitute our own? Since the production of power is necessarily historical and specific, are these commitments compatible with the kaleidoscopic pluralism of our body politic? In chapter 4, we discuss how our theology of power propels the Christian center toward an emphatic pluralism that abjures the right's nativism, the left's idolatry of difference, and the empty center's vacuous pluralism.

Chapter 4

Difference and Commitment

PLURALISM
AND THE
CHRISTIAN CENTER

EMPHATIC CHRISTIAN CENTRISM: OPPOSING THE PLURALISM OF NEGLECT

Ever since the first chapter, we have been mindful of the fear—whether justified or not—that a religious presence in the public square will lead to religious domination and intolerance. We are confident that our argument thus far has avoided any hint of religious domination.[1] Now we confront the issue of pluralism directly. The emphatic Christian center's relationship to other political and religious claims must be argued, not asserted. In opposition to both the ideology of secularism and inclusivists like Richard Neuhaus, we demonstrate two important things in this chapter. First, respect and appreciation for alternative religious and political visions *requires* commitment to a *particular tradition,* not renunciation. Any pretension that one must arrive at some universal standpoint before pluralism is possible runs the risk of dominating oppression of others (as in some nineteenth-century rationalism), or vacuity (as in much pluralism today). Second, the emphatic Christian center is not self-sufficient. For its survival, to say nothing of its value and vitality, it needs powerful exchanges with (at least) other emphatic centers, which will nourish the Christian center partly through similarity, partly through difference. To show this will require an analysis of American perspectives on pluralism.

In American culture, "pluralism" has various connotations. But what all (or almost all) these pluralisms share is tolerance for a diversity of opinions, cultures, and worldviews. This is the sense in which particular liberalism believes itself best suited for contemporary America—within broad parameters, it preserves the sanctity of individual conscience. Susan Moller Okin, for example, argues that pluralism is the primary warrant for liberalism.[2] As John Rawls points out, pluralism is not an unfortunate fact of American life, but the natural outcome when people are encouraged to follow Immanuel Kant's *definition of enlightenment:* "*Enlightenment is man's emergence from his self-incurred immaturity.* Immaturity is the inability to use one's own understanding without the guidance of another. . . . The motto of enlightenment is therefore: *Sapere aude!* Have courage to use your own understanding." In the nuanced liberalisms of today, such as Rawls's, Kant's injunction loses many of its privatistic tendencies.[3] Because "most people need a secure cultural context to give meaning and guidance to their choices in life,"[4] Rawls concludes that associational plurality is also to be valued, even if only as a concession. But we have already eschewed the effort merely to adjust the emphatic Christian center to the culture in which we live. This does not make liberal defenses of pluralism less valid. Rather, it means that, like political liberalism itself, the value of pluralism needs a stronger foundation than liberalism itself is able to provide.

This is not to say that emphatic Christian centrism provides the only valid defense of pluralism. This cannot be the case, unless pluralism is to become the apogee of parentalism. But emphatic Christian centrism can provide, with some structural similarities to Rawls's notion of an overlapping consensus, one such justification. That much might be considered a service to culture without affecting the core of Christianity. But we go farther—the emphatic Christian center must place a high value on pluralism for the sake of Christianity's own vitality. Christian commitment to pluralism is not a magnanimous, self-effacing gesture. It generates power for both the wider culture and Christianity. On the basis of the three grounding principles of the emphatic Christian center outlined in the foregoing chapter—sin, appreciation (love), and power—a commitment to substantial pluralism is inescapable.

Finally, without succumbing to liberal secularism, emphatic Christian pluralism redeems the claim of our first chapter that the proper form of the American state is secular. Emphatic pluralism makes the Christian center more religious, not less.[5]

However, pluralism as it is currently construed is in serious danger of succumbing to the fate of the vacuous center and the intolerant wings. Not surprisingly, many understandings of pluralism shadow the rest of our political culture. On one hand, we are subjected to various extremisms which exclude all "different" groups—racial, religious, sexual, and cultural—as poisoned and poisoning enemies of the social body. We call these "monoculturalism." The only apparent alternative to this xenophobia about our co-citizens seems to be a pluralism that valorizes difference simply because it *is* different, but is unable to explain or even to ask precisely *what* it is that is valuable about difference—and has nothing to say about the limitations of difference. This pluralism for pluralism's sake comes in two distinct but related forms, which we will call "vacuous"[6] and "ideological" pluralism.

Vacuous pluralism, despite its lionization of difference in the abstract (actually, because of it), is a pluralism of indifference. Believing that commitment and pluralism are incompatible, this indifferent pluralism cannot confront questions about the value of difference because it flows from our purely formal public culture of freedom and independence,[7] with its "right" to have one's own (uncontested) opinion. It is a pluralism of neglect, which, at most, is curious about different others, but lacks any substantive relation with them. Like the American ideology of freedom, vacuous pluralism is ahistorical and presumes the basic innocence of humankind; it does not contemplate the possibility that positions and cultures change (sometimes for the better, sometimes not) through confrontation and exchange with others. It simply neglects others' positions, preferring to remain with the likeminded and those who will not challenge us. This indifferent "tolerance" has at least as much to do with insulating us from uncomfortable criticism (that is, from being confronted with our own sin) as it does with respect for others. Indeed, Bernard Williams is not embarrassed to suggest that the secure cocooning of our own beliefs is the signal virtue of tolerance: "If we are asking people to be tolerant, we are asking for something . . . complicated. . . . They will indeed have to lose something, their desire to suppress or drive out the rival belief; *but they will also keep something, their commitment to their own beliefs*"—as if that were self-evidently a good thing![8] Herbert Marcuse aptly described this sort of tolerance as "repressive tolerance."[9]

Indifferent pluralism is likely to share the same fate as the vacuous center and all merely formal conceptions. Its ideas and cultural practices will become less substantive (because less tested by transformative exchanges, which generate power), retained simply because they are "the way we were raised."[10] This opens the door for extremist commitment, which is only too happy to provide the substance lacking in public culture. It is no accident that "pluralism" is simultaneously one of our most prized and vilified terms. Under these conditions, when difference does become public (in, say, the competition for finite resources), the differences become irreconcilable. Then the only solution is (as we argued with respect to the ideology of freedom) to have a contest of dominations. This is why vacuous pluralism easily transforms into its alleged opposite, *ideological pluralism*. Both are based on a conception of politics as the conflict between interest groups whose positions are unalterably established. The newest incarnation of this position is the ideology of "identity politics," in which group identity is a given which cannot be challenged, and the sole goal of political activity becomes to assert "our" identity. Practically, the difference between ideological pluralism and monoculturalism is almost negligible—they both insist on the group's identity as unchallengeable and incommunicable. Each group believes that only its culture matters (at least to itself), and each sees the public sphere as a zero-sum game for domination; whatever it gains, other cultures must lose. The only difference is how many, and which, groups are "tolerated." Neglectful pluralism, like the ideology of freedom, turns on itself, creating the opposite of what it professes. Absolute tolerance is impossible so long as we must come in contact with one another and one another's claims, and the illusion of absolute tolerance paradoxically becomes a recipe for domination.[11]

The alternative to strident monoculturalism and to vacuous and ideological pluralism is a *transformative* or *emphatic pluralism* that engages the *content* of others' positions, worldviews, and cultures. Indifferent pluralism believes that commitment and pluralism are incompatible; transformative pluralism maintains that commitment is the ground of pluralism and that pluralism, in turn, should deepen commitment. Vacuous pluralism avoids decision; emphatic pluralism embraces mutual transformation. Emphatic pluralism makes an effort both to begin to correct the distortions present in others, and to initiate the reduction of our own sin. We variously call this "emphatic pluralism," "transformative pluralism," and "pluralism of commitment." These are not separate pluralisms, but related moments of emphatic pluralism. We identify, then, four positions on pluralism: monoculturalism, vacuous pluralism, ideological pluralism, and the transformative pluralism of emphatic Christian centrism.

Emphatic pluralism is a pluralism of *commitment* that is related to difference in two ways. First, it is a commitment *to* difference as the food that sustains the historical and conceptual movement of each party. Power, as a communication of efficacy, requires *communication;* and communication requires *difference*—though not for its own sake. Second, emphatic pluralism holds to commitments *in spite of* difference, although those commitments are altered through serious and (one hopes) powerful encounters with difference—not mutual *in*difference. Emphatic pluralism preserves tolerance while moving beyond mere tolerance to mutual transformation in power. Emphatic, transformative pluralism maintains *both* that "truths" are neither arbitrary constructions nor merely products of domination, *and* that truths are plural and relative to one another.

Because "pluralism" is frequently equated with vacuous or ideological pluralism, we begin with an account of what pluralism is *not*. This will put us in a position to develop criteria for transformative pluralism and to examine its content. Finally, we will demonstrate how emphatic pluralism can guard against lapsing back into absolutism (in its monocultural or ideological pluralist forms) and vacuous pluralism.

WHAT PLURALISM IS NOT

Emphatic pluralism is not relativism; or rather, because "relativism" is badly misnamed, emphatic pluralism is *real* relativism: namely relatedness, the state of being *related.* What passes for "relativism" in current discourse is the notion that all claims to truth are equal, "relative" merely to the claimant's views. Far from being "relativism," this is actually *ir-*

relativism, nonrelatedness, simply holding that there is no real relationship between rival truth claims. In conservative political rhetoric (such as that of Rush Limbaugh and Richard Neuhaus), "pluralism" (meaning vacuous or ideological pluralism) is simply equated with "relativism" (meaning that all truth claims are equal, that is, indifferent). That equation is simply wrong, as we will see. Their rhetoric, in service to a new monoculturalism, proclaims pluralism to be relativism's secret agent, infiltrating the culture in order to undermine all moral standards.[12] The proposed solution to this breakdown in moral standards usually is either authoritarian or majoritarian, the latter of which we have already seen in Neuhaus. At the very least, as in William Bennett's *Book of Virtues,* Allan Bloom's ironically titled *The Closing of the American Mind,* or the classical American left's Arthur Schlesinger, Jr., we hear wistful or aggressive calls to return to the values (and implicitly, the situation) of the past—a past which African Americans, Hispanics, women, and others rightly criticize for excluding their own cultures.[13]

Such criticisms of pluralism are not without their point; indeed, they are frequently made more plausible by the defenders of the pluralism of neglect.[14] The chief objection raised by these critics is that pluralism is "relativism." This identity mistakes both sides of the equation. The pluralism they criticize is neither realistically nor consistently plural (as we will see). The error is no less basic with respect to relativism, however. American culture understands "relativism" as the obliteration of all interactive claims to truth and value. It is not difficult to see how that understanding emerged. The collapse of the idea of a universally accessible common reason carried the West in a direction it did not anticipate: that claims to truth and value are culturally conditioned and constructed. In combination with the valorization of freedom as independence and an emphasis on personal experience, it is but a short—albeit false—step to the belief that truth and value are relative only to the self: what is true for me may not be true for others, and what is true for others, if it does not comport with my own sense of truth, is certainly not true for me (particularly because I am innocent and no one has a right to tell me what to do).[15]

Despite its individualistic roots, this sort of relativism is not utterly antisocial. Rather, it is socially solipsistic. It seeks out what Robert Bellah and his associates call "lifestyle enclaves," which are not communities at all.[16] In these enclaves, we seek out people like us. Institutions bear complicity in this narrowing of public life, certainly; churches, for example, increasingly advertise themselves as "friendly" places that sell a product to a clientele.[17] Mainline Protestant churches often try to satisfy immediate desires rather than to transform those who attend. Such "relativism" and its co-conspirators—individual, social, and institutional—are not truly relative, except in the extraordinarily narrow sense of being related to what the individual or group believes (or would like to believe). According to this understanding, "relativism" is "the view that the only available standard is some local group or individual."[18] Truth then matters only to the self, or the self writ large in a lifestyle enclave. Nor, within such homogeneous enclaves, are we truly related to the truth claims of others. This relativism has no relation to alternative claims, except to neglect them. What is usually called "relativism," therefore, *is not relativism* at all; it is *antirelativism*.[19] It aims to be *unrelated* to alternative claims, and to those who make them. Antirelativism seeks independence, not relatedness.

The Roots of Antirelativism

What makes this antirelative "relativism"[20] so persuasive to so many Americans? The answer lies in the conceptions of truth and freedom that are our American inheritance. The chief source of American antirelativism is a disappointed universalism. If there is no *one* right answer, we swiftly conclude that there are *none*. In universal liberalism, freedom was traditionally ruled by reason. Freedom was not an end in itself, but unfettered the search for truth. Freedom was the vital *means* to the end of progress in rationality and truth. This confidence held sway in America[21] throughout the nineteenth and twentieth centuries, eroding only slowly after World War I[22] but more rapidly after the 1960s. Once that confidence was lost, freedom was all that remained. Some (though not all) postmodern philosophy is the head cheerleader for this outcome. The postmodern philosophies of Michel Foucault and Richard Rorty, for example, argue not only that it is impossible to have a relation to truth, but that one should not even try. The only truth for Rorty is what works, although what it might work *for* is undetermined and indeterminable.[23] Like Rorty, the later Foucault understands truth in terms of freedom and aesthetic self-creation.

There are no standards beyond private desires that we might use to decide *what* we might most fulfillingly create ourselves to be.[24] The substitution of "Freedom for Truth" is, for Rorty, cause for celebration.[25] John McGowan convincingly argues that postmodernism as a movement is held together by nothing so much as this commitment to the "negative freedom" of independence.[26]

Postmodern proclamations of this antirelativist cast are *post*modern only in the sense of being a disappointed modernism. They have not taken us beyond modernism at all. The term "postmodern" is telling. To describe something as "post-" does not reveal what it is, only what it is supposed to have passed. But if "post-" is the only descriptor, we know that we are still in the clutches of what was supposed to have been overcome. Postmodernism depends parasitically on the very modernism it rejects. This is why postmodernism must put modernity "on *endless* trial"; otherwise, it will die.[27]

If we are truly to cease beating the horse of modernity (which postmodernism repeatedly declares to be dead—and then resuscitates in order to beat again), we must become clear about postmodernism's continuing bondage to modernity. Oddly, although postmodernism is only too happy to provide genealogies and cultural contexts for everyone else's thought, it is often singularly blind about its own origins. For example, postmodernists conclude that we cannot apprehend a universal truth, and have lost confidence that reason alone can lead us to such a truth. The more radical of the postmodern prophets, however, press these conclusions in a particular direction, concluding that there are no truths at all. Nevertheless, one thing in particular has *not* changed: "truth" is identified with self-identical, unitary, universal truth. This is an utterly modern—not peculiarly postmodern—claim. What postmodernism contributes is the inference that truth as such therefore cannot exist.

Postmodernism's obliviousness toward its own origin is all the more surprising because it is Friedrich Nietzsche, to whom postmodernism often appeals, who argues forcefully that nihilism arises from (among other things) the disappointment of beholding that "there is no such universal!" and maintains that the evasion of nihilism begins with critical questions "about the sources of our faith in these ... categories."[28] A wide swath of postmodernism fails in the second task, continuing to live in the shadow—and the kingdom—of final, universal truth. Postmoderns may be rebellious subjects in that realm, but subjects they remain. Their assumption remains modern: truth is entire and singular, or it is nothing. The only difference is that now it is nothing. Rorty maintains that his positions are not arbitrary simply because everyone's positions are equally arbitrary: "Nobody is being any more arbitrary than anybody else. But that is to say that nobody is being arbitrary at all."[29] But why does arbitrariness not admit of degrees? Is it *really* the case that one who maintains that God is the ground of being is *no more* arbitrary than one who asserts that a cauliflower is? or that personal freedom is? All this can be traced to disappointed modernism.

It is no coincidence that postmodern fever is epidemic in France and America, the sites of the great eighteenth-century revolutions of freedom.[30] This suggests two more roots of present-day nonrelative "relativism" and its twin, nonplural "pluralism": egalitarianism and the hostility to particularity.[31] We consider each in turn.

Egalitarianism: In the French Revolution, liberty and equality were linked in the revolutionary slogan itself.[32] In both countries, the language of liberty is increasingly egalitarian. This egalitarian impulse rather easily translates into a naive pluralism. When confronted with difference, it seems natural to escalate egalitarian tendencies, particularly when linked with the American attachment to freedom as independence.

Antirelativism is, in principle, a full and positive egalitarianism. It is the right to one's opinion spread indiscriminately (again, at least in principle) across all cultures and all possible commitments. If we attend to this egalitarian root, it becomes clear why—in spite of its frequent links to "multiculturalism"—antirelative "relativism" emerged only in *a* culture: an upper-middle cultural class, generally privileged and well-educated, largely but not entirely white, American culture. That culture is the inheritor of egalitarian traditions, and that culture is comfortable enough to make cultural, moral, aesthetic, and intellectual *(but not economic)* egalitarianism seem like a real option. One can only be a moral or intellectual egalitarian if there is nothing at stake, if one is sufficiently insulated from injury so that morality and the worldviews from which it springs seem to have no consequences. The limit of egalitarian antirelativism is the limit of solipsistic freedom; its usefulness is confined to situations in which there is no encounter that cannot be resolved on the basis of participants' previous commitments.

Effectively, this is a limit of noninvolvement, the ability to hold challenges from the world at a safe distance. Few victims of political persecution are moral or intellectual egalitarians.[33]

Next, *antiparticularism:* Enlightenment assumptions about the relation between the universal and the particular play a major role in antirelativist pluralism. For Enlightenment thinkers, the particular was validated only in the universal. This brings us back both to James Madison's complaints about faction and Thomas Jefferson's against "sects" (meaning not denominations, but all historical religions). Any particular religion—like any faction, special custom, or particular practice—was valid only insofar as it conformed with universal reason. Postmodernism, as is well known, rejects the universal truth claim of the Enlightenment. But it retains the Enlightenment opposition between particularity and truth.[34] This is why the claim that there is no *universal* truth slides so effortlessly into the claim that there are *no* truths. Particular claims remain, as they were for the moderns, the enemy of truth. The difference is that the judges of universal reason have been impeached, their court disbanded, and now it's everybody for herself.

To be sure, no particular claims are false for postmodernism, either. There are simply no universal criteria, and hence no criteria, by which they could be judged. What is the relationship *between* particular claims of one subculture and another? The postmodern answer is that the claims of various persons and communities are "incommensurable," a term used well before the postmodern explosion by (surprisingly) John Courtney Murray.[35] But whereas incommensurability was not the final word for Murray, for postmodernists such as Rorty, John Rawls, Jean-François Lyotard, and Foucault, it is.[36] It should surprise—and trouble—us that this claim, that comprehensive worldviews and religions are incommensurable, is made *a priori*. Seldom are any *actual* comprehensive worldviews examined to see if this is really so, even though the claim is clearly an empirical one. For a wide swath of postmodernism, the simple fact that traditions which make universal claims (like world religions) are inevitably particular is deemed sufficient to prove their incommensurability and the futility of all mediation between those claims. We do not deny that there are incommensurable and conflicting worldviews and religions. They certainly do not all teach the same thing! But there is no reason to *assume* that in any particular case. Nor is there reason to assume that there are *no* criteria by which such claims might be adjudicated. There are not, to be sure, intransigent universal criteria. It does not follow that no criteria are available; that would be true *only* if particularity cannot generate truth. But why not?

Finally, there is no reason to assume that even demonstrated incommensurability is *permanent*. Neglect of this question among postmodern pluralists indicates that history does not go "all the way down"[37] for them, protestations to the contrary notwithstanding. Their construction of *freedom* is utterly *ahistorical*. In that construction, the egalitarian and antiparticularistic subroots of antirelativist pluralism form a volatile bond. Indeed, this bond is the point at which antirelative "relativism" melts down; it mutates into antipluralism, and its professed multicultural "tolerance" mutates into a strident monocultural monism (under cover of ideological pluralism). Antirelativism becomes antipluralism once the boundaries surrounding oneself and one's group are treated as inviolable not merely by the force of physical domination but also by arguments that might produce power for all were they allowed to occur. Particularity is not taken to be false, but *prima facie* untrue. This, in turn, reinforces the unwarranted assumption that all opinions are equally true and equally untrue. Since none are universal, no one is supposedly any more arbitrary than anyone else.

Thus there are at least three roots in the genealogy of postmodern pseudorelativism: disappointed universalism, unnuanced egalitarianism, and antiparticularism.

The Inevitable Collapse of Antirelativism

What is the effective difference between ideological pluralism, with its uncriticizable "truth for us," and the fanaticisms of monocultural absolute truth? Very little, in cases in which a *decision* has to be made between allegedly "incommensurable" perspectives—in social policy, educational curricula, institutional organization. Bruno Latour opens *We Have Never Been Modern* with the following review of a single newspaper article on the ozone layer:

> The same article mixes together chemical reactions and political reactions. A single thread links the most esoteric sciences and the most sordid

politics, the most distant sky and a single factory in the Lyon suburbs, dangers on a global scale and the impending local elections or the next board meeting. The horizons, the stakes, the time frames, the actors—none of these is commensurable, yet there they are, caught up in the same story.[38]

The story *will* be resolved one way or another. Debate, decision, action, and reflection will continue to occur. In this case, the pluralism of indifference, indebted as it is to egalitarian freedom and antiparticularism, is of little help. This neglectful pluralism is essentially solipsistic, suited to a frontier mentality in which conflicts are resolved by someone's getting out of town by sundown. Intellectual and moral egalitarianism are essentially monadic, leaving one's own thought untouched and beyond the possibility of being touched by another, that is, un-related to anything or anyone. We are no longer (if we ever were) in a world in which this is possible. And when we encounter one another (as we must), when indifference is no longer possible, the pluralism of indifference cannot sustain itself. Vacuous pluralists cannot decide; their options are to fade from the scene or to become ideological pluralists.

Indifferent pluralism largely derives from situations of relative comfort in which no hard decisions must be made, no significant options eliminated.[39] In such cases, it is convenient to value all differences equally, without attention to the value of specific differences. But when differences become important, indifferent pluralism can sponsor no significant efforts to bridge them, much less to transform all parties in the encounter. It lacks any criteria that could launch such an effort.

Still, people make decisions. Apathy and indecision manifest weakness, the opposite of power, but they are not the incomplete and perverted power of domination. They approach nothingness when contact with difference is substantial.[40] A recent example of such powerlessness was the strange controversy over what American policy should be with respect to female genital mutilation in other nations. Some Americans' indifference to the problem was based on the claim that different cultures have different practices, and that difference itself conferred legitimacy on the practice. This shows the extraordinary weakness of vacuous pluralism. Fortunately, our culture was not so utterly enervated, indifferent, and callous; indifferent pluralism lost the argument, and America established a new category of political asylum for women threatened with mutilation. Indifferent pluralism, however, would have been not only repressive in its tolerance, but happily tolerant of repression.[41]

When the choice is made for power beyond self or group, however, one must either pass beyond the worldview of indifferent pluralism (as opponents of genital mutilation did) or remain within that worldview while contradicting it in practice. In the latter case, indifferent pluralism does not have the intellectual resources to reach the *telos* of power, a communication of efficacy. Instead, the truncated power of mere domination comes to the fore. When indifferent pluralism cannot be sustained, it becomes antipluralistic; when neglect is an option no longer, control is.

Tribalistic egalitarianism, without ability or desire to reach beyond the claims of one's own group, is religious in the narrowest, worst sense. It makes practical claims about ultimacy, but its insulation from all competing claims precludes comprehensiveness and self-transcendence. Often, when antirelativist positions confront one another, both quickly have recourse to practical absolutism. The controversy over Leonard Jeffries' chair at the City College of New York is an instructive example. However preposterous his division between "sun people" and "ice people," however lacking in evidence and sensitivity his remarks about Jews, most media reports (and often, the participants in the controversy) refused to debate Jeffries' evidence or lack thereof. Instead, the debate focused on whether whites—Jewish and non-Jewish—were *offended* by Jeffries' attacks, on the one side, and whether Jeffries had a right to academic freedom, particularly in service to African American pride, on the other. The principal question was not evidence or quality of argument but offense, as if human beings have a right to not being offended. However, what made Jeffries' claims racist and anti-Semitic was not their criticism of white Gentiles and Jews, nor the offense that they gave. They were racist and anti-Semitic because the claims were incredibly disproportionate to the evidence—in fact, there was no evidence. The pride of groups is not at issue; the question is whether such pride is supported by the evidence. One of the few sensible voices in this debate (did this make him an antipluralist?) was Kareem Abdul-Jabbar, who insisted that Jeffries "use *facts*—it's as simple as that."[42] It is precisely facts and evidence, however, that moral and intellectual egalitarianism cannot consider. Nor can such egalitarianism contemplate being changed by evidence, for evidence and argument are presumed arbitrary, equal, indifferent. The result is a battle for domination between external wills, nothing more.[43]

These dominations are frequently concealed, as those whose subcultures are marginalized point out (including those who object to the exclusion of institutional religion from public life). We have seen, in the case of some particular liberalisms (Rawls is an exception), that the argument that all nonliberal positions should be excluded from public debate, although it is ostensibly based on pluralism, in fact relies on the *de facto* dominance of liberalism in American culture. No less than some religious inclusionists, particular liberals argue from facticity—because they are dominant, they should continue to dominate. Michael Perry rightly argues that their appeal to "common, shared premises" in fact privileges *their* liberal premises, despite the claim to neutrality.[44] This form of pluralism has commitments, even though it hides them; but it has ceased to be pluralist or multicultural: it has become a nonplural monoculturalism. The role played by domination in these systems is concealed because their advocates rely on extant privilege and do not have to avail themselves of the cruder weapons of force.[45] If criteria are lacking, if criticism is impossible, what good fortune to be among the privileged! Now privilege can be retained with a clear conscience—or conceded as a beneficent, parental gift to the less privileged.

Liberalism is not the only offender. Less sophisticated chanters of the egalitarian "multiculturalism and pluralism are their own ends" mantra, if they do not opt for comfortable indifference, employ it as a blanket indictment of "intolerant" cultures or persons. The cultural situatedness of their own position is obscured thereby. Although the claim derives from a particular culture, it is not presented as one cultural position among others, but as metacultural—a standard that judges all other cultures exactly because its proponents believe themselves (and no one else) free of their cultural and historical conditions.[46]

A pluralism that remains indifferent at least has the virtue of being externally consistent, albeit weak. But the moment it must make a choice, when power can no longer be avoided, it loses its claim to being egalitarian, pluralist, and multicultural. Instead it becomes, for all practical purposes, absolutist, antiplural, and monocultural. It is precisely this hypocritical combination of professed tolerance and *de facto* dominance that the opponents of pluralism rightly detest. And it is in no small part the practical incoherence of the philosophy of neglectful pluralism that leads both to a revival of intolerance (which is at least clear, aboveboard, and minimally self-consistent) and to the inability to defend what truly is valuable and necessary about plurality. As presently constituted, "pluralism" excludes all meaningful commitments or provides license for arbitrary domination.

CONTOURS OF EMPHATIC PLURALISM

Truth Is Plural and Relative (Related)

We have criticized the egalitarian pluralism of indifference as antirelative and, once choices have to be made, effectively absolutist and antiplural. This is largely because it assumes that truth must be single, unitary, and universal. Its results are inseparable from that presupposition. If neither results nor presupposition is satisfactory, that gives us a very good idea of where the emphatic pluralism of transformation should begin.

To begin with, a pluralism of mutual transformation will be *plural*. It follows that it will be relativist in the proper sense; that is, it will *relate* worldviews, religions, and their particular positions to one another. It will assume neither the incommensurability of views *a priori*, nor that presently incommensurable positions cannot be altered for good reasons. Moreover, it will assume not only a need for social cooperation but also a need for conflict, disagreement, and argument in order to generate power for all parties. Within a broad range, there is no need to choose between social order and disagreement, as if every dispute automatically damages order. On the contrary, American constitutional democratic government is founded on the opposite principle. Because positions come into regular dispute in transformative pluralism—and therefore their rationales and symbols invigorate public debate regularly—it is likely that social order in relatively stable societies is strengthened because there will be continual readjustment, assessment, and transformation.[47] That, at any rate, is the democratic gamble.[48] It should also be the religious gamble. The present concern with social order (even among liberals, as we saw in chapter 1), which views forceful debate as a threat, helps to produce a fragile order unable to deal constructively with deep difference.

When radical difference and pluralism do enter public debate, they appear to precipitate a crisis, because a society that valorizes agreement is not accustomed to regular reflection, defense, and alteration with respect to institutional, philosophical, theological, and social arrangements. In relatively stable societies, as in enduring personal relationships, the suppression of difference and disagreement undoes stability more readily than it reinforces it.

Truth Is Particular, Not Universal

Second, the modern and postmodern presupposition that "truth" must be single and universal is in error. Emphatic Christian pluralism still talks about truth and adequacy, even though (or perhaps because) truth is irreducibly particular. Truths are relative in a meaningful sense: that is, truths will be related to one another, which means that they can be compared on certain criteria (also relative to other criteria and to what we are able to discern about the world, humanity, God, history, and nature), and adjudicated in ways that are more and less adequate. To deny that universal reason is available to us is not to deny that there are better and worse reasons for certain conceptions and actions. Truths are precisely relative and related, not antirelative and solipsistic. The division between the universal and the particular that was so vital to rationalism (and is still accepted by many postmodernists as well) is chimerical, indeed downright foolish. The sooner we leave it behind, the better off we will be.[49]

Why the idea of a universally accessible reason is a delusion should be evident from language itself and how we use it, as postmodernism argues. The adage that "we do not speak language; language speaks us" is forceful. The language we speak is a *particular* language which opens certain arenas while closing others: we do not know which until we are confronted with another language that opens what we never knew was there. The terrible, admirable task of translation seeks to make one world of speech, thought, and action comprehensible to another. It always only partially succeeds.[50] No language is universal—the fiasco of Esperanto should have taught us that.

Universality is also absent *within* any language, in at least two ways. First, language changes; terms, sentences, and their referents come in and out of practice, in confrontation with other languages, formulations, and new aspects of the world. Language is historical and responds to history. "Domestic violence" existed long before the term became current; but when it was described as "marital troubles" or "incompatibility" or "he hits her sometimes," these terms did not evoke the universal disapproval—and nondiscursive action—that "domestic violence" now does. Of course, linguistic change is not always progressive, as the fruitful retrievals of various forgotten past perspectives indicate, whether by critical feminists or less critical neoconservatives. In addition, even the fact that "universal" exists as a particular word undercuts the historical possibility of its intended reference. As a particular term within particular languages, it distinguishes itself from what it intends merely by the fact of its differentiation from other terms. The simple existence of the term "universal" is the clearest indication that its referent is impossible to capture within language. Whatever else "universal" means, it means that its content cannot be fully grasped.[51]

Whether "universal" truth actually "exists," even if "universal" includes history, is not particularly important for now. What is incontrovertible is that it cannot be spoken and is therefore of little direct use in the public realm, which is driven by speech and language. Universal truth may or may not "exist" in the "mind of God." But we have no unmediated social or linguistic access to it. The nearly unanimous testimony of Western mysticism is to the point. Whatever the key of mystical music—apophatic or cataphatic, Christian, kabbalistic, Sufi, Platonic, or neo-Platonic, or whether there is union with the divine or not—mystics agree that what unity and universality is had in the mystical experience is neither directly nor completely expressible in language. For some, the experience cannot occur at all unless we, as Augustine says, pass beyond our own souls and our language, only returning to them "with a sigh, leaving our spiritual harvest."[52] At the very least, language sacrifices fullness even as it strives for it; according to the apophatic traditions, language distorts the very universality it tries to express.

It is irrelevant to object, as defenders of universal reason do, that the assertion that truth is particular is itself a universal assertion, and therefore undercuts itself.[53] The objection is as logically true as it is practically empty; its persuasiveness depends upon satisfaction with mere formality.⁵⁴ As Hans-Georg Gadamer notes, whatever the logical truth of the argument, its force is directed at the arguer (the attacker of relativism) and not the intended target, relativism itself:

> However clearly one demonstrates the inner contradictions of relativist views, it is as Heidegger has said: all these victorious arguments have something about them that suggests they are attempting to bowl one over. However cogent they may seem they still miss the main point. In making use of them one is proved right, and yet they do not express any superior insight of any value. That the thesis of skepticism or relativism refutes itself to the extent that it claims to be true is an irrefutable argument. But what does it achieve? The reflective argument that proves successful here falls back on the arguer in that it renders the truthfulness of all reflection suspect. It is not the reality of skepticism or of truth dissolving relativism, but the claim to truth of all formal argument that is affected.⁵⁵

The claim that relativism is inconsistent, if purely formally true, nevertheless fails to establish any extrahistorical, absolute content for truth. The argument gets discernment of firm, universal, established truths exactly nowhere.⁵⁶ An ontology that is historical recognizes that in time, truths are particular. Because we did not always take the power of history and language seriously, because we variously thought that consciousness, intellectual seeing, or the will dominated history and language, we did not notice truth's particularity. Now we do—it is given to us with our time in history.⁵⁷

Does the denial that universal truth is accessible in history throw us back on antirelativism? No, provided we can escape the *illusion* that *truth* is by definition *universal.* The opposition between truth and particularity is maintained by antirelativism and universalism alike.⁵⁸ That opposition is itself ungrounded. There are no arguments to support it that operate in the way that arguments normally operate in order to persuade. What evidence can be adduced in support of the antinomy? The prejudice that the content of truth must be universal is an article of faith in the worst sense. Moreover, there is a good deal of evidence against it. The assertion is clearly ahistorical and cannot account for the real changes that history brings. Progressivist philosophies and theologies of history maintain their universality by completely subordinating history to consciousness—and they have all been unfruitful as explanations for the continuing course of history.

Hegel, in a rare poetic flourish, was one of the few to see the futility of a comprehensive philosophy of history that includes the future: "Philosophy . . . always comes too late to perform this function. . . . When philosophy paints its gray in gray, a shape of life has grown old, and it cannot be rejuvenated, but only recognized, by the gray in gray of philosophy; the owl of Minerva begins its flight only with the onset of dusk."[59] Even Hegel, who thought absolute knowledge of the Spirit within his grasp, never believed that he could capture the Spirit's future. Even if we reject Hegel's timidity for Feuerbach's and Marx's boldness at one point—insisting that philosophy and theology should say something for the future as well as for the past and present—Hegel's admonition that the future remains outside the bounds of consciousness remains prudent. Knowledge of the future is utterly different in kind from knowledge of the past and present. The power and unpredictability of history give better reason to believe that truth is irreducibly particular than that its content is universal in a way accessible to we who are within histories of culture, nature, society, biography, and language.

Truth Is Discussable Even If Not Universal

We have dispatched the idea that truth must be everywhere self-identical. This is only a partial answer to antirelativist relativism. We must also refute the false conclusion derived from its faulty premise—that since truth is not *universal,* it cannot be *discussed.* Antirelativists such as Rorty argue that our lack of sovereignty over language precludes significant discussion of truth claims. We may initially doubt the accuracy of such an assertion simply because we see such discussions occurring regularly (although with increasing difficulty), including in Rorty's own work.[60] We have already suggested that for Rorty, history does not go all the way down, either; it extends neither to conceptions of freedom nor to history itself.

Still, Rorty's case focuses on language. He does not say that things are constituted only by language. (He does not trade Berkeley's perceptual idealism for its linguistic twin.) He does say that "truth" is constituted only in language. The core of his case is worth exploring more fully. Rorty argues initially that "to say that truth is not out there is simply to say that where there are no sentences there is no truth, that sentences are elements of human languages, and that human languages are human creations."[61] This does not necessarily mean that there are not reasons for believing certain sentences to be true: "We shall not be tempted to confuse the platitude that the world may cause us to be justified in believing a sentence true with the claim that the world splits itself up, on its own initiative, into sentence-shaped chunks called 'facts.'"[62] So far, Rorty's criticism extends to universality and correspondence as serviceable ideas of truth.

Rorty maintains more than this, however. From his criticism of universal and correspondent notions of linguistic truth, he moves by a curious route to the more radical position that abandons *all* criteria of judgment and reference of language. He argues that "this conflation" between words and facts, which make us think of a *truth* that is out there and independent of language,

> is facilitated by confining attention to single sentences as opposed to vocabularies. For we often let the world decide the competition between alternative sentences ... e.g., between "Red wins" and "Black wins." ... But it is not so easy when we turn from individual sentences to vocabularies as wholes. When we consider examples of alternative language games—the vocabulary of ancient Athenian politics versus Jefferson's, the moral vocabulary of Saint Paul versus Freud's, the jargon of Newton versus that of Aristotle, the idiom of Blake versus that of Dryden—it is difficult to think of the world as making one of these better than another, of the world as deciding between them.[63]

From this Rorty concludes that there is *no means* to decide between them. But why can we make only a *random* choice—or a choice imposed by the force of domination when a decision must be made? Rorty offers two reasons: (1) language systems as a whole do not have "reference to something exterior to the network";[64] and (2) "notions of criteria and choice (including that of "arbitrary choice") are no longer in point when it comes to changes from one language game to another."[65] In sum, no one can offer arguments (including Rorty, who is "not going to offer arguments against the vocabulary I want to replace"[66]) or produce reasons.

Rorty already prejudices the case with the first reason. Of course a language system *as a whole* does not have an external referent. But this is hardly the issue (or at least it should not be for a pragmatist such as

Rorty). No one speaks a *whole* language system. Even the "rules" of a language game develop through particular instances. We speak and think in particular aspects of language, preeminently in sentences. Now even Rorty does not deny that sentences refer to *something* outside themselves, and even outside the linguistic system as a whole. Sentences make meaning.[67] Rorty's universe of a "language system" is an abstraction every bit as empty as the notion of universal truth.

Sentences, unlike "language as a whole," can be compared, and can even be spoken across languages. Otherwise, how are translation and interpretation possible?[68] How can we become multilingual? How could Freud have translated Greek myth and the Pauline-Augustinian discourse of the will into the new idiom of psychoanalysis? How could the discourse of human dignity have been detached from the discourse of male dignity alone? And how can Western notions of Being and Eastern notions of nonbeing even be understood across "language games," let alone begin to be dealt with constructively? The answer is that no *entire* language is ever in play simultaneously, but only sentences and complexes of sentences with referents that can be discussed, so that the world may or may not give us better and worse reasons to believe. To be sure, the partiality of linguistic play also produces the possibility for misunderstanding. But misunderstanding is possible only as a misunderstanding of *something*, which does imply that there is something there to *be* (mis-)understood. To assert that a language system *as a whole* lacks reference is as tautological as it is irrelevant.

Language, Truth, and Change

This brings us to the question of the possibility of change in language. Rorty asserts that change occurs "no more [as] an act of will than . . . [as] a result of argument." To take a few of his examples, "Europe did not *decide* to accept the idiom of Romantic poetry, or of socialist politics, or of Galilean mechanics. . . . Rather, Europe gradually lost the habit of using certain words and gradually acquired the habit of using others."[69] In a minimal sense—that a good deal of linguistic alteration goes on behind our backs even as it emerges from our lips—this is likely true.[70] We do not and cannot reflect on every utterance used in any particular culture. But to say that Rorty's sweeping claim is overgeneralized is a mild rebuke indeed, especially against one who protests so grandly against universal generalizations. Is it really the case that we acquire new linguistic habits for *no* apparent reason? In some instances, perhaps. But the Romantics themselves, the socialists and their adherents, and Galileo had *reasons* for speaking as they did, and tried to *persuade others* that their new idiom was *more descriptive* and *more creative* than then-current "habits" of language. Europe may not have decided, *but Europeans did*. The criteria for those decisions were the successes of their *references* to the cosmos, political life, linguistic and nonlinguistic experience, and so on. Even those who adopted the new habits without deep reflection found something advantageous in the new vocabulary. It is marvelously glib—and strikingly unhistorical—to suggest that change in vocabularies and idioms occurred without arguments pro and con.[71] Rorty's emphasis on language as a whole—along with his corresponding inattention to particular deployments of speech—drives him to a historically insupportable conclusion. Because he begins with universality, Rorty does not see that new vocabularies did *not* contest the language game as a whole, but substantial *parts* of linguistic referents; and he is blind to the palpable fact that arguments about referents were involved. The arguments may or may not have been correct, and there may have been many other factors involved in the change. But that conclusion would require counterargument, not mere dismissal.

Postmodernism in its Rortian guise fancies itself utterly independent of all predecessors. For just that reason (as we have seen in its conception of truth), it is the most parasitic upon them. Just as "universal" has a referent that cannot be incorporated into language itself, so it is with "language as a whole." If we abandon the deceptive, abstract demand that truth be "universal" and that we have a timelessly valid understanding of language as a whole before *any* argument is acceptable, we are freed to defend, create, and challenge particular truths. Now that would really be "historical all the way through."[72] Nor does this exclude ontology, as some varieties of postmodernism assume. Rather, *ontology itself becomes historical*, freed from the burden of having to find "timeless" truths in history.[73]

This historical turn allows us to discuss "human nature" and all the traditional categories of ontology as historical categories. Claims about "deep human nature," anathema to some postmodernists, are not dogmatic assertions but *interpretations* of available evidence. For example, "sin" is a fruitful symbolic description of the corruption of human life as we have experienced it down to the present, and we have no reason to believe that the evidence on which it is based will require us to abandon the symbol in the near future. To be sure, "sin" is not the only appropriate symbol of human distortion, and its content varies across time and space (as feminist and liberation theologies rightly argue). Moreover, as with all historical religious symbols, we have good reason to think that its content is not adequately expressed, and that the symbol itself might well be distorted in many of its manifestations. But these are precisely the points at which particular arguments are likely to occur, both within and between religious and nonreligious traditions. Theological argument, we suggested in the first chapter, is subject to the same strictures as other arguments. At their best, theological symbols are both malleable and firm, concretely relative and related, incorporating new content within themselves even as they transform it along with themselves. At their worst, they become timeless and ossified, utterly detached from history—or merely current, which is just a different way of being utterly detached from history. Religious and nonreligious arguments alike must engage (not mimic) current symbolic expressions in order to extend their comprehensiveness and self-transcendence. In short, the demand is that religious symbols become more religious.

Two Criteria of Emphatic Pluralism

Vacuous pluralism has no criteria by which to judge difference. Difference is just there. This unwillingness embraces both a powerful truth and a destructive delusion. Building on this insight, emphatic pluralism can offer an account of pluralism which is simultaneously more coherent and less dangerous. This, in turn, yields at least two formal criteria of an emphatic pluralism.

We begin with the observation that, irrespective of any commitment to plurality, all decisions are exclusive by nature. That is, they exclude some things and choose others. That includes the decision to take pluralism seriously or not, and all decisions subsequent to that. The truth of the vacuous center and its twin, indifferent pluralism, lies in their recognition that all action is nonplural in some way. But their delusion is to think that inaction is not also a decision. We ignore both the truth and the delusion only at our own peril. As an ideology of mere tolerance, vacuous pluralism correctly recognizes that any discursive process is curtailed (if not destroyed) by the power of decision and action. The root of "decision" is *decidere*, "to cut off." Vacuous pluralism's mistake is to fancy that it can avoid such "cutting off" by perpetuating the plural discursive process. Extradiscursive action may be postponed for a time but not indefinitely, if conditions outside the conversation are to be altered.

It is beside the point to regret the sharp difference between pluralist procedure and exclusive decisions; within history, the difference is inevitable. It is given to us with our humanity and historicity. To abandon symbols and actions simply because they are not complete is another flawed legacy of the demand that truth be absolute and unalterable. Vacuous pluralism is unable to relate plurality to decision because it views them as unreconciled and irreconcilable enemies. But if we accept the particularity of truth and embrace power as a communication of efficacy, we cannot fail to embrace the need for decision and nondiscursive action.

This yields the first criterion of an emphatic pluralism: plural processes and conversations should have a *telos*, a goal of power. The processes must, at some point, issue in communications of efficacy. Conversation should and must lead to decision and nondiscursive action—the conversation should have a point.[74] Decisions *must* and *will* be made, options must and will be cut off even as others are opened, and all decisions are "absolute" in the sense of absolutely cutting off certain other options. The decision not to act still cuts off some possibilities and opens others. A decision to go to war, to engage in civil disobedience, to have a child, or to lower taxes, is irreversible in that one will never have the option to unmake *this particular decision* about *this particular act or child or tax* at *this particular time* again. Such is the logic of historical decision.[75] We should choose a course based on which route is likely to produce the greatest power in a particular instance. Inevitably, however, we choose some course.

This quickly leads us to the second formal criterion: it is the task of emphatic pluralism, as far as it can, *to retain plural processes* as the environment in which these absolute decisions are made. Power as communication of efficacy cannot sacrifice plurality. That does not alter the absolute character of decision, to be sure. But as a *communication* of efficacy, power *requires* plurality.[76] This means that whatever is chosen in a concrete instance—plural process or singular decision—should be directed to preserving the possibility of the other. If vacuous pluralism is a pluralism of indifferent neglect, emphatic pluralism must be powerfully plural, including the recognition and preservation of the other.[77] Thus should singular decision seek to retain the possibility of plural processes. This will usually mean that even as one decision cuts off debate and dialogue, steps are taken to ensure that no one is cut off from conversation about future decisions. Thus nonviolent action is preferable to violence, inclusive processes to exclusive, equal access to inequality, and so on. These are matters of basic justice for a theology of power.

In other words, *power is more basic than plurality.* Emphatic pluralism values plurality for the sake of power as communication of efficacy, not for the sake of freedom and difference themselves. Both plurality and singularity are required. This in no way reduces the intrinsic conflict between them. They remain conflicting demands, and choices for one over the other must be worked out on a case-by-case basis. Neither plural conversation nor singular nondiscursive action is privileged in principle. Both are essential to processes of power. We consider several such specific relations and issues in the next chapter.

Varieties of Difference: The Material of Emphatic Pluralism

These formal criteria—preserving plural processes and conversations while making singular and nondiscursive decisions—should be examined with respect to the expanse of material affected by pluralism. In contemporary America (to say nothing of American dealings with foreign cultures), plurality is vast, seemingly infinite. It is so wide that we must confine ourselves here to only one sector of society, institutional religions. That will be more than enough, and even if we could exhaust it, that would still leave the question of noninstitutional religions, to say nothing of other ultimate perspectives such as various ideologies and worldviews. Even within our limited example, however, the plethora of material is simply unmanageable if one requires anything like a complete view.[78]

Our question, then, will be how pluralistic overload can be managed without retreat to cultural ghettos. We discuss five related manifestations of institutional religious pluralism: (1) pluralism within major traditions, (2) within subtraditions, (3) between historical periods, (4) in the interpretation of symbols, and (5) between different traditions.

1. Each religious tradition contains within itself a plethora of positions, only some of which are in play at any given time. Thus, even within a tradition, emphatic pluralism plays itself out along a number of axes. First, emphatic pluralism must be pluralistic with respect to existing subtraditions. In Christianity, this includes both denominational subtraditions and extradenominational ones. In denominational subtraditions, theological interpretations of person, society, politics, nature, and the sacred vary considerably between classical Protestant, Roman Catholic, Orthodox, and American evangelical traditions.

2. Moreover, every subtradition has its own internal variations of doctrine, social location, historical time, and so on. Robert Wuthnow and James Davison Hunter point to a major shift in the pattern of traditional denominational disputes in America.[79] The older division, found (for example) in Will Herberg's *Protestant, Catholic, Jew* no longer describes our situation.[80] Hunter argues that "in the wake of the fading Judeo-Christian consensus has come a rudimentary *realignment* of pluralistic diversity. The 'organizing principle' of American pluralism has altered fundamentally such that the major rift is no longer born out of theological or doctrinal disagreements—as between Protestants and Catholics or Christians and Jews."[81] Therefore, "However deep the theological and ideological divisions were *within* each faith community between the 1880s and the 1960s, they were never more consequential than the ideological divisions that still existed *between* faith communities."[82] Now, however, especially with the reduction of religion to morality, disputes within traditions and subtraditions are at least as fractious as those between them. Moreover, these differences are international as well as national. Catholic and Protestant liberation theologians in Central and South America often have more in common with one another than with their own ecclesiastical brothers and sisters in the first world. Thus pluralism also encompasses the plurality within subtraditions themselves.

3. In addition to questions of breadth, there are also diversities of historical depth. Within each tradition and subtradition, a wealth of

historical material and thought is available for critical retrieval. Moreover, the historical traditions often constitute a greater challenge—and therefore greater possibilities for transformation—to present thought and action than a multiculturalism restricted to the present. Thus, despite whatever divergences and oppositions there may be, contemporary North American religion is largely united on the meaning and importance of "freedom." Historical Christian traditions were much more ambivalent about the subject. *True* diversity will embrace this past diversity as well as present. From Augustine through Thomas Aquinas, Luther, Calvin, and Jonathan Edwards, "freedom" was a deeply problematic construct; "authority" of one kind or another was less troubling than it is for most Americans; and questions of guilt, sin, and grace held greater influence than in virtually every current American Christian theology. Emphatic pluralism *cannot* restrict itself to the present; it must equally attend to the ways in which the past challenges the present, and the ways in which reappropriation of the storehouse of traditions might enliven a more powerful future. In other words, where multiculturalism insists that one must begin *here,* where she is culturally, emphatic pluralism also insists that one must also begin with where she is *now.*[53] But that is not where we should stay! We must confront other *cultures* and other *times.*

4. A related question is the multivalence of symbolic interpretation. One boon of African American, feminist, Latin American, South African, and Asian theologies (again restricting ourselves only to Christianity) is that they have emphasized the *specific contexts* in which theology and action are undertaken. That is not a deficiency. It surely is a limit, but every theology is so limited. Every theological symbol, as well as every theological claim, is particular; and particularity is equally the ground of each symbol's power. The question is whether the context is acknowledged (as in most liberation theologies) or concealed (as in Rortian postmodernism). Polyvalence is both the great benefit and the manifest frustration of theological symbols. Many symbols—and certainly Christian symbols and doctrines taken as a whole—are multivalent, applicable to any number of dimensions of human life (inner life or outer life, psychological, social, or political) and are interpretable with respect to all being (witness the new reflections on the meanings of theological symbols for treating environmental ethics). The question is whether such

multivalence is fruitful, and that case must be made in specific instances.

5. Up to now, we have discussed pluralism *within* historically identifiable institutional traditions. This is usually not the arena that comes to mind in discussions of "pluralism." It more commonly refers to heterogeneous traditions. The structural problem, however, is identical. Despite efforts to be comprehensive, every major tradition is particular. Moreover, different religious traditions emphasize different aspects of the divine relation to the world, and thereby also change certain aspects of the world they inhabit. And those alterations and interpretations are expressed through heterogeneous symbols, which may or may not overlap in content with symbols of other traditions. Buddhist discussions of compassion may overlap with Christian discussions of love and grace; Christian complicity in Nazism may parallel Buddhist complicity in Japanese imperialism;[84] Jewish insistence on justice may correct Christian sentimentality; and Hindu or Islamic cosmology may be challenged by astrophysics.

It may seem that, in principle, the material which emphatic pluralism—whether Christian or not—must confront is limitless. That is true, and worth keeping in the forefront of attention. But this also presents a temptation to lapse back into the vacuous pluralism of indifference in the face of too much material, too many differences— the sin of sloth. Or it can just as easily slip into intolerance and domination when decision for power can be postponed no longer. Emphatic pluralism takes another way. It recognizes the partiality of decisions with respect to both their finiteness and situation. In view of the almost limitless material with which it must deal, however, the question is how to make pluralism practical without retreating into either vacuous pluralism or cultural nativism. It is to this question that we now turn.

TWO MOMENTS OF EMPHATIC PLURALISM

1. The Commitment to Difference: Religious Pluralism and Secularity

MERE TOLERANCE

Emphatic pluralism's commitment to difference preserves the plurality of processes, and in this way retains the truth of vacuous pluralism. There are, however, several ways of understanding this commitment. Vacuous pluralism, we maintained, is unable to offer any reason why pluralism is valuable. Sometimes pluralism is presented as an intrinsic good, to be desired for its own sake, like health or knowledge. Among the many perilous absurdities to which this leads is the conclusion that if *some* pluralism is good, *more* would be better. We would then have to attempt to increase diversity as much as possible, regardless of its impact on anything else.[85] According to this view, there is no need to identify just what it is that makes particular differences desirable. Just as the culture of freedom turns the "right to speak" into right itself, and secularism is held to be necessary in order to preserve rights and different realizations of private ends, so most discussions of pluralism emphasize the need for "tolerance." This is no mistake. Tolerance is necessary in order that options may speak, for without conversation there is no communication of efficacy, and no power. Most discussions of pluralism, however, stop here, assuming that tolerance is the final desideratum of pluralism.[86]

Why, one might ask, is it necessary or helpful that plural options are expressed? This remains an open question, and "freedom" does not constitute a sufficient answer. True, tolerance promotes a certain desirable civility, but it is a civility of indifference. Moreover, such civility insulates our worldviews from serious criticism; any objection to our way of understanding or acting within the world can be dismissed with the charge that our interlocutor is being intolerant. "Live and let live" usually means that life continues just the same; it rarely means "live better and help to live better." Moreover, the very plurality that tolerance seeks turns into indifferent homogeneity.[87] Mere tolerance is not especially committed to anything, and it is certainly not committed to difference. Rather, it is committed to more of the same, as long as it is "my same" or that of my group.

BEYOND TOLERANCE: A COMMITMENT TO DIFFERENCE

Emphatic pluralism transcends mere tolerance. This is so for several interrelated reasons: power's intrinsic plurality, the finitude of all historical endeavor, and the distortions of life (described in the symbol of sin). No finite religion will be sufficiently comprehensive or self-transcendent to accomplish what religion intends—an interpretation of ultimacy that includes all penultimate concerns in a proper order and relation to the ultimate and to one another. We have already discussed how finitude, history, and distortion prevent any religion from achieving this goal. When any finite entity is grasped and held as if it did fully and adequately express the divine and all its relations, finitude is distorted into sin, as Reinhold Niebuhr and Paul Tillich argued persuasively. Religions are not only finite, they are distorted. They do not merely "fall short of the glory of God," as if their symbols and adherents were merely not God. Rather, as Paul makes clear, humans also pretend to be gods, violating the glory of God and wounding one another in the process. Sin perverts the glory of God and the divine creation. This provides us with another reason *why* power must be plural rather than singular. When power is understood and executed without plural and mutual communication, it becomes distorted into mere domination.

Nor is "tolerance" a sufficient end for power. Whereas mere tolerance allows each religion and worldview to maintain itself (at least so long as there are no issues that must be decided), power requires that every religion point beyond itself, and become more comprehensive and self-transcendent. The challenge of power beyond domination requires religions to reach beyond themselves vertically and horizontally. Both directions are important. Religion cannot point only to *God* and not also to the *world,* as if divine omnipotence were not also present to and for the world. Reference to God alone, without the world, is arbitrary and self-indulgent. The deistic conception of God as a mere observer who watches the world as we watch TV's *Days of Our Lives* is a peculiarly modern construct. No classical theology, to our knowledge, ever contemplated such an utter dualism between heaven and earth. Nor can religion point only to the world, nor to human experience (nor to any single group's putative "experience"); transcendence requires transcendence both of the self and the self's group (even if that group is the church, Israel, women, one's country, or the Sangha).

Power and plurality are not easy demands for Christian theology or other interpretations of ultimacy. Most of us want desperately to find the fulcrum of truth that stands beyond the risks of history and power. So, certain symbols or doctrines (whether "religious" or "secular") become enshrined, not as what points to the divine now, but as permanent truth. That can deprive religions of genuine mediations of the divine; freeze symbols, doctrines, and truths in time; and dismiss or dominate all that stands outside them. Such fanatical devotion to the infinite truth of finite claims is truly religious in its subjective dimension, but is antireligious referentially, sacrificing the reference of religions to the divine, eliminating claims to comprehensiveness, and destroying the self-transcendence that is part of the real claim of a religion to be truly religious.

Christianity and Christians are hardly guiltless in this respect, nor would we expect them to be. But Christianity is in a position to see this error more clearly than it has. It is a commonplace to say that Christianity is a "historical religion." That is usually presented as a fact, but is really a *challenge*. No less, but probably no more, than other interpretations of ultimacy (including secular ones, as we saw in the case of many liberalisms), Christianity attempts to stop history in its tracks, and in its own favor. The list of claims that Christianity has attempted to exempt from the alterations of history is a long one. It includes apolitical interpretations of "Give unto Caesar what is Caesar's"; Paul's tepid objection to slavery; anti-Judaism (which became assimilated to anti-Semitism); the ideology of self-sacrifice; the authority of the church in Roman Catholicism; and the absence of church authority in Protestantism. The list also includes more productive (but still not absolute) maxims such as "Give all you have to the poor."

It is time for Christians and Christianity to face seriously this alternative: either Christianity is a historical religion or it is not. If it is, then it must recognize that to be in history is to struggle to articulate a vision of the future on the basis of the resources of the past and the present, and that none of those resources possesses an infinite value, exempt from the vicissitudes of historical change. There is no accurate statement of the everywhere-identical "foundations of what Christian doctrine has been throughout the centuries," as Wolfhart Pannenberg asserts.[88] Or, on the other hand, Christians could give up the claim that their religion is historical: then maybe they could have settled conclusions, and enjoy a measure of security. But the price is high. They would have to give up (to begin with) the claim that Jesus' humanity has anything to do with redemption, or the claim that Jesus was fully human. Moreover, they would have to abandon monotheism in several important respects: giving up the God of history, power, justice, and love in time; deifying themselves or a particular tradition; and making the finite infinite. All these are invitations to reduplicate religions' worst abuses of its neighbors, the abuses which secularism arose to fight (even as it added new ones of its own making).

The particularity of truth requires that emphatic pluralism place a high value on plurality. The tendency to privilege one's own tradition is natural and not necessarily wrong. However, in view of the finitude of all historical formulations, our own finitude, and the distortions of life to which the symbol of sin points, *every tradition* loses all *a priori* claims of universal privilege. Moreover, those distortions and limitations are more likely to be pointed out by those who are not adherents of that tradition. Purely internal self-criticism, although vitally important, remains limited to the worldview of the tradition from whence it comes. To be in a plural situation is to have the privilege of having one's own pretensions and blind spots checked, modified, and sometimes overcome by others. And those are the tasks of religions that seek to worship that which should truly be the object of our ultimate devotion and worship.

Emphatic pluralism's commitment is to difference, not indifference. What is valuable about pluralism is not mere plurality or freedom. Instead, difference must be retained and fostered so that all parties may be *transformed* and begin to be redeemed from their limitations and distortions. This commitment to difference is a genuine relativism—relatedness—that seeks deeper and broader power through mutual transformation. In short, emphatic pluralists avail themselves of the discernment of others—in principle, of all others whom we confront. To the extent that we fail to do so, we fail in the religious tasks of comprehensiveness and self-transcendence.

Managing Plurality

The position of Americans, in a land with so much internal diversity, and with extensive contacts with other world cultures, is in some respects enviable. American diversity makes plurality functionally unavoidable for most. The variety of different roles into which most Americans enter, the cross-pollination of influences that most already experience regularly, means that the *question* of plurality is largely ephemeral. In some sense, as Don Browning perceptively notes, most of us are internally multicultural, having received, incorporated, and expressed a variety of formerly distinct cultural strains.[89] In other words, we are more successful pluralists than we think. Even leaving aside the cultural amalgams present everywhere from popular culture (in music, especially) to high modern and postmodern art, who has not been exposed, at some level, to African American, Hispanic, European, and Asian cultures, whether artistically, socially, or politically? Who has not had to confront, in some way, the plethora of claims of ultimacy, whether arising from Christianity, Judaism, Buddhism, Islam, science, philosophies, and so on? The task of emphatic pluralism is to synthesize these contacts by taking them more seriously than mere curiosity about difference and the vacuous pluralism of mere tolerance are able. The latter type underutilizes the transformative capacities endemic to American plurality.[90]

Still, the seemingly unlimited nature of the task is daunting. It must, of course, remain so if we are not to slip back into the comfortable illusion that this is a universal truth that is the possession of a particular tradition or person. Luther's spiritual use of the law that "reveals and teaches how to recognize sin" so that the "conscience is alarmed and humbled"[91] is no less appropriate for intellectual matters than for moral ones. There remains, though, the question of how this expansive plurality can be managed.

First, we repeat: *we already do manage it to a significant degree.* There is no reason to suspect that we cannot successfully extend those accomplishments. Second, although the material of emphatic pluralism is limitless in principle, there are nevertheless *practical* limits. All aspects of even one's own traditions are not equally relevant at all times and across all concerns. The end of dreams of universal, permanently valid philosophies and theologies also liberates us from the burden of having to master all possible alternatives before we speak. To be sure, it is important to know the limitations of one's investigations, and to listen attentively and critically to those who have greater expertise. But it is not incumbent upon anyone or any tradition to have a full grasp of everything. Moreover, because the purpose of emphatic pluralism is to generate *power*, it presupposes the incompleteness of all participants in the processes of debate and decision. Our continuing bondage to the idea of "universal" truth sets the entrance requirements for responsible public debate at impossibly high levels.

Third, there is a difference between simply interacting with the symbolic thought-world and act-world of another tradition and constructive engagement with that world as a whole, in its most profound and comprehensive sense. Although the second is a deeper and more meaningful encounter, it is not the only one; and there are limits to just how many such encounters one can have in a lifetime. One cannot always be stopping to consider whether Taoism or Judaism is the "right" approach to reality. Otherwise, nothing will get done. Whether emphatic pluralists will be fully "converted" to conceive of what is ultimately meaningful and worthy of devotion in terms quite different from their own traditions is somewhat beside the point. Not that conversion is undesirable, provided that it is clear that all options remain particular, but neither is it necessary. Even in so plural a society as America, we have such deep engagements relatively infrequently. Only a few options are "live hypotheses" for any individual.[92] It is *not* that emphatic Christians must become Buddhists, Taoists, Republicans, naturalists, or Jews; it *is* that they must be open to transformation as they interact with those traditions. To view "conversion" as the primary end of mutual transformation expects too much. We can and do employ special symbols of many cultural, religious, and political traditions even if the world from which they come is not, as a relatively comprehensive picture, a live hypothesis. Even when it is not a real option to exchange one religion for another—in other words, in the vast majority of cases—it is still possible to have one's own ultimate commitments transformed through a confrontation with others, and to seek to transform others, without anyone being "converted" to a different religious faith.[93] History is replete with examples.[94]

INCOMMENSURABILITY?

At a quite practical level, the extent of plurality is not typically unmanageable; in fact, we negotiate pluralism fairly well fairly often. What prevents us from seeing the extent to which we actually deal with plurality are the intellectual assumptions of monoculturalists, vacuous pluralists, and ideological pluralists. Our bondage to these views impedes transformative pluralism. Mutual transformation remains impossible so long as we are under the sway of the solipsistic assumption that worldviews are "incommensurable." The belief (actually a dogma) that worldviews and religions are incommensurable is much like discussions of universal truth—we ask too much, and when our unrealistic expectations are disappointed, give up too early. No one puts forth an entire worldview at once; no one could or need do so. Even ultimate religious commitments are expressed through particular claims and symbols, which are united with and adjusted to other claims and symbols. It is true that every particular claim and symbol implies a comprehensive perspective, as Tillich and Franklin Gamwell argue.[95] However, each expression is inevitably fragmentary, and indeed, because of the character of history and human distortion, entire worldviews are also fragments, albeit large ones.[96]

When we understand worldviews and religions as fragmentary, always obligated to move toward (and yet never achieve) greater comprehensiveness and self-transcendence,[97] our expectations change. We no longer demand that others (or ourselves) make the totality of their worldviews comprehensible; but we can (and must) expect that we (and others) can make important parts of these worldviews understandable.[98] Although it may turn out that certain claims are incommensurable with others for now, that judgment must be made *a posteriori*, not *a priori*. To make that judgment *a priori* quickly leads back to the antirelativism that is always in danger of becoming practical absolutism. If, however, incommensurability is not assumed, then all symbols and doctrines are put into potential relation to all others. That relation can take any number of forms: from the intensification of already existent symbols, to the diminution of others in a quest for a more comprehensive balance of symbols and doctrines, to the introduction of new content into particular symbols (the latter of which is particularly likely in encounters with symbols of other traditions and subtraditions).

These transformative strategies, which actually entertain arguments about the value of certain symbols, doctrines, and practices, distinguish emphatic Christian pluralism from Rawls's notion of "overlapping consensus." For Rawls, legitimate public debate is bounded by an overlapping consensus in a pluralistic world. The overlapping consensus constitutes the range of "public reason," and therefore gives a moral duty to each citizen to engage in political discourse and all coercion *only* on grounds that conform to this overlapping consensus.[99] Public reason, it turns out, *is* the overlapping consensus.[100] Therefore, legitimate public debate is morally bounded by its participants, who are supposed to agree not to step outside the bounds of principles that all can endorse,[101] regardless of their "rights." We have already criticized this notion as both conservative and, despite its own intentions, less able to preserve or advance social stability than emphatic pluralism. In emphatic pluralism, it is not only the overlapping consensus that is the legitimate subject of public debate, but also that which stands *outside* the consensus. The defenders of political liberalism need to *engage* the arguments of antiliberal positions instead of sanctimoniously charging nonliberals with immorality *de jure*. Not only is there no moral duty to limit debate to what falls within the overlapping consensus, it is more productive not to impose that limit.

This is not to say that all positions will actually be in play simultaneously. That would be absurd. It is seldom necessary to introduce the entire rationale for particular positions, even if they do presuppose one. There should rather be a principle of parsimony in debate. One should introduce only what is necessary for the particular purpose at hand. In fact, this is what most debaters actually try to do. However, the scope of such discussions changes frequently and forces parties to reveal assumptions and positions that stand behind the particulars. Each particular debate is a thread of a larger fabric, and one may need to follow the thread into its broader context. There is no reason arbitrarily to forbid discussants from following these threads when they lead outside the boundaries of a supposed "public reason."

Our point here is not about stability, but change. Rawls's overlapping consensus is fragile precisely because frozen in time; it is a historically derived conception become ahistorical. If, however, elements beyond the presently existing consensus are subject to public discussion, it becomes possible to change that consensus in order to generate more power for all. There is, of course, no guarantee that the effect will be an increase in power; that is the chance vitality in history always takes.[102] There is, however, evidence that power does increase through such means, and there is good reason to suppose that, in a relatively stable society, these possibilities are not exhausted. We have already made use of several such possibilities in developing the emphatic Christian center, bringing several themes of historical Christian theology into a creative and critical juxtaposition with contemporary American politics and religion in a way that has transformed all three (as well as both authors). A critical review of some of these syntheses will illustrate and develop this point further.

First, our criticism of the unexamined united front with respect to the

North American religion of freedom stemmed from our previous knowledge and study of the Christian tradition's historical diversity. We would have gotten nowhere had we been content to remain with the facile claim that the past was different, or that everyone does not share Christian convictions. So what? Both statements are equally true, and equally irrelevant. If all "differences" were absolute, it would be impossible to read or speak a single sentence. But difference does not imply absolute heterogeneity or incommensurability; differences are usually more or less, not absolute. That sentences and positions of the past make any sense at all indicates that they are not utterly heterogeneous and can meaningfully challenge present understandings. Nor, on the other hand, will it do simply to import past conceptions into current American culture, while ignoring tendencies toward authoritarianism—this we have learned from the sorry story of Christian (and other) attempts to dominate and eliminate rival worldviews, a story better told by non-Christians than Christians. Rather, what is required is critical appropriation of traditions which abandons neither present nor past but instead confronts each with the other—and both with the future. If our criticism of the American conception of freedom is persuasive, it is concrete evidence of power's ability to emerge through encounter with difference.

Although our argument against mere freedom was born of "religious conviction" (to use Kent Greenawalt's language), it did *not* posit conclusions arbitrarily. It proceeded by means of arguments that were in no respect different from those of supposedly "nonreligious" positions. Indeed, we identified how American culture's basic commitment to a particular understanding of "freedom" is no less religious for being "secular." In addition, our criticism of liberalism was not merely polemical; we incorporated liberal insights regarding the dangers of religion even as we did not accept them *in toto*. We shall soon do the same in agreeing upon the need for the formally secular state.

A similar transformation has happened in our appropriation of the symbol of sin. In the Christian tradition, emphasis has been given variously to the seven deadly sins in combination, or to one of them in particular. In Protestant circles, selfishness as the form of pride has been prominent. We have supplemented this with Karl Barth's understanding of sin as sloth. In recent years, arguments that violence is the primal and most significant sin are heard increasingly from feminists such as Marjorie Suchocki as well as René Girard and his followers.[103] But it is not clear that these quite different understandings are "incommensurable" in any significant sense. And if violence is to be understood as a core manifestation of sin, might not the advocates of this view be obliged—even want—to determine how their claims are related to interpretations of sin emphasizing selfishness or the "seven deadly sins"? There is much to be gained by analyzing the ways in which violence does and does not flow from and create "pride," self-interest, and the like.

Such analysis will raise several questions: Is violence always sin? If it is, is nonviolence always the most virtuous answer? What *is* violence? What makes it wrong? What, exactly, does it violate?[104] The answers, in turn, will have marked effects on the conception of proper virtue. The same is true of *agape*, sometimes defined as self-sacrificial love,[105] a notion crucial to Reformation conceptions of virtue but now under considerable fire. If pride is not, as many feminist thinkers[106] have argued, the chief sin of most women (although it may be for many men), then agapic love will not be the universal virtue that Anders Nygren and Glenn Tinder, among others, claim.[107] Liberation theologies, for their part, identify injustice as the chief evil of our time and justice as the chief virtue. Or one may question, as in the "creation spirituality" of Matthew Fox,[108] whether the symbol of the "fall" is necessary or even productive. We have insisted that it is—but not by claiming that our views are "incommensurable" or "different." Evidence for the universal distortion of human existence is far stronger than any for the innocence or unambiguous growth of humanity assumed in progressive philosophies of history, whether they claim to be religious theories of history or not. But it is hard to see what is gained—except self-indulgence—by assuming that these perspectives, to say nothing of secular understandings of evil, are incommensurable.

Our examples so far have been intra-Christian. But there is no good reason to stop there, and many reasons not to. Buddhist and Hindu conceptions of human distortion as arising from *avidya* (ignorance) partly overlap the Christian symbol of sin, but also constitute a challenge to Protestant understandings of sin, especially when the latter maintain that sin emerges only from the will and not also from the moral quality of ignorance. In this respect, the Catholic emphasis on responsibility for ignorance also challenges any attempt to construe sin exclusively as a matter of the will.[109] Moreover, there is also no need to restrict our understanding of these symbols to institutional religions. Philosophy, sociology, political thought, the sciences, and aesthetics are always in play in theology simply because believers also participate in their wider culture.[110] It is not only natural but necessary that religious conceptions and actions respond to the cultures in which they find themselves as they seek to transform—and to be transformed by—those cultures.

In all these instances, emphatic pluralism is obliged to argue its own particular positions in relation to others. Each party assumes the burden to argue for its own particular understandings on the basis of evidence, and argues against or synthesizes other particular truths in relation to its own. Rarely does one find one's own prior conceptions unaltered, unless one has made the *a priori* assumption of incommensurability.[111]

Emphatic pluralism's overlapping consensus insists on argument. Therefore, just as it does not assume incommensurability, neither can it reduce all conceptions to the lowest common—and often trivial—denominator upon which all agree. Rather, it generates debate and provides confidence for judgment and decision for particular truths at particular times through the fires of a stringent commitment to creating or discovering *what is most true and powerful for us now*. Decisions are not arbitrary; nor are they universally and permanently valid. Liberal attempts to insulate liberalism itself from debate are misguided. It is *not* immoral to call that consensus into question or introduce what is outside the current consensus in order to alter its structure and content. What is not part of an overlapping consensus is as important to public discussion in a relatively stable society as what is; and what is outside the consensus may be more likely to explode the longer we summarily dismiss it from public debate. Nonliberal options *may* indeed be immoral, but that must be argued, not piously declared.

What *is* immoral is to exempt one's own positions from argument, as if one had a unique privilege not conferred upon anyone else, and as if that privilege were the only one that mattered.[112] These assertions of privilege, we argued, are sinful. The summary charge that nonliberals are immoral simply because they are not liberal is a fine example. Liberalism's morality becomes immune from criticism, which is particularly ironic in view of liberalism's reflexive disdain for religious authority. Of course, religion is often authoritarian as well. Liberal religion is often authoritarian in precisely the same way as political liberalism (declaring all nonliberal religion to be immoral, or at least backward). Meanwhile, many contemporary conservative Christian positions maintain, in effect, that they have the "right" to object to others' conceptions of political and moral life, but that an attack upon their own conceptions makes one "anti-Christian" and therefore an enemy of morality, as we saw in chapter 1. In a world in which truths are historical, particular, and subject to distortion, there is no such privilege—whether of tradition or revelation, religious or "secular." To be involved in *public* life is to assume its burdens and delights. None is excused from processes of history, discovery, creativity, and guilt, and if we attempt to exempt ourselves we are on the road to the distortion of power into domination.[113] Emphatic pluralism means that the religious task of self-transcendence is ongoing. Our aim is unity, not identity; amending the great Roman Catholic trinitarian formula of "unity in diversity," emphatic centrism seeks unity *through* diversity, not in spite of it.

SECULARITY AND EMPHATIC CHRISTIAN PLURALISM

Precisely because the religious task is historical, the emphatic Christian center must defend secularity. In America, secularity has largely been the good fortune of religions. Following Perry Miller, Sidney Mead argues that the secular state was embraced by Christians only negatively. Although "the original intention of the dominant and really powerful groups was to perpetuate the pattern of religious uniformity,"[114] none could succeed. Rather, "On the question of religious freedom for all, there were many shades of opinion . . . but all were practically unanimous on one point: each wanted freedom for itself. And . . . it had become clear that the only way to get it for themselves was to grant it to all others."[115] Not an auspicious beginning, but it turned out to be a case of evil being turned to good against the wishes of the denominations themselves.

The secular structure of the American state requires that each ultimate, religious commitment—and religions should require this of themselves—confront its own and others' particularity. Secularity does not demand, as secularism would have it, that those perspectives absent themselves from the public sphere. Christianity, under the pressure of a secular space in which countervailing claims are made, argued, and opposed, has had to come to grips with its own historical location, finitude, and (in moments of clearer insight) distortions. Any governmental structure which enthrones one ultimate perspective as perennially true stultifies that capacity. That is even the sociological discovery of the American experiment. Religion is more vital in America than in any other Western democracy, and that is because the American state, before all other Western democracies, chose not to sponsor religion, and finally showed enough flexibility not to enshrine some vague form of Christianity any more than it sponsored a special branch.[116]

What makes philosophical and theological sense of this social fact is the historical character of truth and the human proclivity to hold truths as absolute and unchangeable. Because they could not structurally accommodate the tendency to narrow the boundaries of truth to one special set of denominational or religious symbols, religions within American secularity had to rely on continuous processes of adjustment, argument, and transformation. Both the "conservative" antiprophets of a Christian state and "liberal" secularism want to stall or to reverse these processes; the emphatic Christian center amplifies them. The historical experience of America when compared with European state churches gives reason to believe that were we to become a "Christian America," Christianity would atrophy. In addition, it would expose itself to the substantial danger of state-sponsored churches, that is, becoming captive to the claims of the state. What government sponsorship gives, government can take away—either explicitly or by pressuring its beneficiaries to refrain from criticizing their governmental patron. In being given the "advantages" of state charter, religion lays itself open to manipulation where it must remain most unencumbered, in criticism of governmental policy. If we think that such a thing would not happen here, the recent attempt to destroy the Legal Services Corporation because it brought class action suits against government on behalf of the poor, instructs us otherwise.

Because of its secular structure, contemporary America is fertile soil for vitalizing Christianity through an emphatic Christian pluralism that subjects its own claims and practices to the scrutiny of others, and has the generosity to scrutinize others' claims and practices as well. The emphatic Christian center—indeed, American Christianity itself—requires *for its own vitality* emphatic Jewish, Hindu, Buddhist, Islamic, and humanist centers. Emphatic Christian pluralism is not merely polite or kind in insisting on this; it is also providing a necessity of its own life. As J. Glenn Gray hoped, power and gentleness can be complementary, not conflicting, attributes.[117]

Emphatic Christian centrism, therefore, supports a secular structure in which all are encouraged to participate in the public arena because secularity is the structure that best mediates the conflicting demands of the absolute decision and the plural process. The public arena is certainly a place to decide, to cut off debate and options in order to act nondiscursively. But the aim of secularity is to make decisions in such a way that the public square still can be enlivened by multiple worldviews, both "religious" and "nonreligious."

The overlapping consensus of emphatic pluralism is not merely a consensus about conclusions but also about the importance of processes of mutual transformation and power. Because the latter task is ongoing, the decisions that are made must be made with an eye toward maintaining power's future creativity. Secularity provides space for power to emerge. It participates in power because it keeps potentialities for power more available than a state that irrevocably commits to a single ultimate perspective. The secular public square need not be naked; it can be full. It becomes naked (1) when secularity becomes secularism, when we have nothing left to say to one another because we fear offending one another or—as likely—because we fear having our own cherished views challenged; or (2) if one party can enforce a claim that it and its adherents have superior privilege within it, thereby converting the public square into private property. Power requires plurality. A bustling, cacophonous, loving, rancorous, powerful public life requires a secularity in which all ultimate, comprehensive—religious—perspectives participate. It collapses when none participate, and becomes ripe for an invasion of a dominating single party that claims exclusive ownership of the public arena.[118]

2. Commitment Despite Difference: Strengthening the Center

NOT JUST COMMON GROUND

Commitment to difference runs the risk of lapsing back into the vacuous pluralism of neglect. Tolerance and appreciation of difference can never be infinite. Intellectual and practical decisions—which necessarily impose limits—must be made, even if plural processes are retained as much as possible in secular structures. Therefore, an emphatic pluralism, to be emphatic, must confront the problem of exclusion forthrightly. The alternatives are vacuous pluralism and practical absolutism.

Public life and institutions should serve and manifest power. In a relatively stable society, public institutions provide space in which power is most likely to emerge by maintaining their secularity. Vigilant secularity guards against any single religious perspective gaining unfettered institutional dominance. Secularity, properly distinguished from secularism, serves power by maintaining plural processes beyond particular commitments and decisions. But secularity only provides *favorable conditions* for power to emerge. It *does not* and *cannot* produce power directly because it lacks content. And when secularity becomes secularism—when the religious, ultimate concern is the prohibition of content (as in the American religion of freedom)—it sacrifices the very power that secularity attempts to foster. Secularity promotes participation, not disengagement; secularism does the reverse.

In other words, the more particular religious options are discouraged or precluded from participation in public life, the more that secularity's gain becomes loss. There may certainly be good reason for institutional restrictions on certain religious activities (a question beyond our scope), but there can be none with respect to public life as a whole. We have noted how some religious perspectives seek to exclude others—both secularist versions of liberalism or Christian attempts to make America into a Christian nation. Vacuous pluralism, on the other hand, thinks it can make no true claims, since they would have to be particular, not "inclusive." Or, it may seek peace at all costs. Some early ecumenical and interreligious discussions exemplified the latter approach, seeking "common ground," even if it turned out to be an empty lot.[119] Such attempts were (and in some cases, remain) unwilling to make arguments for truth from and through particular traditions.

NEGATION AND AFFIRMATION: THE PRINCIPLES REVISITED

Emphatic Christian centrism supports claims about the character of the world, the nature of public life, and the structures of contemporary culture. It deepens and extends the possibilities for particular power by deciding for some options and against others. They are particular, but that is no reason to reject or accept them. On the other hand, Christian centrism also seeks to extend the plurality that is essential to power and thereby to overcome the conflict of particular and plural power as far as possible. Taken as a group, the principles of the center—sin, appreciation, and power—contain both affirmative and negative moments, equally directed *both* to those whom Christians engage *and* to Christians themselves.[120]

Negation is most apparent in the symbols of *sin* and *original sin*. Original sin expresses an empirical claim: human existence is distorted and such distortion is not overcome in history, although its primary forms can and do change. Original sin is thus a pluralistic symbol that negates all claims to insularity because it expresses a truth about its *users* as well as others. Because Christian centrists are guilty of both moral and intellectual transgression, Christian centrism knows that other religions and cultures are indispensable to its own continuing reformation. Earlier we linked the symbol of original sin to an appreciation of the depth of others' political commitments; here we extend it to their religious and cultural commitments as well. It also means that all peoples and cultures are in need of justification, that is, *justice*. "Justification" means "making just," and this applies to personal, interpersonal, and political life. Although neither selves nor cultures can be entirely just within history, it is still possible for them to be more just. Thus, the negating impulse of the symbol of original sin provides two interrelated positive imperatives: plurality and justice.

Appreciation, the second principle, is a political expression of love and the most obviously affirmative of our principles. It, too, is intrinsically plural. Indeed, love is especially *not* care only for what is most like oneself. That sort of "love" is merely self-admiration. If love is not to descend into dominating solipsism and idolatry—which eventually rejects in the beloved just those qualities which do not resemble the self—it must be given to those who are really different from the self. "Love your enemies" is a particularly radical formulation of this point. Love is not gooey sentiment but includes a critical component as well. Love embraces negation as well as affirmation. Indeed, criticism is essential to love.[121] "Loving your enemies" may well require confronting them with their error and wrongdoing. Real love and appreciation refuse the indifference of allowing sinful distortion to continue unabated. Love criticizes and attempts to transform others' distortions; conversely, to be loved is also to have one's own frameworks challenged and confronted.[122]

Sin and appreciation make pluralism necessary; divine power makes it *possible*. As God's power communicates power to a world irreducibly *different* from God, so human power must both receive and give power to others. Power as communication presupposes others who are really different from ourselves. Therefore, without alternative emphatic centers, the emphatic Christian center will atrophy and die (the fate of vacuous pluralism) or betray its own deepest insights, becoming extremist and dominating. Thus power is affirmative. But it is negative as well. An emphatic Christian center will not succumb to the temptation of vacuous and infinite tolerance. It will take positions on the basis of its own strongest insights, precisely because it recognizes those insights to be irreducibly particular. Therefore, although we have neither the right nor the ability to outline the specific shape of emphatic centrism that might arise from other traditions, we can be on watch for principles resembling original sin, appreciation, criticism, forgiveness, and confidence in the transformative and constructive power of God as well as for things of which we never dreamed.[123] It is the "resembling" in the foregoing sentence that gives emphatic Christian centrists both the opportunity and the obligation to speak to others in order to transform them—and others the opportunity and obligation to speak to the emphatic Christian center in order to transform it. Principled and emphatic centrisms in many traditions will enable not only political alliances but also transformation of each religious perspective. Each will seek to convert the error and irresponsibility of the other and will also seek to be converted from its own distortions and failures.

For emphatic Christian centrism, unlike antirelativism, commitment in spite of difference is not a more sophisticated way of expressing an urge to domination. Rather, it is a principled pluralism—a true *relatedness*—based on argument over real differences. Emphatic centrism makes decisions but retains the plural processes for ongoing transformation with its allies as well as its opponents. That is, it produces an overlapping consensus—to use Rawls's term—that incorporates demands of continued challenge and alteration. To be sure, it will at various times and places exclude (as any decision must) a multitude of potential allies, but it will also retain the potential for power in shifting alliances with respect to future decisions. For example, although our version of emphatic Christian centrism will advocate stronger involvement of churches in preventing and treating sexual violence, we will oppose efforts to regulate speech that is claimed to be "offensive" to women, men, or any other group, provided that it does not directly incite violence. This will ally emphatic Christian centrism with many groups on one issue, while standing opposed to many of the same groups on the other.

Of course, emphatic Christian centrism does tend to exclude certain people and viewpoints: those who refuse to recognize the historical and social particularity of their own truth claims; those who claim a unique and incontrovertible privilege to their own positions; those who insist on their own innocence, and therefore focus solely on the conversion of others and not themselves; and those who think that everyone is innocent, so that nobody needs to be converted. The ontological principles of original sin, power, and historicity, as well as the imperative of appreciative love, preclude these claims for compelling reasons. Humans are not God, and those claims tend inexorably to the deification of the self and the group, even if the group is the human race as a whole.

Still, this will not exclude occasional alliances with even these groups on specific issues. And such alliances may unexpectedly facilitate transformation on deeper issues of principle and worldview. Moreover, the tendency toward self-deification and positing one's own innocence is not limited to certain groups or positions. The enemy is not only out there; it is also in here. At least in America, for example, all of us are subject to the self-aggrandizing effects of our cultural interpretation of freedom. All ultimate perspectives tend to idolatry, including emphatic Christian centrism.[124] The best we can do is to be *careful*—careful not to place particular historical claims on the throne of universality, careful not to believe that we have discovered the content of the perfect society and thereby undermined historical processes of power, careful not to claim innocence, careful to keep our ears open to those odd and discordant sounds that may be the beginnings of a new harmony, careful, that is, to strengthen the center. And the best we can do is also to *suspect* that our formulation of emphatic Christian centrism is a mixture of weakness and strength, mere domination and power, callousness and gentleness. With that faith in sin and redemption, we can wait upon other media of the divine, Christian and non-Christian, to strengthen our weakness, extend our power, and give sight to our blindness.

We cannot, however, wait to speak and act. *Commitment*—the active committing of self to someone or something,[125] commitment in spite of difference, commitment because of difference—cannot be postponed. If emphatic Christian centrism can overcome the vacuous pluralism of neglect and indifference, this can only be shown in specific ways. It is inevitable that emphatic Christian centrism take positions consistent with its claims on specific issues for particular reasons. Its truth must be validated both by its conceptual structure and its practical commitments; we turn now to the latter.

Chapter 5

Taking Center Stage

THE EMPHATIC CHRISTIAN CENTER AND POLITICAL PRACTICE

*E*mphatic Christian centrism must begin its political practice somewhere. Rarely is it clear *where* political action ought to begin, but choices must be made; and these must be based on intuitions of importance, visibility, proximity, ability to influence the situation, personal interest, and so forth. Our choice of arenas in which to begin reflecting the emphatic center's politics of power—poverty and education, the family, sexual violence, and the environment—is politically intuitive. Each problem illustrates something important about our society, the role of government, and the emphatic Christian center. We intend no comprehensive exploration of these areas: our purpose at this point is to put our perspective in play, and to examine briefly a few of the challenges for American social policy.

We begin with three overviews which frame emphatic centrism's more specific claims. First, we provide a picture of the political citizen for millennial America. Second, we confront the major challenge of the contemporary American conception of politics as a battle between distinct "interest groups" or—more derogatorily—"special interests." Third, we take up the perennial American question of the proper role of government. On each issue, the emphatic Christian center rejects two oft-heard polar claims. Our approach, however, is not the product of mere compromise, but a principled, historically sensitive claim which reflects the political priority of *power.*

FRAMES FOR POLITICAL PRACTICE

The Intelligent Citizen

American culture seems trapped between two rival conceptions of the ordinary citizen's role in political life. Either we pay homage to "expertise," deferring to the claims—sometimes implausible—of "experts," whose knowledge is acquired in the gnostic enclaves of law schools, medical schools, universities, intelligence agencies, and so on; or we distrust and dismiss expertise and training altogether in favor of "choice," picking options on the basis of mere preference, with no regard for evidence and information. Although these tendencies contradict one another, they both contribute to the antipolitical mood of our land—and to political irresponsibility as well. For the Christian center, however, the citizen can and must be relatively well informed, attentive, and active without being expert.

The cult of the "expert" increases political apathy as well as our sense that the world is beyond our understanding or control. It is born, in part, of an overload of information, options, and technical details that policy development and implementation must confront. But it is also the result of the often spurious "expert" claims to superiority. Indeed, we regularly hear claims to expertise that are not just questionable, but downright nonsense. Just how, exactly, does Jack Kevorkian's training as a *pathologist* entitle him to declare that assisted suicide is not a moral, religious, or political issue but merely a medical issue? In this area he is no more an "expert" than any nonphysician; indeed, he is less so than many psychologists, ethicists, clergy, and patients. This attempt to remove an issue with medical dimensions from public debate by reducing it to a question of medicine *only,* ruling all other contributions out of court, treats the medical establishment—here, only one pathologist—as a privileged and unquestionable priesthood.[1]

Claims to possess specially "revealed" knowledge, acquired by privileged training and experience inaccessible to ordinary citizens, seem more frequent in areas that are heavily technological or scientific, such as defense policy, medicine, and economics. Not only there, however. Many Americans increasingly sense that the social and political worlds are getting away from them in almost every respect—systems are too complex, even simple systems produce unforeseeable results, real understanding of an issue demands far too much time when nearly everyone works more hours than a decade ago, and so on. The natural and disastrous response to all this is simply to withdraw from public involvement, particularly with respect to broad, complex, and technical issues. The bumper-sticker aphorism, "Think globally, act locally" is perhaps sound advice; but it can also reflect a desire to retreat from participation in large-scale political initiative.

Communitarian critics of the privatization of American life, although largely correct about its dangers, should more fully acknowledge the psychological impulse to spurn politics that results from the world's daunting complexity.[2] The culture of freedom, of course, prepares the way for this privatizing response: why should I "impose" my views on other people when I'm not even an expert and can't grasp the complexity? The consequences, however, are catastrophic. Believing that we cannot talk about public policies or goals coherently, we simply stop. Or, if we feel the need to make some connection with the political world, we let ourselves become obsessed with private matters that affect political figures—our fascination with their real or imaginary sex-capades, for example. The effect, as Gore Vidal notes, is to give us the illusion of political participation while in reality we escape from public issues of policy and purpose.[3] The phrase "the personal is political," especially popular during the 1980s in—somewhat surprisingly[4]—leftist circles, exemplifies this trend. It reduces politics to personality and makes personal narrative the trump card in political decision making, as we saw in President Clinton's panel on race.[5]

The growing dominance of narrative and personality, in turn, reinforces the canonization of preference. In revolt against the cult of the expert, the flat American egalitarian conception of freedom turns everyone into an equally qualified "expert," *particularly* in religion and politics. All opinions are held to be equal, all narratives equally valid, as if there were neither arguments nor public reasons for deciding whether or how one should be Catholic or Protestant, Christian or Hindu, Democrat, Republican, or neo-Nazi. A particularly vivid example of this widespread phenomenon in American culture was discovered by Robert Bellah and his associates: one of their subjects, a "Sheila Larson," described her religion as "Sheilaism," "just my own little voice." "It's just try to love yourself and be gentle with yourself. You know, I guess, take care of each other. I think He would want us to take care of each other." Like many Americans, Sheila "preferred" her own construction of religious preference but felt no need to explain it.[6] If that may be tolerable in a faith that does not seek to become public, it is intolerably dominating, as we have seen, when such religions insist on their "right" to be heard.

We also see social policy debates regularly reduced to preference contests. The right routinely—and correctly—points out that the amount of money given to a program is no guarantee of success. Still, what it has sought to do in the past several years is to slash money, not to improve programs. And when defense programs are threatened—particularly in Marietta, Georgia—the right suddenly takes money spent as an absolute indicator of military strength. The left, on the other hand, accuses of heartlessness those who question the adequate delivery of services. Routinely absent in these debates is evidence that goes beyond impressions or stories. The recent wrangle over welfare policy exemplified policy-making by willful blindness. There were no data on what decades of welfare policy had accomplished or failed to achieve; more than that, Congressional Republicans—as if to shield themselves from actual evidence that might question an already-drawn conclusion—made certain that there were almost no hearings to examine the issue, much as they had closed off debate with respect to the budget in 1995. What debates there were, were conducted almost entirely in terms of "what I happen to believe" with almost no reference to those who had studied these areas of social policy for years.

The result was caricature—and apocalyptic, inconsistent caricature at that. Jason DeParle characterizes the welfare dispute accurately:

> Bemoaning the "stereotypes," one side argued that long-term welfare recipients were basically like everyone else—just less lucky. Then it argued that new restrictions might cause children to starve. The other side warned of a welfare underclass so dysfunctional it posed a threat to civilization. Then it supposed that a legal finger snap would prompt the poor to stand up and prosper.[7]

When Americans abandon the worship of the expert, they do so with verve, trading it for the worship of "my opinion," no matter how informed or uninformed that opinion may be.

Nor is disdain for expertise confined to Congress. When Supreme

Court decisions are rendered, the news media typically report the "bottom line" without reference to the legal reasoning that the Court used to arrive at its conclusion. What is missing is an *assessment* of the reasoning that might help us—and the Court—make better decisions in the future. So liberals decry *Casey v. Planned Parenthood* while conservatives gnash their teeth about "liberal federal judges" (more than half of whom were appointed by presidents Reagan and Bush), all with little attention to the legal *rationale* involved, which alone could stimulate a public, reasoned debate that might actually *change* our views rather than merely polarize them.

Personalization and preference politics are no more false than the cult of the expert, nor any more true. Both reduce political decision making to one dimension—expertise or personal narrative. Fully parallel to the extremism in American conceptions of authority—either law or self[8]—these false alternatives leave a vast territory of power unexplored: the realm of the well-informed, conscientious citizen, neither an expert nor an ignoramus, who takes both personal narration and professionally gathered data seriously. The latter is the type of citizen that emphatic Christian centrism—not to mention a vital political culture—requires.

The informed citizen respects the results and methods of those who have special expertise, but also recognizes that the claim to expertise is limited, and often masks sinful self-assertion (what is a moral issue cannot be determined by a medical degree).[9] Nor does expertise preclude critical and intelligent questioning by laypersons. True experts can make the *evidence* for their opinions clear. Non-expert citizens, in turn, are obliged to be curious, well-informed, and willing to refine their own opinions and subject them to critical scrutiny. The citizen is not a Renaissance man or woman. Such broad expertise is no longer possible. In a complex democratic society, no other kind of citizen is possible than the one who is well-informed, curious, and committed—but not an expert (except in her own specific areas of expertise). But this neither disqualifies one from public debate (for not being an expert), nor excuses intellectual and moral sloth ("I happen to believe that").

This is the kind of citizenship to which we aspire in this chapter. We are "experts" in Christian theology and ethics. That expertise leads us beyond these areas, however—Christian centrism is concerned in principle about the whole of the divine creation, its history, and its fulfillment. We are not experts on these public policy issues, but we have made an effort to inform ourselves, to think with as much care and concern as we can, and—not least important—to take the risk of error (which the vacuous center refuses to do). We will surely be wrong about some things, thoughtless about others, insufficient in still others. We can, however, begin in good faith and hope to end this exploration of Christian centrism with better positions than those with which we started, and enable our readers to do the same whether they share our convictions and conclusions or not.

Christian Centrism and the Politics of "Interest"

Thoughtful citizens might first come to grips with the reigning conception of political process. American politics is under the spell of "interest" politics, which has led us to many of our present difficulties, including intensified antipolitical sentiment. Yet, as we argued in chapter 3, one typical Christian answer—that to advocate one's own interest is sinful and selfish—is also inadequate. We support a politics that transcends these alternatives, one that recognizes the legitimacy of interest politics without allowing us to stop there. Indeed, because the aim of politics is the generation of power—and conversely, because a healthy politics depends on power—advocating *only* what appears to be in one's own interest is ultimately counterproductive. Moreover, we often misunderstand our own true interests. History is littered with examples of interest groups that bitterly opposed reforms which ultimately proved to be in their own best interests.[10] Power and politics depend on plurality. This leads us to a broader conception of interest than we see in contemporary America. In some ways, actually, we intend to recover the texture of the hoary notion of "enlightened self-interest" without its rationalist undertones.

INTEREST POLITICS AND THE RELIGION OF FREEDOM

Americans think of politics primarily as a contest between "interest" groups. The initial publication of Robert Dahl's *Who Governs?* in 1961 reinforced that conception and turned it into a virtual orthodoxy, despite criticism of Dahl's approach.[11] This politics of interest forms the basis of the inadequate varieties of multiculturalism we analyzed in the foregoing chapter. It is also the fount of identity politics, which understands interests as given principally by one's ethnic, racial, or gender group—paradoxically returning us to an era of "ascribed" status, against which Americans protest vociferously when it is found in other cultures. Interest politics is also a principal source of our dissatisfaction with politics, such that the term "interest" is now usually preceded by the defamatory adjective "special," clearly expressing our cultural belief that interest groups are interested not in a common good, but only their own.

Unsurprisingly, the dominance of interest politics—both descriptively and normatively—has firm roots in the American suspicion of power and the civil religion of freedom. With respect to power, Dahl celebrated interest politics because the claims of competing interest groups seemed to produce a balance of power, ensuring that no group gained too much dominance at the expense of any other—a partial retrieval of Madisonian politics. But interest politics insulates actors from any critical analysis of what their interests actually *are* or *should be* (and once more we emphasize: persons' *actual* interests can, and often are, different from their *perceived* interests). Interest is decided privately, and then brought to the public trough. In fact, according to the American civil religion of freedom, it is *wrong* to subject our conception of our interests to scrutiny (because that would limit our freedom).

This conception of politics is failing us. The proliferation of interests in a pluralistic society and the decline of the "assimilationist" ideal which Dahl thought essential to effective governance[12]—to say nothing of the self-proclaimed immunity of each group from counterargument—leaves public life in its current state: a vicious, self-fulfilling prophecy that politics is nothing but a contest of factions in which, finally, the ability to dominate and coerce wins the day. Under these circumstances, it is not surprising that most people, if they enter politics at all, do so only in order to promote and defend their specific interests, narrowly defined.

The first problem of interest politics, then, is that the several "interests" tend to be formulated *outside* the public arena, reducing politics to being the public instrument by which private wishes are fulfilled. In this view, there can be no way to assess whether affirmative action programs, tax subsidies for business activities, school prayer, and so on, actually *are* or even should be in the interest of their advocates. This is the point at which interest politics diverges from Madison's theory of factions and justice. Madison, believing in the existence of a publicly available universal reason, assumed that the competition of interest groups in a large republic would leave the wheat of the common good after the thresher finished its work. The "public interest" would then triumph and discredit the divisiveness of factions. However, when reason is dethroned and freedom becomes the civil religion—our present situation—*all* (and there are so many!) positions seem merely to be those of "special interests." There is no public argumentative ground that could change people's conceptions of their interests.

From this problem follows a second, namely, that interest politics embodies the worst features of mere selfishness. This is especially true when interest generally means short-term interest; that is, what I think will help me the most now. When power and benefits are conceived as zero-sum questions, arguments like that of David Blankenhorn, president of the Institute for American Values—that providing a child-care benefit for working parents "in effect punish[es] parents" who do not work outside the home[13]—appear less bizarre than they actually are. Every benefit for others must be contested simply because *it is for others*. Both difficulties—the privatizing devaluation of politics and the reduction of interest to selfishness—presuppose the American conception of innocents at home. Simply because they are mine, nothing can be wrong with my private desires, and I therefore have a right to demand that others submit to them.

INTEREST-FREE POLITICS?

Should we, then, have a politics without self-interest? For many major strains of Christian thought, the answer has been "yes." In *The Bondage of the Will*, Martin Luther describes the Christian will as "disinterested" in its own benefit. Although Luther was here arguing for a will that was disinterested in the person's salvation, he employs a similar conception in his discussions of worldly politics.[14] This narrowing of sin to self-interest and selfishness reverberates in the Christian traditions. In the twentieth century, Anders Nygren vigorously argued that the true heritage of the Reformation—against Roman Catholic notions of "charity"—was that it eradicated self-love, replacing it with selfless, agapic concern for God and others exclusively.[15] More recently, Gregory Jones argues—albeit inconsistently—that the practice of forgiveness is a "costly" discipleship in which the benefits to a forgiver should not be counted as part of the moral equation. To do otherwise, Jones maintains, would reduce forgiveness to mere therapy.[16] In political thought, Glenn Tinder believes that the political meaning of Christianity is found in its advocacy of the agapic triumph over selfishness.[17] Jim Wallis's *Who Speaks for God?* is a jeremiad against the politics of self-interest. Wallis dismisses political positions, not with arguments about their merits, but simply because their advocates are pursuing their own interests.[18]

This supposed identity of selflessness and "being ethical" adds yet another ingredient to the antipolitical stew. It is probably not accidental that Luther, one of the strongest advocates of the moral priority of pure selflessness, also tended to political passivity (as compared with Augustine, for example, who maintained a good deal of self-interest in his conception of charity toward others). Mainline "religious" college students come to their first religion classes believing that selflessness is *the* true expression of Christian ethics—and so they dismiss politics as altogether sordid and beneath "real" religion. But since they also recognize the importance of self-interest, they then go on to dismiss Christian ethics as irrelevant or "idealistic." In this bargain, both religion and politics get short shrift. It makes politics evil, and banishes religion to a netherworld of irrelevance that makes it, according to the criterion of comprehensiveness, less religious.

Mere revulsion in the name of an ideal is not ethical unless it *produces power.* In contemporary culture—and many historical cultures as well—selflessness is not a consistent basis for effective political action. Instead, the trumpets of selflessness sound tinny, hollow, and (ironically) self-indulgent and moralistic. Before we insist on the hard road of selfless agape in such an environment, we ought to see whether a politics that both includes and transcends self-interest is as bankrupt as the prophets of selflessness believe. Much of the theological polemic against selfishness and self-interest is supposed to have derived from the letters of Paul and his school. But just as Kant's injunction—that we should never treat another *merely* as a means—becomes almost useless if the "merely" is omitted, it should give us pause to reflect on what, for example, Philippians 2:4 (RSV) actually says: "Let each of you look not *only* to his own interests, but also to the interests of others." This advice may be more helpful and powerful in today's climate than the false radicalization that omits the "only."[19]

Curiously—or perhaps not—the implicit or explicit rejection of selfless love as the ideal of Christian ethics is one of the few points on which both sides of the political spectrum seem to agree. Implicit criticism comes mostly from the political right wing, and especially groups such as the Christian Coalition and Focus on the Family. They are certainly not embarrassed to claim that they represent the interests of their constituents.[20] Those whose interests would be served by taxpayer-funded private school tuition seem to feel little fear that they will be called self-interested because they advocate vouchers as public policy. Nor was the Christian Coalition abashed to advocate tax relief for those who are "families" by its definition, and from whom much of their money is raised. Wallis misses the point when he chides the Coalition primarily for advocating policies in the interests of its constituents. On the contrary, this is rather its political genius—to sanctify the politics of self-interest by claiming that it is "the truth."[21]

More explicit criticism of selflessness as an overarching ideal has come primarily from the left, especially feminist and liberation theologians. To find their critique persuasive is not to deny that there are circumstances in which self-sacrifice can generate power. Rather, we reject the claims of Nygren, Tinder, Jones, and others that selfless agape is the *summum bonum* of Christian life, and that it constitutes a universal and unexceptionable duty. The demand for selfless love is problematic. It is probably not accidental that those who defend agapic understandings of love tend themselves to be in positions of relative privilege. They usually have something to sacrifice that the one for whose sake they contemplate sacrifice needs more than they do. In a strange way, then, agape as an ideal frequently presupposes the real capacity for dominance on the part of the sacrificer. This implies that selfless love is not a universal duty, but either perspectival (more appropriate for some than others), or of short-term significance, until a rough and helpful parity is established between lover and loved.

When selfless love is construed as a duty, however, it is perverted in three ways. First, those who have no one else to speak for them (usually the oppressed) will not be able to call for justice lest they be accused of acting only in their selfish interests.[22] Second, the sacrificer will have to maintain the privilege, even as it is supposed to be divested. There is a certain parentalism inherent in a universal duty to selfless love. Third, there is the main target of the feminist critique, namely that the selfless lover dissipates in weakness. Tillich, Christine Gudorf, and others observe that such love is no longer even self-sacrificial, because there is no real self to sacrifice.[23] For the disadvantaged, the demand for selfless agape prevents the development of a real self in the first place.[24] In this way, agape becomes the enemy of both justice and power.

Some defenders of agape understood this problem. Tillich, for example, maintains that in order to practice productive self-sacrifice, there must be a *self* whose sacrifice produces power for others rather than simply enervating itself.[25] And Reinhold Niebuhr places the agapic ideal within a framework that recognizes that human needs for vitality and self-assertion should not be canceled utterly by agape.[26] Here, self-sacrifice is a privilege. Less subtle defenders of agape, however, such as Jones, Tinder, and Nygren, make sacrifice of self a duty for all Christians and are subject squarely to our objections.

We deny not that self-sacrificial love is ethical, but rather that it *always* is. Instead, we submit the desirability of self-sacrifice to the criterion of power: will it generate a broader and deeper power for the social body in question—which ordinarily includes the self?[27]

There is another decisive objection to selflessness as the primary ground for social policy: the current political climate is not amenable to it. An ethic of power must confront this pragmatic issue. No ethical proclamation that does not produce powerful and just effects can be *concretely* ethical, however desirable it might seem in the abstract. Despite Wallis's well-intentioned attack on our political climate for the sake of the poor, protests of his kind had little discernible effect on the 1997 welfare debate. Christian centrism seeks to expand power, not merely to protest.

Not only is there no indication that polemic grounded in pure selflessness is effective in the present climate, there are reasons—theoretical as well as empirical—to believe the opposite. Theoretically, advocates of the absolute priority of selfless love confront an irresolvable contradiction. On one hand, they inveigh against persistent, deep-seated selfishness, and denigrate the morality of the selfish. On the other hand, those same degenerate, self-interested persons—when informed of their selfishness—are supposed to desire and be able to flick a switch and renounce their self-interest.

THE POWER OF TARGETED UNIVERSALISM

Reinhold Niebuhr understood this dilemma of self-interest and agape, of justice and love. Unable to resolve it, he simply allowed the paradox to stand, taking sacrificial love as the norm of personal relationships, while insisting on justice as the norm for social relationships.[28] The Christian center can respond to this dilemma more creatively. Negatively, the reality of original sin means that one's perceived self-interest is always distorted. There *is* good reason to reject the Christian Coalition's superimposition of "divine will" on a political program that always serves the interests of its constituents. We discussed this problem in chapter 3, arguing that a responsible political program as a whole will have to include elements not in the apparent self-interest of its advocates, and, indeed, counter to some of their apparent interests. This is vital to the religious task of self-transcendence. Affirmatively, the "visional dimension" of emphatic Christian centrism is the maximal expansion of the scope and intensity of power in *communicative events*.[29] This necessarily retains a place for self-interest. Because it concerns power for all parties in an encounter, there is a presumption against utterly abandoning the self's power for the sake of another. In a fulfilling encounter of power, power is communicated to all parties, not merely one or another. Indeed, a stronger *self* should be one result of the power that is generated.

It will not, of course, always be true that power can be increased for all, but it may be possible more often than our current political rhetoric suggests. The weakness of appeals to pure self-sacrificial love is manifest. The 1996 attack on "welfare entitlements," replete with all its stereotyping of the poor (on both sides of the debate) detonated a system of cash assistance that had, in fact, never been popular precisely because it had been targeted at one group and *one group alone*—a group, moreover, with whom the bulk of the American populace felt no special bond. Similar restrictions to relatively narrow target populations increase the balkanization of our political culture in other arenas. Gay rights ordinances are attacked by the political right on the ground that they create "special" rights. Affirmative action programs are subject to the same objection from groups who are not included among "protected classes." In these cases, the vicious interaction of rights, interests, and freedom produces contentious battles in which there can be only one winner. They are games of domination.

When programs seem to benefit only one subpopulation, even their victories are fragile. The cash-assistance system for the poor is largely a thing of the past, voters in Maine in 1998 repealed the state's gay rights law, and affirmative action programs are under assault nationwide, already banned for college admissions and many hiring decisions in two of America's most populous states (California and Texas). The vulnerability of narrowly targeted social programs is nothing new, as Theda Skocpol points out in her discussion of the history of American poverty policy. Nineteenth-century poorhouses and early-twentieth-century mothers' pensions also inspired the combination of vociferous opposition (among those who did not receive benefits) and the stigmatization of beneficiaries that the "war on poverty" triggered later in this century.[30]

A related difficulty for narrowly targeted programs is their tendency to balkanize issues according to "interest group." For example, placing sexual harassment and violence, child support, and abortion within the purview of "women's issues" makes it seem as if men have no stake in such questions, or even that men are the enemy who must lose if women are to win. This restriction can be used as a shibboleth to exclude men from any participation in resolving an issue; for example, claims of men are devalued by some in the abortion controversy simply because they are expressed by men. And if such "interest" politics do not provoke hostility, they will certainly generate apathy among those not included in the interest group. If it is a "women's issue," then men are tempted to leave it to interested women to deal with. Interest group politics creates convenient excuses not to be involved. The same balkanization appears in race relations and economic policy (especially in labor issues), as well as in public policy.

In other words, self-interest *does* drive involvement in the political process, and selflessness is powerless to overcome it. Nor do appeals to selfless love seem to help prevent vociferous opposition to "special interests" that happen not to be one's *own* special interest. Narrowly targeted programs consistent with self-sacrificing agape-ethics seem to be both ineffective and breeding-grounds of divisive opposition. But this is not necessarily bad news.

A contrasting approach is what Skocpol calls *"targeted universalism."* This approach designs and presents policy initiatives with the interests of *all*—or better, a broad spectrum—of citizens in mind.

Within a broad program, particular populations can be targeted, but a wide swath of the population nonetheless sees benefit for themselves as well as others. Targeted universalist policies seem to generate wider and deeper support. At the same time that the narrowly targeted cash-assistance program was under siege in 1996, Social Security benefits and Medicare withstood attack easily. Indeed, that year's election was a boon to the Democrats because they were able, fairly or unfairly, to accuse the Republicans of plotting to gut Medicare.

What accounts for the difference, particularly in light of the fact that it is the poor (as a proportion of their available resources) who are most helped by Medicaid, Medicare, and Social Security? The explanation may be as simple as this: these are programs that "have spread costs and visibly delivered benefits across classes."[31] The contrast to welfare policy, Skocpol suggests, is that "although many working-class and middle-class families surely gained from increases in social benefits to their elderly relatives, they have not perceived gains to themselves from increased welfare transfers to the poor."[32] This may also be why the current welfare-to-work policies enjoy, for the moment, considerable support in America. Most people can conceive a benefit that will accrue to themselves or society at large from another's labor; that is harder to comprehend in the case of simple cash grants.[33]

The lesson seems to be this: it is easier to gain broad support for programs that disproportionately assist certain populations if relatively universal benefits are also included. Such a targeted universalism has several advantages in the current climate. The first is that it works for the objectives that moral jeremiads against selfishness seek but seem unable to advance. Second (and important for Christian centrists), targeted universalism is self-consciously an ethic based in power, in that it does not try to sacrifice one interest for the sake of another. That is, its policies can produce *both* a wider and deeper power for those affected. A third related benefit is that targeted universalism has the potential to detoxify the current political climate. Divisiveness is a nearly inevitable feature of the narrowly conceived interest politics that pits women's interests against men's, African Americans' against European Americans', the health professions against those served by them, environmental protection against labor, and so on. If, however, we can serve most (or at least many) interests in designing a social policy, not only will support be generated but—in tandem with the emphatic center's pluralism and denial of universal argumentative privilege—we might well remove the zero-sum taint of our present approach to social policy.

In turn, this means that targeted universalism is not simply a matter of policy initiatives, but can also be helpful in thinking about what our interests actually *are*. That is, targeted universalism opens a pathway for discussion about interest rather than simply assuming that our interests are determined privately and then expressed publicly without alteration. To begin to think outside the constraints of the zero-sum of interest politics (which even self-sacrificial agape unwittingly promotes) allows us to approach our own apparent interests as overlapping with others'. For example, sexual violence's impact on trust between the sexes (and therefore on concrete relationships between particular men and women), its high medical cost (much of which is atrociously expensive emergency-room service), its effects on children, the occasional abuse of men by women, and its coarsening effect on those who perpetrate it—all this should surely lead us to the conclusion that sexual violence is *not* merely a women's issue. True, a decline in sexual violence would directly benefit more women than men. But the indirect yet real costs of this violence are spread throughout the social body. Prevention and enforcement are thus in the concrete interests of *men as well as women*. Interests are not, in this case, a zero-sum game.

Fulfilled power is an event which communicates efficacy to all parties in an encounter. The targeted universalist approach to thinking about social practices is well-fitted to an ethic that seeks the increase of power for the whole of divine creation. This is not to say that targeted universalism is the *only* appropriate approach for an ethic of power, nor that it is a panacea for all that ails us. But it does seem to be an overdue proposal for late-twentieth-century American culture, which is far too accustomed to a politics based on a zero-sum conception of interests in which *dominance* is prominent, and it is likely to accomplish far more—indeed, it already accomplishes more—than an ethic of pure selflessness. Thus can an ethic of power, concretized in targeted universalist thinking, both transcend and retain self-interest for the sake of the power of the social body as a whole, and for each member of it. To be more specific, as emphatic Christian centrists, we advocate policies that transcend our immediate self-interest, narrowly conceived as male, white, middle-class, college or university-centered and church-centered, and—to our chagrin—at various points of middle age. However, these same policies *are* in our interest and will, we are convinced, generate power for *ourselves* as well as their primary beneficiaries.

Subsidiarity

The foregoing observations are consistent with a retrieval of the Roman Catholic concept of *subsidiarity,* which is enjoying something of a revival as Protestants—on both the left and right—have begun to discover it.

Subsidiarity was first enunciated by Pope Leo XIII in 1891 in the encyclical *Rerum Novarum.*[34] Responding to the dramatic changes being wrought in family and economy by the worldwide industrialization and unprecedented growth of the late nineteenth century, he sought to limit state intrusion into families while at the same time demanding more state support for families subjected to the powerful disruptive forces of the labor market by the cycles of economic boom and bust. For our purposes, we may formulate it thus: social and personal needs are best met by those social structures closest to the needs (e.g., the family, school, or workplace), but these structures both deserve and require the support of broader social structures (e.g., public health, educational funding, unemployment insurance) to ensure that they *can* meet those needs. Remarkably, we have encountered this principle in liberal environmental theology,[35] liberal family theory,[36] and even Ralph Reed![37]

One concrete example of this principle would be the view that families are the best place to socialize and raise children, but that government must both help families do so and intervene when they do not. The institution nearest the need—the family—is then the primary agency, supported by a variety of mediating institutions, all upheld and supported more or less indirectly by the state. For Leo XIII, this included the state's duties not to interfere with the family, to require employers to pay a family wage, to regulate working conditions, and to guarantee employees the right to organize.[38]

The strength of this doctrine lies in its clear understanding of the role of self-interest in motivating and energizing the smaller social units where most human wants and needs are directly met. It should be obvious that, on the whole, families will directly care for children better than governments, and that this is done out of parents' natural love for children, which is usually so strong that it identifies the parents' and children's self-interests as identical. It should be equally obvious that families cannot carry out all these tasks alone, and cannot always be trusted to do so well. They therefore always require support, and sometimes, intervention. As such, subsidiarity meshes nicely with targeted universalism and a frank acceptance of self-interest in politics, and leads directly into our next topic, the place of government.

What Place Government?

In our current climate, the intelligent citizen who advocates targeted universalism must also confront the raging debate about the role of government. We do so only in order to indicate that in its current form, the debate about government (whether the era of "big government" is "over," what exactly "big government" is, etc.), is too abstract to be useful. It diverts us from more significant questions. In some ways, this dispute is much like the theological argument about the origin of original sin that appeared in chapter 3. It is a false choice, a red herring.

It is true that in 1998, for example, Americans' trust in government soared to its highest level since 1989, climbing steadily after 1994. Trust in government stood at a whopping 22 percent.[39] Remarkably, however, in March of the same year, President Clinton's approval rating was over 70 percent; for Congress, over 60 percent; even the hated IRS, the least popular of all governmental entities, was viewed favorably by just under 40 percent of the population.[40] What can we infer from such contradictory data? It is evident that we combine distrust of government in the *abstract* with wide support of it in *particular* cases—indeed, in almost every particular case. There is nothing startlingly new about this phenomenon. Even when Congress as a body had approval ratings which gave new meaning to the term "sub-basement" in the late 1980s, still about 90 percent of incumbents who ran for reelection were returned to office in virtually every election cycle.

Americans, in other words, are two-faced about government. As one of us drove through Indiana on an interstate highway in the late 1980s, he saw graffiti on the overpass which read "Taxes are evil." The vandal was either a particularly good ironist or a little slow. In order to display his message, the artist had to take the government-funded highway and use the government-funded overpass for his canvas. This cultural inconsistency paralyzes our policy choices and, in the end, provides little useful debate that could justify such paralysis. In the American tradition, antigovernmentalism is driven by the worship of freedom. Since power (as domination) and freedom are viewed as intractable opponents, and since government is the prime possessor of dominating power, government is necessarily oppressive. Antigovernmentalism is built into the fabric of the religion of freedom.

Similarly, the emphasis on voluntaristic morality—made into a mantra by Ronald Reagan in the 1980s—assumes the innocence of Americans. Reagan really believed, apparently, that no matter what government programs were eliminated, the good hearts of Americans would step in to fill the gap. Although voluntary efforts did indeed rise in the 1980s, they did so by a pittance in comparison with the level of governmental effort that had been slashed. Of course Reagan did not advocate "voluntary" defense. But is there more reason to believe that poverty is amenable to private solutions without the assistance of economic, educational, and health policy? Indeed, we have seen that support for government increases just at the point when particular questions about the role of government begin to appear.

Our diagnosis of the self-contradictory American attitude toward government says, of course, nothing about the desirability of particular governmental policies or actions. That is as it should be. The current debate is both abstract and ahistorical. Abstract, in that every question of government policy seems immediately slurried into the pipeline of "big government," "small government," or "no government." Ahistorical, in that the historical effectiveness or ineffectiveness of specific government programs is rarely studied as a possible guide to future decisions. In general, the right claims that government has no useful role to play outside national defense, though it tends to support tax policy that favors business above all others (Rep. John Kasich of Ohio is an exception to the latter). However, the right's accusation against the left is sometimes true, that is, that some leftists have never met a problem that they didn't think would be best and first solved by governmental initiative.

Put in the *abstract*, the question of government is irresolvable. Rather, the appropriateness and effectiveness of government or its absence must be measured and argued in each specific case. Communitarian emphasis on "civil society" and Reagan's championing of "voluntarism" are necessary correctives to a tendency to rely on government too heavily. Moreover, true to the right's recovery of the question of states' rights (which dovetails, surprisingly, with postmodern lionizations of "localism"), some arenas of appropriate government action may be better reserved for smaller units of government. All these reflect the wisdom of subsidiarity: there are problems that government is ill-fitted to solve, and there are no problems that government can address and solve alone.

None of those possibilities, however, deserves the weight of presumption in an argument about specific policies. States' rights, after all, fell into deserved disrepute as a rallying cry when it was employed predominantly as an excuse to maintain institutionalized racial segregation. Moreover, we wonder just how, exactly, environmental degradation can be addressed meaningfully by voluntary civic-mindedness alone. It is true that voluntarism and civil society are vital components of environmental policy, but it is hard to imagine how even a superfluity of private morality can tackle more than a small fraction of positive ecological planning or negative pollution and degradation controls. These are national and international matters. Similarly, although churches and other voluntary organizations can and do lessen some of the effects of poverty, no one has provided plausible reason to believe that poverty and its effects can be ameliorated significantly—let alone prevented, which ought to be the aim of public policy—by voluntary efforts alone. This neither diminishes nor dismisses the significance of voluntary organizations' work. We believe, however, that without significant government assistance—at all levels—these efforts will be Sisyphean at best. "Government or no government" is an abstract and meaningless question outside particular policy questions in which the specific roles of government, nongovernmental organizations, and private initiative are concretely assessed.[41]

This simple opposition between government and its absence is also *ahistorical*. In discussions of governmental initiatives, one rarely hears questions of *time* raised. States' rights rhetoric seems divided between those who claim that states were, are, and always will be superior to the national government, on one side, and those who seem to believe that states—because of their sorry record in the 1960s—should always be preempted by other governmental units. Similarly, the New Deal is vilified or lionized, caught in a public debate which claims it was never necessary (for the right) or will always be needed in the same configuration (for the left). We seem unable to recognize that the need for certain legal initiatives changes over time, and requires periodic rejustification.[42]

For the agenda of the emphatic Christian center, this failure of historical imagination is particularly costly in sexual violence policy. Beginning in the 1970s, public campaigns against the legitimacy of spousal battery (presented in films such as *The Burning Bed*) and attacks on the relevance of prior sexual history in cases of sexual assault (to name but two) led to widespread adoption of new criminal laws as well as education about sexual assault and domestic violence for law enforcement and the public. Despite the success of these efforts, however—or perhaps because of it—we remain largely fixated on the legal realm. But precisely because of the success of legal reform, it may be that the legal arena is not *now* the most fruitful one for public action. Certainly, legal issues remain; for example, would "family rights" laws and "father's and husband's protection" laws undo much of the progress of the last twenty years? But such matters as preventing sexual violence and treatment for the abused and the abuser are not fundamentally legal problems. As we will argue, they are exemplary instances of the power of nonlegal, voluntary institutions and communities—if we recognize the opportunity.

There is no single best answer to questions of governments' size, their proper range of action, or their most appropriate agents (international, national, state, local). Nor is there a corresponding rule that could be applied to civic, nongovernmental organizations or private individuals. In most cases, we suspect, hybrid approaches are probably the most appropriate. Once again, our civil religion of freedom prevents focused discussion of real problems. This is another reason that freedom is a religion that is not worthy of our worship.

These three frames for political practice—intelligent citizenship, targeted universalism, and a legitimate role for government—are applicable to many policy questions. We have also tried to provide an outline of the necessary theological, philosophical, and cultural commitments of emphatic Christian centrism. Our account of that center has had, to this point, a fairly theoretical cast. That emphasis was necessary in view of the manifold confusions over the relation of religion and politics; the contemporary American civil religion of freedom, which is a theory without the self-awareness to acknowledge its theoretical or religious character; the anthropological and theological presuppositions of contemporary culture; the terribly confused conceptions of pluralism; and the distorted perspectives on political practice, which we tried to correct at the outset of this chapter. Those theoretical positions now allow us to show their practical value in developing a *policy agenda* for the emphatic Christian center, to which we now turn.

AN AGENDA FOR THE EMPHATIC CHRISTIAN CENTER

The policy agenda of the emphatic Christian center is, in principle, limitless. To say anything at all, however, requires that one select specific problems and forward a particular direction for policy. Our areas of special concern—the interrelated problems of poverty, the family, sexual violence, and the imposing environmental crisis—are neither exhaustive nor any more necessary than any number of other issues. There is no way to determine the "right" issues with which to begin. But we can and must make responsible, well-informed choices for reasons that we are prepared to defend. Nor are our suggestions for public policy necessarily the best; they are the best we can conceive and are likely to be helpful and to generate valuable debate and action.

One more important preliminary note: we are *not* giving "the Christian answer" to these issues. The reasons for this should be obvious. First, their grounding in the principles of an emphatic Christian center, particularly power, should be clear. The preceding four chapters have outlined the rationale for emphatic Christian centrism, which need not be repeated here. As Hannah Arendt offered, "The principle inspires the deeds that are to follow and remains apparent as long as the action lasts."[43] Moreover, there is *no such thing* as the "Christian answer" to economics or poverty or even the family. Faith in Christ does not automatically confer political wisdom or economic insight. Indeed, to bludgeon the reader with so-called Christian answers would impede the selfsame center's pluralism. We offer nothing, so far as we know, that emphatic humanists, Jews, Muslims, or Buddhists could not affirm.

None of our analyses or recommendations requires Christian faith as a precondition for support. Our policy choices are within what we hope will emerge as an overlapping consensus.[44] But the principle of parsimony in public debate that we discussed in the last chapter holds; if asked, we will support again our vision of the emphatic Christian center. We will reiterate our vision if challenged; but this is not the place.

Poverty

THE CHRISTIAN CENTER AND THE POOR

Between 1993 and 1998, the number of welfare recipients declined sharply, by 37 percent, from over 14 million recipients in January of 1993 to under 9 million by May of 1998.[45] The number of families receiving welfare was reduced from just under 5 million in January 1993 to just over 3.5 million in September 1997, a decline of 29 percent, and the number has continued to decline since.[46] These statistics are a source of political pride for both Democrats and Republicans. But this pride, like the welfare reform debate, focuses not on reducing poverty but on reducing welfare rolls. Unfortunately, our success in reducing poverty has been less dramatic. Despite the economic expansion of the 1990s, the poverty rate declined only slightly between 1993 and 1996, from 15.1 percent to 13.7 percent, a fall from 39.3 million persons to 36.5 million.[47]

Thirty-six and a half million people. Nearly one in seven persons in America has a grossly inadequate income. Moreover, the official poverty line is shockingly low. In 1997, a family of *four* is defined as poor if its income is $16,036, just over $4,000 per person.[48] Few readers of this book, we guess, would find such an existence tolerable—certainly, no poor person could afford to purchase this book. One of the computers on which this book was written (a modest machine by contemporary standards) was purchased for about $2000, one half of the *maximum* yearly income permitted for a "poor" person. The poverty line, in other words, is not a close call. It captures only abject deprivation.

The depth of poverty in America is disgraceful. That alone makes it a pressing question for the emphatic Christian center. But there are other reasons. To begin with, poverty already commands the attention of Christian churches as well as other religious and secular organizations. Historically and biblically, the poor have been at the heart of

Christian concern.[49] That shows no signs of abating. Pope John Paul II is persistent in his calls for economic justice, as are the American Catholic bishops, African American denominations, Latin American liberation theologians of all denominations, and Protestants such as Jim Wallis. Moreover, religious organizations, especially churches, have been ceded authority by default for inner-city poverty in the latter half of the 1990s.[50] Both historically and today, Christianity has a long tradition of acting to ameliorate and eliminate poverty.

On the other hand, Christianity has also helped harden us against the misery of poverty. As we saw in chapter 3, the persistent tendency in Christianity to reduce sin to "personal" action without accounting for the social milieu in which sin occurs and is perpetuated, makes us inattentive to social problems by reducing evil to matters of personal responsibility. Emphatic Christian centrism insists that although sin is never simply a result of social structures, those structures can and do contribute to the ease and likelihood of sin and evil. Conversely, God's power is expressed also through material media, and people's material conditions influence— though they do not determine—the quality of their religious power. The material and the spiritual are not opposed but complementary, as Luther insisted long ago in his debate with the radical Protestants.[51]

With this perspective, Christian centrism enters a debate that is in shambles. On the one side—at the moment, the losing side—are those, like Wallis, who berate the heartlessness of those reluctant to maintain permanent cash assistance to the poor. On the other side are stereotypes of "welfare mothers," a picture tinged with not a small racial undertone.[52] The right-wing picture of the "typical" welfare recipient is an adult, usually female, who pilfers the system, has children merely to increase welfare payments, is black or Hispanic, unemployed by choice, probably drug-dependent, supplements income through street crime, and is massively irresponsible. Outside this picture are the male and female working poor,[53] the involuntarily unemployed, the disabled, children, the white non-Hispanic poor (45 percent of the poor in 1996),[54] and the rural poor. This limited portrait allowed welfare's opponents to dismiss their critics as the lowest of all the political creatures of the eighties and nineties—the "liberals." The current debate is long on stereotypes and short on any discussion of what *policies* might best reduce poverty and generate power for the *whole* social body.

It is not clear that the adherents of either wing are a majority. However, the distorted debate discourages adequate analysis. In the 1996 feud over federal welfare reform legislation, for example, the public was presented with virtually no data showing either that the cash assistance system was a long-term help to the poor, or that it had done nothing. We debated hypotheticals when we could have looked to data to guide us. Moreover, the debate centered only on how much the welfare rolls could be reduced. To say the least, that is a bizarre focus. Christian centrism will demand a different question: What policies to combat the suffering and social cost of poverty will generate power for the poor and the nonpoor?

There should be no mistake: the problem of poverty does not affect the poor alone. At a basic level, we know that about 15 percent—one in seven—of our population is not sustained at a level sufficient to maximize their contribution to the social whole. We also know that poverty tends to persist across generations and that the high proportion of children in poverty (40 percent of all the poor are under eighteen years)[55] means that this minimization is likely to continue. There *is* a cycle of poverty, a drain on the whole of society. If we can produce more widely desirable material conditions for many of the 15 percent of our population who are poor, the social payoff for all levels of society is potentially enormous. This prediction is, of course, vague, simply because we do not know what economic, cultural, and innovative capital could be produced by those who now do not have the resources the rest of us enjoy. We do know, however, that we will never find out unless the conditions for their material and spiritual growth are considerably expanded.

Poverty has, of course, current and tangible costs for the entire social body. The strong statistical association between poverty and crime means not only that the lives of the noncriminal poor are damaged by the threat of crime, and that the poor are more likely to be victims of crime, but also that the whole of society must pay the costs of crime and of housing prisoners (at last count, at least $28,000 per year per prisoner, almost twice the poverty level for a family of four), additional police protection, and decaying infrastructure. Especially in the case of urban poverty, there is also an immeasurable cultural cost. Suburban families (of all races) fear entry into the city they surround for cultural opportunities, recreation, and other activities. The enriching experiences of American cities are denied not only to the poor but also to the nonpoor, who fear (either rationally or irrationally) poverty and its effects. In turn, this contributes to the divided character of the American house. The costs of poverty, then, are at least these—economic, material, cultural, and spiritual. Although these costs are imposed with particular weight on the poor, they are not borne by the poor alone. To address the costs and effects of poverty is not in the interest of the poor alone, but of *all*.

Still, the problem seems intractable. It is easy to become paralyzed in the face of its complexity. Entangled in poverty are questions of banking policy, economic stimulus, unionization and wages, the growing gap between the wealthy and the poor (relative poverty), employment policy, health care, crime, housing, education, and so on. This complexity serves as a warning, but the temptation to paralysis—sloth—must be avoided. The emphatic center must identify a point of attack, one that will have the greatest possibilities for generating power now.

Moreover, the center will have to decide about the place of government in addressing poverty. In this case, as we stated earlier, voluntary institutions alone cannot produce an adequate solution. This is not to dismiss their considerable role: they help ameliorate a few of the worst consequences of poverty, and they bring a badly needed moral voice to the problem, reminding us that love requires justice and power, and that "the neighbor" of whom Christian ethics speaks is "simply he or she who is there and in need."[56] The presence of churches can and does provide a glue of communal unity, a sense of responsibility, and care.[57] Churches can help middle-class and upper-class people, for whom poverty remains distant and abstract, grow in awareness of the problem. But none of those efforts approaches the extent of need. Prevention of poverty on a wide scale will require large-scale institutional political will. In our current situation, it will require substantial government commitment.

Even so, the intractability of poverty is great. There are too many interrelated problems and too few political possibilities to commit resources. But we must find a toehold with which to begin. In our judgment, the best place to begin is with a systematic approach to a crucial contributor to poverty: the lack of good primary and secondary education. There are, to be sure, omissions in this approach. Education certainly privileges children at the possible expense of adults. Still, choices must be made, and this choice privileges long-term over short-term strategies, and prevention over amelioration of a chronic condition.[58]

EDUCATION

In *Rosa Lee,* Leon Dash tells the story of Rosa Lee Cunningham, a woman mired in the worst of urban poverty, some of whose children will likely follow in her footsteps. "There is something in [her] life story to confirm any political viewpoint," Dash notes.

> Some may see her as a victim of hopeless circumstances. Others may give her the benefit of the doubt in some cases but hold her personally accountable for what she did to herself, her children, and her grandchildren. A third group might say that Rosa Lee is a thief, a drug addict, a failed parent, a broken woman paying for her sins, and—that it is amazing that even two of [her children] manage to live conventional lives.[59]

Still, Dash concludes—to the unbelief of Rosa Lee herself—that "education is the route," and that she had been worse than ill-served by the school system she had been given.[60] The data on poverty provide support for Dash's anecdotal conclusion. William Julius Wilson's study of Chicago in the 1980s points to the role of inadequate education in perpetuating poverty and the closure of opportunities that the nonpoor take for granted:

> Of the 39,500 students who enrolled in the ninth grade of Chicago's public schools in 1980, and who would have normally graduated from high school four years later—only 18,500 (or 47 percent) graduated; of these only 6,000 [15 percent of the 39,500] were capable of reading at or above the national twelfth-grade level. However, the situation is even more bleak for those black and Hispanic students who attended segregated inner-city high schools and who represented two-thirds of the original class of 1984. Of the 25,500 ninth-grade black and Hispanic students who originally enrolled in these segregated, non-selective high schools in Chicago, 16,000 did not graduate.... Of the 9,500 students who did graduate, 4,000 read at or below the junior level, and only 2,000 read at or above the national average. In these non-selective segregated high schools, then, only 2,000 of the original class of 25,000 students both completed high school and could read at or above the level considered average in the rest of the country.[61]

The data we have suggest a strong link between poverty and lack of educational achievement. That said, the Bureau of the Census does not publish data on the educational attainment of the poor and the nonpoor. This makes further research on this connection our first policy demand.

Anecdotes and current data are, however, enough to press for a concurrent commitment to education—a call for further study cannot be an excuse to study only.[62] There is already a political consensus that "something" should be done about the state of American education and poverty. We advocate tying these policy initiatives together, not as a panacea, but as a place to begin. Education policy became the fashionable issue of the 1998 off-year elections. The new federal surplus and the flushed coffers of many states gave rise to proposals to dramatically increase the level of funding for education. President Clinton as well as Republican governors George Bush (Texas), Pete Wilson (California), Jim Edgar (Illinois), and Christie Whitman (New Jersey), all proposed major increases in education budgets, and others such as Arne Carlson (Minnesota) had done so in previous years.[63] This is all to the good, but we should not forget the persistent claim of the right that mere budgetary increases do not guarantee effective policy. The emphatic Christian center is committed to educational *results* more than educational spending, and here we are committed to them largely as a way to lift out those in poverty, diminish the cycle of poverty, and provide power for the entire social body.

Unfortunately, the current debate about education is in serious danger of being sidetracked into yet another manifestation of the American religion of freedom and its corollary, the fear of government. Judging by the media and conservative politicians, one might think that virtually the only issue in education is school "choice," a debate with permutations ranging from vouchers for private or public schools to charter schools.[64] Moreover, President Clinton's 1997 proposal for voluntary (i.e., choice-based) national competency testing for students ran into a buzz-saw of opposition from those who claimed that such national standards were an intrusion of "big government." How, exactly, national testing was another indication of creeping federal tyranny was never clearly explained. Republican opponents—among them Arne Carlson, who strongly advocated skills testing for Minnesota public school students on the grounds that the state could not help improve schools unless it knew the level its students were achieving—did not bother to explain why testing was inherently a proper state function. As usual, vague antifederal rhetoric substituted for actual arguments.

There may be merit in vouchers, charter schools, and state testing, but the current debate is off-center. The issue should be about generating educational power and achievement, not choice. Whether we want vouchers or would be more satisfied with them is not immediately germane. We cannot afford to be diverted from concrete policy objectives by our reflexive commitment to freedom and choice. Nor can questions of educational policy afford a detour through the pointless drudge of antigovernment polemics. Americans are supposed to be a pragmatic people. It is time for education policy to prove that true.[65]

What would an emphatic Christian centrist policy (with a targeted universalist approach) mean for education initiatives? There are many needs, especially for schools which serve primarily poor populations. But targeted universalism veers away from making such schools our sole focus. Rather, the performance of all schools is at issue. In view of concerns that American schoolchildren are not prepared adequately in comparison with the schoolchildren of other Western industrialized nations, relatively universalist education reforms seem possible. They will, however, have to be formulated carefully. We propose the following as keynotes for a new policy for American education.

1) School Financing, Targeted Universalism, and a New Federalism

To achieve the objectives of better student performance, current structures should be retained as much as possible. This means that the emphatic centrist endorses an education policy which—in the absence of significant countervailing evidence—advocates that (a) most education initiatives be undertaken at the local level, with (b) principal financing discretion (and quality control) at the state level, and (c) significant federal oversight and funding based on the extent of improvement at state and local levels.[66] Curricular decisions, in other words, are probably most appropriately determined locally. A program that works well in New York City may not be similarly effective in Evanston, Wyoming. This is another example of the principle of subsidiarity at work. Teachers, parents, students, and local leaders are closer to the problem, and usually more effective if they are given resources and not hindered by layers of regulation. But their need for support means that "local control," by itself, is not the answer.

We advocate state-based funding policy because such funding promises equalize spending per student better than funding based primarily on local property taxes—especially now that real estate is no longer the chief form of wealth in most communities.[67] Otherwise, school districts with wealthier residents will have resources and facilities far better than those that any district with an economically disadvantaged residential base can possibly achieve, reinforcing the cycle of poverty.[68]

How should states make funding determinations, and how should federal money be distributed? There are many needs in education policy, some of which we will note later. However, a crucial aspect of emphatic Christian centrism is *accountability*. Education cannot simply be a run for the money irrespective of effectiveness. Local governments should have substantial discretion in *how* they will improve their schools, not *whether* they will do so. The same holds true for states. They too must be held accountable, which will require a significant federal role in education. We propose that state financial policy be based on regional achievement (with regions including a diverse mix of poor, middle-income, and upper-income schools and districts), and that federal distribution of block grants be tied to levels of improvement in student achievement on a statewide basis. Moreover, the formula should privilege improvements in student achievement in low-income schools.

Initially based on a five-year cycle (perhaps later extended to ten years), here is how such a program would work. Based on an initial distribution of federal money to states (the state-to-region case is parallel, but for the sake of simplicity we will focus on the federal-to-state case), student performance is assessed at the end of a five-year cycle. Future funding levels to the *entire* state would be determined on the basis of levels of (a) overall improvement of student performance statewide, with (b) significant funding incentives *statewide* for greater improvements in (1) low-income and (2) initially low-achieving districts. Thus, the funding level for all districts (wealthy, poor, initially high-achieving and low-achieving) will depend in part on the level of improvement in impoverished and low-achieving districts. The policy is, therefore, an example of targeted universalism. All schools have an incentive to improve their performance (a, above), but there is special targeting of poor and backward schools (b, above).

In addition, particularly at the beginning, there should be separate funding for educational initiatives of unproved value but great potential, as long as there are clear strategies for assessing such programs as they are implemented. Innovation is risky, and should be encouraged and funded without penalty for programs which do not have salutary effects as, certainly, some will not. However, such a policy will allow for continuing research and innovation in education. Once again, those programs which are directed to the poor or to schools with lower achievement should be especially privileged.

2) THE PLACE OF PRIVATE SCHOOLS

In general, we oppose voucher programs for private schools. We do so not on constitutional grounds—a question beyond our competence—but on educational ones. First, private school vouchers endanger public education in a way that charter schools and public school voucher programs do not. Second, the data on the efficacy of private vouchers for improving education are ambiguous. At the very least, we should wait to see what substantial, long-term data emerge from communities such as Milwaukee and Cleveland.[69] Third, if private schools accept, even indirectly, governmental financing, they should be subject to the same structures of accountability as public schools. Thus, even were private voucher programs implemented, renewal of voucher eligibility for private schools would need to be based on the level of improvement they are able to produce in students. Thus, entrants' private school achievement measures would have to be compared with their achievement measures prior to entry into the private school. That would be cumbersome, but if private schools expect to be funded by government, they must accept the burden.

There is a more serious difficulty with voucher programs, however, which has not yet emerged in primary and secondary education, but was a crucial factor in higher education in the 1980s. Private higher education tuition has priced many students out of the market (either absolutely or in forcing students to carry a huge debt burden upon completion of their undergraduate education), and is in danger of turning quality private higher education back into a preserve of the well-to-do. In the early 1980s, that was not the case. But from the mid-1980s to the mid-1990s, college tuition costs skyrocketed, consistently and dramatically rising well in advance of inflation. Not coincidentally, in the 1980s, Congress sharply increased the maximum loan debt that students could assume as a response to Ronald Reagan's drastic cuts in education grant programs. As the loan limit rose, so did college tuitions, as if colleges and universities could not countenance forcing students to borrow anything less than the maximum.

What does this have to do with private school vouchers? A great deal. Whatever voucher amount is available to pay private school tuition (in some proposals, $2,000 per year, a figure also suggested in some plans allowing parents to establish "educational savings accounts") can become, easily, free money for private schools. A private school that would want to exclude the poor would simply have to raise its tuition well beyond any figure that a family armed with no more than a voucher could afford. In short, if private school vouchers are to become public policy, it is *absolutely necessary* that cost controls be included in the proposal. Otherwise, vouchers and tax-exempt savings accounts will not benefit those who need it most. To our knowledge, none of the proposals for vouchers has addressed this problem. If this difficulty has not arisen in limited experimental programs such as Milwaukee's, that is likely because those are experimental. Given the human penchant for sinful greed, we can expect that if the experiment becomes public policy, many schools will be off their best behavior and will instead approach vouchers as a cash cow.[70]

3) COMPETENCY AND ACHIEVEMENT TESTING

Accountability requires some means of assessment. How else can fiscal responsibility and the effectiveness of new programs be established? For local and regional districts to qualify for state funding, some form of assessment of student achievement should be required.[71] The same should be true if states want to receive federal funds. It is—to say the least—disingenuous for conservatives to oppose any federal conditions on states that receive federal aid. First, there is no federal obligation to assist states. Second, it is primarily conservatives who routinely and rightly object to financing without accountability. Third, many of the same conservatives felt no similar hesitance about states' rights when Ronald Reagan threatened to—and did—withhold federal highway funding unless states raised the legal drinking age. More recently, there was scarcely a murmur about state's prerogatives in the recent welfare reform legislation, which made block grants to states partly contingent upon their ability not to increase or even to decrease abortions. Why education funding should be any different quite escapes us. If it was fair in the case of highway funds or welfare grants to hold states accountable, it is no less fair—and easily as important—to do so in education.

In addition to evaluating improvement in student performance, we urge teacher competency testing, and support for teacher development. On its face, it is disturbing that approximately one-third of public school teachers in academic fields did not receive college majors or minors in that field. And in schools in which 40 percent or more of the students are from low-income families, the number of teachers teaching subjects for which they were not trained in college rises to nearly 50 percent.[72] It is not necessarily the case that teachers are incompetent in areas in which they were not trained, or that those who are teaching in their fields of study are more competent. But statistics such as these are cause for concern. Moreover, because bodies of knowledge change, we cannot assume that competency continues, as anyone who has taught knows all too well. It is as important that teachers be well-versed in the material they are supposed to be teaching as it is to know the levels of student achievement. At the same time, it is important to encourage teachers, who are closest to the problems and possibilities, by providing room for initiative and creative response to the children they teach face-to-face.

4) OTHER PROPOSALS

Much needs to be done to improve American education, and it is quite clear that not all things can be done immediately. Moreover, needs in particular localities will differ in importance. For example, a technologically inadequate school with large class sizes may gain a greater benefit from addressing one problem before the other. The incentives incorporated in our proposals allow precisely this kind of flexibility. *How* improvement is achieved, within broad limits, is the purview of more local decision makers. *That* improvements are made is the function of both these bodies and the supervisory-funding role of broader units of government and policy. Some possibilities, however, are (a) infrastructure improvements for decaying schools, (b) improvements in classroom technology,[73] (c) efforts to increase parental involvement and responsibility in children's education,[74] (d) teacher retention incentives targeted to poorer districts, (e) class size initiatives,[75] (f) carefully designed charter schools,[76] (g) and public school vouchers, preferably neighborhood-based.[77] Which of these proposals, among others, is adopted and when, should be a matter for local and state governments that are held *accountable* for their decisions about their citizens and their schoolchildren.

In short, emphatic Christian centrism endorses an education policy that meets a concern both religious and secular, does so without merely compromising between alternatives, and forwards its own proposals for public debate. Moreover, our proposals are not beholden to the American civil religion of freedom—or rather, we seek to maximize *both* freedom and responsibility through structures of financial accountability. Our approach is directed toward two primary goals: improvement of education for its own sake, and amelioration of poverty, so that the appalling human cost of 36.5 million people living an economically miserable existence can be reduced for the long term. Education is neither self-sufficient nor a panacea; but it *is* an important piece of a broader social policy to address poverty. Yet its own success depends on the health and support of the families in which children are raised. Emphatic Christian centrism must also seek to promote ways to strengthen families, both for their own sakes and for the wider social power that such families could produce.

Family at the Center: Power Without Patriarchy, Difference Without Disintegration

A "Conservative" Issue Adopted by Liberals

During the 1970s and 1980s, the "family"—as a political issue—clearly belonged to the right. The left concerned itself with women's issues and was otherwise content to celebrate the freedom and diversity of nontraditional families. In the early 1990s, however, it became clear that the right's exclusive ownership of the issue was coming to an end. "Liberals" of various stripes began to acknowledge that the family was in crisis. This development was seriously overdue, not because the right was wrong about everything—it was not—but because the right's valid insights were in desperate need of correction, purification, and broader contextualization. The family was, and is, in crisis. But the right's analysis and prescriptions are short-sighted at best, vicious and punitive at worst.

Starting in the 1970s, the right—primarily the Christian right—sounded the alarm that families in America were on the verge of collapse. The causes of this breakdown were usually identified as abortion, feminism, homosexuality, pornography, and the media. Thus Jerry Falwell made defeat of the Equal Rights Amendment a major priority, Donald Wildmon organized against sex and "antifamily" television programming, antiabortion politics came to the fore, and James Dobson defended parental discipline while fighting homosexual rights. Interestingly, divorce was almost never identified as a problem (perhaps because the Christian right was busy helping to elect our first divorced President, Ronald Reagan). The "family" was of little or no interest, however, to the *economic* right, which was primarily interested in curtailing government influence on economic activity; but it was quite willing to form alliances with activists who wanted to limit government influence on the family and schools, even if it had no interest in school prayer or abortion.

Meanwhile, the left, busily defending its newly won right to abortion and nursing its wounds over the defeat of the Equal Rights Amendment, virtually ignored the family. Not that the left was uninterested in family issues; but it viewed them exclusively in terms of women's—and sometimes children's—*rights*. If women were granted equal opportunity, and child care were provided, that would improve the status of both women and children; men and teenage boys did not need any improvement, at least in domestic matters (except, of course, that they needed to support women's rights and to start doing their share of the housework). But the family as such was rarely discussed; when it was, it was viewed almost exclusively in negative terms, a patriarchal institution which enslaved women and called for liberation.[78] With the religious right having played a central role in the defeat of the ERA and now openly calling for women to stay at home, it was easy for the left to dismiss their frenzied warnings about families as the desperate rhetoric of patriarchal, antifeminist reactionaries. This was unfortunate, for it abandoned the issue to the right, which mixed genuine insight into the family crisis with bizarre nostalgia and insidious patriarchy.

Sometime in the late 1980s to early 1990s, this changed; the family became an issue for many on the left as well.[79] Vice President Dan Quayle's (in)famous 1992 "family values" speech, which criticized the television series *Murphy Brown* for weakening moral values by glamorizing its lead character's decision to have a baby out of wedlock, was quickly dismissed by liberals and mainstream culture alike. The defeat of the Bush-Quayle ticket later that year could easily have been interpreted as another defeat for "family values." But Barbara DaFoe Whitehead's 1993 article "Dan Quayle Was Right" called attention to the growing body of scientific evidence that single parenthood produced worse outcomes for children.[80] And in 1994, President Clinton—with greater nuance and sensitivity, and less racism—was echoing many of the same themes as Quayle. "Both saw teenage pregnancies, out-of-wedlock births, and absent fathers as contributing to the poverty of women and children, growing youth violence, and poorer performance in school."[81]

Like most surprises that burst upon the political scene, this was no surprise for those who had been following the topic. During the 1980s, a largely unpublicized but nevertheless overwhelming accumulation of evidence clearly demonstrated that children of two-parent families do better on a wide variety of measures of child welfare.[82] Conservatives and liberals differed, of course, in their interpretation of the data: conservatives saw government programs, especially welfare, as the cause of the problem; liberals looked to government for solutions.[83] But, more important, both acknowledged that there are real problems, which was a real change for the left. Curiously, however, while some if not most political liberals have come to acknowledge the issue, religious liberals and mainline denominations have continued to remain relatively silent about it.[84]

The Family Crisis—What Is It?

Families are under stress from a variety of factors, both economic and cultural. The childhood poverty rate is over 20 percent, and exceeds the poverty rate for the elderly. Liberals have long assumed that race and sex discrimination are sufficient to explain this disaster, and why some families and children are worse off than others. But a growing body of evidence contradicts this view; although race and sex discrimination are part of the cause of family distress, single-parent families clearly have a negative impact as well. Simply put, children in single-parent households "do worse on four of five measures of high school performance—test scores, college expectations, grade point average, and school attendance." They are "one and a half times more likely to be idle and to have difficulty entering and succeeding in the job market."[85] Moreover, this holds true *regardless of race, parent's education, number of siblings, and place of residence* (compounding the impact that these factors do have). Children in single-parent families are more likely to have learning disabilities, and much more likely to have emotional and behavioral problems. The prevalence of emotional and behavioral problems is "8.3% in mother-father families, 19.1% in mother-only families, 23.6% in mother-stepfather families, and 22.2% in other family situations."[86] Where the popular divorce literature of the 1970s and 1980s had promised improved outcomes for children as a result of divorce, the evidence of the 1980s sharply contradicted that hope.[87]

A more complex matter is the economic status of single-parent families. It is clear that single-parent families have, on average, lower income than two-parent families; and this remains true regardless of race and parental education.[88] There is also strong evidence that although economic hardship helps to cause divorce, divorce makes economic hardship worse.[89] In other words, divorce and economic hardship for children go hand-in-hand, each magnifying the effects of the other.

Similarly, parent-child relationships suffer as a result of divorce. The pro-divorce literature of the 1970s and 1980s assumed that parents who were unhappy in marriage would be happier in divorce, and that the children would naturally be happier too, after a period of adjustment. Research has not confirmed this speculation either. "Fathers in general do not spend much time with their children after a divorce or separation."[90] A 1981 national survey of children in divorced families found that only one of six saw the father at least once a week; nearly half had not seen their father in the preceding twelve months.[91] But mother-child relationships do not improve after divorce, either. After ten years had passed in a longitudinal study of divorced families, researchers found that "over a third of the good mother-child relationships have deteriorated, with mothers emotionally or physically less available to their children."[92]

During the period that this research was conducted, the divorce rate skyrocketed, particularly for divorces involving children. "The rate of children involved in divorce doubled between the early sixties and the late eighties," so that one million children per year were affected by divorce *each* year from 1974 to 1990.[93] The overall divorce rate has risen from 7 percent in the 1860s to 50 percent today.[94] By the late 1980s, 27 percent of all children at any given time were living with a single parent;[95] and estimates suggested that for children born from 1970 to 1984, 44 percent would live with a single parent before age sixteen.[96]

Why has this happened? In an important study of religion and the American family debate—a book which is itself a model of emphatic Christian centrism[97]—Don S. Browning and a team of four other researchers identified four competing explanations of the family crisis: (1) cultural individualism, (2) economic transformations both within and without the family, (3) psychological causes within the family, and (4) patriarchy.[98] Each explanation entails important truths about the crisis of the family; none explains it alone. Conservatives point to individualism, liberals to economics, therapists to psychological causes, and feminists to patriarchy, each group usually focusing only on their *own* "favorite" explanation. But Browning's team did not simply find the midpoint between these views; they made a decision, clearly stating that "inordinate individualism—the desire to attain more expressive and utilitarian satisfactions for oneself—is critical."[99] They cut off unlimited debate on one topic so that they could go on to invite all four views—doubtless represented on the team itself—to contribute to the continuing discussion. The four major trends affecting families are divorce, out-of-wedlock births (rising from 5 percent in the early 1960s to over 30 percent today), the correlation of poverty with single parenthood, and the absent father.[100] At the same time, the researchers also identify the positive developments in family life during the same period, especially the growing pressure (largely the result of feminism) to democratize marriage and family life, with equal regard between spouses displacing patriarchy. They also recognize the especially important role played by feminism in de-legitimating physical abuse in marriage. Yet the overall *results* for children at this point in history are clearly negative. This led Browning's team to identify the married two-parent family as clearly superior—*other things being equal*—for both children and society as a whole.

This does *not* mean that all divorces are bad, nor that people should remain in abusive relationships. Yet, according to some estimates, only 10 percent to 15 percent of all marriages that end in divorce involve violence or serious conflict. In the other cases—including emotional separation, boredom, or outside sexual interest—"the child would probably be better off if the parents resolved their differences and the family remained together."[101]

THE FAMILY CRISIS AND THE AMERICAN RELIGION OF FREEDOM

Our contention that the *real* American religion is an unnuanced and even incoherent notion of freedom as independence is dramatically confirmed by this crisis. If there is any place in human relations that one-sided rhetoric about "freedom" and "independence" and "the right to be left alone" are nonsensical, it is in intimate family relations. This is not to say that freedom and rights are unimportant in marriage and family; they are crucial, including the right to marry without unreasonable constraint, the right not to be battered, the right to be provided with the necessities of life insofar as the family is able, and so on. But the moment one speaks of marriage and family *merely* in terms of independence and freedom, one is speaking sheer nonsense. Yet such nonsense is deeply embedded in American rhetoric and, increasingly, American practice.

Mary Ann Glendon has demonstrated the generally low regard in which the family was held by most of the "natural-right" philosophers who gave birth to what we have called the "religion of freedom" (especially Rousseau and Locke). Rousseau's "noble savage was a strong, healthy, solitary wanderer, who mated casually without bonding."[102] These philosophers "envisioned the dependency of infants as a quickly passing stage, and accorded hardly any attention at all to the mother's circumstances."[103] Locke, wishing to discredit the image of the king as the benevolent father of his subjects, went out of his way to attack parenthood in general, building a "case for mistrust of government by casting suspicion on traditional assumptions about the benevolence of parents." It comes as no surprise, then, that cultures largely based on these arguments repudiate any idea of the human person as "'naturally' situated within and constituted through relationships of care and dependency," preferring to view that person instead as "a free, self-determining individual."[104] This latter view—which is clearly contrary to fact—has had a devastating impact on marriage and family. Much Western law now "holds self-sufficiency up as an ideal, suggesting that dependency is somehow degrading"[105]—although it is noteworthy that these tendencies are more pronounced in English, American, and Swedish family law, and less so in French and German.[106]

We are not at all surprised to find low regard for family life so directly linked to the religion of freedom, even in its origins.[107] Whitehead and Browning, calling it "individualism," have (like Glendon) documented its pivotal role in the family crisis.[108] Not that it is the only cause; we have never claimed that it is the sole root of all evil. But it is present in all sources, interacting with and aggravating all the other causes of the crisis—patriarchal, economic, psychological—to make them many times worse.

THE FAMILY CRISIS AND THE PRINCIPLES OF THE EMPHATIC CENTER

The family crisis clearly manifests the relevance of the emphatic center's principles. Browning and his colleagues do not shrink from identifying *sin* as a factor in distorted families. "The best social-science explanations, as important as they are, do not give us a full account of family disruption." Sin "interacts with cultural values, economic patterns, psychological needs, and patriarchal structures."[109]

We argue that sin is present in human life as both *pride* and *sloth*. In the family, pride takes the form of self-exaltation at the expense of others; sloth manifests itself in self-denigration out of fear of others. In both cases, sin combines with and amplifies the social causes of family disintegration and powerlessness which empirical research describes. The subtle interaction between inner (personal-psychological) and outer (social-political) sin plays itself out in manifold dramas of human interaction and conflict. Sin is especially potent here in its intellectual forms, with claims for "freedom" and "family values" so excessive as to leave one wondering just how much self-deception the rhetoric involves.

The central role of *love* and appreciation in the family—including both what Browning calls "equal-regarding love" (or "mutuality") and "sacrificial love"[110]—is so obvious as to be a cliche. Less obvious, however, in many cases, is just where this love is supposed to come from, or just how the broader society can extend and strengthen it rather than undermine it. Glendon, for example, documents how laws and court decisions have presupposed the existence of mutuality and even sacrificial love without much attending to the sorts of conditions which foster these affections. It is of course more likely that the law will be called in only when at least some of these affections have failed. But it seems that both the law and the popular ideology of love presume that such love is "natural," simply happens ("falling in love"), and cannot be cultivated. This is both foolish and dangerous. Churches, voluntary associations, schools, therapists, the law, and not least of all families themselves, must carefully attend to the ways in which love is taught, modeled, and nurtured.

Feminist criticisms of the family have emphasized the disproportionate expectations placed on mothers and daughters for *sacrificial* love, arguing that this has stood in the way of full equality for women.[111] This was, as was discussed, one of the reasons we rejected self-sacrificing agape as the sole norm of Christian love. Browning and his team acknowledge the dangers of self-sacrificial love, but identify it as "a moment *within* a love ethic of mutuality."[112] This harmonizes well with our own view, which does not view love as the absence of power, but as rather an *outcome* of power, and which, in turn, sees sacrificial love as a moment in the production of power for others and the self.

Power is central, we have argued, to all being; we have even argued its ontological priority to love. With respect to the family, this means that love cannot emerge unless families have the power to function. Love relies on strength. Quite simply, what most of our parents told us about the priority of "putting food on the table" was, and is, true. Families, and the social ecologies in which they live—society, culture, school, church, synagogue—must generate power in order to *be*. Domination—distorted power—can destroy families, and the people in them. But that is no reason to remove all power from the family and make it a mere passing association of free, equal, and independent persons along with free, equal, independent persons-in-training. Yet, as Glendon observes, American and Western European law, mirroring their societies, has clearly drifted in this direction: "Despite the rhetoric of partnership and community, concrete legal changes in each system have moved in the direction of emphasis on the separate and equal individuality of the family members, most decisively in the United States, least so in France." Ominously, she continues: "Stamped on the reverse side of the coinage of individual liberty, family privacy, and sex equality, are alienation, powerlessness, and dependency."[113] Of course! Power is a communication of efficacy; the more private and independent the person in the family becomes, the less power there will be for all.

Finally, we join Browning and his researchers in insisting on *justice* in the family: justice for children, who suffer most from family disintegration; justice in response to the undoubted role of racism and poverty in the family crisis; and justice to counter the continuing pernicious effects of patriarchy. There is need for forgiveness and justification; but they too must issue in meaningful public results.

INGREDIENTS OF A SOLUTION

An emphatic center is already in the process of forming in the family debate, as evidenced by the remarkable and apparently growing consensus among chastened liberals that the family is in crisis, and the mostly silent but evident retreat of conservatives from insisting that women must stay at home. Less clearly, perhaps, there is an emerging consensus that the shallow conception of freedom as mere independence is inadequate to the circumstances of intimate life. Another sign of maturity is that the debate has begun to reach the stage where concrete proposals are beginning to surface.

Browning and his team have put forward four concrete proposals for a "practical theology of families." They are (1) the centrality of "equal regard" or "mutuality" in marital love; (2) the necessary but subordinate role of sacrificial love in support of this equal regard; (3) a "life-cycle perspective" on when and to what extent such self-sacrifice is appropriate; and (4) the "subordination of families" to a larger common good.[114] Taken together, these constitute what they call "critical familism."[115] Space precludes our doing justice to these proposals.[116] Two very important moves deserve comment, however. While they repudiate the primary role assigned to sacrificial love in most Christian accounts of marriage, they still retain a central role for self-sacrifice for *both* men and women. Similarly, while they fully repudiate all remnants of patriarchal authority over wife and children, they retain the central role of parental authority, now jointly exercised by wife and husband. In so doing they appropriate many valuable criticisms of traditional marriage, especially feminist ones, but do not make the fatal mistake of attributing *all* problems in marriage to patriarchy.

Browning's team recommends sixteen specific tactics, several with public policy implications, but most directed toward churches. There is a powerful insight here; churches may command more respect for their public policy recommendations—what they think public authorities such as states and schools should do—if they devote more attention to what they themselves can do.[117] These recommendations for churches include (1) critically retrieving their own traditions of marriage and family, neither as patriarchy nor as mere "committed relationships";[118] (2) joining "with other parts of civil society in their local communities to create a critical marriage and family culture";[119] (3) developing a "bilingual theology" that addresses the needs of intact families and also the realities of other family forms;[120] (4) addressing divorce critically as a sign of failure, and yet supporting those who are divorced;[121] and (5) addressing the issue of father absence, which they call the "male problematic."[122] It is worth noting the congruence of these recommendations with Mary Ann Glendon's "ecological" approach to the family, which suggests that "governments might be able to assist families and their members indirectly by attending to the health of surrounding small-scale communities."[123] This is another version of the principle of *subsidiarity*, that the institutions closest to the people and issues should be the first to deal with them, and should be supported, not undermined, by more general, broader institutions.

Browning's public policy recommendations include (1) helping society understand "that public policy should not and cannot maintain value neutrality" on family matters;[124] (2) providing state-supported marriage and family education;[125] and (3) revision of divorce laws in the direction of a modified "fault" divorce law in cases involving dependent children.[126]

To all this we only add two more observations. (1) All persons—single, married, or divorced; gay, straight, or bisexual; liberal or conservative; believers or not—have a stake in the health of the two-parent committed family. It is an issue that concerns all of society. (2) For now, the family crisis should be a more important issue than either homosexuality or abortion, for both the church and the society at large.[127] These issues will have to take a backseat to the family, at least for now. Church leaders and bodies in particular would do well to desist from warfare over these issues and turn that energy to seeking support for families. Indeed, such warfare itself seems to push aside other issues, upon which there is wide agreement but not much activity, perhaps precisely because agreement does not generate a fighting spirit.

Families, both current and future, are threatened by many factors. Browning and his researchers focused, as we have noted, on a variety of factors that undermine healthy and powerful families, choosing individualism as the chief problem. But a very good case can also be made that nothing threatens families today more than *violence* within them. Nevertheless, despite widespread opposition to such violence, voluntary institutions such as churches do much less about it than they could. If we are as interested in stable and loving families as we say, there seem to be few arenas of action more fitting than reducing sexual violence, to which we now turn.

Sexual Violence and the Emphatic Christian Center

THE SCOURGE OF SEXUAL VIOLENCE

By "sexual violence" we mean both domestic abuse and sexual assault. Measures and estimates of the extent of this violence are beyond troubling—they are astonishing. To begin with domestic violence (violence between partners): in any *single year,* four million women are abused;[128] a 1990 survey found that 1.8 million women "were severely assaulted during the 12 months that preceded the survey. That is to say they were punched, kicked, choked, hit with an object, beaten up, threatened with a knife or a gun, or had a knife or gun used on them."[129] Ninety-five percent of spousal battery victims are women.[130] Indeed, the *primary* locus of violence against women is domestic: numerous studies demonstrate that "women are more likely to be attacked, raped, injured, or killed by current or former male partners than by any other type of assailant."[131] The numbers vary slightly between surveys but remain consistently high; whether "only" two or three million or as many as four million women "experience severe or life-threatening assault from a male partner" per year[132] is not paramount for social policy; in either case, the numbers are far too high.

The situation with respect to sexual assault is not much better. It is true that, along with the overall crime rate, rape seems to have declined; the Federal Bureau of Investigation's Uniform Crime Reports registered a 5 percent decline from 1994 to 1995. Still, just under 100,000 forcible rapes were *reported* to law enforcement for a crime for which reporting rates remain low.[133] Yearly reporting, moreover, masks the extent of the problem of sexual abuse. Diana Russell's extensive study found that during the course of American women's *childhoods*—a longer time frame is a more accurate way to judge the extent of damage from sexual abuse than year-by-year incidence—38 percent of women "reported at least one experience of incestuous and/or extrafamilial sexual abuse before reaching the age of eighteen years; 28 percent reported at least one such experience before reaching fourteen years of age."[134] Relatives accounted for 29 percent of the abuse, total strangers only 11 percent.[135] Twenty-six percent of incest perpetrators were under eighteen years of age,[136] as are 20 percent of all rape offenders.[137] A final statistic worth noting is that, at least in the case of child sexual abuse, there is virtually no correlation between its incidence and the demographic characteristics of either victim or perpetrator—whether economic status, occupation, urbanization, ethnicity or race, or *religion*.[138] Thus, the problem of sexual violence is widely and evenly spread across the social body. No gated community—whether enclosed within barriers literal or symbolic (such as, say, the safety of religious sanctuary)—provides a defense.

The cost of sexual violence to the American polity is enormous. It involves the perpetrators themselves, who confuse violence and control with power, and are themselves brutalized through their own acts of brutality. A Christian perspective that strives for the generation of *universal* power will seek it through justice, recognizing that the commandment to love our enemies—even the greatest of evildoers—*cannot* permit us to forget the violence that the perpetrator does. Otherwise, the perpetrators themselves will be badly served—both interpersonally and spiritually.

For the victims, there is the horrific cost of the violence itself, sometimes extending to serious injury and death. Beyond these, there are the extraordinary psychological costs, as a mountain of research on post-traumatic stress disorder, depression, anxiety, the inability to trust, and suicidal tendencies shows.[139] Unsurprisingly, these effects become more severe with the severity and frequency of abuse.[140]

Nor does the cost of sexual violence stop with victims and perpetrators; it reverberates throughout the social body. The fact that 38 percent of female children—nearly four in ten—are victims of sexual abuse, without regard to social class, race, religion, and other factors means that sexual abuse affects all of us. All of us—whether we realize it or not—know the victims. They are our friends, coworkers, clients, students, mothers, siblings, children, social set, religious associates, neighbors.

The effects of violence spiral out centrifugally over the whole of society. One red thread running throughout the literature of sexual violence[141] is the profound and lasting loss of trust in humanity experienced by victims. This distrust is displayed especially, though not exclusively, toward men. Its effects are profound. In an increasingly gender-conscious society, the effects of sexual violence complicate (and sometimes destroy or prevent) decent, nonsexual cross-gender relationships and friendships—to say nothing of casting a pall over all actual sexual relations, particularly those involving former victims. We tend to be trapped—all of us—in close friendships with only those of our own gender, unable even to dine or celebrate occasions with those of the other gender. Suspicion pervades late-twentieth-century gender relationships; although it would be impossible to *prove* that this is a result of a 38 percent rate of sexual abuse, it would be foolhardy not to presume a connection. This loss of trust is tragic. One of the authors, who works for an assault and abuse crisis center, feels in nearly every conversation with a victim both the desperate desire to trust—in another person, law enforcement, a male, religious organizations, God—and the near inability to do so.

This human cost is the most significant result of sexual violence. But there are certainly economic and social costs as well. For instance, even though there is no socioeconomic correlation with abuse, the most severely abused children do tend to be downwardly mobile in adult life. The psychological costs of abuse are not merely internal but affect personal and social economic productivity; addressing sexual violence is, therefore, one component of antipoverty efforts,[142] just as it is essential to strengthening families. In addition, the medical cost of domestic abuse alone—nearly $1 billion per year just in emergency room costs—is staggering, particularly for an expense that is completely unproductive.[143] In an era of escalating medical costs, which all consumers of health care must bear, the presence of a billion-dollar annual drain is unacceptable. Finally, the problem of sexual violence is intergenerational. Those children who were raised in a sexually violent home are, unsurprisingly, substantially more likely to perpetuate the behaviors of victimizer and victim in adulthood.[144] Like poverty, sexual violence establishes a cycle. Paradoxically, that is also ground for hope; if the cycle can be interrupted at one point, what is gained will resound throughout the social body, increasing intergenerational momentum for long-term reduction of sexual violence.

POWER, LOVE, AND JUSTICE: TARGETED UNIVERSALIST APPROACHES TO SEXUAL VIOLENCE

What should the Christian center advocate with respect to sexual violence? In one sense, the problem of sexual violence is not subject to the left-right division we have been employing. Since no one openly advocates sexual violence, it is ill-suited for presentation in a *Crossfire*-like format.[145] That much is good, but it also means that the media lose interest in it as a social problem. The best the media seem willing to do is to present horrific cases of sexual abuse on daytime talk programs, and to play up news reporting of sex crimes for their shock value, encouraging women to fear all men. However, they pay little attention to social policy implications, the role of government, voluntary institutions, or citizens in addressing sexual violence systematically. In questions of social policy, the media seem at a loss to say anything when the shopworn alternative of "on the right" and "on the left" does not apply.

The Christian center, however, is in a position to speak. There are several initiatives that we believe are essential in order to address sexual violence more adequately: (1) We must clear away the smoke of gender politicization. The *entire* social body—women and men, girls and boys—are implicated in the victimization of sexual violence. Unfortunately, the problem of sexual violence has suffered the fate of so many misinterpretations of "pluralism," which ghettoize issues into their presumed "interest" groups: black issues, white issues, Jewish issues, "Christian" issues. Sexual violence thus becomes a "women's issue." This balkanization is a disastrous mistake. Sexual violence is not a "special interest" issue. The tendency to treat it as one is not only false—the effects of sexual violence are spread throughout the social body—but it also encourages men in particular not to concern themselves with sexual violence, and women rightly to resent men for their apparent lack of concern, perpetuating gender division. This tendency is heightened by the overblown rhetoric of a few feminists such as Catherine MacKinnon, whose negative stereotypes of men in fact encourage male apathy toward the problem of sexual violence.[146] Although gender-based moral righteousness may provide psychological comfort, it is a sure way to *limit* the headway we can make against the problem of sexual violence by encouraging men to believe that it is not their problem, or that they lack the capacity to address it.

In addition to emphasizing that sexual violence is universally damaging, primarily to women and girls but also to men and boys, we must recognize (2) that sexual violence is a *political,* that is *public* problem. Feminist criticism of the still-widespread conception that domestic abuse is a "private" question is quite on point. The American tendency to dismiss the significance of all realms other than self and law has been discussed at length elsewhere in this chapter and in chapter 2. Nowhere is this tendency more damaging than in the question of sexual violence. The claim that sexual violence within the family is a "private" problem allows it to continue unabated and unchecked—even uncondemned. Moreover, it enables those with knowledge of sexual abuse among acquaintances and even friends to ignore brutality with an easy conscience, under the moral banner of not wanting to invade the privacy of others—it is, after all, "none of my business."

These two tendencies—balkanization and depoliticization—are the ingredients of a wicked and cruel brew. The depoliticization of sexual violence leaves victims on a lonely island, while its balkanization leaves women and men on separate islands. The cost of these combined tendencies is substantial. One of the many distressing facts about the Nicole Brown Simpson case—and the least noticed in the extensive media coverage—was the shocking fact that *not a single one* of O. J. Simpson's many male friends ever advised him that he needed professional help, nor even that he should stop beating his wife, though it was common knowledge that he was doing so on a regular basis. Stunning though that is, it is precisely what we should expect when we segregate sexual violence into the category of a "women's issue," and when only self and law are legitimate authorities. On the contrary, sexual violence is a universal political issue; but that will become evident only when we stop reducing "political" to "legal." Politics has to do with the health and vitality of the *polis,* the public body—a vitality and power that sexual violence saps.

The Christian center's view that authority and power exceed self and law leads us also to (3) refocusing social policy. In sexual violence, we judge that legal efforts have taken us a considerable distance in addressing the problem; if we are to get farther, the efforts of voluntary institutions—especially religious ones—should be emphasized. In the 1970s and 1980s, the focus of sexual violence policy was quite different, and appropriately so. The legal protections for those victimized by sexual violence were weak, and those that existed were frequently ignored. The 1970s saw an initiation of legal activity that has continued to the present, including the enactment of rape shield laws, the strengthening of spousal battery and child abuse laws, and more recently, antistalking legislation and sexual harassment rulings. In addition, there was a sharp increase in training of law enforcement and medical personnel to recognize and treat sexual violence victims, enforce existing laws, and increase sensitivity toward the victimized. Social services—funded both governmentally and privately—also expanded dramatically.

Effective response to sexual violence requires these components. It is clear that some fine-tuning of legal requirements is called for in light of isolated excesses, such as the prosecution of the staff of the McNaughton school in California and the cloud of suspicion that hung over the entire town of Jordan, Minnesota, in the mid-1980s. These difficulties, however, can pose a challenge to any legal solution and call for adjustment—not abandonment. The Christian center joins in insisting that legal advances already in place be maintained. No legal structure is perfectly safe and secure, and some of those structures have been jeopardized by the introduction of sloppily drafted "family rights" legislation—including a proposed constitutional amendment in Colorado—which threatens to strip children (in particular) of legal protections outside the family.

However, we also believe that the law has accomplished much of what it can do. Changes around the margins are surely important, but they will remain marginal. Yet the focus of American action against sexual violence remains substantially legal. This is unfortunate, though it is what we would expect in a culture for which authority has no "middle" between self and coercive law. This causes at least two problems. First, the effectiveness of efforts to combat sexual violence is likely to slow; if the law has already accomplished much of what it can, and if the only other authority is the self, we will not expect too much more to happen. The second problem—inherent in legal solutions[147] to human victimization—is more serious: the law comes too late. It can intervene only when substantial damage is already done. It can prevent additional injury but ordinarily cannot prevent initial violence, except through education and deterrence. A single-minded emphasis on legal solutions defrauds us; the law cannot *solve* the problem of sexual violence, only reduce the damage done by it. Our attention to law enforcement, medical training, and crisis hot lines is laudable, and they have done much good; but we would be better off if they were less necessary.

The Christian center, particularly in light of its emphasis on power and subsidiarity, naturally inclines toward voluntary institutions and citizens in ordinary relations with friends, colleagues, and acquaintances, which can actually *prevent initial violence*. We recognize, of course, that this prong of social—but not primarily governmental—policy is not self-sufficient; it requires support and maintenance of legal policies. But the problem is the violence itself, and the less we need to use those legal media, the better for all of us—those who do not become victims of sexual violence even once, those who do not become perpetrators, and those who do not have to confront the social aftershocks of violence as frequently.

It is not that there are no voluntary institutions that address sexual violence prevention. We believe, however, that those efforts are far too limited.[148] In our current situation, expanding efforts at prevention is most in line with the emphatic center's emphasis on power, justice, and love. Commitments to justice should not be narrowly restricted to the reparation of injustice, important as that is. We must also seek *positive, relational* justice (as we argued in our discussion of family policy) that is not only juridical but involves the ongoing fair treatment of partners and children—a routine divine providence rather than an extraordinary, heroic one. Justice is tied to love and, of course, to power as the overarching criterion of both love and justice. The Christian center seeks a powerful love that includes sovereignty without tipping over into relations of heartless domination and submission, in which control and its absence become the overwhelming relational fact.

It has become a cliche to say that sexual violence is about power. *That is wrong.* Sexual violence is not about power, but *control*, about relations of domination which prevent power from emerging. Control is a zero-sum game; power is not. The clearest indication of the difference is that relations that include sexual violence typically become more and more violent; they are relationships in which *no* party—abusers or abused—is fulfilled. And eventually such relationships shatter completely. Sexual violence demonstrates the ontological contradiction of domination in a particularly poignant way. When we strive for utter domination, all power is eventually destroyed, all parties become shells of human beings—empty of both content and power.

But when sexual violence is prevented, the social body can turn its attention to communicating power in other ways that go beyond simply restoring the dignity and power that have been lost. In relationships, in economic achievement, in personal integrity—in all these, new power can be generated.[149] The inherent weakness of a predominantly legal approach is that it can only restore—with painstaking uncertainty—what has already been compromised.

If efforts at prevention of sexual violence could reduce the number of victimized women (to say nothing of the men who are 5 percent of the victims of domestic violence) by even *one* percent of the American female population (from 38 percent to 37 percent), that would mean over one million more women who would have *never* experienced sexual violence directly, who would not carry its scars across an entire lifetime and into all life activities. Here, especially, voluntary institutions—and religious institutions most emphatically—have a crucial and largely unexploited role to play.

National church organizations have, of course, decried the level of sexual violence in our culture.[150] The response of churches, however, is primarily at this "macro" level. Local congregations, with some exceptions, are peculiarly silent on the issue.[151] One of the authors conducted an informal survey of about forty church-going acquaintances of most major Christian denominations. All those people together had heard exactly *one* sermon which mentioned sexual violence. None of them were aware of any instance in which sexual violence was included in confirmation classes or adult education initiatives. Many, however, knew that their pastors or priests had dealt with the tragedy of sexual violence within the congregation in counseling and referral to outside organizations.

Why this inattention to sexual violence? It is not because Christians can comfort themselves with the knowledge that no "Christians" are victimizers or victims. Sexual violence is no respecter of religious boundaries. Christians have approximately the same rates of sexual abuse as non-Christians in America. Nor is it that churches refuse to discuss or contribute to social questions—they spend considerable time effecting clothing drives, running soup kitchens, even helping to build houses. Oddly, churches tend to spend much of their social energy on problems—such as poverty—for which their best efforts can only ameliorate symptoms but for which substantial effects require government action.

In the arena of sexual violence, where church efforts actually might help *eliminate* a substantial part of the problem, there is comparative silence. It is surprising that a problem which likely affects about 38 percent of women *in their congregations* (and the men who are victimizing them) goes virtually unaddressed. Is it precisely because, at a deep level, congregations know that the problem of sexual violence is not "out there" but "in our midst," and that once churches begin to address the problem, they will discover how pervasive *in the sanctuary* are the lives made less powerful, less loving, and less just by sexual violence?

What can churches do? At a minimum, the problem of sexual violence can be addressed forcefully and *frequently* in sermons and liturgy. In liturgy, many denominations include in their orders of service confessions of sin and prayers for healing. These should be less generic; instead, they should discuss particular sins and injustices, specific causes of human brokenness and powerlessness. That specificity should regularly include mention of sexual violence. Surely a type of violence and oppression that affects nearly four in ten women deserves specific mention and treatment in religious congregations, which are generally overwhelmingly female.[152] In sermons, vague allusions about violence, sin, and healing should gain similar specificity. Pastors in one author's experience are inclined to use criminal examples of sin such as murder. But it is considerably more likely that there are more victims and friends of victims of sexual violence in the congregation than families affected by murder. There are certainly more likely to be perpetrators of sexual violence than robbers or murderers. If churches are really committed to speaking about the problems of contemporary society concretely, they should at least emphasize sexual violence consistently.

The same is true of confirmation classes. Discussions of the Ten Commandments, for example, routinely deal with injustice of various forms. Yet we are aware of no confirmation class that seriously discusses sexual violence.[153] But the young women and men who attend them are more likely to beat or be beaten, to be rape victim or sexual assailant, than murderer or murdered. And those murders that do occur are often the result of domestic abuse. In view of the fact that between 20 and 25 percent of sexual assaults are committed by juveniles—and that many live in families with domestic abuse—what better use of resources in confirmation classes than to discuss a Christian response to these problems?

In addition, young women can be taught to be more assertive, less submissive, and perhaps less likely to be victimized by sexual assault and violence during their teen years and later. At all levels of religious instruction, then, we recommend the incorporation of serious discussions of sexual abuse and gender relations that, perhaps, can both reduce the incidence of sexual violence and facilitate broader, nonsexualized gender relations that can create power for the entire social body. All this must become part of the "critical familism" we sketched earlier.

To make such an approach work, we also recommend heavy incorporation of training in sexual violence issues in seminary education. A 1982 survey indicated that although 94 percent of pastors and priests regularly counseled congregants on problems related to domestic violence (the survey did not ask about sexual assault), only 30 percent had received *any* training in sexual violence counseling.[154] With respect to sexual assault, there is anecdotal evidence that even minimal training can encourage victims to raise the issue to their clergy.[155]

Condemnatory statements by church bodies are not enough.[156] A concerted effort on the part of churches—and, of course, others—is a strategy that completes the circle of social policy. That is, it connects back to legal strategies that have already proved successful. Not least among these is for churches to take determined, vigorous, and direct action against perpetrators in the clergy and church staff positions—ensuring above all else that they are not put back into positions of trust involving children. But nonlegal efforts address initial prevention, which means that a legal strategy needs to be employed less frequently. Moreover, heightened attention to sexual violence is likely to lower the threshold of legal and mental health intervention, so that such measures will be employed somewhat earlier in the cycle of violence, and the damage will be less severe, not only for direct victims and perpetrators, but for the social body as a whole, so that divine and human power for the world grow.

One does not need to be reflexively suspicious of government to agree with conservatives that it is not the balm for all that ails us. The emphatic Christian centrist commitment to an ethic of power thus imposes a new responsibility: to turn the insight that government is limited into practical action and social policy. Otherwise, the claim that government cannot do all becomes an empty and powerless abstraction, another exemplar of the sins of sloth and indifference. A sweeping and ubiquitous public opposition to sexual violence will open up a vast space in which to address, with power, justice, and love, the tremendous cost of sexual violence, a cost that is nearly universal.

The interrelated problems of poverty, education, the family, and sexual violence are elements of emphatic Christian response to domestic politics. Our agenda is grounded firmly in emphatic Christian principles, including the plurality that will be necessary to address any of those problems effectively. We believe that this program will generate the creative power that is foremost among our principles, and will do so in a cost-effective way. Moreover, the foregoing program demonstrates the Christian center's nuanced approach to the productive use of government and traditional Christian ethics.

The Earth at the Center

Our book, both by choice and by necessity, has been about American politics and American religion. By choice, because we believe the topic requires urgent consideration. By necessity, because the relationship of politics and religion in America—by virtue of both our peculiar constitution and our particular mix of historical religions—is unique. No other country deals with religion and politics in quite the way we do.

It might seem that with the subject of the environment, however, we are moving beyond our boundaries, since the earth is clearly not the problem of any one nation, but of the entire planet. Yet this is not entirely true. The environment *does* transcend political boundaries, but so too do families and poverty. Yet the nation remains one of the entities best suited to act in this arena, even if it is by itself clearly inadequate (too large for some problems, and too small for others). Here we will limit our attention almost exclusively to ecopolitics in American culture and religion—but without thereby implying that it is only a national issue.

The Environment and the Family

The crisis of the environment offers some striking parallels to the crisis of the family. Like the family, the environment was long the concern of only one of the political wings, and virtually ignored by the other. The difference, of course, is that it was the left (though not all of it) that embraced the environment, while the right disregarded or positively disparaged it, as vividly illustrated by former Interior Secretary James Watt's and Ronald Reagan's gaffes.[157] But, just as some of the left has begun to acknowledge that there is a family crisis, some of the religious right, at least, is beginning to accept that ecocrisis is real.[158] There is not yet an emphatic center with respect to the environment, though the contours of one, even if rather inchoate, are beginning to form.

Another similarity is that the environmental crisis, like the family crisis, results in part from the flawed notion of freedom as independence: here our presumed independence from *nature* is both cause and symptom of a potentially fatal distortion of our relationship with the complex biological systems that sustain both life and civilization. Furthermore, a disregard for science, especially the *biological* and *human sciences*, has exacerbated the crisis in both cases. One of the most vivid connections is illustrated by Mary Ann Glendon's call for an "ecological" approach to the family.[159] Hence any solution will presuppose both a critique of the religion of freedom and careful attention to our biological and social ecology.

Ecocrisis: The Potential for Catastrophe

The evidence of impending massive and potentially catastrophic environmental upheaval is impressive. First, consider climate change. The evidence for global warming may be ambiguous,[160] but evidence that carbon dioxide (CO_2) is now being discharged into the atmosphere at rates unparalleled for the last 165,000 years is not.[161] Atmospheric levels of CO_2 increased from 315 to 355 parts per million over 1958–1990.[162] Evidence that chlorofluorocarbons have contributed to developing a hole in the earth's protective ozone layer is not ambiguous in any way. Other evidence for global climate change includes

> the diminishing size of polar ice caps, the bleaching of coral reefs, the northward retreat of heat-sensitive plant species, the extinctions of equatorial amphibian species, the disruption of established climatological patterns (such as rainfall), [and] the overall twentieth-century increase in temperature.[163]

Second, consider the overwhelming evidence of unprecedented species depletion and the consequent threat to biodiversity. According to one estimate, at least 3 species become extinct *per day* (i.e., more than 1,000 per year), and the figure may be much higher, since we do not know whether there are 5 million or 40 million species on earth.[164] E. O. Wilson estimates that the loss was at least 1,000 per year in the 1970s, escalating to 10,000 per year in the 1990s.[165] Loss of habitat, conversion of land, and climate change all drive this loss. It is true that there have been other mass extinctions in natural history; but it is also true that such mass extinctions have radically altered the conditions of life for *all* creatures on earth at that time, even to the point of eliminating the dominant form of life at that time.

This brings us to the third reason that we must speak of ecocrisis: the close tie between the health of the environment and the social and cultural health—even survival—of humankind. If global warming is indeed taking place on the scale that some data suggest, it is *already too late* to avoid massive changes in our economic, cultural, and social landscape. Reversal of the trend will take decades, likely centuries. Yet there is clear historical evidence that the development and disappearance of cultures and civilizations is powerfully influenced, if not determined, by their interaction with their environment: food, water, land, trees.[166] The disappearance of species may be a harbinger of our own future: "The process, in terms of human time, is relatively slow and insidious. The earth is not degraded all at once; the sky doesn't fall. But there comes a time when environmental ruin leads to cultural breakdown."[167] Clearly, given the complexity of the food chain alone, there is a limit to how much biodiversity may decline before the decline has adverse, even catastrophic consequences for human cultures and civilizations.[168] And we have not even considered the psychological and spiritual impact of a life lived in alienation and separation from the natural environment.[169]

THE FAILURE OF ECOPOLITICS ON THE LEFT AND THE RIGHT

As already mentioned, the politics of ecocrisis closely mirror the politics of the family, except that the poles are reversed. The right trumpeted the importance of "family values" while the left paid homage to personal "choice" in lifestyles; but when it came to the environment, it was the left that demanded change while the issue scarcely existed on the right's horizon. This is still mostly the case for the secular right, which either ignores the problem, or portrays environmentalists as alarmists who just really favor big government and oppose economic development. (One place there *has* been a change has been on the evangelical wing of the *religious* right, which we will take up later.)

As we have repeatedly noted, the left prefers to make choice sovereign in personal matters, but not in economics. It has remained largely consistent on this with respect to the environment, treating it like economics, as an area where choice is *not* the supreme value. They have largely embraced environmental regulation as another form of economic regulation, necessary to protect the environment from the free choices of individuals who might otherwise destroy it.[170] Nevertheless, most of the environmental left has almost instinctively turned to the language of "rights" and "liberation" when it comes to nature: animal rights and the liberation of nature from human enslavement are common themes. The left's unnuanced egalitarianism and absolutist conceptions of individual freedom have attained environmental expression in the insistence that all sentient beings have rights, and that one species ought not to be valued over another. A particularly vivid formulation of this individualism-cum-egalitarianism is the "biocentric equality" offered by the authors of *Deep Ecology:* "All things in the biosphere have an equal right to live and blossom and to reach their own individual forms of unfolding and self-realization within the larger Self-realization," and that all organisms and entities "are equal in intrinsic worth."[171] Equally consistently, human power in regard to nature is viewed as domination, and therefore as evil. Thus Tom Regan insists that our approach to nature should be one of "nondestruction, noninterference, and generally, nonmeddling"[172]—all the opposite of power. Indeed, one is struck by the left's general failure to recognize any positive role for power, *even in nature.*[173] Similarly, Peter Singer seeks to liberate animals, to maximize, as it were, animals' "choice."[174]

The left's deep suspicion of power is also manifested in much of the environmental movement. Thus Devall and Sessions, in *Deep Ecology,* repeatedly endorse the "decentered" and "nonhierarchical" approach of what they call the "minority tradition," opposing it to the "centralized authority" of the dominant tradition,[175] which is "anthropocentric, egoistic, and exploitive."[176] Boundaries, which are part of what makes power—communication of efficacy—possible, are characteristically rejected.[177] Yet, despite their ostensible rejection of anthropocentrism and egocentrism, they still choose "self-realization" as their first principle, while their second principle of "biocentric equality" also remains highly anthropomorphic.[178]

The environmentalist left's shortcomings have been exacerbated by its disdain for culture in general,[179] and religion in particular. Max Oelschlaeger has identified a significant blindness in the environmental movement toward religion—indeed, he calls it a prejudice, "a refusal to consider evidence contrary to a foregone conclusion."[180] Yet "the global ecocrisis continues to worsen despite people's efforts to respond"—what Oelschlaeger calls "the paradox of environmentalism."[181] He takes it as self-evident that the purely scientific approach has proved inadequate.

> Many ecologists who are gravely concerned about biodiversity, overpopulation, climate heating, and other environmental issues remain part of a scientific silent majority, deeply involved with their research and little else. And the paradox of environmentalism suggests that neither scientific nor ethical arguments have caused environmentally harmful public policies and social norms to be replaced by productive ones. In other words, the environmental movement has not proven itself adequate to the task of creating a democratic consensus on sustainability. Religious discourse, if nothing else, is one way a democratic people might . . . create the political will to elect leaders who in turn would create public policies that lead toward sustainability.[182]

This is nothing less than a call for emphatic religious centers—including an emphatic Christian center.

On the right, the situation is almost completely reversed. Larry Rasmussen sums up the situation on the secular and economic right very neatly in a comment on Michael Novak: "Novak's thought, as most neo-conservative thought, is ecologically empty."[183] And where the right has not been empty, it has engaged in a direct attack on environmentalism, especially in the guise of the "wise use" movement, which has successfully portrayed environmentalists as radicals who have no concern for economic growth, or for human culture generally.[184] The anti-environmental wing of the religious right has condemned environmentalism for its hostility to the Judeo-Christian tradition and its alleged pantheism. Thus Robert Sirico, writing in the *National Review*, castigates religious celebrations of Earth Day by associating them with the "declared atheist" Carl Sagan and with Matthew Fox's attack on "Christofascism," and expresses puzzlement that

Jews and Christians "would sign on to such a movement" which is clearly the "opposite" of their views. Sirico clearly privileges economic growth, which "fosters a more humane existence," over ecological concerns. While he admits that we should "strive to preserve the beauty of the earth for future generations of men and women," he is quite emphatic that it is not part of "God's law." "There is no commandment against polluting or mixing trash—that is taken care of by civil law—but there is a very straightforward one about worshipping false gods."[185]

The right's idolatry of personal choice is frequently tied to an insistence that there is nothing really wrong. This refusal to acknowledge ecocrisis is a hallmark of the anti-environmental right. Thus Milton and Rose Friedman characteristically treat environmental issues in the context of a criticism of the inefficiencies of government regulation, and go on to say that "if we look not at rhetoric but at reality, the air is in general far cleaner and the water safer today than one hundred years ago . . . [and] cleaner and . . . safer in the advanced countries of the world today than in the backward countries."[186] Despite the absence of any evidence for this claim, one might well agree that the water we drink is, on the whole, cleaner than what was available in heavily settled areas of the United States at the close of the nineteenth century; great advances were made in public health as a result of improved water supply, and unsafe drinking water is still one of the gravest threats to child health worldwide. But it is simply incredible to claim that the whole of the world's water supply is cleaner today, or that the whole of the atmosphere is cleaner.[187]

In contrast to the economic and political religious right, there is a clear awakening of environmental interest among some evangelicals,[188] particularly those who are scientists. Quietly but unambiguously accepting evolution and other biological descriptions of human and nonhuman life, they seek to apply biblical teaching as they understand it to the clear environmental dangers that their science describes. Thus Calvin DeWitt identifies "seven degradations of creation,"[189] Bouma-Prediger and Vroblesky find clear theological reasons to support the Endangered Species Act,[190] and Reichenbach and Anderson construe humankind's divinely mandated task of "tending" or "caring" for the creation specifically to include tropical rainforests.[191] Evangelicals generally prefer the stewardship model drawn from Genesis, especially chapter 2, in which the first man and woman were placed in the Garden of Eden to tend and care for it. They are also quick to dispute environmentalist accounts that place major or even primary blame on Judaism and Christianity for ecocrisis, though they do not seek to minimize either the seriousness of ecocrisis or human complicity in it.

Religious liberals were much quicker to pick up the environmental issue. Unlike evangelicals, they have been quick to admit Christian responsibility for ecocrisis, and have usually held the stewardship model to be inadequate.[192] Thus Larry Rasmussen, while not rejecting stewardship outright, expresses concern that it may mask "a continuing homocentrism" as well as being unscientific and tainted by racism and imperialism.[193] Sallie McFague specifically disavows the "Christic paradigm" as a starting point and insists on "contemporary science" instead.[194] Both are quick to ascribe much blame to Christianity for the crisis, Rasmussen with more nuance[195] and McFague with less.[196] They also attribute some authority to statements of the World Council of Churches, which evangelicals completely ignore; but the hard science present in many evangelicals' work is lacking in most liberal studies—with the utmost irony in the case of McFague, who professes fealty to science above all in these matters.[197] Liberals are also quick to reject "environmental racism" and to demand that environmental justice must coincide with social justice, especially for Third World peoples.[198]

Most interesting, while liberal theologians are eager to use ecocrisis to attack traditional and biblical understandings, they seem to find that ecocrisis confirms rather than challenges their *own* theological commitments—especially to process theology and panentheism.[199] This is especially striking given that evangelicals, though unwilling to criticize the Bible, seem more willing to entertain the need to revise *their own* theological conceptions.[200]

The religious left, then—quite consistently—views power as evil or at least rarely beneficial, emphasizes love as the chief virtue, and embraces the religion of freedom in its *liberation* version, looking for the liberation of creation—of animals and plants and oppressed peoples. The political religious right (except for some evangelicals) disregards or attacks environmentalism, viewing nature as valuable only in the service of human freedom. Meanwhile, those evangelicals who take ecocrisis seriously endorse stewardship of the creation, but remain largely uncritical of Christianity.

Sources of Ecocrisis

There are obviously more sources of ecocrisis, and more barriers to solution, than can be identified here. We will focus on three: the false dichotomy between nature and culture, the religion of freedom, and barriers to dialogue between religion and science.

One of the most deeply embedded dichotomies in our discourse about nature is the supposed distinction between "natural" and "artificial," where "natural" means "good" and "artificial" means "bad." The model of a "balance of nature" in which human beings have "interfered" is still widely influential in a variety of realms of discourse, from advertising ("all natural ingredients") to science, philosophy, and theology.[201] John Stuart Mill stated the dichotomy clearly in the nineteenth century, to nature's detriment: "All praise of Civilization, or Art, or Contrivance, is so much dispraise of Nature."[202] But this dichotomy between "nature" and "culture" is as violent and incoherent a dualism as any concocted in history. Any reasonable account of human "nature" must *include* culture; indeed, culture is *natural* for human beings. For human beings, "culture is second nature."[203] Or, as Rolston so eloquently puts it, "The human hand and brain are evolutionary products that result in culture, and fortunately so."[204] Only the "fortunately" in that sentence can possibly be disputed, and that even only at the cost of self-contradiction, for it takes cultural tools to dispute it.

But it is equally indisputable that human culture and consciousness have had negative, indeed disastrous and potentially catastrophic, effects on nature. Thus those philosophers, scientists, and theologians who have identified difference between nature and culture have not been wrong to do so. What *has* been wrong has been (1) to make this difference absolute and (2) to attribute nothing but evil to it.[205] What is required is a balanced and nuanced account of this difference. Such a balanced and nuanced account is still to be found in the theology of Reinhold Niebuhr, who affirmed that human beings are both *in* nature and *out* of it:[206] *in* nature in that we are animals, part of the food chain, products of evolution; *out* of nature in that we can survey, study, organize, predict, and manipulate it.[207] Dualism's mistake lies not in distinguishing ourselves from nature, but in making that distinction absolute, in failing to realize that everything we do to nature we also *do to ourselves*. It is not the mere fact that we act upon nature that is the source of the problem; it is the *way* in which we act, as though we could degrade plants and animals and species and environments without degrading ourselves.

A second source of ecocrisis is quite familiar to the reader by now: our mistaken, indeed fatally flawed, notion of freedom as independence. The view that nature is some kind of "tyrant" from which we must achieve "independence" by the same means as independence from George III or Hitler or Stalin is so bizarre and ridiculous it would not require refutation were it not so prevalent. It is incredible that we should not see that a war of independence from nature is nothing less than a war against ourselves. As Oelschlaeger says, "The Enlightenment definition of freedom as individual control over daily life and independence from governmental obstruction is increasingly inadequate."[208]

The third aspect of the problem to which we wish to call attention is the great dangers we risk, and the very high price we pay, for the lack of a meaningful dialogue between science and religion. The history of their conflict is long, interesting, and complex, and important to the task at hand; but much *more* important is that they learn to work together for the solution of ecocrisis.[209] "Both religious and scientific discourse are necessary conditions for the resolution of ecocrisis. Religious discourse offers legitimating narratives that remain outside the framework of utilitarian individualism."[210] Nor do we primarily mean the sort of theological and philosophical critiques of science associated with the work of Langdon Gilkey and Sandra Harding, for example, important as that work is.[211] We rather mean the need for religion to learn from science and for science to accept religion's legitimacy as a realm of discourse different from, but not unconnected to, scientific discourse. The ecocrisis is one of the chief areas where science, ethics, and religion intersect, and there are some environmentalists who seek to bring them together.[212] This sort of dialogue and common cause—seeking an increase in the power of both—is essential to respond to ecocrisis.

ECOCRISIS AND THE PRINCIPLES OF THE EMPHATIC CENTER

The relevance of the Christian center's first principle, *sin*, should be self-evident. Surprisingly, it is not. Even the otherwise judicious Oelschlaeger writes as though only religious conservatives could find the symbol of sin relevant to ecocrisis.[213] Some of these conservatives, he says, also say that "nothing . . . will make a difference [in the ecocrisis] unless we let Jesus into our lives."[214] We are *not* religious conservatives; we reject the view that we must "let Jesus into our lives" before we can solve the ecocrisis; but we *do* attribute ecocrisis, in large measure, to human sin—both as pride and as sloth. We have already alluded to Reinhold Niebuhr's discussion of our curious place both *in* and *out* of nature, utterly subject to its limitations, and yet able to alter it *almost* without limit. It is precisely at this point of tension that sin arises. Feeling ourselves (quite rightly) to be *above* nature in certain respects, we are tempted to pretend (quite wrongly) that we can live *without* nature, or (worse) that we can do anything to nature we please. This is the sin of pride against nature. Or, recognizing ourselves (quite rightly) to be *part* of nature, we are tempted to think (quite wrongly) that we should and can do *nothing* beneficial for nature, and should simply leave it alone. This is the sin of sloth against nature. Instead, we need to seek ways in which power can be increased for both humankind and nature.

There is probably no better environmental expression of our second principle, *love,* than Rolston's forthright injunction, *"Keep Life Wonderful!"*[215] That wonder may be experienced and expressed in myriad ways, from appreciation of a sunset to awestruck fear before the power of a flood or a tornado to overwhelming fascination with the variety of plant species in a single acre of grassland. One who has lost the capacity to wonder at such truly wonderful things is to be pitied; but a culture that has lost this capacity threatens itself with destruction. We also propose that Browning's emphasis on love in the family should be extended to the biosphere: we can and must learn to love *life* in a way analogous to the way that family members should love one another: in mutual respect and regard, and, when necessary, self-sacrifice. We must respect and regard nature as necessary to our lives, and as valuable in itself. And we will need to sacrifice *some* human desires (e.g., for unlimited auto emissions) in the interest of the environment—which will still be in our own interest.

Environmental discourse about the third principle, power, is particularly confused. The false dichotomy between nature and culture, and the inadequacy of the American religion of freedom, converge in this discourse, blinding us to the need for *power* in dealing with ecocrisis. If nature and culture were merely opposed, then any increase in power for nature would have to mean a corresponding decrease in power for culture; and any increase in nature's freedom would have to mean a decrease in human freedom.[216] Thus Devall and Sessions, following Thoreau, argue for the value of nature as explicitly *opposed* to culture and human power, and tie an increase in wilderness to a decrease in human power.[217] But if power consists in communication of efficacy, then it must be possible—perhaps even necessary—for both human and natural power to be increased. Indeed, if we depend on nature for our very existence, then our power depends on nature's power, and we cannot threaten it without threatening ourselves. If it is pride to deny or to seek to dominate *natural* power, yet it is sloth to disavow or abdicate *human* power in light of ecocrisis. Rather than try to expand human "freedom" without limit or try to expand the "liberation" of nature without limit, we must seek to *increase* power for both as a communication of efficacy between humankind and nature, society and ecosystem, plant and animal, earth and inhabitants. Although this may well mean imposing certain kinds of limits—certainly on chlorofluorocarbons, probably on fossil fuels, and perhaps on human population—it does not mean simply limiting all human activity.

ECOCRISIS AND THE CONTOURS OF SOLUTION

Discourse on the ecocrisis lags behind discourse on the family. Although we do not yet have a broad consensus that the family is in crisis, we are at least much farther down the road toward developing a vocabulary and concepts to describe it. "Ecocrisis" does not enjoy the currency of "family values," however troubling that latter term may sometimes be. Thus a major part of any solution will have to be *conceptual* as well as *concrete*. We turn to the conceptual issues first.

Although there is much disagreement among the various parties to ecological discourse, there is a remarkably wide-ranging consensus, extending from evangelicals to deep ecologists,[218] over the appropriateness of (1) an ethic of *stewardship* and *care* for the earth. In this regard, at least, an emphatic center does seem to be emerging. Theistic versions of this ethic specifically refer to the story of Adam, according to which God "took the man and put him in the garden of Eden to till it and keep it" (Gen. 2:15), often suggesting that God will call all humankind to account for their care of the creation.[219] Nontheistic versions trace this human care to the factual ascendance of humankind in evolution, but with much the same result.[220] This ethic of stewardship must be supplemented, however, by a powerful sense of (2) the *absolute dependence* of the human race on nature for survival. This is a simple statement of a complex and yet elementary state of affairs, even though we rarely appreciate the severity of this dependence.[221] Closely linked to this is the need (3) to recognize that human culture and consciousness are *thoroughly* natural, and nevertheless *different* from the rest of nature. Rolston's injunction, (4) *"Keep life wonderful!"*[222] cannot be improved upon. (5) Any and all hint of environmental racism must be eliminated. Economic community, social community, and environmental community must be seen in the close relationship that they truly have. The widely used concept that Rasmussen calls (6) *"sustainable community"* is instructive in this respect, even if vague.[223]

What Rolston calls (7) a *"sense of residence"*[224] in a local environment must be assiduously cultivated, reminding human beings of their close physical relationship to their cultural and natural environment. (8) The centrality of *biology* and scientific knowledge must be acknowledged in thought and practice, without making science and scientific discourse absolute.[225] (9) A deep sense of *humility* with respect to our natural environment should be cultivated. Just as *humus* is of the earth, so true humility links us to the earth.[226] Notwithstanding this, however, (10) the central role of *power* in both nature and culture must be fully appreciated. "In this ethic, knowledge is power, as also is love, with faithfulness. There is a penultimate place for superior human standing, and the ultimate lesson is that the meek inherit the Earth."[227] This meekness, however, must not be understood as the opposite of power, but as its condition and expression. Finally, an emphatic Christian center will have to insist that, even though the earth is the necessary presupposition of all life that we know, and even though humankind is absolutely dependent on nature, (11) *neither* the earth *nor* nature is *absolute*. It is well to recall in this connection that there have been demonic and destructive earth faiths, Nazism and Social Darwinism in particular.[228] Comprehensiveness is reserved to God alone.

So much for conceptual elements of a solution. They will mean nothing, will have no power, will not even exist without concrete, practical elements as well. The first concrete step to be taken is (1) to *cultivate* the attitudes and concepts outlined in the preceding paragraph.

Oelschlaeger is particularly perceptive on this point. Indeed, he wrote his book largely because he is convinced that no amount of scientific knowledge or technology can solve the ecocrisis without a political will to do so, and that religion may be the most effective tool for building that will: "Religious discourse is essential to creating a democratic consensus on an environmental agenda. . . . New metaphors such as 'caring for creation' can lead to solidarity on an environmental agenda . . . possess[ing] the *moral authority* that reform environmentalism now lacks."[229] A similar conviction led Carl Sagan and other scientists to appeal to the religious community for help in cultivating a sense of ecocrisis.[230] Oelschlaeger offers concrete suggestions as to how these attitudes can be cultivated in faith communities, including prayer and liturgy, lessons on stewardship (based on Noah's ark) for children, planting trees for teens, and adult study of city planning documents.[231]

Careful attention must be paid to (2) calculating and accounting for the environmental and social *costs* associated with economic growth. Pathbreaking work in this regard has been done by Cobb and Cobb with their Index of Sustainable Economic Welfare.[232] Of course, there is room for important debate over what costs are included (air pollution) and not (aesthetic values), and a strong case could be made to include other social costs (unstable families and measurable decreases in child welfare). Nevertheless, they do propose a way to calculate costs rather than simply opposing economic growth to environmental values as though they represented a zero-sum game.

Finally, although legislative activity on environmental questions over the last three decades has been significant,[233] there is certainly (3) much important public policy work to be done. International treaties limiting the use of chlorofluorocarbons have marked an important advance, and progress needs to be made with respect to reducing emissions of CO_2.[234] More could be done to encourage grassroots initiatives (in accord with the principle of subsidiarity), from encouraging the building of small urban parks that would be safe communities for people, plants, and animals, to gardening as part of education and child care. It is also important that more research and experimentation in the use of market mechanisms, especially the so-called pollution tax or effluent charges, be undertaken as a way of tuning the economy in a way that issues in greater power for nature and culture—sustainable growth.[235] But none of these will avail—nor even be likely to happen—without the changes addressed in the foregoing two paragraphs.

Thus the task is large, and the need great. Important differences remain among those who agree that ecocrisis is real. But what Oelschlaeger says of religious groups can be enlarged to include political and cultural groups as well: "Solidarity on an environmental agenda does not require theological orthodoxy."[236] To summarize, then, the emphatic center insists on increasing power for the whole of creation, including nature and human culture, which are not opposed, but in tension. We need to reduce emissions by just means that do not place an unfair burden on developing countries at the same time that we cultivate a deep love and respect for nature that recognizes our mutuality with the ecosphere.

AN INFRASTRUCTURE FOR THE CHRISTIAN CENTER

What follows is the shortest section in this chapter, indeed in the entire book. Yet, it may prove to be the most important. The emphatic Christian center cannot be a mere cluster of ideas about religion and politics, God and power, sin and justice. If the center is to be a center, it must happen *somewhere*. One reason, we believe, that the center has been silent in the recent American past is that it has lacked a *place* where it can happen—where ideas can be exchanged, where a sense of isolation can be overcome, where power can be generated through communications of efficacy. This is another way of saying that the vacuous center lacks power. If one looks at the far more effective Christian right, one can immediately see its infrastructure, particularly Pat Robertson's multimillion-dollar broadcasting and political network. Robertson's ideas have someplace to *happen*.

We began this book with the observation that, for some time now, the center has been silent. This was not always so. At midcentury, powerful voices like Paul Tillich and Reinhold Niebuhr lashed out at the grave menaces to peace and justice, first fascism and Nazism, and later at Stalinist communism (even as both of them continued to be informed by Marxian categories). Why are such voices not heard today? The reasons are complex: the intrinsic ineptness of the vacuous center that has allowed the left to persuade it that power is evil; the declining numbers, in both relative and absolute terms, of historic Protestants (so-called mainline Protestants); the mainstreaming of Catholics after John F. Kennedy's election to the presidency and Vatican II; a culture increasingly hostile to or at least indifferent to religion, at least historic American religion; and the determined efforts of the right. But there is another reason: the old outlets for public expression of the Christian faith have declined or been surrendered, while new outlets have not been cultivated.

In the mid-1980s Robert Bellah complained that the mainline churches had, for some time, failed to produce a Paul Tillich or a Reinhold Niebuhr who could command the attention of the public. At roughly the same time, Richard W. Fox, in his well-written if controversial biography of Reinhold Niebuhr, concluded that Niebuhr, if he were alive today, would not be an influential figure, in part because the Christian college lecture circuit, on which he so tirelessly traveled, is gone.[237] One need not share Fox's controversial conclusions about Niebuhr the man to see the truth of this observation. Henry Luce, son of Chinese missionaries, recognized Niebuhr and Tillich and gave them voice in his Time-Life publication empire; today Time Warner has no ear for centrist religion. Martin E. Marty has long been aware of this need, and is now, with his Public Religion Project, assiduously cultivating a media presence for religious scholarship and voice, seeking to articulate religious convictions and their significance clearly and disinterestedly. This is an important start, led by (one is tempted to say) the perfect person for the job. Yet it is but a start.

It is interesting to note in this connection that in at least one of the specific issues with which we dealt, the family, important progress finally occurred when some observers on the left began to take the issue seriously and to sort out the actuality from the fantasy in the right's rhetoric. Serious attention to ecocrisis may well wait upon such a phenomenon occurring on the right. This is not, as we have been at pains to insist, simply a question of the "midpoint" on a spectrum between the "extremes," but a genuine communication of efficacy across boundaries that produces not an average, but new insight.

It is an infrastructure for this kind of communication of efficacy that the emphatic Christian center so desperately needs to help it realize power. Power is not evil, but good; not wrong in its use, but its abuse; not the opposite of humility, but its fruit and its root.

There are some signs of hope, and we call attention to them as we conclude our study. The already-mentioned Religion, Culture, and Family Project of the University of Chicago and the Lilly Endowment was a particularly bright spot, and one can only hope for more such projects in the future, perhaps beginning with ecocrisis and going on to include such topics as poverty and sexual violence. The Wabash Center on Teaching and Learning Theology and Religion, also sponsored by the Lilly Endowment, marks an important step toward improving one key element of public discourse on religion. The Public Religion Project, headed by Martin E. Marty and funded by the Pew Charitable Trusts, is an extremely important attempt both to promote and to improve public awareness of religion, particularly among journalists. The Christian Center project of Messiah College, while different from our conception of the emphatic Christian center, is nevertheless a fine example of the infrastructure that is necessary, promoting discussion between evangelicals, Roman Catholics, and traditional-liberal Protestants.

There are no doubt other such projects and programs, of which we are not aware. The Lilly Foundation and the Pew Charitable Trusts are to be congratulated especially for their support of these programs. Perhaps an important next step would be to begin to create an infrastructure like—but doubtless quite different from—that Christian college lecture circuit mentioned by Richard Fox, on which the future Reinhold Niebuhrs and Paul Tillichs, including their Catholic and female and African American and other successors, can begin to emerge.

ENVOI

If frustration and hopelessness are the symptoms of the politics of interest and domination, then tragic optimism and cautious hope are the signs of the politics of the emphatic center. We owe the term "tragic optimism" to the late psychoanalyst and concentration camp survivor Viktor Frankl, in his essay of that title,[238] although the term could also describe the mature Reinhold Niebuhr's political convictions[239] or Martin Luther's "nevertheless"—by grace, despite sin and death (and injustice, we may add)—"*nevertheless* we shall still live."[240] The epigram with which Frankl closes another essay bears repeating: "We have come to know man as he really is. After all, man is that being who has invented the gas chambers of Auschwitz; however, he is also that being who has entered those gas chambers upright, with the Lord's Prayer or the *Shema Yisrael* on his lips."[241] To this we might add, neither Hitler's nor Stalin's infamies, for as much evil as they did, were able to survive for long.

We do not face anything in America today as drastic as those gas chambers. However, our problems are substantial, and manifest greatness, goodness, pettiness, and evil. And it is with only some kind of tragic optimism—neither wallowing in self-pity nor basking in self-righteousness—that these realities can be faced.

Tragic optimism must be *tragic* in knowing that every solution we propose and every action we take will necessarily be incomplete, finite, and, in some sense, sinful. It must never shrink from a full recognition of the ways in which all our actions—and especially our religious ones—can become idolatrous. This is not the self-pitying tragedy of people who are too good for this evil world, but the optimistic tragedy of people who suffer and even commit great evil and yet continue to live in a world in which power and good are *nevertheless* more basic— more powerful—than impotence and evil.[242]

Tragic optimism must also be *optimism* by continuing to act in confidence that nevertheless, God is God and not any less, that power is more basic to being than impotence, love more basic than hate, justice more basic than sin, and joy more basic than sorrow. It must never forget to remember the manifold ways in which power and love and justice continue to thwart sin, impotence, and perverted power. Indeed, the recognition that Christianity and the Christian center do not pose universal, eternal solutions to temporal problems, that time's boundaries and our own finitude must be respected, may partly reduce the likelihood that finitude will be perverted into sin, or that power will be frozen into relations of domination.

No one could ever prove that it is less "rational" (in some disembodied abstraction of reason) to despair than to hope. But despair is less powerful than hope. Hope can act, despair cannot; hope can trust, despair does not. Hope takes the sufferings, the perversions, the tragedies of its time, and does what it can to alleviate them, not forever and not completely but as much as possible for now. If *tragic* remains the first word in "tragic optimism," the last word continues to be *optimism*.

Notes

INTRODUCTION

1. For example, Jack Rogers, *Claiming the Center* (Louisville, Ky.: Westminster/John Knox Press, 1995).
2. An excellent presentation of these political split personalities is given by E. J. Dionne, *Why Americans Hate Politics* (New York: Simon and Schuster, Touchstone, 1991).
3. Arlen Specter's short-lived 1995 presidential campaign, in contrast, at least attempted consistency. Specter represented a libertarian option, which advocated reduction of public involvement in both economic and social spheres. The abject failure of Specter's campaign cannot be written off entirely to the dominance of the right wing in Republican primaries. Rather, his failure should have been surprising, because he advocated essentially what the successful 1994 Republican sound-bytes trumpeted: the reduction of government's role in all arenas of life. This is truly curious: it may mean that Americans are not, ultimately, as antigovernment as they say.
4. In this respect, the "passionate center" of Tsongas et al., is a half-improvement. It does provide concrete proposals and directions; but it fails to explain the underlying commitments and principles that produce those proposals. The passionate center may be passionate, but not necessarily coherent.
5. John Heilemann, "Washington's Last Loud Liberal," *The New Yorker*, August 5, 1996, 23.
6. *New York Times*, January 10, 1996, A10, Chicago edition.
7. The charge of extremism has been a factor in American political campaigns for some time. Some argue that Goldwater's 1964 campaign was doomed from the moment he uttered his famous statement that "extremism in defense of liberty is no vice; moderation . . . is no virtue." The appeal of portraying one's opponent as an extremist can be seen in the Johnson campaign's famous retort, to Goldwater's slogan "In your heart, you know he's right," "In your guts, you know he's nuts." What is disturbing about more recent developments, however, is that now charges of extremism are rarely accompanied with explanation.
8. Hendrik Hertzberg, "Big Talk," *The New Yorker*, September 9, 1996, 5.
9. George Stephanopoulos, Concordia College public lecture, April 1997.
10. J. Glenn Gray, *The Warriors*, 2nd ed. (New York: Harper and Row, 1970), 226.
11. James Davison Hunter, *Culture Wars* (New York: HarperCollins, Basic Books, 1991). Mr. Buchanan seems to have read no more than the title of Hunter's illuminating work in constructing his speech at the 1992 Republican National Convention.
12. Gray, *The Warriors*, 230.
13. We should note at least two exceptions: (1) Ironically, even as the general cultural tolerance for *religious* politics continues to decline, the culture manifests a growing desire for a more *spiritual* politics; (2) there is also a broad cultural desire within many religious communities—particularly among conservative Christians and non-mainline groups—for a broader religious presence in politics and culture. Yet, apart from these qualifications, our original statement holds true for the culture at large.
14. We use "public" in a broader sense than "political." Hannah Arendt, *The Human Condition* (Chicago: University of Chicago Press, 1958), and *On Revolution* (London: Penguin, 1965), draws a strict distinction between the "political" (the sphere of governmental action and var-

ious direct efforts to influence government) and "social," which is public but nongovernmental.
15. The emphatic Christian center, while critical of attempts to "secularize" public life by the exclusion of religious meanings, *must* support formally secular political institutions. See chaps. 3 and 5.
16. These principles are outlined also in Kyle A. Pasewark and Garrett E. Paul, "The Emphatic Christian Center: A Call to Political Responsibility," *The Christian Century* 111, no. 24 (August 24-31, 1994): 782-83. We understand power *not* as domination or control, but as a *communication of efficacy*. This is discussed at length in Kyle A. Pasewark, *A Theology of Power* (Minneapolis: Fortress Press, 1993).
17. Here the postmodern critics, ironically, turn out to be more modern than the modernists themselves. In particular, the postmodern insistence on the "incommensurability" of various discourses actually *reinforces* modernity's emphasis on interest group politics. In this sense, as in its understanding of freedom, postmodernism often appears less "post-" than *hyper*-modern: "largely another attempt to carry out the old Enlightenment program of demolishing tradition, ritual, cult and historical narrative, except now without the Enlightenment's faith that reason and technology can assume their place." Garrett Paul, "Why Troeltsch? Why Today? Theology for the 21st Century," *The Christian Century* 110, no. 20 (June 30, 1993): 676-82.
18. This section of the book involved a sharper division of labor than the rest, reliant on the authors' differing expertise and interests. Pasewark wrote the sections on poverty and education, as well as that on sexual violence. Paul wrote the sections on the family and the environment.
19. In a longer book, this would be the place to develop a public ecclesiology for the emphatic Christian center.
20. The phrase is drawn from Robert T. Handy, *A Christian America* (New York: Oxford University Press, 1981).

CHAPTER 1. A COMMON FAILURE: THE SECULARIST STATE AND ITS RELIGIOUS CRITICS

1. Hannah Arendt, *On Revolution* (London: Penguin, 1965), 185-86.
2. For an excellent brief analysis of the shortcomings of the "wall of separation" language in jurisprudence and culture, see Ronald F. Thiemann, *Religion in Public Life* (Washington, D.C.: Georgetown University Press, 1996), 42-71. Also see David Hollenbach, "Contexts of the Political Role of Religion: Civil Society and Culture," *San Diego Law Review* 30 (Fall 1993): 877-901. Still, the language of separation and its accompanying mind-set have not disappeared. Franklin I. Gamwell, *The Meaning of Religious Freedom* (Albany: SUNY, 1995), 208-9, argues that it underlies Jürgen Habermas's interpretation of religion. Stephen L. Carter, *The Culture of Disbelief* (New York: HarperCollins, BasicBooks, 1993), 105-23, finds the metaphor unproblematic, despite objecting to some of its interpretations; and Robert Wuthnow, *The Struggle for America's Soul* (Grand Rapids, Mich.: Wm. B. Eerdmans, 1989), 8, 57, 107, employs the language without complaint.
3. Our argument is restricted for the most part to the United States, because no other nation or culture in the world has quite the same dynamics of religion and politics. Formally, India is one of the closest parallels, but the division of the officially secular country between an antagonistic Hindu majority and Muslim minority is obviously very different. A comparison with Europe is easily misleading: France is much more militantly anti-ecclesiastical than the United States, England and Germany have established churches, and so on. In particular, the low church attendance rates in Western European countries should not automatically be interpreted as secularization. Churches and religious communities have a public presence in most Western European countries that is still quite noticeable, and largely supported by the populations, even if they do not attend worship. How else can it be explained that the city of

Dresden has insisted on rebuilding the Frauenkirche—over the objections of the Evangelical Church? The dynamics of religion and politics in Europe are different, and facile comparisons should be avoided.
4. On "secularism," see Reinhold Niebuhr, *The Children of Light and the Children of Darkness* (New York: Charles Scribner's Sons, 1972), 128-34, and Richard John Neuhaus, *The Naked Public Square*, 2nd ed. (Grand Rapids, Mich.: Wm. B. Eerdmans, 1986), ix, 25. Although certainly all forms of secularism are not "liberal," there are two reasons for linking the two. First, in the United States, secularism has tended to be defended most strongly by those who stand within the liberal traditions. Second, at least in contemporary thought, liberals present the most compelling and interesting arguments for the exclusion of religious perspectives from public life.
5. It is possible that the claims bear more directly on the relation between political life and monotheistic religions, though that is by no means certain.
6. Neuhaus, *Naked Public Square*, does not sufficiently appreciate this. His argument is directed primarily to obtaining a public hearing for Christianity. Consequently, he persistently and erroneously equates "pluralism" with "relativism," an identification that receives attention in chapter 4. If Neuhaus's argument succeeds, it is hard to understand how the public square remains public. This may be why Neuhaus is fundamentally antipolitical; the political is desirable insofar as it improves private life, but he remains suspicious, at points even contemptuous, of public life as such. On the contrary, because of the principle of divine power outlined in chapter 3, politics is inseparable from plurality, as Arendt, *On Revolution,* maintains for different reasons.
7. *New York Times,* September 10, 1996, A16, Chicago edition. Scholarly literature sometimes shows an equal lack of subtlety. The persistent invocation of "separation" by Robert Audi, "The Separation of Church and State and the Obligations of Citizenship," *Philosophy and Public Affairs* 18, no. 3 (Summer 1989): 259-96, is all the more remarkable because Audi recognizes that church-state issues are distinct from religion–public life questions, but proceeds to take the former as the paradigm for determining the latter. Much is wrong with Crasswell's Christian radicalism but not because it is Christian and radical. On the contrary, it is not enough of either.
8. Clifford Geertz, *The Interpretation of Cultures* (New York: Basic Books, 1973), 90.
9. Gamwell, *Religious Freedom,* 224.
10. David Tracy, *Plurality and Ambiguity* (San Francisco: Harper & Row, 1987), 84. For a more extensive analysis of what Tracy means by "limit questions," see Tracy, *Blessed Rage for Order* (New York: Seabury Press, Crossroad, 1978), 91-118. Tracy's qualification—that he is not attempting a narrow "definition" of religion, but seeking to elucidate "family resemblances"—applies also to what follows.
11. Paul Tillich, *Dynamics of Faith* (New York: Harper & Row, 1957), 1.
12. Paul Tillich, *Theology of Culture,* ed. Robert C. Kimball (London: Oxford University Press, 1959), 40. Thus, what Tillich means by "religion" comes quite close to what John Rawls, *Political Liberalism* (New York: Columbia University Press, 1996), means by a "comprehensive perspective," in which he customarily includes "religious, philosophical and moral" comprehensives. Rawls employs a narrower definition of religion than we do, although we doubt that a merely moral viewpoint is capable of being finally comprehensive.
13. Kent Greenawalt, "Religion as a Concept in Constitutional Law," *California Law Review* 72, no. 5 (September 1984): 806-11. For a similar point, see Gamwell, *Religious Freedom,* 156-57.
14. This procedure is not unusual. Judicial interpretation often selects one among many possible meanings for use. Think, for example, of the judicial interpretation of "speech," which is broader than some philosophical and cultural uses, narrower than others. We need be troubled by the differences in breadth of meaning only if we think words are univocal and that judicial interpretation determines proper meaning.
15. This says nothing prejudiced about church bodies, congregations, synagogues, and other religious institutions. Our point here is only that limiting a definition of religion to specific insti-

tutions blinds us to the full range of religion's real presence in American (or any other) culture. Institutions play a key role in this, but are not the whole story. In fact, hostility toward all institutions, and especially religious ones, is central to the American religion of freedom. Nevertheless, it is highly unlikely that religion—even in its noninstitutional and anti-institutional forms—can survive without the presence of institutions that concretely nurture it. See our discussion "An Infrastructure for the Christian Center," in chapter 5.
16. The encompassing, comprehensive character of ultimate concerns is discussed in more detail on pp. 33-35.
17. Augustine, *On Christian Doctrine*, trans. D. W. Robertson, Jr. (Indianapolis: Bobbs-Merrill, 1958), I.4, p. 9.
18. Perhaps Augustine's (and Tillich's) definition is most difficult to grasp for those who think primarily in terms of the *use*, not the *enjoyment*, of things.
19. Greenawalt, "Religion," 808.
20. Hannah Arendt, *Between Past and Future* (Harmondsworth, England: Penguin, 1968), 102.
21. "Cultural forms" include institutions such as churches, synagogues, temples, schools, colleges, universities, amateur athletics, choral societies, food shelves, and museums; but they also include cultural activities such as music, sports, dance, philosophy, literature, and entertainment.
22. See especially Gamwell, *Religious Freedom*, 28.
23. See, for one example, *New York Times*, June 17, 1996, A8, Chicago edition, for a description of California as "a place where . . . being young and on the cusp is its own religion."
24. David Remnick, "The War for the Kremlin," *New Yorker*, July 22, 1996, 44.
25. For Dole, see *New York Times*, September 4, 1996, A12, Chicago edition. An identical claim was made by former Turkish Foreign minister Tansu Ciller, who, during the 1996 tensions in Cyprus, declared "Our flag is holy and sacred. If [the Greek Cypriots] stretch their hands to our flag they will be broken" (*New York Times*, August 16, 1996, A4, Chicago edition).
26. For simplicity's sake, we will consider only one expression of ultimacy in a religion (abstracting from the multiplicity internal to every religion and from the question of hypocrisy) and one believer's possible response to her religion's claim about ultimate reality.
27. One analytic possibility excluded is the fully adequate delineation of ultimacy (God) and all divine relations to reality. We borrow the phrase "relative adequacy" from Tracy, *Blessed Rage*, 80, and *Plurality*, 98-99. The analytic possibility of the perfect religion and the perfect believer are excluded because, for reasons that appear later, neither is a realistic possibility within history.
28. This happens frequently in American religion, when America or capitalism or middle-class mores or wealth or health is worshiped under the name of God.
29. This is particularly widespread in traditional American Protestant churches.
30. This argument has structural similarities to Anselm, *Proslogion*, in *The Prayers and Meditations of Saint Anselm*, trans. Sister Benedicta Ward (Harmondsworth, England: Penguin, 1973), 238-67. Whether Anselm "proves God's existence" (or intends to) is not germane. The point is simply that whatever is claimed to be God (or a system of gods) is "that than which nothing greater can be thought." It is not clear how far from Anselm's own purpose this takes us. The *Proslogion* was, after all, a prayer within which an argument was contained. Thus, it arises from within preexistent faith, which a strictly rational proof (if one were available) need not do in order to persuade.
31. This does not mean that every religious symbol or doctrine must be simultaneously and completely comprehensive. Rather, the system of symbols taken as a whole can be judged according to its comprehensiveness.
32. Karl Rahner, *Foundations of Christian Faith*, trans. William V. Dych (New York: Crossroad, 1978), 20.
33. "It is very questionable, despite many protestations to the contrary, despite the prevalence of self-pity among some moderns because 'God is dead,' that anyone has ever yearned for radical faith in the One God" (H. Richard Niebuhr, *Radical Monotheism and Western Culture* [New York: Harper & Row, 1960], 31). Niebuhr's discussion of Christian henotheism, 58-60, is still very much to the point.

34. Human finitude prevents any individual from establishing a constructive practical or conceptual relation to all spheres of being. Still, if a religious tradition as a whole excludes realms of being from religious significance, the confinement is not only upon one adherent but upon the whole body of believers. The consequences of this can be enormous, as the exclusion of nature from the body of Christian thought has been.
35. Augustine, *Concerning the City of God Against the Pagans,* trans. Henry Bettenson, ed. David Knowles (Harmondsworth, England: Penguin, 1972). Augustine's analysis, in its turn, is indebted to Hebrew prophetism's focus on idolatry. To mistake something not ultimate for one's final "enjoyment" is idolatry. It is not accidental that Augustine is one of the first Christian theologians to recover the prophets for something more than their supposed foretelling of Jesus' incarnation, although he affirms that as well.
36. Ludwig Feuerbach, *The Essence of Christianity,* trans. George Eliot (New York: Harper & Row, 1957).
37. For an example of such a process in India, see Milton Singer, *When a Great Tradition Modernizes* (Chicago: University of Chicago Press, 1972).
38. The qualifier "directly" is important. God may well, as Augustine and most of the Christian tradition have maintained, turn evil to good without making evil less evil. God is presumed to have a positive relation even to evil, but not directly so: God must *turn* evil to good.
39. Thus were Roman and European pagan customs incorporated into Christmas and Easter celebrations and the cult of the saints. It is noteworthy that some of the Christian sects, such as the Jehovah's Witnesses, vigorously repudiate such Christianized celebrations.
40. Paul Tillich, "The Formative Power of Protestantism," in *The Protestant Era,* trans. James Luther Adams (Chicago: University of Chicago Press, 1948), 212. For additional discussions of theonomy, see Tillich, *The Religious Situation,* trans. H. Richard Niebuhr (New York: Meridian Books, 1956), 216; *Systematic Theology,* vol. 1 (Chicago: University of Chicago Press, 1951), 85; and *Systematic Theology,* vol. 3 (Chicago: University of Chicago Press, 1963), 245-82.
41. By "finite" we mean the simple (though much-disregarded) empirical reality that human beings, their culture and society, are all *limited,* i.e., *not infinite.* We later distinguish between finitude, which is not evil, from *distorted* finitude, or sin, which *is.*
42. Many religious disputes (particularly Reformation debates about the priority and meaning of "faith" and "works") were not primarily about theological or sacramental elements, but about their proper placement in relation to each other and to God.
43. An excellent analysis of American primitivism is Richard T. Hughes and C. Leonard Allen, *Illusions of Innocence* (Chicago: University of Chicago Press, 1988).
44. See Pauline Maier, *American Scripture* (New York: Alfred A. Knopf, 1997).
45. See Walter Rauschenbusch, *A Theology for the Social Gospel* (Nashville: Abingdon Press, 1978), and John Dewey, *A Common Faith* (New Haven, Conn.: Yale University Press, 1934).
46. This is the same criticism Ernst Troeltsch directed against positivism, including John Stuart Mill and especially Auguste Comte: "In positivism there are only new combinations of old elements." Ernst Troeltsch, *Der Historismus und seine Probleme* (Tübingen: J.C.B. Mohr [Paul Siebeck], 1922), 379.
47. Nor has this attitude disappeared. Without a shred of evidence, Gordon Graham ("Tolerance, Pluralism, and Relativism," in *Toleration,* ed. David Heyd [Princeton, N.J.: Princeton University, 1996], 50), simply "supposes" both moral progress and that "the first efforts of humans in morality and religion are fumbling." Many Jews, Rwandans, and Cambodians would be alive had we continued so to fumble.
48. H. Richard Niebuhr, *The Responsible Self* (New York: Harper & Row, 1963), 91.
49. An exciting discussion of Social Darwinism remains Richard Hofstadter, *Social Darwinism in American Thought* (Boston: Beacon Press, 1992).
50. Langdon Gilkey, *Through the Tempest,* ed. Jeff B. Pool (Minneapolis: Fortress Press, 1991), 9-10, notes the alliance between primitivist theology and technological dominance among

"conservative" Christians. This is a tradition of long-standing: witness early fundamentalism's claims to be "true science," as George M. Marsden, *Fundamentalism and American Culture* (New York: Oxford University Press, 1980), notes frequently. For Reaganism's additional impetus, see Garry Wills, *Reagan's America* (Garden City, N.Y.: Doubleday and Co., 1987), 378-88, and "It's His Party," *New York Times Magazine*, August 11, 1996, 30ff.

51. Walter Benjamin, *Illuminations* (New York: Harcourt, Brace and World, 1968), 263. Benjamin is discussing progressivist visions of history but the same is true of primitivist interpretations.
52. In American literature, Edith Wharton, *The Age of Innocence* (New York: Barnes and Noble, 1996), is an exemplary critic of this tendency.
53. The distinction between power, potentiality, and actuality is developed in greater detail in Kyle A. Pasewark, *A Theology of Power* (Minneapolis: Fortress Press, 1993), 207-14. See also Jean-François Lyotard, *The Postmodern Condition,* trans. Geoff Bennington and Brian Massumi, *Theory and History of Literature,* vol. 10 (Minneapolis: University of Minnesota, 1984), for an account of progressivism as an inevitable outgrowth of modernism.
54. The same holds true for what Tillich called "the demonic," the destructive and dangerous (as well as the creative). See Tillich, *Dynamics of Faith,* 2, 15-16.
55. Hannah Arendt, *The Human Condition* (Chicago: University of Chicago Press, 1958), 233.
56. On inevitability, see Tillich, *Dynamics of Faith,* 104.
57. The mission is a religious one, even if phrased in secular terms.
58. An excellent brief presentation of the ambiguity of the symbols of the chosen people in America is Robert N. Bellah, *The Broken Covenant,* 2nd ed. (Chicago: University of Chicago Press, 1992).
59. Reinhold Niebuhr, *The Nature and Destiny of Man, vol. I* (New York: Charles Scribner's Sons, 1964), 26-53, 104-5. Niebuhr's notion of vitality is double-sided: vitality is both creative and destructive.
60. Tracy, *Plurality,* 82.
61. Chapter 4 discusses the implications of this claim for religion, political life, and emphatic Christian pluralism.
62. Dwight D. Eisenhower, quoted in E. J. Dionne, Jr., *Why Americans Hate Politics* (New York: Simon and Schuster, 1991), 218.
63. One inclusionist argument that will not be considered here is Franklin Gamwell's rationalist defense of religious participation in public debate. Gamwell's position depends on an Enlightenment confidence in universal reason, and does not take the problem of the failure of a universalizable language seriously enough. The problems of universal reason are considerable, and will appear in our consideration of universal liberalism and in chapter 4.
64. Neuhaus, *Naked Public Square,* 25.
65. Carter, *Culture of Disbelief,* 40 (emphasis added).
66. For a biting criticism of the primacy of "rights-talk" in contemporary cultural life, see Mary Ann Glendon, *Rights-Talk* (New York: Macmillan, Free Press, 1991).
67. Carter, for example, links "rights," "fairness," and political (not legal) discourse in *Culture of Disbelief,* 72.
68. Kent Greenawalt, *Religious Convictions and Political Choice* (New York: Oxford University, Press 1988), 4.
69. Ibid., 144 (emphasis added).
70. Michael J. Perry, "Religious Morality and Political Choice: Further Thoughts and Second Thoughts On *Love and Power,*" *San Diego Law Review* 30 (1993): 706.
71. Ibid., 717.
72. Michael J. Perry, *Love and Power* (New York: Oxford University Press, 1991).
73. Carter, *Culture of Disbelief,* 113.
74. Neuhaus, *Naked Public Square,* 9.
75. Carter, *Culture of Disbelief,* 101.
76. "Good reason" here does *not* mean a universal truth that can be demonstrated scientifically;

nor does it mean a truth that can be deduced from foundational, universally established truths; a "reason" can even be *nonrational* in the sense that it cannot be deduced from other reasons, but is still at least understandable to those who do not share it. For example, non-Jews can understand Jewish feelings about the Holocaust or Israel even though these are not universal. See n. 199.
77. This claim receives attention in chapter 4.
78. This accounts for the apparently odd fact that although Neuhaus argues for the inclusion of religious positions in public debate on specifically pluralist grounds, he persistently attacks pluralism as equivalent to relativism. Perhaps because Carter, Greenawalt, and Perry are legal scholars, their arguments do not shift into a majoritarian gear. The link between the argument from facticity and majoritarianism is not necessary, but it is common, and there is at least some tendency to slide from one to the other, particularly if one does not attend closely to the essentially liberal American constitutional tradition.
79. Neuhaus, *Naked Public Square*, 26.
80. Ibid., 94-113. This limitation leads Neuhaus to the frankly bizarre claim that "the religious freedom of those outside the Judeo-Christian consensus is best protected by grounding such freedom in that consensus" (146).
81. Ibid., 176 (emphasis added).
82. Ibid. Note, first, that this is a Christian "Jerusalem." Second, the two American understandings of history are both present.
83. Even when Neuhaus is critical of some expressions of the Christians who are the majority, he places blame on "leaders of . . . negative dispositions" (ibid., 178). Those who are not leaders remain innocent, a point related to Neuhaus's opposition to political life in general, which is discussed momentarily.
84. We will discover in chapter 4 that these constitutional impediments are the good fortune of religions, including Christianity.
85. Neuhaus, *Naked Public Square*, 82.
86. Ibid., 80.
87. Ibid., 86, 87 (emphasis added).
88. For examples of this persistent theme, see ibid., 29-34, 50, 80-82, 180. Part of the problem is Neuhaus's continual equation of power with domination. Neuhaus's argument also reveals a deep affinity between American neoconservatism and some postmodern thinkers, particularly French postmodernists such as Foucault and Lyotard. Both understand power as inevitably dominating and centralizing. Consequently, they are often blind to factors in public discussion other than the drive to domination, and insensitive to the group-based dominations that their philosophies foster. Martha C. Nussbaum, "Human Functioning and Social Justice," *Political Theory* 20 (May 1992): 204-13, provides a sustained argument on this point, and also points to its majoritarian implications. In theology, the link between postmodernism and neoconservatism is present in, for example, Stanley Hauerwas, *Community of Character* (Notre Dame, Ind.: University of Notre Dame Press, 1981) and Robert Jenson, "Modernity's Undermining of Its Own Foundations," *Trinity Seminary Review* 18, no. 1 (Summer 1996): 5-12.
89. Neuhaus, *Naked Public Square*, 29.
90. Richard Rorty is the most notable exception. Aspects of his thought will be considered in chapter 4.
91. For an excellent critique of liberalism's storybook image of religion, see Robin W. Lovin, "Perry, Naturalism, and Religion in Public," *Tulane Law Review* 63 (1989): 1517-39. One core assumption is that liberalism conceives religion as restricted to institutional religions rather than more broadly as ultimate concern. That assumption has already been considered and need not detain us.
92. Dean C. Hammer, "The Rhetoric of Origins: The Construction of a Puritan Tradition in Revolutionary, Federalist, and Whig Thought," unpublished manuscript, 102-27, demonstrates that this bias pervades the literature concerned with the nation's founding.

93. The subtitle of *Culture of Disbelief* is "How American Law and Politics Trivialize Religious Devotion." While liberals base their opposition to religion on anything but a view that it is trivial, such trivialization in the broader culture may be the indirect consequence.
94. Alexander Hamilton, *The Federalist*, ed. Isaac Kramnick (London: Penguin, 1987), IX, 118.
95. In theology, Reinhold Niebuhr was the most forceful modern proponent of this duality. Reinhold Niebuhr, *Moral Man and Immoral Society* (New York: Charles Scribner's Sons, 1960), 12-23.
96. This points to an ever-widening contradiction on the right wing. Those conservatives who make crime into a perennial campaign issue require the strong central government that they otherwise reject. Although many on the right have long held these two conflicting attitudes simultaneously, the force of the antipolitical, anti-government movement is splintering the right. Clear evidence of this is the recent sympathy within Congress (from Representative Helen Chenoweth and others) for militia resistance to law enforcement agencies, and the attacks by the right wing on law-enforcement agencies such as the FBI.
97. Hamilton, *Federalist* I, 90.
98. Isaac Kramnick, "Editor's Introduction," in *The Federalist*, 58.
99. James Madison, *Federalist* X, 123. See also Hamilton, *Federalist* I, 87.
100. Much of this suspicion may have to do with the continuing influence of the Federalists. Daniel Howe, "The Political Psychology of *The Federalist*," *William and Mary Quarterly*, 3d series, XLIV, no. 1 (July 1987): 509, claims *The Federalist* has attained the status of "secular scripture."
101. Madison, *Federalist* X, 123.
102. Ibid., 124.
103. Ibid., 125; also see Madison, *Federalist* LI, 321.
104. In governmental structure, this solution is partially recapitulated in the separation of powers (Hamilton, *Federalist* IX, 119).
105. Madison, *Federalist* LI, 321. For other instances of the parallelism, see Hamilton, *Federalist* I, 88.
106. Hamilton, *Federalist* IX, 120. For the source of Hamilton's argument, see Montesquieu, *The Spirit of the Laws*, trans. and ed. Anne Cohler, Basia Miller, and Harold Stone (Cambridge: Cambridge University, 1989), 9.1, 131-32.
107. Madison, *Federalist* LI, 322.
108. Ibid.
109. Thiemann, *Religion and Public Life*, does not sufficiently appreciate this aspect of Madison's claim. He appropriates the antimajoritarian impulse of Madison's pluralism without recognizing that it undercuts his own effort to find in plural, particular groups some enduring significance that fosters truth and justice. For Madison, particularities were merely strategic antonyms for each other.
110. James Madison, *Memorial and Remonstrance Against Religious Assessments*, in *The Writings of James Madison*, vol. II, ed. Gaillard Hunt (New York: G. P. Putnam's Sons, 1901), 184. This element of Madison's argument is the one usually emphasized, perhaps because it has more resonance with the Jeffersonian solution.
111. Thomas Jefferson, *A Bill for Establishing Religious Freedom, 1777*, in William Lee Miller, *The First Republic* (New York: Alfred A. Knopf, 1986), 557.
112. Ibid.
113. Two excellent accounts of rationalism in relation to religion are Sidney E. Mead, *The Lively Experiment* (New York: Harper & Row, 1963), and Edwin S. Gaustad, *Faith of Our Fathers* (San Francisco: Harper & Row, 1987). So entrenched was this attitude among cultural and political leaders that disagreements among rationalists sometimes took the form of attacking the other's rationality. For example, Paine's *Age of Reason*, which argued that one "learns the theory of religion by reflection" alone rather than instruction from others (a hyper-rationalist position), was blasted by John Adams for the worst of all rationalist crimes, that of "promot[ing] rather than retard[ing] the cause of revelation." Paine's "billingsgate,

stolen from [others], will never discredit Christianity." See Thomas Paine, *The Age of Reason*, in *The Complete Writings of Thomas Paine*, vol. I, ed. Philip S. Foner (New York: Citadel, 1969), 506. John Adams is quoted in Gaustad, *Faith*, 89.
114. Thomas Jefferson, *Jefferson's Extracts from the Gospels*, ed. Dickinson W. Adams (Princeton, N.J.: Princeton University Press, 1983), 350. Jefferson here invokes the Quaker preacher Richard Motte to his interlocutor. Both Jefferson and Paine thought that of all the sects Quakerism was closest to the universal truth of reason. Still, Jefferson objects (ibid., 346) that Quakerism does not have loyalty to America alone (America apparently being the apotheosis of reason!); Paine (*Reason*, 498) will only concede that the Quakers have approached reason more closely than other sects, not that they have attained his height of reason.
115. Paine, *Reason*, 506.
116. Jefferson, *Extracts*, 328. The future state was conceived in a Pelagian fashion: the future state was our incentive to act well now (ibid., 326, 336).
117. On simplicity, see Jefferson, *Extracts*, 352, and Paine, *Reason*, 498.
118. There were no benign motives in errors about essentials or in adding obfuscating superfluities, such as the divinity of Jesus (see Jefferson, *Extracts*, 331, 333) or the "Platonic mysticisms" of the Trinity (ibid., 347).
119. Jefferson, ibid., 328. On universality, see ibid., 330. For Paine's similar comments, see *Reason*, 477, 505, 509.
120. Also like the recent Jesus seminar, Jefferson (ibid., 352) sought to "select . . . the very words only of Jesus."
121. Ibid., 328.
122. Paine, *Reason*, 512.
123. Jefferson, *Extracts*, 345 (emphases added).
124. Paine, *Reason*, 504.
125. Ibid., 506.
126. Ibid., 464.
127. They agreed on a good deal more, of course. For the purposes of appropriations of liberalism, we have distinguished them more sharply, perhaps, than they themselves did. But in the late twentieth century, the distinction between Madison's claim that government's purpose is justice and Jefferson's emphasis on truth is significant.
128. Jefferson, *Religious Freedom*, 558.
129. Ibid.
130. Jefferson, *Extracts*, 320.
131. Langdon Gilkey, *Message and Existence* (New York: Seabury Press, 1979), 244. Richard Rorty is one of the few postmodernists who continues to speak of progress, probably because of his Deweyan heritage.
132. Dewey, *Common Faith*. Dewey differs from the rationalists in rejecting primitivism. Other than that, he says of scientific reason exactly what Jefferson and others said of reason.
133. See, for example, Jefferson, *Letters*, 343.
134. Paine, *Reason*, 515.
135. Jefferson, *Extracts*, 328. Medieval Judaism was not much better, Jefferson says, ibid., 351.
136. Conversely, of course, it was illegitimate for public authority to inquire into religious opinion that exceeded minimalist morality (Jefferson, *Letters*, 331).
137. Pasework, *Theology of Power*, 9-10. In governmental policy, of course, the claim conceals power as well. Jefferson's trade embargo included one of the most severe restrictions of civil liberties in American history in the names of freedom and reason. Robert W. Tucker and David C. Hendrickson, *Empire of Liberty* (New York: Oxford University, 1990), provide other examples of similar contradictions in Jefferson's administration.
138. Clive James, "Sex and Reason," *The New Yorker*, December 9, 1996, 106.
139. In chapter 4 we will find cause to agree with these suspicions and to deny the claims of universal reason.

140. Gaustad, *Faith*, 89.
141. Jefferson, *Extracts*, 350. See also ibid., 333, 347.
142. See, for example, Jefferson's summary dismissal of the "dominion of the clergy, who had got a smell of union between church and state, and began to indulge reveries which can never be realized in the present state of science" (ibid., 324). Note the alliance between a lust for power and unreason, especially forceful in Jefferson's reduction of his opponents to the animalistic "smell" rather than thought. Jefferson has no need to deal with arguments, for he assumes none can be made against his "science."
143. Some, of course, believe that moral (not technical) truth has already been discovered and need only be proclaimed. That is, of course, a pre-Enlightenment perspective.
144. Rawls, *Political Liberalism*, 4.
145. Jefferson, *Letters*, 347.
146. Michel Foucault, "Two Lectures," trans. Kate Soper, in *Power/Knowledge*, ed. Colin Gordon (New York: Pantheon, 1980), 90.
147. Ralph Reed, quoted in Sidney Blumenthal, "Christian Soldiers," *New Yorker*, July 18, 1994, 31.
148. Bruce Ackerman, "Why Dialogue?" *Journal of Philosophy* 86, no. 1 (January 1989): 8.
149. Ibid., 6.
150. Ibid., 9.
151. Ibid., 13.
152. Ibid., 14.
153. Ibid., 16.
154. Ibid.
155. Ibid.
156. The closest recent approximation to Ackerman's conception was Michael Dukakis's 1988 nomination acceptance speech, in which he declared, "This election is not about ideology; it's about competence." Apparently not; George Bush made the election about ideology, and won in a romp.
157. Which is not to say, of course, that the abolitionists provide us with the ideal model of how to go about persuading or converting one's political opponents.
158. Greenawalt, *Religious Convictions*, 57.
159. Ibid.
160. Ibid., 58.
161. George M. Marsden, *Fundamentalism and American Culture* (Oxford: Oxford University Press, 1980), 15-18, 215-21.
162. Greenawalt, *Religious Convictions*, 59-63.
163. Ibid., 64-69.
164. Ibid., 166.
165. Ibid., 69.
166. Ibid., 145.
167. Ibid., 53.
168. Ibid., 71.
169. Ibid., 144-45.
170. Ibid., chaps. 4–6.
171. Audi, "Separation of Church and State," 280-83.
172. Kent Greenawalt, *Private Consciences and Public Reasons* (New York: Oxford University Press, 1995), 163-64, responds to this criticism by arguing that (1) omission of certain kinds of reasons for one's decision is not deceptive; and (2) whatever deception remains is surely worthwhile, for (although Greenawalt gives no evidence) opposing "religious" (in the narrow sense) positions will lead to more acrimony and division than, apparently, opposing nonreligious positions. Both arguments are inadequate. To omit certain minor reasons for one's position may not be deceptive, but that claim is less defensible if one omits the *determinative* reason. And if Greenawalt is correct that religious grounds are uniquely divisive—as Audi agrees—then the simpler solution is Audi's: religious people of good conscience should simply be silent.

173. Greenawalt, *Religious Convictions*, 220.
174. Rawls, *Political Liberalism*, 281-85.
175. Ibid., 190-206, 368-69.
176. Ibid., 100, 108, 140, 150, 302, 386.
177. Ibid., 312, 368-71.
178. Ibid., 138.
179. Ibid., 94.
180. Ibid., 40-43. Rawls, then, is not a privatist with respect to truth, as Gamwell claims in *Religious Freedom*, 45-75.
181. Rawls, *Political Liberalism*, 129.
182. Ibid., esp. 173-211.
183. Ibid., 206, 420.
184. Ibid., esp. 133-72, 289-371. The basis of this consensus in freedom and equality is clear throughout *Political Liberalism*.
185. Rawls claims that this conception of political liberalism is "freestanding"; that is, it does not depend on any special comprehensive doctrine in order that it be endorsed. "Freestanding" is a misleading characterization. In fact, while the political conception does not depend on the presence of any *one* comprehensive doctrine, it does depend on the presence of *at least two* comprehensive supports. Thus, Rawls's conception may be freestanding with respect to *any* special comprehensive doctrine but not with respect to *every* such doctrine.
186. Rawls, *Political Liberalism*, 217.
187. Ibid., esp. 281-85, 324-31.
188. Ibid., xli-xlii. This is a significant revision of his 1993 argument.
189. Ackerman, "Why Dialogue?" 6.
190. Rawls, *Political Liberalism*, 73; see also 214-17, 367.
191. Ibid., xxv-vi, 329.
192. Audi, "Separation of Church and State," 270, 287. Also see ibid., 278.
193. Greenawalt, *Religious Convictions*, 204.
194. Ibid., esp. 94-95, 203-30.
195. Ibid., 73; Greenawalt, *Private Consciences*, 41.
196. Our thanks to Chris Wheatley for this formulation.
197. This argument bears some similarity to but also differs with the interpretation of the relation between reason and revelation in Paul Tillich, *Systematic Theology*, vol. 1 (Chicago: University of Chicago Press, 1951), 81-94, 147-54.
198. Faith is "a personal, practical trusting in, reliance on, counting upon something . . . as able to bestow significance and worth on our existence" (H. Richard Niebuhr, "Faith in Gods and in God," in *Radical Monotheism and Western Culture*, 116, 118).
199. We do not have space here to develop a complete phenomenology of universal rationality, public rationality, irrationality, nonrationality, antirationality, and suprarationality. Suffice it to say that particular liberalism here seems to recapitulate universal liberalism's error: that is, the presumption that there is one, universal, everywhere-identical "reason," and that *everything* that is not *rational* in this sense is *false* or at least useless. And since irrationality and antirationality are supposedly *both* wrong (because not rational), there is no need to distinguish between them. But there *are* clear, and relevant differences: antirationality, such as "scientific creationism," *contradicts* commonly established reason; irrationality is that which cannot be deduced from that which preceded it, including all *historical novelty* (which, as we have noted, progressive liberalism cannot account for); nonrationality is that which does not operate according to reason, such as Buddhist meditation, which explicitly seeks enlightenment outside rational structures. But liberalism conflates all these, and more.
200. On the exclusion of "unreasonable" comprehensive perspectives, see Rawls, *Political Liberalism*, 138.
201. In particular liberalism, this seems to be the result of an odd philosophical move. The particularists recognize that reason has a history. This is why they will not make broad claims

about the "truth" of liberalism but resort instead to particularist formulae of "public reason" for our culture. However, to this Hegelian conception of the history of reason, they append a neo-Kantian ahistorical understanding of the contents of truth, having recourse to moral absolutes that are not affected by history in any appreciable way. Rawls's Kantianism is more explicit than that of other particular liberals, but the assumptions about truth are common.
202. Rawls, *Political Liberalism*, 387, insists that he is not (like Greenawalt) valorizing stability but only stability "for the right reasons," that is, in view of the presuppositions of freedom, equality, and justice. Very well, but then we have to judge how "right" these reasons are, and we are entitled to ask whether the liberal state is the best way to achieve these objectives. At just this point of qualifying his argument from facticity, Rawls should open the door to comprehensive (religious) challenges to liberalism.
203. *New York Times*, October 12, 1997, Internet edition.
204. This, of course, is an assumption that the inclusionists do *not* share. Yet they seem remarkably uninterested in how their religious commitments might *strengthen* public debate. They seem more interested in being *heard* than in contributing to the debate itself.
205. *New York Times*, September 18, 1997, A15, Chicago edition.
206. See esp. Paul Tillich, *The Religious Situation*, trans. H. Richard Niebuhr (New York: Henry Holt, 1932; repr. New York: Meridian, 1956), esp. 47-49 (repr. ed.). On the limitation of humanistic symbols see Tillich, *Systematic Theology*, vol. 3 (Chicago: University of Chicago Press, 1963), 86. A fuller discussion of these issues in Tillich is given in Pasewark, *Theology of Power*, 251-60.
207. See esp. Paul Tillich, *The Socialist Decision*, trans. Franklin Sherman (Washington, D.C.: University Press of America, 1977), 13-23.
208. Although Neuhaus, *Naked Public Square*, 20-37, also talks about "public religion," he means something much closer to civil religion than we do.
209. Langdon Gilkey, *Reaping the Whirlwind* (New York: Seabury Press, 1975), 45.

CHAPTER 2. LET FREEDOM REIGN: CONTEMPORARY AMERICAN POLITICAL PRACTICE

1. Arthur M. Schlesinger, Jr., *The Vital Center: The Politics of Freedom* (Cambridge: Riverside; Boston: Houghton Mifflin, 1962), chap. 11.
2. Nor did Schlesinger think it was the case by 1962, when his "Introduction" (ibid., ix-xvii) declares victory for principles of freedom among American liberals.
3. Indeed, Schlesinger himself has begun to wonder about his "faith." His *Disuniting of America: Reflections on a Multicultural Society* (New York: W. W. Norton, 1992), is a sometimes bitter, sometimes wistful reflection on the fragmentation of the contemporary language of pluralism. He does not seem to recognize, however, that it is due precisely to a devotion to the faith of freedom that such fragmentation seems so intractable.
4. *New York Times*, November 6, 1997, Internet edition. On the question of the language of freedom in affirmative action referenda, also see *New York Times*, November 4, 1997, Internet edition.
5. A "myth" is not a false story, but a religious symbol which discloses religious, i.e. ultimate, meaning. This meaning may be true (or better, "relatively adequate,") if it meets the criteria of comprehensiveness and self-transcendence we described in chapter 1), or it may be demonic (as were the powerful Nazi myths of blood, race, and soil). See Tillich, *Dynamics of Faith* (New York: Harper & Row, 1957), 48-54, for an introductory discussion of "myth."
6. *The New Yorker*, August 11, 1997, 4.
7. Even grief, outrage, and glee seem capable of expression as "rights." Richard Thornton, the spouse of one victim of Karla Faye Tucker, said minutes after the latter's execution, "I want to say to every victim in the world, demand this. Demand this. This is your right" (*New York Times*, February 4, 1998, A17, Chicago edition).

8. See also Garrett E. Paul, "Why Troeltsch? Why Today? Theology for the 21st Century," *The Christian Century* 110, no. 20 (June 30, 1993): 676-82.
9. Harold Bloom, *The American Religion* (New York: Simon and Schuster, 1992), comes the closest to suggesting this religious component of freedom. Bloom largely endorses such a religion, however.
10. One reason for this is that there is little if any support in the New Testament for the conservatives' version of "family values." For example, in the Gospel of Luke, Jesus says, "Whoever comes to me and does not hate father and mother, wife and children, brothers and sisters, yes, and even life itself, cannot be my disciple" (Luke 14:26). The Gospels as a whole show very little interest in family structure; the authentic letters of Paul (e.g., 1 Cor. 5:1-5; 7:1-40) show some interest in the issues; but only the later deutero-Pauline and general epistles (e.g., 1 Tim. 2:9–3:5, 1 Pet. 3:1-7) have more detailed treatments. For a comprehensive approach to the perspective on family in the New Testament, see Arland Jacobson, "Jesus Against the Family: The Phenomenon of the Dissolution of Family Ties in the Gospel Tradition," unpublished manuscript, Concordia College, December 1997.
11. Christian Coalition, *Contract with the American Family: A Bold Plan to Strengthen the Family and Restore Common-Sense Values* (n.p., n.d.), 5-7, 12-16.
12. Kyle A. Pasewark and Garrett E. Paul, "Forming an Emphatic Christian Center: A Call to Political Responsibility," *Christian Century* 111 (August 24-31, 1994), 780-83.
13. For the "neither/both" language, see *New York Times,* December 12, 1996, A16, Chicago edition.
14. Actually, we call for the emergence of several emphatic centers, as we will argue in chapter 4. For now, however, we will speak of it in the singular.
15. James Davison Hunter, *Culture Wars* (New York: HarperCollins, 1991); Pat Buchanan's speech to the 1992 Republican National Convention.
16. Robert Hughes, *Culture of Complaint* (New York: Oxford University, 1993).
17. John Updike, *Self-Consciousness* (New York: Random House, Fawcett Crest, 1989), 156.
18. H. Richard Niebuhr, *The Responsible Self* (New York: Harper & Row, 1963), esp. 56-68.
19. Alan Brinkley, "The Vital Center Will Not Hold," *New York Times Magazine,* January 19, 1997, 32. Brinkley, of course, is using the nontechnical definition of "myth" as "falsehood," not the technical philosophical definition given above in n. 5.
20. On the absoluteness of this "negative freedom," see Mary Ann Glendon, *Rights Talk* (New York: Free Press, 1991), 17-46. For the classic defense of the notion of freedom as purely negative, see Isaiah Berlin, *Four Essays on Liberty* (London: Oxford University, 1969).
21. There are other combinations, of course. Libertarian analysis embodies the dubious virtue of utter consistency, abjuring any and all "interference" with "freedom" in matters both personal and economic, while a more diffuse and unorganized populism countenances regulation in both personal and economic matters. See E. J. Dionne, Jr., *Why Americans Hate Politics* (New York: Simon and Schuster, 1991), 277. Dionne builds on William S. Maddox and Stuart A. Lilie, *Beyond Liberal and Conservative* (Washington, D.C.: Cato Institute, 1988), 111.
22. Glendon, *Rights Talk,* esp. 145-70.
23. Oliver Stone, in Ken Auletta, "What Won't They Do?" *New Yorker,* May 17, 1993, 47.
24. Kathleen Norris, *Dakota* (New York: Ticknor and Fields, 1993), 97-98. Norris continues: "Blaming others wouldn't do. Only when I began to see the world's ills mirrored in myself did I begin to find an answer; only as I began to address that uncomfortable word, sin, did I see that I was not being handed a load of needless guilt so much as a useful tool for confronting the negative side of human behavior." It is also significant that she realized that this is something "that the human potential movement of the late twentieth century never seemed to address" (ibid.). In our view, the human potential movement largely functioned to justify the needs and wants of educated upper-middle-class persons while shielding these needs and wants from criticism.
25. On this point, see Dionne, *Why Americans Hate Politics,* esp. 324-25.
26. This reflects the deeply held American conviction that private life is utterly separable from,

and utterly uninfluenced by, public life (including economics). The Christian right regularly ignores the impact of economics on its vaunted "family values"; there is no way in their scheme of things to take account of the increase in child abuse that accompanies increased unemployment. Meanwhile, the left refuses to pay attention to the growing evidence that two-parent families are, other things being equal (a major qualification!), better for children. See chapter 5.

27. For a brief comparison of conceptions of freedom in the West, see Ernst Troeltsch, "Die deutsche Idee von der Freiheit," *Die Neue Rundschau* 27 (1916): 53-71. Troeltsch's analysis of the differences between English, German, American, and French ideas of freedom is still remarkably accurate, though the latter two have moved closer together, as we argue in chapter 4.

28. For a more extended argument on this point, and for an analysis of its deleterious interpersonal consequences, see Kyle A. Pasewark, "The Troubles with Harry: Freedom, America, and God in John Updike's *Rabbit* Novels," *Religion and American Culture: A Journal of Interpretation* (Special Issue: Religion and Twentieth-Century American Novels) 6, no. 1 (Winter 1996): 3-5.

29. Not surprisingly, one of the few other writers about whom the same can be said is Ayn Rand, a pop-culture version of an American Nietzsche. See Mary Midgley, *Can't We Make Moral Judgements?* (New York: St. Martin's, 1993), 119-27.

30. Perry Miller, "Afterword: Walden—The Secret Center," in Henry David Thoreau, *Walden, or Life in the Woods and On the Duty of Civil Disobedience* (New York: Penguin, Signet, 1980), 249-50.

31. People for the American Way, *Democracy's Next Generation: A Study of Youth and Teachers* (Washington, D.C.: People for the American Way, 1989), 14.

32. See the verbatim answers in ibid., 67-75.

33. Thoreau, *Walden*, 10.

34. Ibid., 21.

35. Ibid., 118.

36. Ibid., 10.

37. Ibid., 10-11.

38. Ibid., 48.

39. Ibid., 136, 110.

40. See, e.g., ibid., 48. Ironically, Thoreau largely reproduces the viewpoint of the Yahwist narratives in the Bible (esp. Genesis 2:4b–11:9, which includes the stories of the fall, Cain and Abel, the flood, and the tower of Babel). These biblical narratives also view civilization as the result of a fall. Hence a socially produced, cultural, and traditional document reinforced (if it was not actually the chief source of) Thoreau's antisocial and anti-traditional views.

41. Thoreau, *Walden*, 119.

42. On "savages," see for examples, ibid., 17-18, 25, 48, 51, 99-100 (although Thoreau is occasionally derisive toward "savages" as well); on animals, see 46; and for children, see 69, 71.

43. Ibid., 209.

44. Ibid., 64.

45. Ibid., 73.

46. Garry Wills, *Reagan's America* (Garden City, N.Y.: Doubleday, 1987).

47. For a more detailed account of this paradox of reason, and why it will turn almost inevitably into domination, see Pasewark, *Theology of Power* (Minneapolis: Fortress Press, 1993), 260-70.

48. *New York Times*, October 26, 1997, 4:1.

49. The failure of the right to enact that agenda illustrates two things. First, the inconsistency of the agenda; that is, the government was supposed to stay out of "private lives"—except of course those lives of which it disapproved, such as gay, poor, immigrant, and female life. Second, the Republicans' antipoliticalism coincided with their antigovernmentalism. But the public, which resoundingly supported President Clinton's efforts to maintain some govern-

ment presence (see Garry Wills, "The Clinton Principle," *New York Times Magazine,* January 19, 1997, 28ff.), did not see things the same way. The public came to understand certain kinds of government programs as *supportive* of antipolitical tendencies, and hence distinguished what the Republicans had identified. Clinton's brilliant turn of nonpoliticization into support for government (government should give people opportunities "to make the best of their *own* lives") was, as one might expect, based on the ideals of autonomy and freedom. The Republican effort was more philosophically consistent in this respect.

50. For an accessible and thoughtful criticism of this idea of a sacrosanct "private" sphere, see Midgley, *Can't We Make Moral Judgements?* 35-76.
51. See Christian Coalition, *Contract,* 5-7, which explicitly promotes religious liberties "in public places."
52. For the phrase "lifestyle enclave," see Robert N. Bellah, Richard Madsen, William M. Sullivan, et al., *Habits of the Heart* (New York: Harper & Row, 1985), 71-75.
53. Hence the American obsession with sincerity; if a desire is *not* innocent, it must somehow be insincere, impure.
54. On the "intolerance" of the left in a dramatic instance at Harvard University, see Jeff Jacoby, "Those Who Preach Tolerance Should Try to Practice It as Well," *Minneapolis Star Tribune,* November 10, 1997, A9.
55. See Richard T. Hughes and C. Leonard Allen, *Illusions of Innocence* (Chicago: University of Chicago Press, 1988). The Southern Baptist Convention is the best example of this today. An explicitly nonhierarchical "Convention" (which does not call itself a "church") and one based on congregational autonomy is purging its seminaries and agencies of moderate professors and officials in ways of which no Catholic or Anglican hierarchy could dream.
56. *New York Times,* March 9, 1998, A12, Chicago edition; *New York Times,* March 13, 1998, A1, A15, Chicago edition.

CHAPTER 3. WHERE SHALL WE GO? WHO SHALL WE BE? A THEOLOGY FOR THE CHRISTIAN CENTER

1. Augustine, *Concerning the City of God Against the Pagans,* trans. Henry Bettenson (Harmondsworth, England: Penguin, 1971), 2.20, p. 71.
2. It is true that great missionary religions—Buddhism, Christianity, and Islam—are "universal" in the sense that they are *intended* for everyone. But the hope of a Buddhist "Universal Emperor," a worldwide "Christendom," or an ever-expanding "House of Islam" are fading, perhaps irretrievably. The universal thrust of these religions is not going to go away, but will, we predict, have to be profoundly altered.
3. Persons familiar with Christian theology may recognize in our views a trajectory of thought that extends from the Hebrew prophets and Jesus through Paul, Augustine, Luther, and Tillich. Close observers of the American theological scene will probably note that our accents are more those of Hyde Park than New Haven, Morningside Heights, Cambridge, or Berkeley. Let us, then, submit this trajectory and accent to scrutiny by other trajectories in the Christian tradition and other non-Christian and nonreligious trajectories. But the particularity of our trajectory is no reason to reject our arguments.
4. See chapter 4.
5. The extent to which the peculiarly American religious context—Puritan commonwealth, official disestablishment, religious freedom, sectarian proliferation, and an officially nonreligious (yet unofficially highly religious) politics—has caused this peculiarly American confusion about freedom and power, is a tantalizing question, but one that lies beyond the scope of this volume.
6. We refer here only to North American liberation theology, which, while partly homegrown, is also partly inspired by the many Latin American (and, to a lesser extent, African and Asian) liberation theologies, which, in turn, were part homegrown and part influenced by German political theol-

ogy of the 1970s. The groundbreaking Latin American work is Gustavo Gutiérrez, *A Theology of Liberation*, trans. Caridad Inda and John Eagleson (Maryknoll, N.Y.: Orbis Books, 1973). Also see Gutiérrez, *Essential Writings*, ed. James B. Nickoloff (Minneapolis: Fortress Press, 1996). A good discussion of the relationship of Latin American liberation theology and German political theology is Rebecca S. Chopp, *The Praxis of Suffering* (Maryknoll, N.Y.: Orbis Books, 1986). A somewhat dated but quite useful survey of liberation theologies in South America, Africa, and Asia is Deane William Ferm, *Third World Liberation Theologies* (Maryknoll, N.Y.: Orbis Books, 1986).

7. In comparison, Jerry Falwell's influence, which was quite strong during the Reagan administration, has faded considerably. Although persons without knowledge of the differences between Falwell's Separatist Baptist background and Robertson's pre-millennial charismatic drive may have seen little difference, it is noteworthy that the enthusiastic, apocalyptic, and charismatic Robertson has overtaken and surpassed the stern and serious Falwell.

8. There is also a poorly defined third wing, a vague but widespread Christian liberalism which is neither as powerful and visible as the right nor as committed and focused as the left, but is pervasive nonetheless. It is largely an unemphatic version of the left, similar in many ways to the vacuous center described in chapter 2.

9. Adlai E. Stevenson, *Major Campaign Speeches of Adlai E. Stevenson* (New York: Random House, 1953), 45, 188, 196 (including a reference to the "anti-Christ"), 235, 247-50, 268. Jimmy Carter, of course, made references to his "born-again" Christianity, but more as a means of personal self-identification than as an element of public discourse. John F. Kennedy's response to a question about the Supreme Court decision abolishing teacher-led prayer in the public schools was that any child could pray in private. While this accelerated the exclusion of religion from the public sphere—in this case appropriately—it is noteworthy that Kennedy showed no embarrassment in making public reference to the act of prayer.

10. See Martin Luther King, Jr., *Strength to Love* (Philadelphia: Fortress Press, 1963), esp. 139-46; Malcolm X, with Alex Haley, *The Autobiography of Malcolm X* (New York: Grove, 1965), 169-382. More generally, see Martin Luther King, Jr., *A Testament of Hope: The Essential Writings and Speeches of Martin Luther King, Jr.*, ed. James M. Washington (San Francisco: HarperSanFrancisco, 1986). On the religiosity of the Civil Rights movement as a whole, see David J. Garrow, *Bearing the Cross: Martin Luther King, Jr., and the Southern Christian Leadership Conference* (New York: Random House, 1986).

11. We should note two qualifications. First, in this chapter we are more concerned with the cultural situation as a whole than with academic and scholarly literature. Second, we do not consider a vital exception to our characterizations, namely, African American churches. These churches strike the authors as a fecund source for American religious renewal, but we do not have sufficient competence to address that topic fully.

12. See, e.g., Christian Coalition, *Contract with the American Family, A Bold Plan to Strengthen the Family and Restore Common-sense Values* (n.p.: n.d.), 8-19.

13. The Christian Coalition has lately made overtures, greeted with qualified suspicion, to African American churches on poverty policy (*New York Times*, January 31, 1997, A15, Chicago edition), and in 1996 raised funds to restore and rebuild burned Southern churches. Its entrance into the health-care debate was simply as an opponent of the Clinton plan, on the grounds of "limiting physician choice."

14. For example, Mississippi Governor Kirk Fordice's proclamation that America is and must be a "Christian nation" at the 1992 Republican National Convention.

15. It is worth recalling in this connection that more U.S. Presidents have been Episcopalian or Congregationalist by far than any other affiliation. Not only have there been no Jews and but one Roman Catholic, but also no Lutherans, Mennonites, Greek or Russian Orthodox, Mormons, Dutch Reformed, and others.

16. This was not always so. Christian liberalism, at least broadly defined, has had a long history of distinguished and influential public leaders, including in this century Walter Rauschenbusch, Harry Emerson Fosdick, Reinhold Niebuhr, and Paul Tillich. Why there are none today is a question we will raise at the end of chapter 5.

17. Indeed, the use of such general terms may be closer to imperialism than inclusivity; it is an arrogance akin to Jefferson's to take a movement with particular Christian roots and then call it "spiritual" as though it were simply identical with all true human religious aspiration.
18. This was exemplified by the folding of *Christianity and Crisis*, for many years the chief organ for left-leaning and liberationist Protestantism in this country. Its disappearance leaves *Christianity Today* as the organ of conservative evangelical Protestantism and *The Christian Century* as the organ of liberal Protestantism, but no comparable outlet for liberationist thought. See Leon Howell, "To Celebrate, and Say Goodbye," *Christianity and Crisis* 53 (April 12, 1993): 75; and Maxine Phillips, "A Better Choice of Comrades," *Dissent* 41 (Winter 1994): 134-36.
19. Two recent examples—both, characteristically, dealing with sexuality—may be cited. When the Task Force on Human Sexuality of the recently merged Presbyterian Church (U.S.A.) prepared a study on sexuality which suggested "justice-love" as the sole criterion of sexual relationships, it provoked a strong negative reaction. Later, an amendment directed against homosexual clergy and elders, requiring "fidelity within the covenant of a man and a woman or chastity in singleness," won approval of the required majority of presbyteries, and a recent attempt to moderate the language to "fidelity and integrity in marriage or singleness" appears headed for defeat. See David Heim, "Sexual Congress: the Presbyterian Debate," *Christian Century* 108 (June 26, 1991): 643-44; John J. Carey, "Sexuality: What We Couldn't Say," *Christianity and Crisis* 51 (August 19, 1991): 258-59; John P. Burgess, "Can't Stop Talking About Sex," *Christian Century* 110 (July 28, 1993): 732-34; and "Presbyteries Say No to Amendment," *Christian Century* 115 (January 21, 1998): 50. Many congregations, especially in the South, continue to withhold funds from the national church in protest over these matters. (The significance of the subsequent disappearance of *Christianity and Crisis* is underscored by the fact that it alone, of the weekly Protestant organs, published an essay suggesting that the Task Force had not gone far enough.)

    In the Evangelical Lutheran Church in America, a study document on sexuality which was released to the press before it was even sent to clergy, generated similar controversy for its acceptance of homosexual relationships (eclipsing, unfortunately, the rest of the document). A revised statement has been prepared, and the discussion is continuing. See "More Reaction to ELCA Sexuality Report," *Christian Century* 110 (December 22, 1993): 1295-96, and "More Reaction to ELCA Sexuality Report," *Christian Century* 111 (November 23, 1994): 1105.
20. Of course, this may be because there can be no intelligently conceived criticism. Gay advocates frequently point to the ignorance of their critics. Yet to advance any criticism leaves one vulnerable to the charge of "homophobia." See Don S. Browning, *Religious Ethics and Pastoral Care* (Philadelphia: Fortress Press, 1983), 72-98, esp. 87-95, for a rare example of a careful and reflective criticism of a simple acceptance of homosexuality.
21. Catholics in general, including the bishops in this instance, seem to be able to cross the left-right divide better than their Protestant counterparts. But the antagonism of the left and right in U.S. Catholicism should not be underestimated.
22. The local importance of African American congregations again warrants special comment. These are frequently quite "conservative" on cultural issues but "liberal" on economic ones, a mixture that the Christian right is beginning to appreciate for its potential links to its own program. Moreover, African American churches frequently serve as the centers of neighborhoods and communities, and have lately been in the forefront—following massive cuts in government spending—of social service delivery, housing construction, etc.
23. Our choice of the term "metaphor," though intended to be neutral, is actually a concept favored by the left. The left speaks of "metaphors" for God; the right is confident that it speaks for no metaphor, but for God.
24. H. Richard Niebuhr, *Christ and Culture* (New York: Harper & Row, 1951), 15, notes that "the virtue of Christ which religious liberalism has magnified beyond all others is love." Also see ibid., 15-19, for Niebuhr's appreciation and criticism of this approach. He cites both

Adolf Harnack and, interestingly, his own brother, Reinhold Niebuhr (15n.), as representatives of this liberal view.
25. Jim Wallis, *Who Speaks for God? An Alternative to the Religious Right: A New Politics of Compassion, Community, and Civility* (New York: Doubleday, Delacorte, 1997).
26. John J. McNeill, "Homosexuality: Challenging the Church to Grow," *Christian Century* 104 (March 11, 1987): 244.
27. Alfred Tennyson, *In Memoriam A. H. H.*, stanza 56, "Man . . . Who trusted God was love indeed/And love Creation's final law—/Tho' Nature, red in tooth and claw/With ravine, shriek'd against his creed," cited in James M. Gustafson, *A Sense of the Divine* (Cleveland: Pilgrim Press, 1994), 50.
28. Browning, *Religious Ethics and Pastoral Care*, 82-87. The metaphor of God as judge is also missing, although Browning does not make this observation.
29. With these questions we tread on the ground of the hoary question of theodicy: if God is all-powerful, all-knowing, and just (or loving), how can there be evil in the world? We are not going to solve this question here; it may not even be a fruitful question, even if it is impossible to avoid asking it. Evil happens, and the real question is not so much "Why?" or "Why me?" or even "Why not me?" but "What are we being called to do in response to what is happening?" See H. R. Niebuhr, *The Responsible Self: An Essay in Christian Moral Philosophy* (New York: Harper & Row, 1963), 67, and James M. Gustafson, *Ethics from a Theocentric Perspective*, vol. 1, *Theology and Ethics* (Chicago: University of Chicago Press, 1981), 327. Also see Gustafson, *Ethics*, 224-25, where the question "Why me?" has no place among the four basic religious questions: "In whom or what can we have confidence?" "To whom, or to what, do we owe loyalty?" "For what can we, and ought we, to hope?" "What are the appropriate objects of human loves and desires?" These are all far more practical than asking, "Why me?"

For a typically provocative attack on the questions which underlie theodicy, framed in the context of the death of children, see Stanley Hauerwas, *Naming the Silences: God, Medicine, and the Problem of Suffering* (Grand Rapids, Mich.: Wm. B. Eerdmans, 1990).
30. For criticism of male imagery, see Carol P. Christ, "Symbols of the Goddess and God in Feminist Theology," in Carl Olson, ed., *The Book of the Goddess Past and Present* (New York: Crossroad, 1985). When Sallie McFague chooses the metaphors of "mother," "lover," and "friend" for God, it is not clear whether she means to complement or to replace male metaphors; she says that her metaphors are in addition to the traditional male metaphors, but a few pages earlier she identifies her project as part of a "monistic" tradition in theology, radically opposed to the monarchical "dualistic" tradition of male imagery. Sallie McFague, *Models of God* (Minneapolis: Fortress Press, 1987), 97, 92-93. Patrick M. Arnold, *Wildmen, Warriors, and Kings* (New York: Crossroad, 1992) and John W. Miller, *Biblical Faith and Fathering* (Mahwah, N.J.: Paulist Press, 1989) are attempts to reclaim and to reinterpret biblical male imagery for God. A popular gnostic-Jungian attempt to achieve the same results is Robert Moore and Douglas Gillette, *King Warrior Magician Lover: Rediscovering the Archetypes of the Mature Masculine* (San Francisco: HarperSanFrancisco, 1991). A more perceptive approach, although not focused on the issue of God-language, is James Dittes, *Driven by Hope: Men and Meaning* (Louisville: Westminster John Knox, 1996).
31. See, e.g., James Cone, *Black Theology and Black Power* (New York: Seabury Press, 1969), 118. Sharon D. Welch, *Communities of Resistance and Solidarity* (Maryknoll, N.Y.: Orbis Books, 1985), simply bases her "definition of freedom" on the experience of liberation from sexism (p. 81). This is a very personal experience, evidently self-authenticating, with a strongly nihilistic flavor (pp. ix-x, 13-14, 87-90). Welch resolutely resists attempts to generalize her definition of freedom for fear of reintroducing oppression, 83-85. A more careful phenomenology of human needs and rights, distinguishing needs from preferences, informs Daryl F. Trimiew, *Voices of the Silenced* (Cleveland: Pilgrim Press, 1993), 65-79.
32. African American and Latin American liberation theology continue to refer to God as "Father," but this symbol of God is rarely used in other forms of North American liberation theology.

33. An early example of this is in the groundbreaking, and still quite insightful, work of Paulo Friere, *Pedagogy of the Oppressed*, trans. Myra Bergman Ramos (New York: Seabury Press, 1970), 134n: "Once a popular revolution has come to power, . . . the new power has the ethical duty to repress any attempt to restore the old oppressive power. . . . Dialogue between the former oppressors and the oppressed as antagonistic classes was not possible before the revolution; it continues to be impossible afterward." Nevertheless, the revolution supposedly maintains its "dialogical character" despite this refusal. José Porifirio Miranda's treatment of Jesus' involvement in politics and violence ultimately finds no distinction between politics and violence. See Miranda, *Communism in the Bible*, trans. Robert R. Barr (Maryknoll, N.Y.: Orbis Books, 1982), 67-78. Welch, *Communities of Resistance*, flatly asserts that ontological analysis "is based *solely* in the experience of men of a certain class" (p. 38, emphasis added). The deceptive and astonishing claim implied in this remark is that knowledge *only* expresses the experience, quite narrowly construed, of the knower. Under such circumstances it is no surprise that dialogue with the "oppressor" group is impossible.

    This is not to say that the conditions of structural violence to which liberation theology calls attention—such as widespread malnutrition and chronic unemployment—do not call for action, nor that the victims of such evils do not have a special knowledge of them to which we must carefully listen. We mean only that a too simple analysis of all such evils as traceable to the dichotomy of oppressor-oppressed easily leads to dismissal of whomever one chooses to label "oppressor."
34. The right continues to capitalize pronouns for God, e.g., "He" and "Him," and we shall do so while recounting their views.
35. Jerry Falwell, *Listen, America!* (Garden City, N.Y.: Doubleday, 1980), 19-20, 263-64, and *passim*. Also see Pat Robertson and Bob Slosser, *The Secret Kingdom* (Nashville: Thomas Nelson, 1982), 29: "In some cases God intervenes directly to destroy the antichrist society before it reaches full flower. . . . But always there is destruction." Also see ibid., 21-34.
36. For the case of the American Anglicans, see H. Richard Niebuhr, *The Social Sources of Denominationalism* (New York: Henry Holt, 1929), 23-24, 209.
37. Both Falwell, *Listen*, 29-50, and Pat Robertson, *America's Dates With Destiny* (Nashville: Thomas Nelson, 1986), 60-115, have remarkably one-sided accounts of the Revolution and early republic. One would never gather that Jefferson was a deist from their accounts!
38. See, e.g., Steven J. Keillor, *This Rebellious House: American History and the Truth of Christianity* (Downers Grove, Ill.: InterVarsity, 1996).
39. A good portrayal of the genesis of that anger among lower-class whites is in E. J. Dionne, Jr., *Why Americans Hate Politics* (New York: Simon & Schuster, 1992), 90-97. Dionne's discussion emphasizes the way in which lower-class ethnic whites were angered by liberal (and individualist) support for measures which they perceived as threats to their neighborhoods and economic survival.
40. Falwell, *Listen*, 13; Pat Robertson, *America's Dates*, 283-91.
41. Falwell, *Listen*, 12, 19.
42. "Our religious heritage and our liberty can never be separated" (ibid., 28). See ibid., 69-81 for Falwell's discussion of how government threatens liberty.
43. Esp. in ibid., 107-13.
44. Robertson is especially enamored of conspiracy theories; see Pat Robertson, *The New World Order* (Dallas: Word, 1991), 95-115.
45. See ibid., 219.
46. Reinhold Niebuhr, *Moral Man and Immoral Society* (New York: Scribner's, 1933), 64. Of course, Niebuhr here describes religion as simultaneously *both* "humility before the absolute *and* self-assertion in terms of the absolute" (emphasis added). But these days humility seems to be largely absent from the equation.
47. Of course, their racism and sexism is not intentional, but caused by society. James M. Gustafson has repeatedly underscored the un-self-critical character of this sort of piety by pointing to the enormously widespread (mis)interpretation of Paul Tillich's sermon "You Are

Accepted" (Paul Tillich, *The Shaking of the Foundations* [New York: Scribner's, 1949], 153-63): "How often versions of Paul Tillich's famous sermon 'You are accepted' have been preached in my presence with the implication and sometimes outright claim that now one can live freely, at least with an internal freedom that is not nagged by guilt" (Gustafson, "Don't Exaggerate!" *Christian Century* 114 (October 29, 1997): 964; also see Gustafson, *Ethics from a Theocentric Perspective* 1:18-23.
48. H. Richard Niebuhr was particularly sensitive to the way in which judgment directed against some may take the form of the innocent suffering of others: he refers to God's "grace that will change our minds while, at the cost of innocent suffering, it heals the wounds we have inflicted and cannot heal" (*Christ and Culture*, 241). Also see Niebuhr, "War as the Judgment of God," in *Christian Century* 59 (May 13, 1942): 630-33.
49. Alexis de Tocqueville, *Democracy in America*, vol. 2, trans. Henry Reeve (New York: Schocken Books, 1961), 38.
50. This perspective is also deeply hostile to the body at the same time that it strives for youth. See Gilbert Meilaender, "Terra es animata: on having a life" in *Hastings Center Report* 23 (July-August 1993): 25-33, and Stephen Sapp, "Living with Alzheimer's: Body, Soul, and the Remembering Community," *Christian Century* 115 (January 21, 1998): 54-60.
51. Daniel C. Maguire, *The Moral Core of Judaism and Christianity* (Minneapolis: Fortress Press, 1993), 243.
52. Paul Tillich, *Theology of Culture*, ed. Robert C. Kimball (London: Oxford University Press, 1959), 44.
53. Augustine responds at length to Julian in *Against Julian*, trans. Matthew A. Schumacher, Fathers of the Church, vol. 35 (Washington, D.C.: Catholic University of America, 1957).
54. Augustine of Hippo, *The Spirit and the Letter*, in *Augustine: Later Works*, trans. and ed. John Burnaby, Library of Christian Classics, Ichthus ed. (Philadelphia: Westminster, 1955), 195, 196.
55. It is important to emphasize that original sin is a *condition*, a state of being, and not a specific *act*. It is a state of alienation from God, from one another, and from our own true selves—which issues in specific acts of wrongdoing. Traditional theology distinguishes *actual sins* (plural) such as lying, stealing, and murder, from the *state* of *original sin* (singular).
56. Langdon Gilkey, *Shantung Compound* (New York: Harper & Row, 1966), 233.
57. On the relation between finitude and sin, see Paul Tillich, *Systematic Theology*, vol. 2 (Chicago: University of Chicago Press, 1957), 66-75.
58. If one had to choose between these idolatries, one would have to choose the Catholic. The Protestant notion of "Scripture alone" ignores the fact that the canon was only determined finally in the fifth century—by the church. Thus, even the form of the scriptures is determined by tradition. "Scripture alone" is self-contradictory as an exhaustive claim to authority.
59. See, e.g., Gustavo Gutiérrez, *The Power of the Poor in History* (Maryknoll, N.Y.: Orbis Books, 1983), 208, and Stanley Hauerwas, *A Community of Character* (Notre Dame, Ind.: University of Notre Dame Press, 1981).
60. See Glenn Tinder, *The Political Meaning of Christianity* (San Francisco: HarperSanFrancisco, 1991), 41-52; Tinder follows Niebuhr's reduction of "pride" to selfishness.
61. See, for example, Reinhold Niebuhr, *The Nature and Destiny of Man*, vol. 1 (New York: Charles Scribner's Sons, 1964), 40-42, on vitality as the "will to power." For a tragicomic example of this phenomenon, see Gilkey, *Shantung*, 19, on a guerrilla war that was fought to capture sixteen inches of space.
62. Indeed, there is one good reason not to overemphasize the interests of the claimant, namely, that it diverts us from the content and merit of the claims. For defenses of an emphasis on the content, not the arguer, see Alexander Hamilton, *The Federalist*, ed. Isaac Kramnick (London: Penguin, 1987), I, pp. 87-88, and more recently, Hans-Georg Gadamer, *Truth and Method* (New York: Crossroad, 1982), esp. 235-341, 491-98, on truth claims.
63. By "self-interest" is usually meant short-term interest rather than "enlightened self-interest," which generally takes a longer view. That distinction becomes important in chapter 5.
64. Rahner explains original sin solely in terms of the "original and permanent co-determination

by others' guilt." In other words, we bear "the stamp of the guilt of others in a way which cannot be eradicated." Karl Rahner, *Foundations of Christian Faith*, trans. William V. Dych (New York: Crossroad, 1982), 109, 111.
65. Elsa Tamez, *The Amnesty of Grace* (Nashville: Abingdon Press, 1993), 106.
66. Walter Rauschenbusch, *A Theology for the Social Gospel* (Nashville: Abingdon, 1978), 53.
67. Rauschenbusch continues: "A theology for the social gospel would have to say that original sin is partly social. It runs down the generations not only by biological propagation but also by social assimilation" (ibid., 60-61). In fact, Rauschenbusch went farther than saying that original sin was *partly* social (which is something with which we agree). Because he thought that the human race was gradually progressing biologically, the "inner cause" of original sin would be soon removed, leaving only the social form in place.
68. See John Bunyan, *Grace Abounding to the Chief of Sinners* (Grand Rapids, Mich.: Baker, 1978); Philip Jacob Spener, *Pia Desideria*, trans. Theodore G. Tappert (Philadelphia: Fortress Press, 1964).
69. On the importance of these passages, see, e.g., Martin Luther, *To the Christian Nobility of the German Nation Concerning the Reform of the Christian Estate*, in *Luther's Works*, vol. 44, trans. and ed. James Atkinson (Philadelphia: Fortress Press, 1966), 131, and *Temporal Authority: To What Extent It Should Be Obeyed*, in *Luther's Works*, vol. 45, trans. W. A. Lambert, rev. and ed. Walther I. Brandt (Philadelphia: Fortress Press, 1962), 85-86.
70. Luther was followed in this regard by Kierkegaard. For Kierkegaard's existentialism, in its reflexive opposition to Danish Hegelianism, see Søren Kierkegaard, *Concluding Unscientific Postscript*, trans. David F. Swenson and Walter Lowrie (Princeton, N.J.: Princeton University Press, 1941).
71. It is remarkable that Luther took this position, because in every other theological doctrine (the doctrine of the Lord's Supper, the relation between faith and works, etc.), external circumstances were vital for faithful inward life. "Faith" was not independent of obedience and action. See Pasewark, *Theology of Power* (Minneapolis: Fortress Press, 1993), 124-30.
72. Luther was not a perfectionist. There is no one, under the conditions of existence, who is perfectly faithful. All are sinners, and no work is a perfectly good work. See Martin Luther, *Treatise on Good Works*, in *Luther's Works*, vol. 44, trans. W. A. Lambert, rev. Atkinson, 34-39. However, in the hands of American perfectionists, this concept of sin becomes nearly abusive, laminating all weakness with the epithet "sin."
73. See, e.g., Martin Luther, *Against Latomus*, in *Luther's Works*, vol. 32, trans. and ed. George Forell, 151-224.
74. For criticisms of this view, see Gilkey, *Shantung*, 109-11.
75. The Eagles, "Peaceful, Easy Feeling," *The Eagles: Their Greatest Hits, 1971–75*, Elektra, 1976.
76. This much is Aristotle's view as well.
77. John Calvin, *Institutes of the Christian Religion* (1559), trans. Ford Lewis Battles, ed. John T. McNeill, Library of Christian Classics, vol. XXI (Philadelphia: Westminster, 1960), 4.20.2-3, pp. 1487-89.
78. See Gilkey, *Shantung*, 112; Tillich's term (*Systematic Theology*, 2:47-64), like Augustine's, is "concupiscence."
79. See, e.g., Langdon Gilkey, *Message and Existence* (New York: Seabury, 1979), 142, 246-47; and *Society and the Sacred* (New York: Crossroad, 1981), 152-53.
80. See Gilkey, *Shantung*, 19, for a chronicle of a failed attempt to govern without compulsion.
81. Friedrich Schleiermacher, *The Christian Faith*, trans. H. R. Mackintosh and J. S. Stewart (Edinburgh: T. & T. Clark, 1928), 288. "We are conscious of sin partly as having its source in ourselves, partly as having its source outside our own being" (279).
82. This dynamic received brilliant artistic expression in the films and television of Alfred Hitchcock. Hitchcock constantly and masterfully plays with the viewer's suspicion of various characters. Is the strange, quiet man in *The Lodger* guilty of murder? His behavior is very suspicious. Could the dapper, smooth Joseph Cotten in *Shadow of a Doubt* really be a murderer?

He seems too nice. In *Strangers on a Train,* Hitchcock leads the viewer to think that the likable, mild-mannered, and utterly innocent Farley Granger has become so desperate that he will murder Bruno's father. The message is clear: anyone, under the right circumstances, might be led to contemplate murder. By extension we say, *anyone* is capable of *anything.* The fault we condemn in others, we share (at least in potential) with them.

83. See Valerie Saiving (Goldstein), "The Human Situation: A Feminine View," in *Journal of Religion* 40 (July 1960), 100-112.
84. It was in Augustine's dispute with the Pelagians, which reached full throttle in the early 410s, that he made this unfortunate mistake. The Pelagians asked him, If original sin is universal, if all of us are inevitably polluted by it, how does that happen? The question was about the *mechanism* of original sin. Augustine did not demur to answer. He did not say that original sin is a descriptive symbol to aid understanding rather than a causal explanation. Instead, he answered that sin is transmitted through the seed of the male from the time of Adam's sin forward, and because of that sin. See, e.g., Augustine, *A Treatise on the Grace of Christ, and On Original Sin,* 241, and *On Forgiveness of Sins, and Baptism,* 23, in *Saint Augustine's Anti-Pelagian Works,* trans. Peter Holmes and Robert Ernest Wallis, rev. Benjamin B. Warfield, Select Library of the Nicene and Post-Nicene Fathers of the Christian Church, vol. 5, ed. Philip Schaff (Edinburgh: T. & T. Clark; Grand Rapids, Mich.: Wm. B. Eerdmans, 1991). This had two unfortunate consequences. It narrowed the focus of the doctrine of original sin to the body, leading some Christian circles to disdain the body. Second, it tended to emphasize the individual's role in the propagation of sin *at the expense of thinking about social origins* of sin. Original sin became a supposedly biological fact, not a social one. That tradition has been unwittingly followed by most Protestants, including those who conceive original sin as selfishness and self-interest.
85. "At Rome I was at once struck down by illness, which all but carried me off to hell loaded with all the evil that I had committed against you [God], against myself, and against other men, a host of grave offenses over and above the bond of original sin [originalis peccati], by which we have all died with Adam" (Augustine, *Confessions,* trans. R. S. Pine-Coffin [London: Penguin, 1961], 5.9, pp. 101-2).
86. See esp. ibid., 1.9, pp. 29-31.
87. Examples of Augustine's intensifications of sin are replete throughout the first five books of the *Confessions.*
88. Likewise Tinder, *Political Meaning of Christianity,* 38, correctly notes that original sin does not "explain the origins of sin."
89. See Wallis, *Who Speaks for God?* 58-60.
90. A fine defense of the need to link "justification" to its root term, "just," is Tamez, *Amnesty of Grace.*
91. Tinder, *Political Meaning of Christianity,* 151-95, advocates a go-slow, incremental approach to justice because of his emphasis on original sin. Our position differs from his. Caution that is attentive to potential social and personal distortions of political justice does not necessarily imply preference for small-scale changes. Incremental approaches are not obviously more immune from sinful distortion. In addition, it is hard to understand how an American, a beneficiary of one very sharp political shift—from monarchy to constitutional government—can deny the possibility of positive revolutionary transformation.
92. They are more likely to be heroes who have more chances to recover from their mistakes. The "heroic" conception of faith also has a bias against the poor, whose mistakes tend to be more damaging—because they have a smaller margin for error—than the mistakes of the non-poor. On this point, see Suzannah Lessard, "The Split," *New Yorker,* December 8, 1997, 80.
93. Martin Luther, *An Open Letter on the Harsh Book Against the Peasants,* in *Luther's Works,* vol. 46, trans. Charles M. Jacobs, rev. and ed. Robert C. Schultz (Philadelphia: Fortress Press, 1967), 64-68.
94. Augustine, *City of God,* 19.21-25, pp. 881-91. This is also a central argument of Niebuhr, *Moral Man,* though he takes a slightly different view in *Nature and Destiny,* 1:285, 293-95.

95. For an indictment of this insulation of narratives in the present "dialogue" on race, see, "The Honest Dialogue That Is Neither," *New York Times,* December 7, 1997, 4:5, Chicago edition.
96. Responsibility entails answerability, as noted in chapter 2.
97. *New York Times,* November 30, 1997, 4:1ff., provides a good, brief summary of the Vatican's efforts.
98. *New York Times,* October 1, 1997, Internet edition.
99. Quoted in Joseph Fletcher, *Situation Ethics: The New Morality* (Philadelphia: Westminster, 1966), 91.
100. This is not to say that a victim should never forgive; but such forgiveness comes at great cost to the victim, and whoever asks the victim to pay such a great price ought to consider very carefully who may ask her to do it, and when and how.
101. Dietrich Bonhoeffer, *The Cost of Discipleship,* trans. R. H. Fuller (New York: Macmillan, 1963), 54-60.
102. See L. Gregory Jones, *Embodying Forgiveness* (Grand Rapids, Mich.: Wm. B. Eerdmans, 1995).
103. Consider the example of an adult child of an alcoholic. The scars left by alcohol-induced fits of rage or missed birthday parties last a lifetime. For such a child to forgive such a parent—which would be a good thing, of benefit to both parent and child—will be no easy matter.
104. Tamez, *Amnesty of Grace,* 21-22.
105. David Tracy, "Literary Theory and Return of the Forms for Naming and Thinking God in Theology," *Journal of Religion* 74, no. 3 (July 1994): 307, says that "the major candidate for the modern naming of God is still deism—a warmer deism perhaps than the eighteenth century's, but deism nonetheless."
106. Curiously, given the Christian right's contempt for Islam (frequently portraying it as a fanatical, almost inherently terroristic religion), they and orthodox Islam have almost exactly the same perspective on God as a strict rewarder of good and punisher of evil.
107. Hobbes was also the early apostle of the complete separation of the private and public spheres for subjects of the commonwealth.
108. Donald Shriver, *An Ethic for Enemies* (New York: Oxford University Press, 1995), 3.
109. For a more detailed exposition of how this might be accomplished, see Kyle A. Pasewark, "Remembering to Forget: A Politics of Forgiveness," *Christian Century* 112, no. 21 (July 5-12, 1995): 683-85 (a review of Shriver's *Ethic for Enemies*), and Pasewark, "'We Shall Be Released:' The Communicative Power of Forgiveness," unpublished address at Harvard Divinity School, April 1996.
110. Calvin, *Institutes,* 3.3.1, pp. 592-93.
111. Our criticism of the right, as we will see in chapter 5, is not that it includes self-interest, but that self-interest is so narrowly understood.
112. Where other world traditions stand on the question of power is beyond the immediate scope of this argument. Suffice it to say that Islam, Hinduism, Confucianism, and Shinto all accept power as a good. Buddhism too acknowledges the importance of power, although it generally shows less interest in politics and statecraft, and, like Hinduism, views spiritual power as superior to political power. Only Taoism seems consistently to hold all power in disdain, and yet has co-existed for millennia in China alongside Confucianism's reverence for power. Western fantasies about "Eastern" religions (itself an incoherent category—Confucianism is more like modern secularism than it is like Buddhism) that are free from power's stain tells us much more about Western views of power than about these religious traditions. We *do* have many things to learn from these traditions, but the belief that power is hopelessly evil and corrupt is *not* one of them.
113. For a penetrating criticism of Acton's epigram, see Arnold A. Rogow and Harold D. Lasswell, *Power, Corruption, and Rectitude* (Englewood Cliffs, N.J.: Prentice-Hall, 1963).
114. A very nice account of one disastrous outcome of Tolstoy's disavowal of power is given by H. Richard Niebuhr, *Christ and Culture,* 75.

115. Kyle A. Pasewark, *A Theology of Power*, 52-53.
116. This claim, and most of the argument that follows, borrows heavily from the fuller exposition in Pasewark, *A Theology of Power*.
117. G. van der Leeuw, *Religion in Essence and Manifestation*, 2 vols., trans. J. E. Turner (London: George Allen and Unwin, 1938; repr., Gloucester, Mass.: Peter Smith, 1967).
118. Rudolf Otto, *The Idea of the Holy*, trans. John W. Harvey (New York: Oxford University Press, 1969).
119. See, e.g., Paul Tillich, *Systematic Theology*, vol. 1 (Chicago: University of Chicago, 1951), 235-36, 261, and *Love, Power, and Justice* (London: Oxford University, 1954), 35.
120. Thus do the ecumenical Christian creeds (Apostles, Nicene, Athanasian, Chalcedonian) all begin with belief in God the *Creator:* "We believe in God the Father Almighty, Creator of heaven and earth" (to quote the Symbol of Nicea). Although some world religions are largely silent on the issue of the world's creation (e.g., Confucianism and Taoism), only Buddhism positively denies that there is a creator. Yet the power of the Buddha, cultivated by wisdom and compassion, is quite effectual and inspires devotion.
121. Or, perhaps, to pretend that they do not exist.
122. Pasewark, *Theology of Power*, 200. Also see Georg Simmel, *Domination and Freedom*, in *The Sociology of Georg Simmel*, trans. and ed. Kurt Wolff (New York: Macmillan, 1978).
123. For this argument, at one with many postmodern philosophies, see Pasewark, *Theology of Power*, 245-70.
124. Paul Tillich, *The Courage To Be* (New Haven, Conn.: Yale University Press, 1952), 185.
125. Pasewark, *Theology of Power*, 198-201.
126. Ibid., 246.
127. The same is true of reason's attempt to be the ultimate power, as we saw in chapter 1, and is argued more fully in Pasewark, *Theology of Power*, 260-70. The inherent plurality of power as communication of efficacy is also our principal difference with the conception of power forwarded by Hannah Arendt and Tillich. For Arendt, see ibid., 211-13, 246-49; for Tillich, see ibid., 273-313.
128. Also see Hannah Arendt, *The Human Condition* (Chicago: University of Chicago Press), 199-212.
129. See Reinhold Niebuhr, *Nature and Destiny of Man*, 2:269, where he identifies two contrasting views of "government" in the Bible: "According to the one, government is an ordinance of God and its authority reflects the Divine Majesty. According to the other, the 'rulers' and 'judges' of the nations are particularly subject to divine judgment and wrath because they oppress the poor and defy the divine majesty." Taken together, "These two approaches do justice to the two aspects of government." Today our culture admits only the second view, forgetting its rationale; we hate government not for its tendency to oppress the poor, but just because it governs.
130. Pasewark, *Theology of Power*, 319.
131. For a masterly discussion of sin as sloth, see Karl Barth, *Church Dogmatics* 4/2, *The Doctrine of Reconciliation*, trans. G. W. Bromiley (Edinburgh: T. & T. Clark, 1958), 403-83. "The sinner is not merely Prometheus or Lucifer. He is also . . . a lazy-bones, a sluggard, a good-for-nothing, a slow-coach and a loafer" (ibid., 404).
132. Pasewark, *Theology of Power*, 329-30.
133. We do not here provide a definition of justice. That task lies beyond our scope. Definitions of justice ("to each his own," "from each according to her ability, to each according to her need," "due process," "equal opportunity," etc.) can serve a useful purpose, but often limit the discussion in advance. In terms of our argument, an adequate conception of justice would have to take account of at least the following: human historicity and finiteness; original sin and corruption; moral and intellectual pretension; social and personal responsibility; the need for love; freedom; and the ubiquity and necessity of power.
134. We do not, of course, claim that these are *exclusively* Christian principles; but neither do we claim that they are identical with supposedly *universal* principles, or the political principles of other religions. That is a question for detailed comparative research, not for universal schemes.

CHAPTER 4. DIFFERENCE AND COMMITMENT: PLURALISM AND THE CHRISTIAN CENTER

1. That is, we have "avoided any hint of religious domination" unless all power is taken to be domination—a view we have taken great pains to refute.
2. Susan Moller Okin, "Humanist Liberalism," in *Liberalism and the Moral Life*, ed. Nancy L. Rosenblum (Cambridge, Mass.: Harvard University Press, 1989), 40.
3. Immanuel Kant, *An Answer to the Question: "What Is Enlightenment,"* in *Kant's Political Writings*, ed. Hans Reiss (Cambridge: Cambridge University Press, 1970), 54; John Rawls, *Political Liberalism* (New York: Columbia University Press, 1996), 37.
4. Amy Gutmann, "Introduction," in *Multiculturalism and "The Politics of Recognition,"* ed. Amy Gutmann (Princeton, N.J.: Princeton University Press, 1992), 5.
5. A similar position is taken by Edward Schillebeeckx, *World and Church*, trans. N. D. Smith (New York: Sheed and Ward, 1971), 86.
6. Indeed, some discussions of pluralism are formulated as attempts to create a "middle ground." See T. M. Scanlon, "The Difficulty of Tolerance," in *Toleration*, ed. David Heyd (Princeton, N.J.: Princeton University Press, 1996), 226-27.
7. The tie between toleration and freedom is argued in Bernard Williams, "Toleration: An Impossible Virtue?" in *Toleration*, ed. Heyd, 22-25. Martha C. Nussbaum, "Human Functioning and Social Justice," *Political Theory* 20 (May 1992): 212, notes the close link between "relativism" and the lionization of freedom.
8. Williams, "Toleration," 19.
9. Jürgen Moltmann, "Is 'Pluralistic Theology' Useful for the Dialogue of World Religions?" in *Christian Uniqueness Reconsidered*, ed. Gavin D'Costa, Faith Meets Faith Series (Maryknoll, N.Y.: Orbis Books, 1990), 149-56, makes a similar argument.
10. In the fourth century, Augustine, *Confessions*, trans. R. S. Pine-Coffin (Harmondsworth, England: Penguin, 1961), 3.4-6, already warned against relying on upbringing as the overriding factor in religious commitment. Augustine, who was set ablaze by the "love of wisdom" he discovered in the pagan Cicero, fell into his disastrous affinity for the dualistic Manichaean sect precisely because the latter possessed the "name of Christ" (though not its meaning), upon which Augustine's "infant heart had been suckled dutifully."
11. The logic of this paradox is argued by Lesslie Newbigin, "Religion for the Marketplace," in *Christian Uniqueness Reconsidered*, ed. D'Costa, 135-48, and noted by Gordon Graham, "Tolerance, Pluralism, and Relativism," in *Toleration*, ed. Heyd, 46.
12. For an academic expression of this equivalence, see Paul Taylor, "Ethical Relativism," in *Moral Philosophy*, ed. George Sher (Orlando, Fla.: Harcourt Brace Jovanovich, 1987), 146-60.
13. Neoconservative literature rarely raises, let alone answers, problems of the past's oppressiveness to certain groups, or the relation of that oppressiveness to the very "virtues" and thinkers who are valorized. The question is raised neither in William Bennett, ed., *The Book of Virtues* (New York: Simon and Schuster, 1993), nor in Allan Bloom, *The Closing of the American Mind* (New York: Simon and Schuster, 1987). Bloom is also a good example of the equation of pluralism and relativism. Arthur M. Schlesinger, Jr., *The Disuniting of America* (New York: W. W. Norton, 1992), is at least attentive to the need to include the new literature of previously marginalized groups in his canon, even though he averts his eyes from the seamier sides of the traditional classics.
14. For a good review of this literature in theology, see Scott Cowdell, *Is Jesus Unique?* (Maryknoll, N.Y.: Orbis Books, 1996), 237-78.
15. Nussbaum, "Human Functioning," 209, 243, calls this subjectivism the extreme of relativism. It is certainly the pole to which many Americans are committed intellectually.
16. See chapter 2. On the other hand, communitarians such as Amitai Etzioni, *The Spirit of Community* (New York: Crown, 1993), understand communities as a collection of individu-

als who may be (and probably are) highly similar. Although Etzioni also advocates the pluralism of multiple communities, we are entitled to wonder how far such an effort can reach. If a really different other is not included in the very constitution of "community," it is unlikely that an insular group will suddenly discover the virtues of difference. On that point, see Mary Douglas, *Cultural Bias* (London: Royal Anthropological Institute of Great Britain and Ireland, 1978). Linell Elizabeth Cady, *Religion, Theology, and American Public Life* (Albany: SUNY, 1993), also has a persuasive critique of such insularity.

17. See Marsha Witten, *All Is Forgiven* (Princeton, N.J.: Princeton University Press, 1994). This problem need not be historically unique to remain a serious concern. Laurence Moore, *Selling God* (New York: Oxford University Press, 1994), examines continuities and transformations in the religious "market" in American history.
18. Nussbaum, "Human Functioning," 243.
19. This antirelativist attitude reflects the victory of radical Protestant conceptions of the "church" and other organizations. For a comparison of this view with Martin Luther's quite different conception of the church as a community of moral difference, see Kyle A. Pasewark, "The Body in Ecstasy: Love, Difference, and the Social Organism in Luther's Theory of the Lord's Supper," *Journal of Religion* 77, no. 4 (October 1997): 511-40.
20. Henceforth what is normally called "relativism," we will call "antirelativism," "antirelative relativism," etc., because that is what it is.
21. I.e., political and intellectual America, as well as a broad swath—but not all—of Christian America.
22. The same process unfolded much more quickly in Europe, especially France and Germany.
23. For Rorty's pragmatism, focused on the metaphor of the tool, see Richard Rorty, *Contingency, Irony, and Solidarity* (Cambridge: Cambridge University Press, 1989), 11-13; for the indeterminable nature of that for which the tool is used (outside of private ends that cannot be evaluated), see Rorty, *Essays on Heidegger and Others, Philosophical Papers, vol. 2* (Cambridge: Cambridge University Press, 1991), 196-97.
24. See especially Michel Foucault, *The Care of the Self*, trans. Robert Hurley (New York: Random House, Pantheon, 1986), and "The Ethic of Care for the Self as a Practice of Freedom," trans. J. D. Gauthier, in *The Final Foucault*, ed. James Bernauer and David Rasmussen (Cambridge, Mass.: MIT Press, 1988), 1-20. For a more complete argument on Foucault's relation to freedom, see Kyle A. Pasewark, *A Theology of Power* (Minneapolis: Fortress Press, 1993), 33-55.
25. Rorty, *Contingency*, xiii. Some postmodernists such as Lyotard have more subtle positions. Our concern is principally with American thought, however, which Rorty exemplifies. Of the French, the most influential in America are probably Foucault and Jacques Derrida.
26. John McGowan, *Postmodernism and Its Critics* (Ithaca, N.Y.: Cornell University Press, 1991).
27. Leszek Kolakowski, *Modernity on Endless Trial* (Chicago: University of Chicago Press, 1990).
28. Friedrich Nietzsche, *The Will to Power*, trans. Walter Kaufmann and R. J. Hollingdale, ed. Walter Kaufmann (New York: Random House, 1967), 12, 13.
29. Richard Rorty, "The Priority of Democracy to Philosophy," in *The Virginia Statute for Religious Freedom*, ed. Merrill D. Peterson and Robert C. Vaughan (New York: Cambridge University Press, 1988), 273.
30. For an excellent treatment of the initial different meanings of "freedom" in each revolution, see Hannah Arendt, *On Revolution* (London: Penguin, 1965).
31. The opposition between universality and particularity is not specifically French or American, but combined with egalitarianism, it has a specific way of playing itself out.
32. Arendt, *On Revolution*, 61-66, 215-22, argues that even among Americans the French Revolution is the paradigm of the nature of revolutions. This is confirmed in Rorty, *Contingency*, 3, and *Essays*, 19.
33. This point is made forcefully in the criticism of pluralistic "dialogue" offered by John Milbank, "The End of Dialogue," in *Christian Uniqueness Reconsidered*, ed. D'Costa, 183-84.

34. See below, pp. 166-73.
35. John Courtney Murray, *We Hold These Truths* (New York: Sheed and Ward, 1960).
36. These thinkers have somewhat different reasons for their investment in incommensurability. Rorty's thought is under consideration presently. For Rawls the incommensurability of universal doctrines that are inevitably particular is the ground for a specifically *political* liberalism that makes no comprehensive claims (see chapter 1). For Foucault, as well as Jean-François Lyotard, *The Postmodern Condition*, trans. Geoff Bennington and Brian Massumi, Theory and History of Literature, vol. 10 (Minneapolis: University of Minnesota Press, 1984), incommensurability is a desideratum in order to prevent the onslaught of the great postmodern bogeyman, "totalization." Echoing Foucault, incommensurability is necessary in order to prevent the subsumption of everything and everyone in the "power" of the "system." This wing of French postmodernism essentially reduplicates the earlier fear of the totalizing tendencies of technology, although the totalizing force is now the vaguer "system." Hence, whereas Rawls seeks consensus, Lyotard ("Answering the Question: What Is Postmodernism?" trans. Régis Durand, in *The Postmodern Condition*, 77-82), fears it as the shepherd of domination.
37. Rorty, *Contingency*, xiii.
38. Bruno Latour, *We Have Never Been Modern*, trans. Catherine Porter (Cambridge, Mass.: Harvard University Press, 1993), 1.
39. In a recent classroom discussion, one student offered the following cop-out in response to Aristotle's discussion of the virtues: "What he means by generosity and what I mean by generosity are completely different" (meaning, of course, that Aristotle was completely irrelevant—unrelated—to his life, and could hence be safely disregarded). When challenged to explain how their views differed, he demurred. Another student said, "Our times are different from his." In response to both comments, the instructor challenged, "Different in what way? How, exactly, are these views different? How do you know that your views are *completely* different? Just because some views are different, that does not mean that *all* views are *completely* different." A spirited discussion followed. Later, after having established that language itself, despite all differences in the way we use words, would be impossible if *everyone's* views about *everything* were *completely* different, the instructor went on to ask, "Why, then, are we automatically inclined simply to say that these views are different and leave it at that?" With remarkable insight and honesty, one of the students who had spoken earlier said, "Because it's easier that way." It would be difficult to put it any better than that. (The section under discussion was *Nicomachean Ethics* II, 1107a:26-1108b:6.)
40. It is true that separatist and sectarian groups can generate some (though not full) power for their own members, so long as isolation remains a live option.
41. On this point, see also Newbigin, "Religion," 145.
42. *New York Times Magazine*, October 13, 1996, 50.
43. See also Graham, "Tolerance," 46. The French postmodern fear of "totalization" is hardly the only or even the most important threat of domination. Granted that plurality is helpful in preventing hegemony, we should not neglect the dangers of intragroup hegemony and the desire for domination that antirelativist pluralism produces. The current state of affairs, in which no moral or political point can be argued, was clearly described more than fifteen years ago by Alasdair MacIntyre in *After Virtue* (Notre Dame, Ind.: University of Notre Dame Press, 1981), esp. 1-11. What we call "moral egalitarianism" is very close to what MacIntyre calls "emotivism," which he also traces to the Enlightenment.
44. Michael J. Perry, *Love and Power* (New York: Oxford University Press, 1991), 8-28, and "Religious Morality and Political Choice," *The San Diego Law Review* 30 (1993): 712. This is related to the claim of chapter 1 that such conceptions also inoculate political debate against change.
45. As observed more than half a century ago by Reinhold Niebuhr, *Moral Man and Immoral Society* (New York: Charles Scribner's, 1932), 129: "No society has ever achieved peace without incorporating injustice into its harmony. Those who would eliminate the injustice are therefore always placed at the moral disadvantage of imperilling its peace. The privileged

groups will place them under that moral disadvantage even if the efforts toward justice are made in the most pacific terms" (also see ibid., 233).

46. For a similar point, see Mary Douglas, *Risk and Blame* (New York: Routledge, 1992), 25-32, and Milbank, "End of Dialogue," 175.

47. Of course, disagreement and vigorous argument can also collapse into weakness and domination. That the result in any particular case cannot be foreseen with certainty is part of the risk and unpredictability inherent in power's generation.

48. This is not to say that any debate is or should be entirely open. Some issues are effectively removed from public debate for long periods, and should be.

49. This problem of the relation between "universals" and "particulars" mars otherwise interesting efforts at something similar to emphatic pluralism. For examples, see Gavin D'Costa, "Christ, the Trinity, and Religious Plurality," and Christoph Schwöbel, "Particularity, Universality, and the Religions," in *Christian Uniqueness Reconsidered*, ed. D'Costa, 16-29, 30-46, respectively.

50. For a penetrating analysis of the *moral* dimensions of translation, see Alasdair MacIntyre, "Tradition and Translation," in MacIntyre, *Whose Meaning? Which Rationality?* (Notre Dame, Ind.: University of Notre Dame Press, 1988), 370-88. MacIntyre observes that the translation of a differing moral viewpoint from one language (tradition) to another may enable persons in the target language (tradition) to identify "the limitations, incoherences, and poverty of their own beliefs" (ibid., 387-88). Translation frequently involves stretching the target-language to express ideas, concepts, sensibilities, and values that are not part of its common vocabulary and worldviews; perhaps it involves coining a new term, like "human sciences" for *Geisteswissenschaft*, or simply not translating a key word, like *Blitzkrieg*. Sometimes it works; sometimes not.

51. Consequently, efforts to establish "universal" truth without reference to the problem of language, such as Taylor, "Ethical Relativism," are naïve repetitions of an already stale debate.

52. Augustine, *Confessions*, IX.10. In Augustine, *The Literal Meaning of Genesis*, vol. 2, *Books 7-12*, trans. John Hammond Taylor, Ancient Christian Writers 42, Book 12, 178-231, Augustine distinguishes the highest type of vision, the intellectual, as incapable of error. In this "face to face" vision of God's "own divine essence," God "speaks—in an *inutterable* converse where no man beholds Him while living this mortal life in the senses of the body" (218-19, emphasis added). Only if one is taken out of the mortal body, as Augustine thinks Paul was, is this vision possible, and, in any case, its content cannot be *expressed*. Our thanks to Roy Hammerling for clarifying this.

53. See Franklin I. Gamwell, *The Meaning of Religious Freedom* (Albany: SUNY, 1995), for a recent example of this well-traveled argument.

54. We omit from this account that this objection presupposes—generally without argument—the universal validity and usefulness of a particular form of binary logic. We do not want to deny the considerable validity and wide usefulness of such language, but its advocates need to make the further case that they often do not, i.e., that it is universally applicable, useful, and valid.

55. Hans-Georg Gadamer, *Truth and Method* (New York: Crossroad, 1982), 308-9.

56. If binary propositional logic must be satisfied, one might say this: "As far as we are able to argue under the conditions of history, all propositional truths—except this one—are partial, incomplete, relative to one another, and conditioned by history and culture." The logical problem is solved; existentially and in terms of the content of "truth," nothing has changed. We resist that solution for two reasons. First, it is as facile as the logical problem. Second, it too would declare history closed by reason.

57. One of the best contemporary theological arguments for the notion of comprehensive rather than localized truth—while still incorporating pluralism—is the body of Langdon B. Gilkey's work. For an assessment of Gilkey's perspective, see Kyle A. Pasewark, "Power, Freedom, and History: The Symbol of Divine Providence," in *The Theology of Langdon Gilkey: Systematic and Critical Studies*, ed. Kyle A. Pasewark and Jeff B. Pool (Macon, Ga.: Mercer University Press, 1999), chap. 12.

58. For example, Taylor, "Ethical Relativism," 147, 154. Nussbaum, "Human Functioning," 213, makes a point similar to ours.
59. G. W. F. Hegel, *Elements of the Philosophy of Right*, trans. H. B. Nisbet, ed. Allen W. Wood, Cambridge Texts in the History of Political Thought (Cambridge: Cambridge University Press, 1991), 23. Postmodern reflections on the future—and the place of philosophy—sometimes sound much like Hegel. Foucault's archaeological method, for example, depends on the dissolution of the age under analysis. In Michel Foucault, *The Order of Things* (New York: Random House, Vintage, 1970), 75, he maintains: "The Classical age was no more able than any other culture to circumscribe or name its own general system of knowledge." To the extent that Foucault begins to be able to perform an "archaeology of the present" (Gilles Deleuze, *Foucault*, trans. and ed. Seán Hand [Minneapolis: University of Minnesota Press, 1988], 50), this is because modernity has, in his view, already collapsed.
60. Moreover, we are entitled to doubt the sharp dualisms that Rorty promotes in order to build his case—the oppositions between "discovery" and "creativity," "intrinsic" and "historical," "argument" and "taste," as well as the identity between "argument" and "ahistoricism"—because he gives us no reason to believe them. Moreover, he denies the need to do so.
61. Rorty, *Contingency*, 4-5.
62. Ibid., 5.
63. Ibid.
64. Ibid., 10.
65. Ibid., 6.
66. Ibid., 9. Once more we note how fortunate it is to be socially privileged if argument is impossible.
67. An extended defense of the priority of the sentence in the construction of meaning (in contrast to the denotative word) is Paul Ricoeur, *The Rule of Metaphor*, trans. Robert Czerny, Kathleen McLaughlin, and John Costello (Toronto: University of Toronto, 1977).
68. Again, see MacIntyre, "Tradition and Translation."
69. Rorty, *Contingency*, 6.
70. However, Anthony Giddens, *Central Problems in Social Theory* (Berkeley: University of California Press, 1979), and *The Constitution of Society* (Berkeley: University of California Press, 1984), offers a compelling argument that sociological theory generally overestimates the extent of actors' ignorance.
71. Thomas S. Kuhn, *The Structure of Scientific Revolutions*, 2nd ed. (Chicago: University of Chicago Press, 1970), is a brilliant analyst of the way changes in scientific paradigms have actually occurred. Kuhn demonstrates, without recourse to a notion of unitary truth, that scientific revolutions nonetheless occur for reasons that are persuasive to actors.
72. Rorty, "The Priority of Democracy to Philosophy," 258.
73. A classic analysis of this problem is Ernst Troeltsch, *The Absoluteness of Christianity and the History of Religions* (Richmond, Va.: John Knox, 1971). His later brilliant and sustained discussion of value, knowledge, individuality, and cultural synthesis in a thoroughly historicized framework is *Der Historismus und seine Probleme* (Tübingen: J. C. B. Mohr, 1922), esp. 164-220 and 656-772, trans. David Reid and Garrett E. Paul, *Historicism and Its Problems* (Atlanta: Scholars Press, forthcoming).
74. It is true, of course, that some conversations are their own purpose. Generally, however, political discussions have purposes outside themselves, either to other discursive acts or to action beyond discourse. And even conversations that are their own purpose (including the divine conversation which believers call worship) will still affect what goes on outside them.
75. This is, by definition, what history is all about, and any philosophy that claims to be "historical all the way down" must take account of it. Historical events and decisions are unrepeatable. Wellington never faced Napoleon before, nor will again. See Ernst Troeltsch, *Der Historismus*, 27-67. Also see Troeltsch, "Historiography," in *Encyclopedia of Religion and Ethics*, ed. James Hastings, 6:716-23, and "Modern Philosophy of History," in *Religion in History*, ed. James Luther Adams, trans. James Luther Adams and Walter F. Bense (Minneapolis: Fortress Press, 1991), 273-320,

esp. 285-87. Cf. Wilhelm Dilthey, *Introduction to the Human Sciences*, ed. Rudolf A. Makkreel and Frithjof Rodi (Princeton, N.J.: Princeton University Press, 1989), 214-19.
76. For a more complete argument, see Pasewark, *Theology of Power*, 196-214, 311-31.
77. Charles Taylor, "The Politics of Recognition," in *Multiculturalism and "The Politics of Recognition,"* ed. Gutmann, 25-73, gives a nuanced and persuasive argument for a pluralism based on the largely Hegelian emphasis on recognition. The remainder of the volume and its companion, *Multiculturalism: Examining the Politics of Recognition,* ed. Amy Gutmann (Princeton, N.J.: Princeton University Press, 1994), contain enlightening responses to Taylor's proposal.
78. On this point, see Karl Rahner, *Foundations of Christian Faith*, trans. William V. Dych (New York: Crossroad, 1982), 9.
79. Robert Wuthnow, *The Struggle for America's Soul* (Grand Rapids, Mich.: Wm. B. Eerdmans, 1989); James Davison Hunter, *Culture Wars* (New York: HarperCollins, Basic, 1991).
80. Will Herberg, *Protestant, Catholic Jew,* rev. ed. (Garden City, N.Y.: Doubleday, Anchor, 1960).
81. Hunter, *Culture Wars,* 77. It is possible, of course, to contest the notion of a "Judeo-Christian" consensus (as Arthur Cohen does), and to doubt whether the disagreement is more about the sources of moral truth than anything else, as Hunter maintains. Still, the point is that denominational battles are no longer, politically, the crucial ones.
82. Ibid., 86.
83. Langdon Gilkey, *Message and Existence* (New York: Seabury Press, 1979), 8.
84. See Klaus Scholder, *The Churches and the Third Reich,* trans. John Bowden, 2 vols. (Minneapolis: Fortress Press, 1987–88), and James W. Heisig and John C. Maraldo, eds., *Rude Awakenings* (Honolulu: University of Hawaii Press, 1995). Our thanks to John Cha for alerting us to the existence of the Japanese Buddhist discussion as a parallel to the German church question.
85. To treat health as an intrinsic good also leads to various practical contradictions; if *more* health is always better, then there is no limit to how much we should spend on health care, even compared with other goods such as education or reducing poverty.
86. An exception is the helpful discussion by George P. Fletcher, "The Instability of Tolerance," in *Toleration,* ed. Heyd, 158-72.
87. Douglas, *Risk and Blame,* 25-30.
88. Wolfhart Pannenberg, "Religious Pluralism and Conflicting Truth Claims," in *Christian Uniqueness Reconsidered,* ed. D'Costa, 96-106.
89. Don S. Browning, *A Fundamental Practical Theology* (Minneapolis: Fortress Press, 1991), 44-46. Browning argues persuasively that a fatal flaw in more dogmatic narrative theologies such as those of George Lindbeck and Stanley Hauerwas is that they fail to recognize that nearly all of us take part in several narratives, not just one. This multiple participation is significant for several reasons, one of which is that one simply cannot disentangle the influence of the "Christian narrative" from the "American," the "female," or any other community in which one participates. This rules out any tendency to place the Christian story on a plane exempt from the usual processes of culture and criticism.
90. This book has been a considerable exercise in managing and transforming plurality for its authors, who, despite many outward similarities and inner agreements, nevertheless frequently challenged and criticized each other's views. Only once was the disagreement sufficient to require a note, and here it is.

The authors find themselves divided over the value and coherence of the sectarian option in Christianity. The Christian "sect," as defined by Max Weber and Ernst Troeltsch, is a gathered community of believers which actively separates itself from the "world," and absolutely refuses any compromise with it, in a quest for greater purity and authenticity. See Ernst Troeltsch, *The Social Teachings of the Christian Churches,* trans. Olive Wyon (New York: Harper & Row, 1960), 1:993-1002, also 691-94 and 724-38. The sect frequently looks forward to the overthrow and disappearance of the present world, particularly its economic, social, and national arrangements. It may be radically egalitarian (the Levellers or Diggers and Fifth

Monarchy Men of seventeenth-century England, or the Amish of today) or radically reactionary (Hal Lindsey's popular doomsday book *The Late Great Planet Earth* [Grand Rapids, Mich.: Zondervan, 1970] and Pat Robertson's Christian America). Sects also differ widely; they may take conversionist, introversionist, adventist, or gnostic forms (see Bryan Wilson, "An Analysis of Sect Development," in *American Sociological Review* 24 [February 1959]: 3-14, cited in J. Alan Winter, *Continuities in the Sociology of Religion* [New York: Harper & Row, 1977], 160-61).

Both authors of this book acknowledge the (nigh) insufferable self-righteousness and arrogance of many sects, including the "sect" of liberal secularism. Given the major role played by the Protestant sects in ushering in the modern world (quite against their wishes), and given our criticism of modernity, it is natural that we would be critical of the sects as well. But Garrett Paul sees much more value in the consistent, nonviolent, noncompromising sect; value for itself, and (altogether ironically) value for the very world it seeks to avoid or even overthrow. Such sects point to the ultimately secondary character of all politics, all nations, all peoples, all civilizations, all cultures, and even this planet in comparison with the infinite transcendence of God. From the viewpoint of the sect, democracy and communism are, in important respects, equally distant from the divine holiness, and never a substitute for it. Sects also have often been the first to resist the absolute claims made by demonic governments, as when the Jehovah's Witnesses were among the first Christians to stand up to the Nazis, or when Quakers first rejected slavery. The sect is also far and away the preferred social form in African American Christianity. Professor Paul feels more strongly that the "sect" is one of *three* valid and yet contradictory social forms Christianity can take (church, sect, and mystic); they are mutually contradictory, exclusive, and exhaustive, and yet all three are necessary.

Also see H. Richard Niebuhr's characterization of the sect (which he restricted to its introversionist form) as "A Necessary and Inadequate Position," *Christ and Culture,* 65-82. For an Anabaptist rebuttal which nevertheless concedes a good deal to Niebuhr, see Charles Scriven, *The Transformation of Culture* (Scottsdale, Pa.: Herald Press, 1988).

91. Martin Luther, *Against the Heavenly Prophets in the Matter of Images and Sacraments,* trans. Bernard Erling, ed. Conrad Bergendoff, in *Luther's Works,* vol. 40 (Philadelphia: Fortress Press, 1958), 82.
92. The notion of the "live hypothesis" as distinct from the theoretically possible is from William James, *The Will to Believe,* in *The Will to Believe and Human Immortality* (New York: Dover, 1956), 2-3.
93. A very helpful Christian theological model for accomplishing this mutual transformation is provided by Francis X. Clooney, "Reading the World in Christ: From Comparison to Inclusivism," in *Christian Uniqueness Reconsidered,* ed. D'Costa, 63-80. Clooney's discussion centers on how his own notion of Christian love was altered by a Hindu song of love to Krishna. Clooney maintains that his process moved from comparison to evaluative conclusions which altered his own conception of love.
94. To give some examples of the diversity of such transformations: Christianity adopted the natural law ethic of Stoicism to supplement the ethics of the New Testament; Thomas Aquinas adopted Aristotelian categories to help interpret the Christian faith; Gandhi was deeply influenced by Leo Tolstoy; and Martin Luther King, Jr., in turn, adopted Gandhi's thoughts and applied them in Alabama.
95. See Paul Tillich, *Systematic Theology,* vol. 3 (Chicago: University of Chicago Press, 1963), 3-7; Gamwell, *Religious Freedom.*
96. The term "fragments" is drawn from Søren Kierkegaard, *Philosophical Fragments, or A Fragment of Philosophy,* trans. David F. Swenson, rev. Howard V. Hong (Princeton, N.J.: Princeton University Press, 1962).
97. Of course, not all traditions actually move toward greater comprehensiveness. Some, such as anti-Semitism and white supremacy, actually resist it and move toward more *exclusive* goals.
98. For example, we need not expect a Christian to provide a convincing proof of the existence of God or the sacredness of Scripture; but we can expect a Christian to provide a meaning-

ful account of what it means to believe in God—to take the "leap" that proclaims life and reality meaningful despite the evidence against it. Likewise, a conservative Christian could be challenged to explain why the biblical passages which condemn homosexual acts are more important than the more numerous passages that condemn abuse and neglect of the poor—and liberals asked why they ignore the former while insisting upon literal interpretation of the latter. And both could be asked to make their claims meaningful and as convincing as possible to those who do not share their other beliefs.

99. See, e.g., Rawls, *Political Liberalism*, 217 and chapter 1, herein.
100. Ibid., esp. 212-54.
101. Ibid., 61, 97, 161-63.
102. Reinhold Niebuhr's discussion of vitality, reason, and the risk of loss of vitality, remains invaluable. See Niebuhr, *The Nature and Destiny of Man*, 2 vols. (New York: Charles Scribner's Sons, 1964), *passim*.
103. Marjorie Hewitt Suchocki, *The Fall to Violence* (New York: Continuum, 1994); for Girard, see e.g., René Girard, *Violence and the Sacred*, trans. Patrick Gregory (Baltimore: Johns Hopkins, 1977).
104. Whatever it is that makes violence wrong, it will not be merely that it "violates" the sacred boundaries of individuality. It will have more to do with integrity and dignity than mere identity.
105. The translation of the Greek "agape," one of several Greek words for love, is a fine example of the promise and peril of translation. Since English does not have a word which corresponds to it, any translation will have to stretch and bend the English word "love" with only partial success. (Other possible translations include "self-giving love" and "unconditional love.")
106. See, e.g., Judith Plaskow, *Sex, Sin, and Grace* (Washington, D.C.: University Press of America, 1980).
107. Anders Nygren, *Agape and Eros*, trans. Philip S. Watson (Philadelphia: Westminster, 1953); Glenn Tinder, *The Political Meaning of Christianity* (San Francisco: HarperCollins, HarperSanFrancisco, 1991).
108. Matthew Fox, *Original Blessing* (Santa Fe, N.M.: Bear, 1983); Fox and Rupert Sheldrake, *Natural Grace* (New York: Doubleday, 1996).
109. The one-sided volitional reading of sin in Protestantism may have to do with a limited reading of Luther's *Bondage of the Will*. In fact, Luther's understanding of sin, even in *Bondage*, was never so narrow. Rather, Luther understood sin as emerging from the "heart," a spiritual center that underlies the traditional faculties of reason, will, and emotion.
110. A simple example: Augustine's understanding of the relation of sin, lust, and freedom would likely have been quite different had he known that somnambulant erections indicate rapid eye movement sleep and not necessarily sexual desire.
111. From this perspective, debates about the *uniqueness* of Christianity are misplaced. "Uniqueness" alone tells us little—every religion, like every historical phenomenon, is unique. In the political sphere, the issue is not whether there is some special content that gives Christianity a perennially privileged relation to truth, but whether *distinctive* Christian claims of thought and practice are helpful in constructing productive frameworks for public life. There is simply no need for a pitched battle about whether *only* Christianity, Buddhism, or humanism contains a particular insight. It is enough that each does contain insights, and for the future of civility and power, better that some of those insights are similar. See John Hick and Paul F. Knitter, eds., *The Myth of Christian Uniqueness*, Faith Meets Faith Series (Maryknoll, N.Y.: Orbis Books, 1987), D'Costa, ed., *Christian Uniqueness Reconsidered*, and Cowdell, *Is Jesus Unique?*
112. A question we do *not* raise here is whether intrareligious beliefs and commitments, beliefs for which one does not demand space in the public square, are exempt from this requirement. Examples might include observance of dietary laws and dress requirements. Even these might require public space in that peoples' rights to believe and observe thus should be honored, without being subject to public debate, but also without public consequence.

A related question also not addressed here concerns whether the requirement that truth must be truth *now* also extends to such intrareligious beliefs.
113. See chapter 3 for a fuller discussion of privileges.
114. Sidney E. Mead, *The Lively Experiment* (New York: Harper & Row, 1963), 20.
115. Ibid., 35.
116. One should not be too quick to presume, however, that the American way is the only way, or even the best. True, religion shows more vitality in the United States if that vitality is measured by worship attendance and other forms of participation. Yet the established and semi-established churches in Germany and the Netherlands, for example, have a *public* presence that American religious institutions might well envy, despite very low attendance (by American standards). At the same time, European institutions seem to be less adept in dealing with plurality. This topic, however, exceeds the bounds of this investigation.
117. Søren Kierkegaard, *Kierkegaard's Attack Upon "Christendom,"* trans. Walter Lowrie (Princeton, N.J.: Princeton University Press, 1968), has an early—and typically odd—form of the argument that what Christianity most needs is non-Christians, contained in his vituperative objections to "Christendom" and official Christianity. Our thanks to Steven Gallien for pointing out this connection.
118. We emphasize again that our concern is with public debate, not the legal questions of rights and public funding that have been so emphasized in the recent cultural discussion. An examination of those issues with respect to an "ideal state" is found in John Kekes, *The Morality of Pluralism* (Princeton, N.J.: Princeton University Press, 1993). The principal difficulty with Kekes's argument is that it only concerns an "ideal state," which leads to the odd result that Kekes attempts a quasi-eternal solution to what are clearly historical, culture-specific (i.e., pluralistic) problems. State support for *all* substantive plural values as a substitute for state neutrality strikes one as wonderful—and hopeless.
119. For a good criticism of least-common-denominator interreligious discussions, particularly those advocated by John Hick, see J. A. DiNoia, "Pluralistic Theology of Religions: Pluralistic or Non-Pluralistic?" in *Christian Uniqueness Reconsidered,* ed. D'Costa.
120. Of course, these are not the only symbols that can produce this dialectic of affirmation and negation, or which can provide pluralistic impetus. Paul Tillich, *Systematic Theology,* vol. 2 (Chicago: University of Chicago Press, 1957), 97-138, finds similar features in the relation between "Jesus" and "the Christ," whereas D'Costa, "Christ," discovers them in the doctrine of the Trinity.
121. Several first-year college students, schooled on near-vacuous high school slogans like "love not hate," were recently astounded to read a saying of Confucius that "only the humane man can love men and hate men" (Analects of Confucius 4:2, in William Theodore De Bary, ed., *Sources of Chinese Tradition* [New York: Columbia University Press, 1958], 1:26). This saying actually goes farther than we do here, since we counsel only criticism and the attempt to transform distortions, not "hate" as such. But given a choice between Confucius and Lennon-McCartney on this point, we would definitely have to say that "Love is *not* all you need!"
122. E.g., "If another member of the church sins against you, go and point out the fault when the two of you are alone" (Matt. 18:15; also see 1 Cor. 5:1–6:8, Eph. 4:25-26, and Gal. 6:1, etc.). The frequently quoted New Testament injunctions against *judging* (e.g., Matt. 7:1, James 4:11, Rom. 14:13) must be read in light of the former exhortations; there is a difference between criticism and judgment, and between judging *actions* or *attitudes* and judging people.
123. In the case of original sin, for example, a secular perspective with some overlapping—but also some disparate—claims is George Soros, "The Capitalist Threat," *Atlantic Monthly* 280, no. 2 (February 1997): 45-58, and "Toward a Global Open Society," *Atlantic Monthly* 281, no. 1 (January 1998): 20-24ff.
124. As we argued in chapter 1.
125. H. Richard Niebuhr, "Faith in Gods and in God," in *Radical Monotheism and Western Culture* (New York: Harper & Row, 1960), 117.

CHAPTER 5. TAKING CENTER STAGE: THE EMPHATIC CHRISTIAN CENTER AND POLITICAL PRACTICE

1. We owe this formulation of the medical priesthood to Langdon B. Gilkey.
2. See, e.g., Franklin I. Gamwell, *Beyond Preference* (Chicago: University of Chicago Press, 1984), and *The Meaning of Religious Freedom* (Albany, N.Y.: SUNY Press, 1995); Mary Ann Glendon, *Rights Talk* (New York: Macmillan, Free Press, 1991); and Amitai Etzioni, *The Spirit of Community* (New York: Crown, 1993). Robert N. Bellah, Richard Madsen, William M. Sullivan, et al., *Habits of the Heart* (New York: Harper & Row, 1985), 207-8, acknowledge the role of complexity in discouraging active citizenship, but they tend to write as though Americans are merely too lazy or selfish to deal with it: "Americans prefer to avoid . . . coming to terms with this invisible complexity" (ibid., 207). The ensuing discussion of "administrative despotism" (ibid., 208-11) is highly instructive. Also see Bellah, et al., *The Good Society*, (New York: Alfred A. Knopf, 1991), 20: "Complexity is real enough, but it should not be a cover beneath which undemocratic managers and experts can hide. . . . There is no reason a modern citizenry cannot participate in this larger world much more knowledgeably and actively than is presently the case."
3. Gore Vidal, "Coached by Camelot," *The New Yorker*, December 1, 1997, 88.
4. Ibid.
5. "The Honest Dialogue That Is Neither," *New York Times*, December 7, 1997, 4:5, Chicago edition.
6. Bellah et al., *Habits of the Heart*, 221.
7. Jason DeParle, "Welfare to Work: A Sequel," *New York Times Magazine*, December 28, 1997, 14.
8. See chapter 2.
9. Notwithstanding their sometime aspiration to priestly authority, the scientific community probably has a better record in truth telling and candor in explanation than either the religious or the political communities. The massive educational effort whereby the American public of the 1950s and 1960s became quite knowledgeable about the physical mechanics of satellites and space travel is a case in point, where scientists, government managers, and the media effectively cooperated. See H. Richard Niebuhr, "Science in Conflict with Morality," in Niebuhr, *Radical Monotheism and Western Culture* (New York: Harper & Row, 1960), 127-41, esp. 134-36.
10. Business interests' opposition to the New Deal and Southern opposition to integration are two noteworthy examples. Both ultimately profited from the changes they opposed. New Deal reforms strengthened the banking system and bolstered American currency, and integration released important economic forces which segregation had kept bottled up.
11. One of the most trenchant criticisms remains Thomas R. Dye and Harmon Zeigler, *The Irony of Democracy*, 8th ed. (Pacific Grove, Calif.: Brooks/Cole, 1990).
12. Robert A. Dahl, *Who Governs?* (New Haven, Conn.: Yale University, 1989), esp. 32-51.
13. *Washington Post National Weekly Edition*, February 2, 1998, 12.
14. Martin Luther, *The Bondage of the Will*, in *Luther's Works*, vol. 33, trans. and ed. Philip S. Watson (Philadelphia: Fortress Press, 1972), 212. For the question of self-interest in Luther's political thought, see Kyle A. Pasewark, *A Theology of Power* (Minneapolis: Fortress Press, 1993), 119-28.
15. Anders Nygren, *Agape and Eros*, trans. Philip S. Watson (Philadelphia: Westminster, 1953).
16. L. Gregory Jones, *Embodying Forgiveness* (Grand Rapids, Mich.: Wm. B. Eerdmans, 1995), esp. 35-69.
17. Glenn Tinder, *The Political Meaning of Christianity* (San Francisco: HarperCollins, HarperSanFrancisco, 1989). Although Tillich, the Niebuhrs, and Gilkey never went this far,

they still hold agape as the paramount expression of human and divine love, while the most grievous and common sin, for Reinhold Niebuhr and Gilkey, remains selfishness.
18. Jim Wallis, *Who Speaks for God?* (New York: Delacorte, 1996), 6-9.
19. Emphasis added. We do not, of course, pretend to resolve the New Testament debate here. Yet we hold that our emphasis on power constitutes at least as good a preunderstanding with which to read the New Testament as the more typical presupposition that selflessness is the highest form of love.
20. Indeed, many in the Christian right, such as James Dobson and his Focus on the Family group, are threatening to desert the Republican Party precisely because it has not served their interests adequately. Gary Bauer, president of the Family Research Council, complains, "There is virtually nothing to show for an 18-year commitment" (*New York Times*, March 23, 1998, A1, A12, Chicago edition).
21. One may object that the Coalition makes little effort to include the interests of anyone *else* in their policies, but this is a distinct issue which will be discussed later.
22. In fact, this is precisely the charge that Luther, though sympathetic with their demands, lays against the peasants in his *Admonition to Peace*, in *Luther's Works*, vol. 46, trans. Charles M. Jacobs, rev. and ed. Robert C. Schultz (Philadelphia: Fortress Press, 1967), 22. Four centuries later Reinhold Niebuhr explicitly rejected the moralistic idea that the proletariat must practice self-sacrificial love: "The moralist places an unjustified moral onus upon advancing groups which use violent methods to disturb a peace maintained by subtler types of coercion" (Reinhold Niebuhr, *Moral Man and Immoral Society* [New York: Charles Scribner's Sons, 1933], 233). Also see ibid., 129-30 and 139-41.
23. See, e.g., Paul Tillich, *Love, Power, and Justice* (New York: Oxford University Press, 1954), 68-71; Christine E. Gudorf, "Parenting, Mutual Love, and Sacrifice," in Barbara Hilkert Andolsen, Christine E. Gudorf, and Mary D. Pellauer, eds., *Women's Consciousness, Women's Conscience* (San Francisco: Harper & Row, 1985), 175-91.
24. Valerie Saiving, "The Human Situation: A Feminine View," in Carol P. Christ and Judith Plaskow, eds., *Womanspirit Rising* (San Francisco: HarperCollins, HarperSanFrancisco, 1992), 25-42; Judith Plaskow, *Sex, Sin, and Grace* (Washington, D.C.: University Press of America, 1980).
25. Tillich, *Love*, 117-27.
26. Reinhold Niebuhr, *The Nature and Destiny of Man*, vol. 1 (New York: Charles Scribner's Sons, 1964), 26-53. "Natural vitality is not evil of itself; and redemption does not therefore consist in a rational enervation of or transcendence over natural impulse" (ibid., 49). But Niebuhr never fully resolved the problem. He later lapses back to interpreting Jesus' summary of the Torah, "You shall love the Lord your God with all your heart, and with all your soul, and with all your mind [and] your neighbor as yourself" (Matt. 22:37, 39) as the demand for "an action in which regard for the self is completely eliminated" (ibid., 287). In *Moral Man and Immoral Society*, esp. 257-59 and 270-72, he similarly distinguished between the virtues of love and justice, consigning love and self-sacrifice to the realm of personal relations ("moral man") while assigning justice to social and political relations ("immoral society"). To the extent that he viewed women as the chief governors of the domestic sphere and men as the chief actors in the political sphere, this meant that he implicitly assigned love to women and justice to men (see ibid., 46-47 and 63), a move which feminist theologians have rather justly criticized.
27. "Ordinarily," because there are certain acts of self-sacrifice, including those which lead to death, in which the self cannot participate in the fruits. But in even such an act of self-sacrifice as Dietrich Bonhoeffer's willingness to face death as a consequence of his participation in the conspiracy to kill Adolf Hitler, it can be argued that he could still at least hope that those he loved, and perhaps even he himself, would live to enjoy the fruits of the Third Reich's demise.
28. Niebuhr, *Moral Man*, 270-71. It is this paradox in Reinhold Niebuhr's thought, perhaps more than any other, that justified his brother H. Richard Niebuhr's classification of Reinhold,

along with Paul, Luther, Roger Williams, Kierkegaard, and Ernst Troeltsch, in the category of "Christ and Culture in Paradox," the "dualist" type of Christ and culture. See H. Richard Niebuhr, *Christ and Culture* (New York: Harper & Row, 1951), 183 n. 30.

29. The term "visional" is borrowed from the excellent discussion of practical moral thinking in Don S. Browning, *A Fundamental Practical Theology* (Minneapolis: Fortress Press, 1991), summarized at 105-9.
30. Theda Skocpol, *Social Policy in the United States* (Princeton, N.J.: Princeton University Press, 1995), 253-59.
31. Ibid., 259. Medicaid is a partial exception to this general rule.
32. Ibid., 258.
33. The successful—from labor's point of view—1997 UPS strike is another example. After years of labor dormancy and failure to garner public support, UPS reversed these trends by focusing on UPS management's effort to add more part-time workers without benefits at the expense of full-time workers with benefits. The union was successful because the substitution of full-time by part-time labor is a growing tendency *throughout* the American economy. Thus, UPS policy seemed to be a real threat to all workers, from service employees to blue-collar and white-collar workers.
34. Pope Leo XIII, *Rerum Novarum,* in Michael Walsh and Brian Davies, eds., *Proclaiming Justice and Peace* (Mystic, Conn.: Twenty-third Publications, 1991).
35. Larry L. Rasmussen, *Earth Community Earth Ethics* (Maryknoll, N.Y.: Orbis Books, 1996), 336-40.
36. Don S. Browning, Bonnie J. Miller-McLemore, Pamela D. Couture, K. Brynolf Lyon, and Robert M. Franklin, *From Culture Wars to Common Ground* (Louisville: Westminster John Knox, 1997), 224, 238-42.
37. Ralph Reed, *Active Faith* (New York: Free Press, 1996), 275, cited in Browning et al., *From Culture Wars,* 235.
38. *Rerum Novarum,* 28, cited in Browning et al., *From Culture Wars,* 241.
39. *The Economist,* January 24-30, 1998, 19. The Pew Center reports a somewhat higher figure, 34 percent (*Washington Post National Weekly Edition,* March 16, 1998, 35).
40. For the IRS, see *Washington Post National Weekly Edition,* March 16, 1998, 35.
41. During the course of writing this book, the authors found themselves in the midst of two natural disasters—the flooding of the Dakota-Minnesota border in the spring of 1997, and devastating tornadoes in southern Minnesota in the spring of 1998. Voluntary efforts during both disasters were nothing short of remarkable. However, none of those efforts would have been successful had it not been for shrewd and astute planning for the flood that descended upon Fargo-Moorhead, and tornado warning systems and coordinated clean-up efforts in southern Minnesota. Of course, both were coordinated and largely funded by government, although tornado warning systems depend also on voluntary efforts of citizens (*New York Times,* March 16, 1998, A10, Chicago edition). For an outstanding account of the necessity of both voluntary and governmental initiatives in the flooding disaster, see Stewart W. Herman, "Coming Together in Fargo," *Christian Century* 114, no. 22 (July 30-August 6, 1997): 694-98.
42. For example, Social Security worked very well at virtually eliminating poverty among the elderly in the twentieth century, but there is serious question whether it can continue to function in the twenty-first century. Similarly, IRAs and tax-deferred retirement savings worked very well at generating capital and building wealth for the elderly, but do not seem able to address the question of what happens to the poor when they "retire."
43. Hannah Arendt, *On Revolution* (London: Penguin, 1965), 213.
44. This is the grain of truth contained in the otherwise senseless saying that "religion and politics don't mix." This book is largely devoted to a careful refutation of that hackneyed cliche. But it is true that religion—and especially Christianity—does not contain a revealed body of knowledge about how to solve the political and social problems of everyday life. The Bible does not contain the solution to inflation, nor did Jesus lay down the ground rules for the labor move-

ment or for socialism or for Pat Robertson's campaign. But religion and politics *do* mix all the time insofar as religious faith reorients and redirects a person's *entire* life toward God, self, and the neighbor. In this sense, religion can leave *nothing* untouched. Adolf Harnack put it well a century ago: the gospel contains not a social *program*, but an energetic social *message*. See Adolf Harnack, *What Is Christianity?* trans. Thomas Bailey Saunders (New York: Harper & Row, 1957), 97-98.
45. *New York Times,* June 19, 1998, A21, Chicago edition.
46. Administration for Children and Families, U.S. Department of Health and Human Services (http://www.acf.dhhs.gov/news/case-fam.htm). In "welfare," we include Aid for Families with Dependent Children (AFDC) and Temporary Assistance for Needy Families (TANF).
47. The last year for which data were available to us was 1996. The comparative data are from Leatha Lamison-White, *Poverty in the United States: 1996,* U.S. Department of Commerce, Bureau of the Census (http://www.census.gov/prod/3/97pubs/P60-198.PDF), March 17, 1998, and Bureau of the Census, *Analysis of Income and Poverty Data: 1993* (http://www.census.gov/hhes/income/incpov93/analysis.html). In the 1996 statistics, the Census Bureau employs a number of definitions of poverty, which range from the official measure (which we have cited) to a measure that includes the value of government benefits (which reduce the measure of actual poverty by measuring actual poverty after benefits are computed rather than calculating poverty based on eligibility) to effects of taxation and other disposable-income reductions (which increase the poverty rate). The only significant decline in poverty after all benefits are accounted for (to 10.2 percent) occurs after the Earned Income Credit is taken into account. This has two implications. First, it means that the credit is the single most effective current policy for reducing income poverty. Second, because one can only claim the credit if one is working, it highlights the high proportion of the poor who are employed. These claims are also confirmed in *New York Times,* March 15, 1998, 18, Chicago edition: (1) Without the Earned Income Credit, the poverty rate for young children would be 23 percent higher; (2) 63 percent of poor children are in families with at least one working parent.
48. *New York Times,* March 15, 1998, 18, Chicago edition.
49. This has been so well demonstrated by liberation theology that we need only refer the reader to a few biblical texts: Exod. 22:21-27; Amos 2:6-8, 4:1-3, 5:7-13; Isa. 5:8; Matt. 25:31-46; Luke 6:20-25; 1 Cor. 11:17-22; James 2:15-18. There are far, far more passages in both Testaments that condemn abuse of the poor than deal with homosexuality or personal self-realization.
50. Joe Klein, "In God They Trust," *The New Yorker,* June 16, 1997, 40-48.
51. See esp. Martin Luther, *Against the Heavenly Prophets in the Matter of Images and Sacraments,* in *Luther's Works,* vol. 40, trans. Bernhard Erling and Conrad Bergendoff, ed. Bergendoff (Philadelphia: Fortress Press, 1958), 79-223.
52. Jill Quadagno, *The Color of Welfare* (New York: Oxford University Press, 1994), argues that race is the "red" herring of opposition to the poor in America. She maintains that the stereotyping of the poor as minority poor allows white society to both stigmatize and ignore the poor.
53. See n. 47, above.
54. Lamison-White, *Poverty,* cover graph.
55. Ibid., vi. Richard J. Murnane, "Education and the Well-Being of the Next Generation," in Sheldon H. Danziger, Gary D. Sandefur, and Daniel H. Weinberg, eds., *Confronting Poverty* (New York: Russell Sage Foundation, 1994; Cambridge, Mass.: Harvard University Press, 1994), 296, notes that "in 1991, 21 percent of children lived in families classified as poor, an increase from 16 percent in 1969." Moreover, poverty is an enduring condition for many children. Mary Jo Bane and David Ellwood estimate, for example, that "the average poor black child today appears to be in the midst of a poverty spell which will last for almost two decades."
56. Langdon Gilkey, *Message and Existence* (New York: Seabury Press, 1981), 172.

57. This may be especially true of African American churches. For a detailed analysis of one such congregation, see Browning, *Fundamental Practical Theology,* 26-33, 243-77.
58. We do not, of course, oppose expansion of other antipoverty efforts but believe that attention should be centered on education and perhaps housing, the latter of which we will not discuss. But we do not call for declaration of a new "war on poverty." Why not? It seems to us that the budgetary disaster of the 1980s, at least at the federal level, precludes such a declaration, however satisfying it might be. In early 1998, the national debt stood at $3.8 *trillion,* with a debt-to-gross-domestic-product-ratio at a dangerously high 50 percent (*Washington Post National Weekly Edition,* March 23, 1998, 19). If we are to avoid the consequences of this level of debt, as well as begin to free resources now devoted to interest payments on the debt, the best policy in the short-term is modest new spending initiatives combined with a concentrated effort to pay down the debt. That strategy accomplishes three things. First, it allows us to address one significant problem (education) with substantial resources. Second, it allows pursuit of limited additional antipoverty tactics in order to discover (through smaller, less expensive programs *combined with research that assesses their effectiveness along the way*) what types of other initiatives might reduce poverty. Finally, in the longer term our strategy allows major commitments to those programs that are successful without straining the nation's budgetary capacity, *if we have the political will to pay down the debt.*
59. Leon Dash, *Rosa Lee* (New York: Basic Books, HarperCollins, 1996), 251.
60. Ibid., 252.
61. William Julius Wilson, *The Truly Disadvantaged* (Chicago: University of Chicago Press, 1987), 57-58.
62. The call for further study also applies to the troubling tendency of most poverty study to be directed only at urban poverty. With the exception of Michael Harrington's *The Other America* (published in the early 1960s), rural poverty has been inadequately studied. This is a vital omission, not only for policy studies, but for the attention of media, legislatures, and other institutions. Indeed, Lamison-White notes that "the nonmetropolitan poverty rate in 1996 (15.9 percent) was higher than the rate inside metropolitan areas (13.2 percent)."
63. *New York Times,* March 16, 1998, A1, A16, Chicago edition. Not only Republican governors proposed increases. Notable among Democrats was Zell Miller (Georgia).
64. See, e.g., the testimonies of proponents and opponents of charter schools in *Hearing on Charter Schools,* Subcommittee on Early Childhood, Youth and Families of the House Committee on Education and the Workforce, April 9, 1997 (Washington: U.S. Government Printing Office, 1997). Amy Stuart Wells's testimony notes that the policy assumptions of charter schools—and one could say the same for vouchers—resonate with "long-held American beliefs about liberty and individualism" (148). The Christian Right's impassioned advocacy of "school choice" is yet another indication that, far from being critics of the American civil religion of freedom, they are captive to it.
65. There are, of course, significant constitutional questions about the propriety of vouchers for private—particularly religious—schools. And it is possible that certain kinds of federal initiatives might also raise legal questions of federalism. These are matters for the courts and beyond our immediate competence or concern. With respect to private school vouchers, however, we think there is good reason—even without constitutional questions—to restrict them, as we will argue. Vouchers might be allowed to public schools, however, if forthcoming data supports their effectiveness.
66. Paul C. Bauman, *Governing Education* (Boston: Allyn and Bacon, 1996), discusses the relative values of "centralization" and "decentralization." Bauman's proposals are not as helpful as his presentation, however, because he seems concerned with the formal question of centralization more than its results. Consequently, his argument tends toward a "vacuous center," which is interested in "balancing" centralization and decentralization.
67. Many residents of school districts have far more wealth in IRAs and other retirement vehicles, all invested outside their communities, than in their real estate. Even when most communities had significant taxable income-producing property, the property

tax was not an equitable vehicle for financing schools; today it is utterly unsuitable.
68. For the relative equity of state-based funding, see *New York Times*, March 16, 1998, A1, A14, Chicago edition. For the importance of school financing in general, see Deborah A. Verstegen, "Reforming American Education Policy for the Twenty-First Century," in James G. Cibulka and William J. Kritek, eds., *Coordination Among Schools, Families, and Communities* (Albany, N.Y.: SUNY, 1996), 269-96.
69. Preliminary data from Milwaukee suggests improvement by the third year of student participation in the program. See Paul Peterson and Chad Noyes, "School Choice in Milwaukee," in Diane Ravitch and Joseph P. Viteritti, eds., *New Schools for a New Century* (New Haven, Conn.: Yale University Press, 1997), 144-46.
70. We also sidestep here the question of parochial schools, especially Catholic and Lutheran schools, but some conservative "Christian" schools as well, which have primarily served their own members and others without high tuitions, rather than serving as private schools for the wealthy. There are of course serious constitutional questions involved in vouchers for parochial schools, as well as the questions of economics we raise here. But if there were accountability for public dollars spent, and standards for subjects covered (which might well include evolution and critical religious history), perhaps the other problems would not be insuperable.
71. We sidestep the important and thorny issue of how student performance is assessed. This is an area in which quantitative research is done, and professional opinions should be taken seriously—and asked for clear explanation. We do, however, have questions about minimal competency testing. Many students, rightly, take this as an insult to their intelligence. Worse, teachers are tempted to teach "for the test" rather than for knowledge and creativity. Nor is it in accord with targeted universalism and subsidiarity. It also seems to tend to stifle creativity in students, who may well begin studying "for the test" rather than for knowledge. We have already begun to see the ill effects of this in college students. There must be better ways to assess improvement for *all* students besides a *minimal* test that seems more than a little punitive for teachers and students alike. Thus, while we do not *oppose* minimal competency testing, and think it preferable to *no* assessment at all, we hope that finer and less minimalist instruments would be employed.
72. Diane Ravitch, "Put Teachers to the Test," *Washington Post National Weekly Edition*, March 2, 1998, 27. Ravitch cites a 1997 U.S. Department of Education report.
73. See William Julius Wilson, *When Work Disappears* (New York: Alfred A. Knopf, 1996), 210-11.
74. See the essays in Cibulka and Kritek, eds., *Coordination*.
75. Attempts to reduce class size must avoid drawing qualified teachers away from poorer districts as more positions open in wealthier districts. California's attempt to reduce class sizes led to that problem (*Washington Post National Weekly Edition*, March 23, 1998, 31).
76. The data on charter schools' educational effectiveness is currently thin, as Wells, *Hearing*, 152-54, notes. Still, the promise is considerable, argues Louann A. Bierlein, "The Charter School Movement," in *New Schools*, ed. Ravitch and Viteritti, 37-60. We depart from Bierlein's desire to remove virtually all oversight from charter schools, which Bierlein justifies largely on the basis of—unsurprisingly—parental and student *satisfaction*, even as she admits that data on student *performance* is inadequate. Indeed, *New Schools* as a whole is a virtual mantra to choice for choice's sake.
77. See Peterson and Noyes, "School Choice," in Wilson, *When Work Disappears*, 214, and for neighborhood-basing, *The New York Times*, February 24, 1998, A19, Chicago edition.
78. Susan Brownmiller, *Against Our Will* (New York: Simon and Schuster, 1975), linked rape to Western family structure. Marilyn French's gripping novel, *The Women's Room* (New York: Summit Books, 1977), describes several suburban families during the 1950s in flashback from the standpoint of an escapee who has learned to frame her experiences, and those of her friends, purely from the standpoint of a liberation struggle. By the conclusion of the book, the reader is at a loss to see any value in family life whatsoever, and this is, no doubt, the only possible conclusion from French's point of view. As will be seen later in this chapter, howev-

er, the stories from the children's points of view might well have been very different. See Barbara DaFoe Whitehead, "The Children's Story of Divorce," in Whitehead, *The Divorce Culture* (New York: Alfred A. Knopf, 1997), 107-28.
79. The following account of this transformation, indeed the argument of this entire section, is heavily indebted to Don S. Browning, Bonnie J. Miller-McLemore, Pamela D. Couture, K. Brynolf Lyon, and Robert M. Franklin, *From Culture Wars*, 29-49.
80. Barbara DaFoe Whitehead, "Dan Quayle Was Right," *Atlantic Monthly* (April 1993), 47-84, cited in Browning et al., *From Culture Wars*, 32.
81. Browning et al., *From Culture Wars*, 31-32.
82. See ibid., 52-58.
83. This is argued at length by Charles Murray, *Losing Ground: American Social Policy, 1950–1980* (New York: Basic Books, 1984). Dan Quayle and Diane Medved, *The American Family: Discovering the Values That Make Us Strong* (New York: HarperCollins, 1996), follow the conservative view; Hillary Rodham Clinton, *It Takes a Village: And Other Lessons Children Teach Us* (New York: Simon & Schuster, 1996), takes the liberal view.
84. See Browning et al., *From Culture Wars*, 44-47. The Evangelical Lutheran Church in America's 1993 proposed social statement *The Church and Human Sexuality: A Lutheran Perspective* (Chicago: Division of Church in Society, 1993) received much media attention for its controversial statements on homosexuality; completely ignored by the press, however, was its condemnation of adultery and its strong statement that, from the standpoint of the church, there are no "no-fault" divorces. Browning et al., 43, criticize the statement for drifting "toward a language of poorly defined 'committed' and 'loving' relationships," and ignoring information "on the situation of children, the burdens of mothers, the absence of fathers, and the emerging culture of nonmarriage and divorce."
85. Browning et al., *From Culture Wars*, 57, drawing on Sara McLanahan and Gary Sandefur, *Growing Up with a Single Parent: What Hurts, What Helps* (Cambridge, Mass.: Harvard, 1994), 44 and 50-51.
86. Nicholas Zill and Charlotte A. Schoenborn, "Developmental, Learning, and Emotional Problems: Health of Our Nation's Children, United States, 1988," *Advance Data* 190 (Nov. 16, 1990), 4.
87. See Whitehead, *Divorce Culture*, 85-90, for a summary of the benefits promised to children when unhappy parents divorce.
88. McLanahan and Sandefur, *Growing Up*, 84.
89. Ibid., 86-87.
90. Browning et al., *From Culture Wars*, 54.
91. Frank F. Furstenberg and Andrew Cherlin, *Divided Families: What Happens to Children When Parents Part* (Cambridge, Mass.: Harvard, 1991), 35-36, cited in Browning et al., *From Culture Wars*, 54.
92. Judith S. Wallerstein and Sandra Blakeslee, *Second Chances: Men, Women, and Children a Decade After Divorce* (New York: Ticknor & Fields, 1989), 187. The comparable figure for fathers reported in this study is one-half.
93. Whitehead, *Divorce Culture*, 83.
94. Browning et al., *From Culture Wars*, 52. Of course, divorce statistics are disputed: recordkeeping practices have changed, and changes in demographics make the simple practice of dividing the number of divorces in a year by the number of marriages misleading. (If 100,000 couples marry and 50,000 divorce in a single year, that does not directly tell us how many of those 100,000 marriages will end in divorce.) But the changes are so dramatic that no reasonable allowance for statistical error can totally discount them.
95. Donald Hernandez, *America's Children* (New York: Russell Sage Foundation, 1993), 65, cited in Browning et al., *From Culture Wars*, 53.
96. Larry Bumpass and James Sweet, "Children's Experience in Single Parent Families: Implications of Cohabitation and Marital Transitions," *Family Planning Perspectives* 21 (November-December 1989), 256-60, cited in Browning et al., *From Culture Wars*, 53.

97. *From Culture Wars* was the result of the Religion, Culture, and Family Project, sponsored by the Lilly Endowment and the University of Chicago, and directed by Don S. Browning. It is the first of eight projected volumes in the Westminster John Knox Press series "The Family, Culture, and Religion."

   Although we have dismissed the relatively static metaphor of a "common ground" in favor of the more dynamic idea of an emphatic center, Browning's book is an excellent example of just the sort of discourse and action we advocate. It does not use "freedom of religion" as a trump to guarantee its "right" to occupy the public square; instead, it argues in categories accessible to "believers" and "nonbelievers" alike. At the same time, it does not pretend to discover "universal" truths of reason that just happen to coincide with Christian teaching; the discussion of marriage and family is thoroughly contextualized. It pays distinct attention to sin, and uses a broader range of metaphors for God than vague "love" or vindictive "judge." The authors mix appreciation with criticism, recognize the positive role of power in family relations, and insist on justice within the family as well as in society. Moreover, it is a collaborative endeavor by five authors—men and women, white and black—who struggled, at times, to find a common voice. "There were times during these years we thought the book might never be completed, that our differences were too large, or that changes in vocations" would make it logistically impossible. But "a richer argument has evolved because it has weathered the storms of our conflicts and the complexities of our family and work lives" (x). In particular, the discussion of the teachings and practice of African American churches with respect to the family is especially commendable (225-31).

   With such an intentional commitment to diversity and through diversity, it is not surprising that they came very close to what we mean by an "emphatic Christian center." Nor is it accidental that our argument here relies heavily on theirs.
98. Browning et al., *From Culture Wars*, 50. See 50-72 for the entire argument.
99. Ibid., 51.
100. Ibid., 52-54. On the correlation of single-parent families and poverty, they cite data that fewer than one-third of children receive the full child support to which they are entitled (McLanahan and Sandefur, *Growing Up*, 81, cited in Browning et al., *From Culture Wars*, 53). In this connection, Mary Ann Glendon's comment on "no-fault" divorce law and property settlements is illuminating: "Support laws that start from the principle that no support should be available treat as exception what is in fact statistically the most frequent case: that of a spouse whose capacity for self-support is impaired because of her child-care responsibilities." The time has come to recognize "that many rules of marital property and support law which may be well suited to the situations of childless couples are inappropriate to the circumstances of families with children" (Mary Ann Glendon, *The Transformation of Family Law: State, Law, and Family in the United States and Western Europe* [Chicago: University of Chicago Press, 1989], 235).
101. McLanahan and Sandefur, *Growing Up*, 30-31, quoted in Whitehead, *Divorce Culture*, 97.
102. Mary Ann Glendon, *Rights Talk* (New York: Free Press, 1991), 68.
103. Ibid., 69.
104. Ibid., 70.
105. Glendon, *Transformation of Family Law*, 297.
106. Ibid., 197-98.
107. Of course, the absolutist defense of absolute rights continues unabated in some liberal circles. For example, Iris Young, rightly objecting to the right's uncritical stance toward patriarchy, and deeply desiring that single mothers be not blamed but helped, instinctively turns toward the left's favorite (only?) good, the *right* to do or be something. In this case, it is the right to motherhood. Browning et al. argue that this is "an implicit notion of separative motherhood." They criticize her for attempting "to create a women-centered politics in which the biological family is valued primarily as it relates to women's freedom" (ibid., 167-68, citing Iris Marion Young, "Making Single Motherhood Normal," *Dissent* [Winter 1989], 91). Very little distinguishes Young's appeal to freedom from the free-market view that legit-

imates a man's decision to have as little to do with his child(ren) as possible if such a decision maximizes his own "freedom." Indeed, an absolute "right" to motherhood would seem to imply an absolute "right" to engage in biological fathering without any obligation to participate in actual parenting.

108. Whitehead, *Divorce Culture*, 56-61; Browning et al., *From Culture Wars*, 51, 58-59. In this, both are following Bellah, *Habits of the Heart*, 32-35, 142-63. Whitehead goes on to call contemporary divorce "expressive divorce," following Bellah's description of "expressive individualism," for which Walt Whitman is the defining example (*Habits*, 33-35).
109. Browning et al., *From Culture Wars*, 70.
110. Ibid., 101-28.
111. See Gudorf, "Parenting, Mutual Love, and Sacrifice"; Barbara Hilkert Andolsen, "Agape in Feminist Ethics," *Journal of Religious Ethics* 9 (1981): 64-83; and Judith Plaskow, *Sex, Sin, and Grace: Women's Experience and the Theologies of Reinhold Niebuhr and Paul Tillich* (Lanham, Md.: University Press of America, 1980), all cited in Browning et al., 351 n. 96.
112. Browning et al., *From Culture Wars*, 127.
113. Glendon, *Transformation of Family Law*, 147.
114. Browning et al., *From Culture Wars*, 272.
115. Ibid., 306-34.
116. Again, however, it is worth commenting on Browning's exemplary method. Their proposals command a space in the public square, but not merely on the basis of "who we are" or "the right to our opinion" or "the Bible says." (In this connection it is worth noting that the researchers discovered that more recent writings from the profamily Christian right actually draw very little on biblical teachings, 235-38.) The proposals reflect a theological, indeed Christian impetus, but are not based on mere religious authority. They reflect engagement with social scientific evidence, feminist criticisms of patriarchy, African American family practice and church teaching, the Christian right, and many others.
117. A family therapist—himself not a Catholic—once told one of the authors that he had great respect for the Marriage Encounter programs of the Roman Catholic Church. As he put it, the church is saying, in effect, "We insist on the sacrality of marriage, and reject divorce. Now, here is what we will do to help you stay married." The scarcity of such programs in Protestantism speaks volumes about Protestant commitment to marriage.
118. Browning et al., *From Culture Wars*, 307. We do not follow Browning's numbering.
119. Ibid., 310.
120. Ibid., 315.
121. Ibid., 318-19.
122. Ibid., pp. 320-21. Browning has addressed this concept of the "male problematic" elsewhere, notably in *Fundamental Practical Theology*, 250-77.
123. Glendon, *Transformation of Family Law*, 308.
124. Browning et al., *From Culture Wars*, 322; also see Glendon, *Transformation of Family Law*, 307: "Family support [of family members] will in all likelihood remain an indispensable mechanism through which society as a whole deals with the dependency of the young, the disabled, and the frail elderly." Again, 308-9: "'Modern governments cannot avoid influencing families, directly and indirectly, in countless ways,' [and] individuals benefit, not only from having 'rights,' but also from being surrounded by certain kinds of social arrangements."
125. Browning et al., *From Culture Wars*, 328-29.
126. Ibid., 332-33. The specificity of Browning's recommendations compares favorably with the vagueness of Whitehead's chapter "Dismantling the Divorce Culture" in *Divorce Culture*, 182-95, where she is able to do little more than to say that we must change the way we "think" about divorce and marriage. This is doubtless true; but we will not change our thinking without also making structural changes that will require concrete action.
127. During the 1970s and 80s, liberal Christian groups were just as preoccupied with abortion and homosexuality as the Christian right, though (obviously) with different goals. They did

not, however, attend to family issues except in the context of the critique of patriarchy. See Browning et al., *From Culture Wars*, 44-45.
128. Esta Soler, in *Domestic Violence,* Hearing before the Subcommittee on Crime and Criminal Justice of the House Committee on the Judiciary, June 30, 1994 (Washington, D.C.: U.S. Government Printing Office, 1994).
129. Mary P. Koss, Lisa A. Goodman, Angela Browne, et al., *No Safe Haven* (Washington, D.C.: American Psychological Association, 1994), 43.
130. According to Department of Justice estimates, cited in "The Health Care Response to Domestic Violence" (http://www.fvpf.org/fund/the_facts/health_response.html), 1.
131. Koss, et al., *No Safe Haven,* 41.
132. Ibid., 44.
133. Federal Bureau of Investigation, "Uniform Crime Reporting Program Press Release" (http://www.fbi.gov/ucr/ucr95prs.htm), 3.
134. Diana E. H. Russell, *The Secret Trauma* (New York: HarperCollins, 1986), 61. Russell's study is the most complete and methodologically rigorous we have found. This evaluation of rigor is shared by the survey of the literature in Koss et al., *No Safe Haven,* 43. In Russell's study, "abuse" does not include all encounters that might be construed as of a sexual nature (Russell, *Secret,* 40-42).
135. Russell, *Secret,* 219.
136. Ibid., 220.
137. Lawrence A. Greenfeld, *Sex Offenses and Offenders* (Washington, D.C. Bureau of Justice Statistics, 1997), 4.
138. Russell, *Secret,* 102-14. The only exceptions in Russell's study were for Asian Americans and Jews; for both these groups, child sexual abuse occurred at lower-than-average rates.
139. See Koss et al., *No Safe Haven,* 75-76, for a list of the disorders spurred by sexual abuse, as well as Christine A. Courtois, "Treating the Sexual Concerns of Adult Incest Survivors and Their Partners," in Robert Geffner, Susan B. Sorenson, and Paula K. Lundberg-Love, eds., *Violence and Sexual Abuse at Home* (New York: Haworth, 1997), 293-310, and Paula K. Lundberg-Love, "Current Treatment Strategies for Dissociative Identity Disorders in Adult Sexual Abuse Survivors," in Geffner et al., eds., *Violence,* 311-33. For narrative accounts of some of these problems, see essays in Carol J. Adams and Marie M. Fortune, eds., *Violence Against Women and Children* (New York: Continuum, 1995).
140. Koss et al., *No Safe Haven,* 79.
141. Mention of the loss of trust is nearly ubiquitous. We will not re-cite literature already cited in this section. One example not cited is Marie M. Fortune, *Sexual Violence* (Cleveland: Pilgrim Press, 1983), 140-75.
142. Russell, *Secret,* 201-2.
143. Department of Justice, "Health Care Response," 2. About one-quarter of women who visit emergency rooms do so because of symptoms related to ongoing domestic abuse (Pat Schroeder, in *Crimes of Violence,* Hearing Before the Subcommittee on Civil and Constitutional Rights of the House Committee on the Judiciary, November 16, 1993 [Washington: U.S. Government Printing Office, 1994], 94).
144. Koss et al., *No Safe Haven,* 21-25; Honore M. Hughes, "Research Concerning Children of Battered Women: Clinical Implications," in Geffner et al., eds., *Violence,* 225-45.
145. The left and the right do differ here on one key point, however: the left sees sexual violence as a "women's issue," an issue that pits all women against all men (see Brownmiller, *Against Our Will*), while the right views it as a "law and order" issue, pitting law-abiding citizens against criminals.
146. Catherine MacKinnon, *Only Words* (Cambridge, Mass.: Harvard University, 1993). See Kyle A. Pasewark, "Who May Speak?" *Christian Century* 110, no. 33 (November 17-24, 1993), 1164-67, for a critical review of MacKinnon's position. This section is an installment in making actual Pasewark's claim at his review's conclusion, that men should understand the "right" to speak as including a *responsibility* to speak about sexual violence.

147. Especially in the United States, with its legal presumption of innocence. Sexual offender notification laws—laws which require law enforcement authorities to inform people in a neighborhood when a convicted sexual offender moves into their neighborhood—are an example of rare legal attempts to prevent violence.
148. For a listing of agencies that deal with prevention as well as treatment and adjudication, see *Domestic Violence*, 130-76.
149. A similar point can be made, conversely, by asking whether good sexual relationships are possible—or even desirable—*without* power. We are not likely to celebrate *powerless* sexual relationships. Indeed, our common discourse itself betrays the truth whenever we speak of a "powerful" experience.
150. Koss et al., *No Safe Haven*, 246-47.
151. The only data we are aware of that treat the responses of individual congregations are John M. Johnson, "Church Response to Domestic Violence," in Adams and Fortune, eds., *Violence*, 412-21, and John M. Johnson and Denise M. Bondurant, "Revisiting the 1982 Church Response Survey," in ibid., 422-27. Neither discusses church response to sexual assault.
152. Some suggestions for liturgy are given by Marjorie Procter-Smith, *Praying with Our Eyes Open* (Nashville: Abingdon Press, 1995), 115-50, and Procter-Smith, "'Reorganizing Victimization': The Intersection Between Liturgy and Domestic Violence," in Adams and Fortune, eds., *Violence*, 428-43, and "The Whole Loaf: Holy Communion and Survival," in ibid., 464-78.
153. One of the authors, teaching a seventh-grade confirmation class for the first time in several years, did include a brief discussion of sexual violence and respect in his treatment of the Sixth Commandment (Seventh in some numberings), "You shall not commit adultery." Martin Luther's explanation of the commandment—routinely used for instruction in Lutheran churches—includes the statement that "we are to fear and love God so that husband and wife love and respect one another" (Martin Luther, *The Small Catechism* [Philadelphia: Fortress Press, 1968], 6). The instructor suggested to the class that the Sixth Commandment is not just about husband and wife respecting each other, but *men* and *women* respecting one another. He then asked, "What are some ways in which men and women do *not* respect one another?" The students' answers quickly turned to sexual abuse as well as dirty jokes, stereotypes, "blonde jokes," telling stories about people, and so on. Our thanks to Hans Paul for helping recall the discussion.
154. Johnson, "Church Response," 418.
155. Fortune, *Sexual Violence*, 127.
156. In addition, of course, clergy should be well trained to know the *limits* of their competence and should, therefore, develop working relationships with mental health, medical, and law enforcement personnel.
157. Watt, when asked about conserving forests for future generations, replied that we don't know how many generations are left until Jesus returns. Reagan, of course, said that trees cause acid rain.
158. We draw the term "ecocrisis" from Max Oelschlaeger, *Caring for Creation: An Ecumenical Approach to the Environmental Crisis* (New Haven, Conn.: Yale University Press, 1994), 2.
159. Glendon, *Transformation of Family Law*, 308.
160. A particularly cold winter in Minnesota or mild summer in Texas is no evidence against global warming; the average temperature of the globe could easily increase by one degree Fahrenheit in the same year that St. Paul or Fort Worth has temperatures averaging even as much as ten degrees below normal.

It has come to our attention that global warming may manifest itself less in increased temperature and more in increased rates of *evaporation*. While we are not going to jump to any conclusions, the dramatically increased tornadic activity of January 1999 would be consistent with those increased rates of evaporation. But again, fluctuation in weather patterns is normal, so there is no way to be sure that this is related to global warming—yet by the time that it does become indisputable (if it ever does), it will then be too late to turn back the clock even to 1990 levels of CO_2 without a long and protracted period of social, economic, and technological change.

161. "Ice core samples establish a natural baseline and a variability in carbon dioxide levels (for the past 165,000 years) that are far below the present levels and rate of increase" (Oelschlaeger, *Caring for Creation*, 240 n. 2).
162. Oelschlaeger, *Caring for Creation*, 20.
163. Ibid., 15.
164. Calvin DeWitt, "Introduction: Seven Degradations of Creation," in DeWitt, ed., *The Environment and the Christian: What Does the New Testament Say About the Environment?* (Grand Rapids, Mich.: Baker, 1991), 15.
165. Edmund O. Wilson, *Biophilia* (Cambridge, Mass.: Harvard University Press, 1984), 122, and *The Diversity of Life* (Cambridge, Mass.: Belknap Press, 1992), 351, both cited in Oelschlaeger, *Caring for Creation*, 20.
166. See Clive Ponting, *A Green History of the World: The Environment and the Collapse of Civilizations* (New York: St. Martin's Press, 1992). Also see Crispin Tickell, *Climatic Change and World Affairs* (Cambridge, Mass.: Harvard Studies in International Affairs, 1977).
167. Oelschlaeger, *Caring for Creation*, 22-23, citing John Perlin, *A Forest Journey: The Role of Wood in the Development of Civilization* (New York: W. W. Norton, 1989). Also see DeWitt, "Introduction," 21.
168. Another measure of cultural degradation as a function of environmental degradation is proposed in Clifford W. Cobb and John B. Cobb, Jr., *The Green National Product: A Proposed Index of Sustainable Economic Welfare* (Lanham, Md.: University Press of America, 1994). They propose and execute a different measure of net economic performance based on the Gross National Product (GNP), but which deducts several costs not usually taken into account: auto accidents, commuting, urbanization, water and air pollution, loss of farmland and wetlands, depletion of nonrenewable resources, and long-term environmental damage. For the United States, they calculate that this Index of Sustainable Economic Welfare peaked in 1979 at 849.9, and declined, though neither continuously nor precipitously, through 1986. The lowest figure after 1979 was for 1982, 786.8; it was followed by a slow increase thereafter to 822.1 in 1986, the last year for which they calculated it (ibid., 82-83).
169. One thinks of the absence of flowing water, trees, grass, and horticulture in many urban neighborhoods; but these are usually absent too from indoor suburban shopping malls.
170. This has not been true of the entire left; in particular, Marxism did not attribute a particular value to nature in theory or in practice, focusing on society instead.
171. Bill Devall and George Sessions, *Deep Ecology* (Salt Lake City: Peregrine Smith, 1985), 18. They attribute this concept to the Norwegian environmentalist Arne Naess.
172. Tom Regan, *All That Dwell Therein* (Berkeley: University of California, 1982), 200, cited in Bruce R. Reichenbach and V. Elving Anderson, *On Behalf of God: A Christian Ethic for Biology* (Grand Rapids, Mich.: Wm. B. Eerdmans, 1995), 97.
173. A notable exception to this is Langdon Gilkey, who emphasizes power as the first category under which we experience nature. See Gilkey, *Nature, Reality, and the Sacred* (Minneapolis: Fortress Press, 1993), 87.
174. Peter Singer, *Animal Liberation* (New York: New York Review Books, 1975).
175. Devall and Sessions, *Deep Ecology*, 18.
176. Ibid., 53.
177. "There is no bifurcation in reality between the human and the non-human realms. To the extent that we perceive boundaries, we fall short of deep ecological consciousness" (Warwick Fox, "The Intuition of Deep Ecology," unpublished paper, cited in *Deep Ecology*, 66).
178. Devall and Sessions, *Deep Ecology*, 66-67. What makes "biocentric equality" anthropomorphic is that "equality" is a social construct, derived from mathematics, not biology. Of course Devall and Sessions reject the "socially programmed" self of Western culture in favor of our "unique spiritual/biological personhood," which seeks to free itself from social influence.
179. Except, usually, for scientific culture.
180. Oelschlaeger, *Caring for Creation*, 23. See 22-27 for the complete discussion. He does not, however, attend to the popular versions of Buddhism, Taoism, and cosmic selfhood on the

environmental left. See, e.g., Charlene Spretnak, *The Spiritual Dimension of Green Politics* (Santa Fe, N.M.: Bear & Co., 1986).
181. Oelschlaeger, *Caring for Creation*, 4.
182. Ibid., 22-23.
183. Larry L. Rasmussen, *Earth Community Earth Ethics* (Maryknoll, N.Y.: Orbis Books, 1996), 58.
184. Oelschlaeger, *Caring for Creation*, 21.
185. Robert A. Sirico, "The Greening of American Faith," *National Review* 46, no. 16 (August 29, 1994), 42-46. Of course, as is the case with most one-sided attacks, a half-truth lurks in the distortion. Some environmentalists and naturalists *do* speak of human beings and human cultural activity, including economic activity, as though they were intrinsically opposed to the environment and therefore of either no value, or positively opposed to environmental values. See, e.g., Thomas Berry, *The Dream of the Earth* (San Francisco: Sierra Club Books, 1988), 154-57, 173-76, 192-93. Cf. the thoughtful critique of sentimental species-egalitarianism in Holmes Rolston III, *Environmental Ethics: Duties to and Values in the Natural World* (Philadelphia: Temple University Press, 1988), 71-78. Nor can it be denied that some environmentalists may have used "scare" tactics in trying to alert the public. Yet the ambiguity of certain data, particularly that which concerns global warming, make it difficult to distinguish genuine cause for alarm from honest but misled attempts to alert, and both of these from dishonest and manipulative attempts to create alarm.
186. Milton and Rose Friedman, *Free to Choose: A Personal Statement* (New York: Harcourt Brace Jovanovich, 1980), 218.
187. This rhetorical flourish and other put-downs mar the Friedmans' preceding discussion of pollution, which explores the important question of the merit of using market forces rather than regulations to control pollution (pp. 213-18). These points could have been made without the dismissal of environmental concerns that the right seems to think requisite for any discussion.
188. When we use the term "evangelicals" as a *noun*, we are referring to relatively conservative (but nonfundamentalist) American Christians who belong to a broadly populist religious movement within the Reformed and Calvinist heritage (as opposed to, say, a Catholic or Lutheran or Wesleyan heritage); they emphasize biblical authority, individual decision, a personal relationship with Jesus Christ, and conversion. This is a quite different meaning from "evangelical" as an *adjective* applied to a church body, as in the "Evangelical Lutheran Church in America" (or Germany or El Salvador or Tanzania or the Ukraine), where it refers to a called community based on the gospel and sacraments.
189. DeWitt, "Introduction," 13-23.
190. Steven Bouma-Prediger and Virginia Vroblesky, *Assessing the Ark: A Christian Perspective on Non-Human Creatures and the Endangered Species Act* (Wynnewood, Pa.: Crossroads, 1997).
191. Bruce R. Reichenbach and V. Elving Anderson, *On Behalf of God: A Christian Ethic for Biology* (Grand Rapids, Mich.: Wm. B. Eerdmans, 1995), 52-53, 73-86. One also finds—in marked contrast to most evangelical *theology*—positive references to liberal Christians and secular environmentalists. Thus Loren Wilkinson, "Christ as Creator and Redeemer," refers approvingly to Dietrich Bonhoeffer and Larry Rasmussen, in DeWitt, *The Environment and the Christian*, 42, and Bouma-Prediger and Vroblesky, *Assessing the Ark*, 11-13, draw heavily from Holmes Rolston.
192. Nor have they cited evangelical environmentalists in the way that evangelicals have cited liberal environmentalists.
193. Rasmussen, *Earth Community*, 235-36.
194. Sallie McFague, *The Body of God: An Ecological Theology* (Minneapolis: Fortress Press, 1993), 103.
195. Rasmussen, *Earth Community*, 270-72.
196. McFague, *Body of God*, 14-22, 136-41, 151-57.
197. Holmes Rolston is a noteworthy exception to this rule among liberals. A nice example of

sloppy science is Rasmussen's misuse of evidence taken from Paul Hawken, *The Ecology of Commerce, A Declaration of Sustainability* (San Francisco: HarperBusiness, 1993), 21-22, which says that every day the world burns 10,000 days' worth of stored (i.e., fossil fuel) energy. Rasmussen says, "It hardly takes rocket scientist intelligence to read 'unsustainability' writ large here, if such a way of life goes on for very long, in earth terms." But how long is that? Taking Hawken's rate, and taking the earth's age as 4 billion years and no change in consumption, this rate could continue for 400,000 years.

We are not trying to discredit Rasmussen's overall argument, only pointing out his rather slipshod use of scientific evidence, which is quite embarrassing alongside the work of some evangelicals. Presuming that Hawken's figure is accurate (which we have no reason to question), it does raise serious issues. But Rasmussen's slip here does raise questions about the status of his other scientific and quantitative claims.

198. Rasmussen, *Earth Community*, 75-83, 291; McFague, *Body of God*, 129, 201.
199. Rasmussen, *Earth Community*, 239, 273-76; McFague, *Body of God*, 140-50.
200. Thus Reichenbach and Anderson, after reviewing the three "biblical injunctions" to fill, rule, and tend (care for) the land (pp. 49-52), baldly assert, "But things differ today" (54).
201. See Oelschlaeger, *Caring for Creation*, 165-81, for a summary of what he calls "radical creation stories" and "alternative creation stories." These stories, while quite different, are united in their general rejection (or subordination) of history and culture as modes of divine revelation, in favor of nature. Despite its fervent philosophical rejection of dualism, Devall and Sessions's *Deep Ecology* continues to draw a very strict division between human society and wilderness, 110-14. This abrupt dualism has recently been criticized from within the secular environmental movement by William Cronin, "The Trouble with Wilderness," in Cronin, ed., *Uncommon Ground: Toward Reinventing Nature* (New York: W. W. Norton, 1995), 69-90, esp. 83. Our thanks to Bob Moline for alerting us to this book.
202. John Stuart Mill, "Nature," in John Stuart Mill, *Collected Works* 10, *Essays on Ethics, Religion, and Society*, ed. J. M. Robson (Toronto: University of Toronto Press, 1969), 373-402; here, 400. Cited in Rolston, *Environmental Ethics*, 40. Of course, Mill is only giving clearer expression here to what many, many others have believed and taught in manifold ways.
203. Rasmussen, *Earth Community*, 59.
204. Rolston, *Environmental Ethics*, 335.
205. Ironically, one of the sources of this second mistake has been a one-sided reading of the Bible itself: specifically, the Yahwist creation story and primeval history in Genesis 2:4–11:32, which begins with the creation and the first sin and climaxes in the destruction of the earth in the flood.
206. Reinhold Niebuhr, *The Nature and Destiny of Man*, vol. 1, *Human Nature* (New York: Charles Scribner's Sons, 1941), 181-82. Niebuhr never extended his analysis to the ecocrisis in this way, yet to do so is both true to his best insights and fruitful for understanding.
207. The same holds true for humanity's relationship to history and culture; we are *in* and *out* of history, *in* and *out* of culture and society. We cannot be human without them, but we are not limited to them, and we can shape and manipulate them.
208. Oelschlaeger, *Caring for Creation*, 12. Also see Midgely, *Can't We Make Moral Judgements?* 61.
209. "Such collaboration [between religion and science] is difficult to describe from either a religious or a scientific standpoint—both presuppose that there is but one true account of reality" (Oelschlaeger, *Caring for Creation*, 33). In other words, the classic conflicts between religion and science—Galileo vs. the Catholic Church, fundamentalism vs. Darwin—have been between two contestants, each of which was equally sure (1) that there could be only *one* true account of reality and (2) that *it* had the right one. In other words, only science or religion could be true—not both. It is this paradigm that each must shatter if they are to cooperate meaningfully in responding to ecocrisis.
210. Ibid., 41.
211. Gilkey, *Nature, Reality, and the Sacred*, 1, traces ecocrisis to the "scientistic" understanding

of nature as a "realm of external relations, . . . mindlessly hurrying here and there . . .void . . . of any trace of inwardness." Such an understanding objectifies nature into mere "raw material for our use." He also identifies religion's complicity in this error, 79ff. Also see Sandra Harding, *Whose Science? Whose Knowledge? Thinking from Women's Lives* (Ithaca, N.Y.: Cornell, 1986), cited in McFague, *Body of God,* 243 n. 76.

212. Much of the work of environmentally minded evangelicals is exemplary in this respect. See, e.g., Bouma-Prediger and Vroblesky, Reichenbach and Anderson, and DeWitt. Rolston too is excellent on this count. Constructive engagement with science is less widespread among liberal religious thinkers. McFague, despite her endorsement of Harding's critique, largely subordinates the discourse of religion to that of science, which leaves one wondering just what it is that religion, on her account, has to contribute beyond the fact that it is somewhat important to McFague. Her "bottom line" is "coherence or compatibility between the scientific view and the interpretation of our basic doctrines" (p. 76). Thus "the religious/secular/modern picture of human reality is a lie" (108) (but not, evidently, the scientific picture). For a perceptive account of the current state of the dialogue (or lack of one) between science and religion, see Philip Hefner, "Confessions of a Scientist-Theologian" (a review of John Polkinghorne, *Belief in God in an Age of Science* [New Haven, Conn.: Yale University Press, 1998], in *Christian Century* 115 [May 20-27, 1998], 533-39).

213. Oelschlaeger, *Caring for Creation,* 7.

214. Ibid., 8.

215. Rolston, *Environmental Ethics,* 26; McFague expresses similar views throughout *Body of God,* e.g., 79 and 209.

216. "The scale of human activity relative to the biosphere has grown too large. Further growth beyond the present scale is overwhelmingly likely to increase costs more rapidly than it increases benefits" (Herman E. Daly and John B. Cobb, Jr., *For the Common Good: Redirecting the Economy Toward Community, the Environment, and a Sustainable Future* (Boston: Beacon Press, 1989), 1. Similarly, McFague, *Body of God,* 102, chooses to emphasize the categories of nature and space over those of history and time.

217. Devall and Sessions, *Deep Ecology,* 109-29. They open by quoting Henry David Thoreau's essay "Walking": "In short, all good things are wild and free" (109), cited from Charles R. Anderson, ed., *Thoreau's Vision: The Major Essays* (Englewood Cliffs, N.J.: Prentice-Hall, 1973). This close link between wilderness, individual freedom for individual organisms, and disdain for society and culture deserves careful attention. It is the incoherent but vastly influential presupposition of much American thought.

218. Even McFague, who rejects most traditional creation imagery, speaks of human beings as "stewards of life's continuity on earth and partners with God in solidarity with the oppressed" (201). Devall and Sessions "agree in some respects on practical grounds but not on philosophical grounds" with the "revised Christian version of stewardship," but go on (without evidence or documentation) to say that it is "narrowly utilitarian" and regards "natural resources primarily for human use" (*Deep Ecology,* 125). This is quite different from Reichenbach and Anderson's sense of holding the creation in trust for the Creator.

219. This is the central thrust of Reichenbach and Anderson, as reflected in the Reformed audacity of their title, *On God's Behalf.* The paradigm of "the creator and his stewards" (43ff.) runs throughout the book. Human rule over the creation "is to take into account the interests of the Landlord, ruler, and ruled, [and] not *only* to serve human interests" (ibid., 96). But the outcome of their book is not very different from that of Rolston: a special role for humankind is affirmed, but so too are the inherent goodness and interests of the creation.

220. See Rolston's discussion, "Humans as Moral Overseers on Earth," *Environmental Ethics,* 335-41. Some critics of the stewardship ethic hold that it is merely inadequate—a view with which we concur: "You can't solve the whole problem of nature's care by stewardship. . . . [Stewardship is] not a big enough doctrine; it's not central enough." Nature is not "neutral or mute," but "defines the human place in the world" (Joseph Sittler, *Gravity and Grace: Reflections and Provocations* [Minneapolis: Augsburg, 1986], 13). Those who reject the

stewardship model altogether usually tend toward a species of egalitarianism that is neither biologically nor morally defensible (see Rolston, *Environmental Ethics*, 335-51).
221. Gilkey, *Nature, Reality, and the Sacred*, calls for a "Mother's day for nature to remind us of our ultimate dependence on her" (143).
222. Rolston, *Environmental Ethics*, 26.
223. See Rasmussen, *Earth Community*, 15-16, 142-46, 153-54. "Vague," however, is an understatement. A similar concept is Devall and Sessions's "self-regulating community" (*Deep Ecology*, 19).
224. Rolston, *Environmental Ethics*, 346; also see Devall and Sessions, *Deep Ecology*, 22-23.
225. In this respect Oelschlaeger's approach is preferable to both McFague's near-absolutization of science and Gilkey's near-demonization of it.
226. "Humility respects the human scale of things, eschews overweening ambition, does not build towers in Babel nor embark upon social engineering that gets out of hand and ends up in a Holocaust" (Charles M. Murphy, *At Home on Earth: Foundations for a Catholic Ethic of the Environment* [New York: Crossroad, 1989], 141). Devall and Sessions, *Deep Ecology*, emphasize "cultivating the virtues of modesty and humility," 110.
227. Rolston, *Environmental Ethics*, 354.
228. Rasmussen powerfully makes this point concerning Nazism, 298-302. Citing the account of Luc Ferry's "Nazi Ecology" in Ferry, *The New Ecological Order*, trans. Carol Volk (Chicago: University of Chicago Press, 1995), 90ff., Rasmussen observes that the Nazi laws of 1933–35 protecting nature and animals were among the first pieces of environmental legislation anywhere. Rasmussen dryly concludes, "Nazi ecology was, it turns out, not incompatible with genocide" (299 n. 16). The reference to Social Darwinism is on 315. Rasmussen could have added Shinto to the list as an at least occasionally demonic earth faith; in Shinto, what we call "nature" is sacred, but *only in Japan*. Indonesian rain forests do not have *kami*.
229. Oelschlaeger, *Caring for Creation*, 13.
230. See Rasmussen, *Earth Community*, 183-84. This is the appeal which upset Robert Sirico so much in "The Greening of American Faith."
231. Oelschlaeger, *Caring for Creation*, 205-13. An excellent example of the latter, conducted not by a church but by a team of researchers that included theologians, is Strachan Donnelley, ed., "Nature, Polis, Ethics: Chicago Regional Planning," a Special Supplement in *Hastings Center Report* 28, no. 6 (November-December 1998).
232. Cobb and Cobb, *The Green National Product*. This is a measure they propose to substitute for the Gross National Product as a measure of the economy's performance. See above at n. 169.
233. See Rolston, *Environmental Ethics*, 249-53, for an extensive listing of legislation in the U.S. during 1955–87. Remember, however, Oelschlaeger's "paradox of environmentalism," namely, that "the global ecocrisis continues to worsen despite people's efforts to respond" (*Caring for Creation*, 4).
234. It is vital that Americans treat the Kyoto accords more seriously than we have. As of this writing, even debate on the accords is on hold in Congress, typical for a body that would evidently rather fight than have hearings. However, Congress's apparent unwillingness to expose the public to environmental debate, as though there were toxins present in the words, need not preclude the public itself from bringing the issue to the fore. We are doing ourselves a disservice to wait on our legislators. A good, readable review of the current environmental situation is Bill McKibben, "A Special Moment in History," *Atlantic Monthly* 281, no. 5 (May 1998): 55-78.
235. This is preferred by several economists, including Milton and Rose Friedman: "Instead of requiring firms to erect specific kinds of waste disposal plants or to achieve a specified level of water quality in water discharged into a lake or river, impose a tax of a specified amount per unit of effluent discharged. That way, the firm would have an incentive to use the cheapest way to keep down the effluent. Equally important, there would be objective evidence of

the costs of reducing pollution" (*Free to Choose*, 217). We are much less sanguine than the Friedmans that this proposal will almost automatically be just to the victims of pollution, but this is not a reason not to experiment with it.
236. Oelschlaeger, *Caring for Creation*, 211.
237. Richard W. Fox, *Reinhold Niebuhr: A Biography* (New York: Pantheon, 1985), 295. Niebuhr's participation in that lecture circuit was also directly due to the interest the wealthy Sherwood Eddy (an influential leader in the YMCA movement when it still had church associations) had taken in him. It was Eddy who enabled Reinhold to take his first trip to Europe in 1923 and, starting in 1924, provided him with a budget of $2,500 per year to cover his travel expenses on the lecture circuit as well as the cost of an assistant pastor for his congregation in Detroit (ibid., 77-81). Neither Ted Turner nor Bill Gates seem to have any such interests today.
238. See Viktor Frankl, "The Case for a Tragic Optimism" in Frankl, *Man's Search for Meaning* (New York: Simon & Schuster, 1985), 161-79.
239. As in his memorable epigram, "Man's capacity for justice makes democracy possible, but man's inclination to injustice makes democracy necessary" (Reinhold Niebuhr, *The Children of Light and the Children of Darkness: A Vindication of Democracy and a Critique of Its Traditional Defense* [New York: Charles Scribner's Sons, 1945], xi).
240. "Even though I shall be buried and be consumed by worms, nevertheless I shall live. 'But you will die,' objects the flesh. . . . To be sure, I shall be turned to ashes. Nevertheless, I shall live." Martin Luther, *Lectures on Genesis*, trans. Jaroslav Pelikan, *Luther's Works* 4 (St. Louis: Concordia Publishing House, 1964), 118. Luther here paraphrases Isaac's thoughts as he is bound to the sacrificial altar and sees his father Abraham raise the knife (Gen. 22:10).
241. Viktor Frankl, "Logotherapy in a Nutshell," in *Man's Search*, 119-57; here, 157.
242. The real question is not "Why do bad things happen to good people?" but "Why, in the light of all that is evil, does good continue to go on?" The quick answer to the latter question is, as Augustine saw, because evil is parasitic on good. Without good, no evil can exist. As Augustine puts it, all things are good by nature, and nothing is evil by nature. Evil is a result of a misdirected will which puts good things to bad uses. See Augustine, *City of God*, trans. Marcus Dods (New York: Modern Library, 1950), 381-88, esp. 386: "For when the will abandons what is above itself, and turns to what is lower, it becomes evil—not because that is evil to which it turns, but because the turning itself is wicked. Therefore it is not an inferior thing which has made the will evil, but it is itself which has become so." The evil will, then, has only a "deficient" cause, not an efficient cause (ibid., 387). Also see H. Richard Niebuhr, *Radical Monotheism*, 37-38, where he insists that "whatever is, is good," but immediately goes on to insist that this is *not* to say that "whatever is, is right." Whereas Augustine identifies the evil will as the cause of evil, Niebuhr identifies wrong *relations* between good things as the source of evil. In either case, however, good is both logically and ontologically prior to evil.

Index

Abortion, 67, 78, 80, 96, 111, 113-15, 121, 203, 211, 229, 231-32, 240
Ackerman, Bruce, 64-66, 69, 73
Antipolitics, 42, 50, 65, 77, 81, 144, 200, 204, 215
    See also Majoritarianism
Arendt, Hannah, 25, 30-31, 38, 59, 82, 219
Audi, Robert, 68, 73
Augustine of Hippo, 29, 33-34, 39, 109, 127-28, 129, 131, 135-36, 168, 178, 207

Bellah, Robert, 85, 157, 201-3, 264
Bennett, William, 157
Blankenhorn, David, 206
Browning, Don, 117, 183, 234-36, 260
Buchanan, Pat, 39, 89
Bush, George H. W., 76

Calvin, John, 127, 134, 138, 142, 178
Carter, Stephen, 43-47, 52, 75
Center, emphatic Christian
    compared with political wings, 14, 17-18
    compared with vacuous center, 13-14
    principles, 13, 17-18
Centrism, current (vacuous), 13-15, 204
    See also Pluralism, vacuous
Christian Coalition. *See* Right, the religious
Citizenship, 200-204, 218
Civil Rights movement, 65, 78, 112, 115
Clinton, William, 15-17, 65, 76-77, 225
Crasswell, Ellen, 27, 76

Dahl, Robert, 204-5
Dash, Leon, 223-24
Democratic Party, 16, 46, 212, 220
Dewey, John, 37, 40, 54, 59, 60
Dole, Robert, 31

Domination, 50, 63, 70, 76, 78, 81, 152, 155, 162-66, 171, 181-82, 190-91, 193-94, 196, 202, 205, 215, 242, 247
    authority and, 73, 188, 190, 203

Education, 199, 223-31
    See also Poverty
Egalitarianism, 160, 163-64, 166, 201
Eisenhower, Dwight, 42
Environment, 21, 38, 113, 114, 178, 199, 214, 217, 219, 251-53
Exhaustion, politics of, 15-17, 76

Faith, 31, 39, 64, 169
    argument, reason and, 51, 66-68, 73-74, 188
Falwell, Jerry, 113, 121, 231
Family, 35, 199, 206, 208, 214, 219
Feminist, feminist thought, 52, 68, 96, 111, 114-15, 132-33, 135, 140, 168, 174, 188, 189, 208
Feuerbach, Ludwig, 34, 40, 131, 170
Finitude, 35, 38, 180-83
Forgiveness. *See* Love, forgiveness and
Foucault, Michel, 60, 63, 157, 160
Freedom
    political and cultural discourse and, 14, 43, 45, 59, 66, 69, 71, 73, 75, 77, 79-80, 82, 160, 162, 178, 180, 201, 210, 215, 225-26
    religion of, 28, 154, 158, 187-88, 204-6, 230-31

Gadamer, Hans-Georg, 168-69
Gamwell, Franklin, 28, 62, 185
Geertz, Clifford, 28
Gilkey, Langdon, 59, 82, 127, 129, 134, 259
Glendon, Mary Ann, 85, 92, 237-39, 251-52

God, 18, 266-67
  and comprehensiveness, 31-35
  and history, 35-38
  and power, 145-49
  and the world, 141-42, 181, 195
  as ultimate concern, 27-29
  as viewed by rationalism, 56-59
  freedom as a god, 84-86, 102
  in contemporary American religion, 111-25
Government
  attitudes toward, 215-16, 225
  roles of, 214-19, 223, 243-46, 250
  voluntary institutions and, 216-17, 246-48
  See also Antipolitics
Gray, J. Glenn, 17, 193
Greenawalt, Kent, 28-29, 44, 47, 64, 66-69, 71, 72, 73, 76, 188
Gudorf, Christine, 208-9

Hamilton, Alexander, 53, 55
Hegel, Georg Wilhelm Friedrich, 61, 169-70
History, change, and the new
  implications of, theological and philosophical, 31, 36-38, 50, 167-70, 172-75, 177-78, 180-82, 185-87, 190-92, 216-19, 245-47
  philosophies and theologies of, 36-37, 57, 59, 61, 62, 162, 169, 172-74, 189
  political relation to, 34-36, 65-66, 154-55
  power and, 37-38, 178, 197
  religious relation to, 34-35, 46
Hobbes, Thomas, 52, 54, 142
Hunter, James Davison, 17, 177

Interests and self-interest, 189, 199, 204-15
  Federalists and factions, 54-56

Jefferson, Thomas, 25, 54, 56-61, 63, 73, 83, 93, 102, 160
Jesus, 57-58, 60, 61, 116, 127, 182, 259
Jones, L. Gregory, 206, 208, 209
Justice, 69, 71, 176, 182, 195, 206, 208, 247, 248

Kennedy, John, 27
Kevorkian, Jack, 200
Kierkegaard, Søren, 38
King, Martin Luther, Jr., 112
King, Rodney, 64

Lamm, Richard, 13
Latour, Bruno, 162
Left, the political, 14, 36, 201, 202, 221, 243
Liberalism, 26, 45, 51, 190-91
  conservatism of, 65-66, 74-76, 186-87
  particular, 51, 62-80, 153, 165
  universal, 51, 53-62, 70-71
Locke, John, 95, 236
Love, 112, 116-20, 137, 179, 182, 189, 195, 208-11, 213, 237-38, 247, 260, 267
  appreciation and, 19-20, 138-40, 153
  forgiveness and, 139-41
Luther, Martin, 61, 127, 138, 178, 184, 206-7, 221, 266

Madison, James, 54-56, 59, 62, 63, 70, 75, 97, 161, 205-6
Majoritarianism, 47-50, 54-55, 74-76, 78, 81, 165
Marx, Karl, 148, 170
Mill, John Stuart, 95, 257
Monoculturalism, 154-55, 156, 162, 165, 185
Murray, John Courtney, 161

Neuhaus, Richard, 43-44, 46-50, 75, 122, 152, 156
Niebuhr, H. Richard, 37, 91, 116
Niebuhr, Reinhold, 39, 123, 127, 129, 134, 135, 148, 181, 209-10 258, 264, 266
Nietzsche, Friedrich, 130, 159
Nygren, Anders, 188, 205, 207, 208

Okin, Susan Moller, 153

Paine, Thomas, 56-61, 73
Paul, 181, 207
Penny, Tim, 13
Perot, Ross, 42, 65

INDEX

Perry, Michael, 45, 47, 164
Pluralism
   antipluralism and, 47, 162, 165 (*see also* Monoculturalism)
   commitment and, 156, 165-66, 193-98
   difference and, 152, 156, 160, 176-93
   emphatic Christian center (pluralism of commitment) and, 18, 26-27, 40, 41, 81, 152-98, 219, 250 (*see also* Power, aim of politics as)
   Federalist conceptions of, 53-56, 64
   ideological, 154-56, 162-65, 204-5
   particular liberalism, in, 62-80
   tolerance and, 53-61, 153-56, 162, 165, 174-75, 179-84, 193
   vacuous (pluralism of neglect and indifference), 45, 47, 154-56, 160-66, 174-76, 180, 183-84, 194-95, 198
Polarization in politics and political discourse, 13-14, 16-17, 76-77, 154-58, 166, 212, 221, 243-44
Politics and religion. *See* Religion and politics
Poverty, 15, 47, 68, 78, 192, 199, 209, 210-32, 217, 219-31, 243
Power, 37-38, 57, 59-60, 152-53, 155, 156, 163-64, 185, 191, 196-98, 207, 210, 212-13, 219, 242, 247
   aim of politics as, 18, 175, 184, 190, 194-99, 204, 209, 231, 247
   plurality and, 156, 175-76, 178, 181-98, 204 (*see also* Pluralism, emphatic Christian center and)

Rauschenbusch, Walter, 37
Rawls, John, 62, 63, 66, 69-73, 76, 78, 153, 161, 165, 186-87, 196
Reagan, Ronald, 15, 37, 216, 228, 229
Reason, 51, 54-55
   particular, 62-82, 161 (*see also* Liberalism, particular)
   universal, 18, 56-63, 70, 71, 158, 161 (*see also* Liberalism, universal)
   See also Faith, argument, reason and
Reed, Ralph, 64, 95, 105, 216
Relativism

   antirelativism, as, 156-67, 169-70, 186, 196
   relatedness, as, 156, 166-67, 172-76, 180-83, 186
Religion, definition of
   culture and, 30, 161 (*see also* Freedom, religion of)
   effects on religion and politics and, 26-27, 34, 39, 65, 69-70, 81
   religious institutions and, 27-28, 65
   ultimate concern and normative criteria, 26-41, 68-69, 74, 75-76, 78-82, 164, 174, 180-82, 186, 210
Religion and politics
   conceptions of relation
   emphatic Christian centrism, 26-27, 42, 78, 81-82
   exclusionism, 45, 50-80, 82
   inclusionism, 41, 43-50, 51, 61-62, 75, 76, 77, 80, 82
   particularist, 41, 62-80
   reduction to law, 44-45
   universalist, 41, 50-62
Republican Party, 16, 46, 76-77, 202, 212, 220
Right, the political, 14-15, 36, 53, 202, 216-17, 221, 243
Right, the religious, 35, 63, 78, 79, 191, 208, 210
Rights, 43-48, 50, 51, 75, 80, 180, 186, 191, 210, 218
   See also Freedom
Robertson, Pat, 73, 76, 78, 111, 113, 123, 125, 264
Rorty, Richard, 158-59, 161, 170-73, 178
Rousseau, Jean Jacques, 98, 236

Secular state, 25-26, 48, 62, 72, 77-79, 154, 191-93
Secularism, ideology of, 26, 79-82, 152, 154, 193
Secularity, 26, 79-80, 82, 154, 193
   emphatic Christian center and, 26, 191-93
Sexual violence, 167-68, 197, 199, 211, 213, 218, 219, 240-50
Sin, 34, 35, 58, 153, 156, 181, 183, 185-

(sin continued)
    86, 188-90, 195, 203, 216, 248
    descriptive category, as, 18, 174
    pride and selfishness, as, 40, 189, 204, 206-8
    sloth as, 40, 188
Skocpol, Theda, 211-12
Subsidiarity, 214-15, 217, 246
Suchocki, Marjorie Hewitt, 188

Targeted universalism, 209-15, 218, 226-27, 243-50
Thoreau, Henry David, 98-101, 103, 260
Tillich, Paul, 28-31, 35, 69, 79, 127, 134, 145, 181, 185, 208-9, 264
Tinder, Glenn, 127, 188, 206-8

Tracy, David, 28
Truth(s), 44, 57-60, 62-67, 70, 75-76, 156-74, 181
    incommensurability and, 69, 72, 81, 161, 162, 166, 185-91
    language and, 40, 167-74
    particularity and, 158-66, 170-74 *(see also* Reason, particular)
    postmodernism and, 158-66, 170-74
    universality and, 158, 161-62, 166-74, 184, 192 *(see also* Reason, universal)

Violence, 176, 188-89, 197
    See also Sexual violence

Wallis, Jim, 207-9, 220-21